# WITCHCRAFT, POWE

# Anthropology, Culture and Society

Series Editors:
Dr Richard A. Wilson, University of Sussex
Professor Thomas Hylland Eriksen, University of Oslo

# WITCHCRAFT, POWER AND POLITICS

## Exploring the Occult in the South African Lowveld

ISAK NIEHAUS

WITH ELIAZAAR MOHLALA
AND KALLY SHOKANE

## David Philip
CAPE TOWN

Pluto Press

LONDON · STERLING, VIRGINIA

First published 2001
by PLUTO PRESS
345 Archway Road, London N6 5AA
and 22883 Quicksilver Drive,
Sterling, VA 20166–2012, USA

www.plutobooks.com

Published in Southern Africa 2001
by David Philip Publishers
208 Werdmuller Centre, Newry Street,
Claremont 7708, South Africa

British Library Cataloguing in Publication Data
A catalogue record for this book is available from
the British Library

Library of Congress Cataloging in Publication Data
Niehaus, Isak A. (Isak Arnold)
Witchcraft, power, and politics : exploring the occult in the South
African lowveld / Isak Niehaus, with Eliazaar Mohlala and Kally Shokane.
    p. cm. — (Anthropology, culture, and society)
Includes bibliographical references.
ISBN 0–7453–1563–1 (hardcover) — ISBN 0–7453–1558–5 (pbk.)
1. Witchcraft—South Africa. I. Mohlala, Eliazaar. II. Shokane,
Kally. III. Title. IV. Series.
BF1584.S6 N54 2001
133.4'3'0968—dc21

00–012646


ISBN 0 7453 1563 1 hardback (Pluto)
ISBN 0 7453 1558 5 paperback (Pluto)
ISBN 0 86486 379 9 (David Philip)


10  09  08  07  06  05  04  03  02  01
10   9   8   7   6   5   4   3   2   1

Designed and produced for the publishers by
Chase Publishing Services, Fortescue, Sidmouth EX10 9QG
Typeset from disk by Stanford DTP Services, Northampton
Printed in the European Union by TJ International, Padstow, England

# CONTENTS

## LIST OF MAPS

## LIST OF TABLES

## LIST OF CASE STUDIES

Contents                                          vii

## LIST OF FIGURES

# ACKNOWLEDGEMENTS

As the research and writing of this book has extended over a decade, the number of people and institutions who have given valuable assistance towards its successful completion are literally legion. Here, I can mention but a few of those to whom I am indebted.

Selecting lowvelders to whom to offer explicit thanks is a difficult task. Kindness, patience, hospitality and helpfulness were general to the hundreds of people with whom I had dealings. I wish to thank the former director of the University of the Witwatersrand Rural Facility (WRF), John Gear, and his staff for facilitating my research. Eliazaar Mohlala and Kally Shokane are superb hosts, expert research assistants and my most valued friends. I am also very grateful to others who aided my work as informants and in countless other ways. They include the late B. Chiloane, Enios Chiloane, chief Nkotobona Chiloane, Philipina Chiloane, 'doctor' Gumede, Trafi Maatsie, Elmon Machate, Freddy and Joyce Makhubela, Justice Malatsi, Phileon Malapane, John Malathole, Harry Maluleke, Valley Mapaile, the late 'doctor' Marule, Sešhieng Mashego, Doris Mathebula, *ngwa* Modike, Elphas Mogale, Alec Mohlala, MacDonald Mokgope, Caswell Mokoena, Timothy Monareng, Milton Morema, Lakios Mosoma, Sabina Ndlovu, Jabulane Nokeri, Sidney Nyathi, Nelson Sekgobela, Willias Sekgobela, Exom and Girly Shokane, Meita Shokane, Daniel Thobela, Eric Thobela, Feita Thobela and Nana Tlou. I hope that in some way this book may contribute to preserving the history of this part of the lowveld for their descendants and towards realising their aspirations to build a prosperous country in which mis-understanding, intolerance, violence and fear knows no place.

I also wish to acknowledge the contributions of Peta Katz, Edwin Ritchken, Graeme Rodgers and Jonathan Stadler. As fellow researchers in the lowveld they kindly shared their information with me and shaped the development of my research.

Many individuals assisted me during the trying task of writing up the book. I especially wish to thank Adam Kuper who supervised the original PhD thesis on which this book is based. Adam provided intense intellectual stimulation, expert comments on the drafts of chapters and, along with Jessica Kuper, selflessly accommodated me during my stay in London. I am also extremely grateful to Peter Geschiere, Suzette Heald, Patrick McAllister and Richard Wilson who read and commented upon the entire manuscript.

I presented drafts of successive chapters as seminar papers to the Department of Social Anthropology and the Institute for Advanced Social Research at the University of the Witwatersrand (Wits); Department of Social Anthropology, University of Cape Town; Department of Anthropology, Yale University; Department of Human Sciences, Brunel University; Department of Anthropology, Venda University; Council for the Development of Social Research, Dakar; and to the American African Studies Association and the Association for Anthropology in Southern Africa. I thank all participants for their insightful comments, criticism and encouragement. It is again difficult to select individuals for whom to offer explicit thanks. I none the less feel obliged to mention Russel Alley, Leslie Bank, Gina Buijs, Dianne Ciekawy, David Coplan, Jim Campbell, Gotfried Dederen, Peter Delius, Don Donham, Stuart Douglas, Ronald Frankenburg, David Gellner, Carolyn Hamilton, David Hammond-Tooke, Deborah James, Prudence Mnisi, John Middleton, Ras Niehaus, Murray Last, Tom Lodge, Justine Lucas, JoAnne Pannell, Patrick Pearson, Graeme Reid, Hal Scheffler, John Sharp, Karen Shapiro, Owen Sichone, Jan Simpson, Andrew Spiegel and Charles van Onselen. I am grateful to Carla Lodge for skilfully preparing the maps.

Most of all I wish to thank my parents, Anita and Hennie Niehaus, to whom I dedicate this book, for their unfailing love and support throughout the years. I also thank Elaine and Victor Katz, and Lorraine and Paul Thiel, for feeding me in Johannesburg.

Financial support was provided by the Human Sciences Research Council (Centre for Science Development) and by Wits University. Funding from the latter institution included a University Council grant; financial support for sabbatical leave by the office of the Deputy Vice Chancellor, Academic Affairs; and allocations from the Department of Social Anthropology's research incentive scheme. The views expressed in this book do not reflect those of the funding bodies.

Because my project has spanned some years, some of my observations have already found their way into print. Earlier versions of chapters two, three and six were published as 'Christianisme, apartheid et genese de la sorcellerie dans le Lowveld Sud Africain', in Veronique Faure (ed.) *Dynamiques religieuse en Afrique australe*, Paris: Karthasla/CEAN, pp. 207–38, 2000; 'Witches of the Transvaal Lowveld and their Familiars. Conceptions of Duality, Power and Desire', *Cahiers d' Études Africaines*, XXXV (2–3), 138–9, pp. 513–40, 1995; and '"A Witch Has No Horn": The Subjective Reality of Witchcraft in the South African Lowveld', in Patrick McAllister (ed.) *Culture and the Commonplace: Anthropological Essays in Honour of David Hammond-Tooke*, Johannesburg: Witwatersrand University Press, pp. 251–78, 1997. My articles 'Witch-Hunting and Political Legitimacy: Continuity and Change in Green Valley, Lebowa', 1930–91, *Africa*, (63), 4, pp. 137–60, 1993; and 'The ANCs

Dilemma: The Symbolic Politics of Three Witch-Hunts in the South African Lowveld', *African Studies Review*, (41), 2, pp. 93–118, 1998, summarise some findings from Chapters 7 and 8.

Isak Niehaus
Hatfield, Pretoria

# NOTES ON TERMINOLOGY

Colloquial, official, vernacular and analytical terms play a major role in this book and must therefore be carefully defined. Owing to the nature of my arguments, the truest definitions of terms are left to the main text. For easier reference, however, I provide a basic definition of some colloquial and official terms, a glossary of vernacular terms used more than once in the text and a list of abbreviations.

## COLLOQUIAL AND OFFICIAL TERMS

**African, black and white** Former South African legislation classified the country's population into four main categories as Black, Coloured, Asian and White (cf. West 1988). The former three have been officially described as non-white, but many people thus classified prefer the generic reference black, which is how I have used the term. I use the term African to describe the category designated Black (previously Native or Bantu) in legislation. I do not use them to imply support for any system which classifies people in racial terms for purposes of political discrimination.

*baas* (Afrikaans: 'boss'). A term used to denote employers and sometimes white male persons in general.

*Bantustan* No term used to describe the Bantustans/homelands/national states is politically neutral. I have used the term Bantustan because it most clearly reflects rejection of the policy of creating separate political-geographic entities for different categories of the South African population.

**Comrades** Nationally used to denote supporters of the liberation movements. In the lowveld the term was used to include almost any youth who was seen to support the liberation struggle.

**currency** Prices are expressed in pounds sterling (£) until 1961, when the Union of South Africa became a Republic, and in South African rands (R) thereafter. The rate of exchange was £1 = R2 until devaluation of the pound in 1967, and fluctuated through the 1970s, 1980s and 1990s. The value of the Rand has declined sharply against many other currencies in recent years. On 26 April 2000 the exchange rate was £1 = R10.65 and US$1 = R6.70.

*ipimpi* (Zulu). Used by supporters of the liberation movements to refer to 'sell-outs', reactionaries and police informers.

*marula* (pl. *marulas*). The deciduous tree *Scerocarya birrea* common in the hotter parts of South Africa. Its fruit, also known as marulas or marula berries, is used for making jam and jelly and for making beer.

*ndumba* (Tsonga). Small round, thatched-roofed homes built specifically for the ancestors and alien spirits to dwell in. Nearly all diviners and herbalists treat their clients in *ndumba*.

*psyanga* (Tsonga: 'rebel'). The name of a youth gang from Acornhoek.

*rondavel* A round, thatched-roofed home.

*shebeen* (Gaelic: 'small house') An illegal private house of entertainment selling beer and liquor.

*sjambok* (Afrikaans: 'whip', verb *sjambokked*). Usually manufactured from rhinoceros or hippopotamus hide or from strong plastic.

*xirwalo* (Tsonga 'bring beer'). A ritual visit by a man's affines. Also denotes the beer and presents brought by the affines.


GLOSSARY OF NORTHERN SOTHO TERMS

Unless specified otherwise, all vernacular terms in the text are in the Sepulana dialect of Northern Sotho, as spoken in the lowveld.

*bonyatsi* long-term, extramarital love affair.

*bjang* grasses used for thatching.

*difeka* an affliction caused by the transgression of seniority rules. As a consequence women are unable to bear children.

*duma* innate, natural, desire.

*fiša* heat and pollution.

*go loma* 'to bite', rite of the first fruits.

*go hlaola* 'to select', a fine paid by the progenitor of a child to free himself of any paternal obligations.

*hlabologileng* civilisation.

*ila* (pl. *diila*) taboo.

*kgoro* (pl. *dikgoro*) a ward or moot/court of a chief or headman.

*kgoši* (pl. *magoši*) chief.

*lehufa* envy and jealousy.

*lekgowa* (pl. *makgowa*) white person.

*lešako* reeds for manufacturing mats and thatched grass.

*letšwa sehlare* placed on a corpse which causes the witch or killer to die in a similar manner as his or her victim.

*maatla* power, strength.

*madi a magolo* 'big blood', an ailment.

*mafulara* an affliction caused by the transgression of funeral rules. Its symptoms include chest pains and profuse coughing.

*maitshwaro* virtuous conduct and character.

*makgoma* an affliction brought about by contact with someone who has touched a corpse or is polluted by sexual intercourse. Its symptoms include convulsions and a shortness of breath.

*makgoweng* 'place of the whites'.

*malome* mother's brother.

*mamlambo* a snake-like witch-familiar.

*mmamogolo* mother's elder sister or senior co-wife.

*mmangwane* mother's younger sister.

*mmele* corporeal and visible body.

*morgen* a unit of measuring land.

*mošate* chief's headquarters.

*motho* (pl. *batho*) person, also used to denote Africans.

*motse* (pl. *metse*) family or village.

*moya* air, breath, wind or spirit.

*mshoshaphanzi* a potion used by male witches to have sexual intercourse with women from a remote distance.

*ngaka* (pl. *dingaka*) healer, herbalist, diviner.

*ngaka moloi* (pl. *dingaka baloi*) doctor-witch, consulted by clients to harm their enemies.

*ngwa* from, daughter of.

*nyatsi* (pl. *dinyatsi*) paramour, extramarital lover.

*phasa* to call or invoke the ancestors.

*pheko* (pl. *dipheko*) prescription by the ancestors or alien spirits, could include a sacrifice.

*pitšo* (pl. *dipitšo*): public meeting or assembly organised by chief or headmen.

*rakgadi* father's sister.

*ramogolo* father's elder brother.

*rangwane* father's younger brother.

*sefolane* paralysis of the legs.

*sefolo* a type of *sehlare* witches lay on footpaths to cripple their enemies.

*sehlare* (pl. *dihlare*) a compound of plant and animal substances used either to heal or to harm. A local equivalent of the Zulu term *umuthi*.

*sejeso* a slow poison.

*sekgowa* 'ways of the whites'.

*seriti* a person's shadow or aura.

*setšo* culture, tradition.

*seše manyane* 'twitchy eyes', a sty.

*šibeka* a type of sehlare made from human blood. Used by witches to cause drought.

*sporiani* a disease, the symptoms of which are red spots.

*tawana* sehlare used to harm thieves.

*tlhaga* forest or bush, that which is primordial.

*tokolotši* an ape-like witch-familiar.

*tšhwene* baboon.

*thwasane* (pl. *mathwasane*) the apprentice of a *ngaka*.

# ACRONYMS

| | |
|---|---|
| ANC | African National Congress |
| AWB | *Afrikaner Weerstands Beweging*, Afrikaner Resistance Movement |
| BENBO | Bureau for Economic Research re. Bantu Development |
| CODESA | Convention for a Democratic South Africa |
| Contralesa | Congress of Traditional Leaders of South Africa |
| DBSA | Development Bank of Southern Africa |
| DTA | Democratic Turnehalle Alliance |
| ESCOM | Electricity Supply Commission |
| LDE | Department of Agriculture |
| MEC | Member of the Executive Council |
| MK | *Umkhonto We Sizwe*, Spear of the Nation (Armed Wing of the African National Congress) |
| NEHAWU | National Education, Health and Allied Workers Union |
| NTS | Native Affairs Department |
| PAC | Pan African Congress |
| RDP | Reconstruction and Development Programme |
| SACR | South African Court Records |
| SAIRR | South African Institute of Race Relations |
| SWAPO | South West Africa People's Organisation |
| UDF | United Democratic Front |
| ZCC | Zion Christian Church |
| ZINATHA | Zimbabwe National Traditional Healer's Association |

Map 1: South Africa

LEGEND
Bophuthatswana
Lebowa
Gazankulu
Kwandebele
Venda
Kangwane

0   20  40  60  80
Kilometres

ZIMBABWE

Thohoyandou

KRUGER
NATIONAL
PARK

MOZAMBIQUE

Giyani

Pietersburg

Phalaborwa

SEKHUKHUNELAND

Acornhoek

MHALA

MAPULANENG

Garankuwa

Nelspruit

Waterval Boven

Pretoria

Witbank

Johannesburg

SWAZILAND

Map 2: Northeastern South Africa, Including former Bantustans

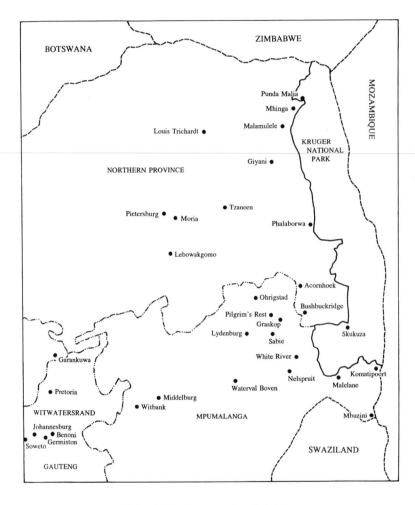

Map 3: Northeastern South Africa

Map 4: The Wider Bushbuckridge Region, Indicating Villages

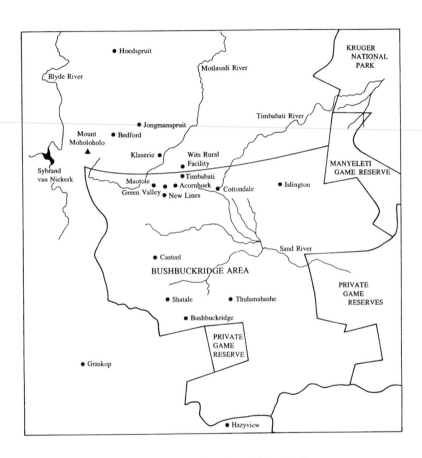

Map 5: The Wider Bushbuckridge Region

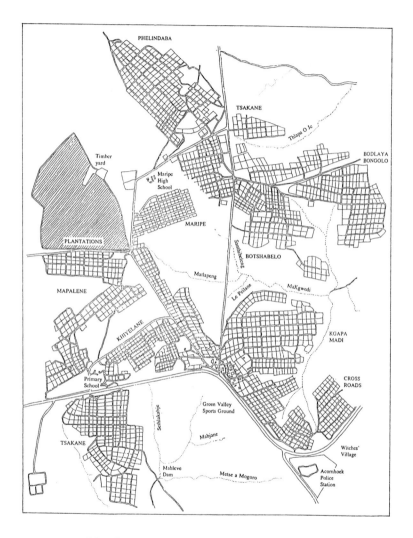

Map 6: Green Valley, Including Village Sections

# 1 INTRODUCTION: EXPLORING WITCHCRAFT, POWER AND POLITICS

Early ethnographic studies of the Tsonga and Northern Sotho-speaking inhabitants of the areas now comprising the Northern Province of South Africa do not portray witchcraft as particularly problematic. Junod (1966:534) recorded only one witch execution among the Tsonga at the turn of the century and writes that chiefs usually fined witches a few goats or £1. Krige and Krige (1965:250–71) document 50 witchcraft accusations among the Lobedu in the 1930s and note that witches were forced to leave the area only if they were suspected of having harmed a number of people. Sansom (1972) observed that during the 1960s witchcraft accusations, in the full sense of public denunciation, hardly ever occurred in Sekhukhuneland; whilst Hammond-Tooke (1981) insists that traditional cosmologies among the Kgaga of the lowveld emphasised pollution rather than witchcraft.

In stark contrast to these accounts, witchcraft accusations and the killing of suspected witches has reached alarming proportions in recent years. An official investigation, headed by Victor Ralushai, documents 389 witchcraft-related killings in the Northern Province between 1985 and 1995 (Ralushai et al, 1996).[1] In one episode alone, during April 1986, members of the Sekhukhuneland Youth Organisation 'necklaced' 47 alleged witches.[2] Police uncovered their corpses in pits and in bushes. A man told reporters how he had seen his wife burnt to death while her young assailants sang 'freedom songs'(*Sunday Times*, 20 April 1986).

The study of witchcraft has always been a staple topic in anthropology, but anthropologists have remained remarkably silent about witchcraft in contemporary South Africa. Our basic knowledge of witchcraft in the Republic still depends on chapters in the holistic studies of particular ethnic groups, such as those by Junod (1966) and by E. and J. Krige (1965), written chiefly in the 1930s and 1940s.[3] Whilst these works contain sensitive descriptions of indigenous beliefs, they are largely devoid of theoretical analysis. Witchcraft is simply treated as a peculiar feature of local cultures. Only a few essays have been devoted to theoretical discussions.[4] The predominant anthropological concern in South Africa has been the analysis of politics, economics and the predicaments engendered by apartheid (Gordon and Spiegel, 1993). Witchcraft was deemed to be a component of religion, somehow removed from these concerns and unworthy of serious scholarly investigation. Anthropologists have also sought to contrast the inhumanity of apartheid with the humanity of dominated people. It was possibly feared that representations of seemingly illogical beliefs and violence could augment the racist stereotypes held by the dominant white minority.[5]

Drawing from ethnographic fieldwork conducted since 1990 in Green Valley – a village situated in the Bushbuckridge district of the South African lowveld – my monograph attempts to break this silence. Green Valley has a rich and varied history. Since the passage of the 1913 Native Land Act the area was set aside for the exclusive occupation by Africans. During the era of apartheid, Green Valley formed part of the Bushbuckridge Native Reserve, and later of the Lebowa Bantustan. In 1994, with democratisation and the disestablishment of all Bantustans, Bushbuckridge was transferred to the newly established Northern Province.[6] Today Green Valley is sub-divided into eight residential sections and has an estimated population of 20,000.[7] Official identification of the village with the Northern Sotho Pulana belies its ethnic and linguistic heterogeneity. Residents also include Roka, Pedi, Kone, Kgaga and Lobedu (Northern Sotho); Hlanganu and Shangaan (Tsonga); Ndebele and Swazi.

The central concern of this study is to provide a detailed ethnographic and historical account of the escalating fears of witchcraft. Theoretically, I use the rich body of literature on witchcraft elsewhere in Africa, and also in Melanesia, to illuminate the local situation. But I also draw on my fieldwork to reflect critically upon some assumptions of the literature. I specifically aim to investigate the connections between three different dimensions of witchcraft: cosmological and symbolic formulations of witchcraft as a type of mystical power; patterns of witchcraft accusations and their significance in the domestic domain; and the involvement by political actors in witch-hunting. In short, I treat witchcraft in relation to symbolic system, social structure and political action.

## CHANGING WITCHCRAFT

My fieldwork in Green Valley lends credence, at the micro-level, to the general observation of an increasing regional concern with witchcraft. Elderly informants insisted that there were once only a few witches in Green Valley, but these were well-known and witchcraft was often tolerated as a legitimate form of revenge against enemies and thieves. Only when witches killed innocent victims were they regarded as malefactors and fined a specific number of cows. But even then, witches were hardly ever assaulted, expelled or executed. These elders believed that anxiety about witchcraft has grown in recent times and certainly, during the course of my research, virtually any person might be suspected of practising witchcraft. Moreover, there is now no tolerance of witchcraft. All forms of witchcraft, including vengeance magic, have come to epitomise evil. Public witch-hunts and the violent punishment of witches are commonplace.

These changes are captured by the very different experiences of *ngwa* ('from', 'daughter of') Mokgope – who was accused of witchcraft in the 1950s – and those of her son, Aaron Mashile, who suffered the same fate two decades later. My discussion of these cases is based on the recollections of their kin and neighbours.

### Case 1.1: The Headman's Wife

In 1955 *ngwa* Mashile – who was a widow and the sister of Ben Mashile, the headman of the Kgapa Madi settlement in Green Valley – planned to host a feast at which she would divide her cattle amongst her two sons. In preparation for the feast she went to brew beer at her brother's home on the northern outskirts of the village. *Ngwa* Mashile returned in the dusky hours of the early evening, but fell down as she was about to cross a river stream. People who lived nearby recalled hearing her screams, but did not investigate because it was already too dark. Early the next morning a boy notified elders that he had discovered *ngwa* Mashile's corpse. At *ngwa* Mashile's burial some of her relatives speculated that witch-familiars (*dithuri*) might have beaten her to death.

Two years after this traumatic event Edna Siboye – Ben Mashile's daughter-in-law – became pregnant and returned from her work in Nelspruit to give birth at his home. Edna's child died only one day after its birth. She recalled, 'There is an olden method that stillborn babies have to be buried in the corner of the house. The elderly women buried the baby's corpse before sunrise and covered the hole, nicely, with cow dung. Early in the morning I found a small hole in the ground. I was surprised and suspected that a rat had come out from the ground. That night we put two snares near the hole. To our surprise the snares were not there in the morning. They had been taken away. Because we suspected something strange we called the *baruti* [Zion Christian Church ministers] to fortify the home. The next morning we caught the rat... In the day we heard dogs barking outside our home. They barked furiously and pursued something which climbed up a maroela tree... Children told us that they had seen a bush baby [*nganaka-lla*] in the tree. This monkey-like creature is the size of a hen. Its hind legs are like those of a dog, but its forearms are like those of a human being. Although it has a tail and fur on its body, its face is clean like that of a human being. It also makes the sound of a human baby. The witches keep bush babies and send them on errands during the night. Maybe they sent it to kill my child.'

Edna asked her father-in-law, Ben Mashile, who was the headman of Kgapa Madi, to consult a witch-diviner (*mungoma*) to find out what was wrong. 'Although we insisted, Ben was reluctant to go. He refused! Because of this we suspected that he was the witch and that the creature [bush baby] belonged to him.' Eventually Ben conceded to the demands of his own kin and accompanied *ngwa* Mashile's sons to a witch-diviner in Phundu Malia, near Venda. Upon their return to Green Valley, *ngwa* Mashile's sons informed the chief (*kgoši*) and their neighbours that the diviner had beaten Ben on the knee. This meant that Ben was not a witch, but that his first wife – *ngwa* Mokgope – was responsible for the deaths at their home. The chief instructed her to compensate *ngwa* Mashile's sons with four head of cattle.

This procedure allayed the curiosity and fears of Kgapa Madi's residents. A neighbour explained: 'Because she was fined and exposed she was not expelled from Green Valley. Nothing else happened to her.' Few informants doubted *ngwa* Mokgope's guilt. They recalled that before her death the old woman was completely insane. There were even rumours that she once told others: 'children's livers are very tasty'.

*Case 1.2: The Headman's Son*

When Ben Mashile died in 1975, his son Aaron returned from the Witwatersrand, where he had worked as a migrant labourer, and was installed as Kgapa Madi's new headman. Aaron was already middle-aged by then.

Shortly after Aaron's return many deaths occurred amongst his kin. *Ngwa* Mashego (Ben's second wife) died in 1978. In the late 1960s and 1970s four of *ngwa* Mashego's sons (Aaron's half brothers) passed away. One son died mysteriously after he had been circumcised, two died after they started coughing and the fourth son, Simon, was knifed to death by his best friend, Lekgowa. This incident was truly mysterious: whilst drinking beer the two friends inexplicably started quarrelling and fighting. The other deaths were those of Aaron's two paternal uncles, his mother's brother's son, sister's child, sister-in-law and his sister's two children.

The remaining members of Ben Mashile's second house publicly accused Aaron of witchcraft. *Ngwa* Mnisi, Aaron's sister-in-law, explained the reasons why she suspected witchcraft as follows. 'We could understand that some deaths, such as those of my father and mother-in-law were natural. But not all the deaths! They occurred too frequently. They were untimely and unnatural! People were dying like flies – every three months or so. The one after the other.' *Ngwa* Mnisi recalled that whilst *ngwa* Mashego was terminally ill, the old woman screamed, 'Here is a horrible thing. It has come to suck my blood!' 'She said the creature was the size of a 25-litre water container. It had no mouth, nose nor ears. It was very large and resembled a worm in its movements. The thing sucked her blood without leaving any marks on her body.'

*Ngwa* Mnisi herself had an uncanny experience when she dug soil at the spring early one morning. 'Just across the spring I saw a very horrible person. It was a pitch-black man who seemed to be naked. He had long, uncombed, hair. The thing was very close range. I wanted to scream, but withheld and just continued walking. I was frightened, rigid and dumb. I stood still for a long time. I did not collapse, but all my senses were completely gone... From afar I saw two boys sitting on a fence. I called them and asked whether they had seen anything, but they said "No. We saw nothing." I then proceeded to dig the soil and asked the boys to accompany me home. That evening I dreamt that my grandmother came towards me with a bucket full of water. She was angry and shouted, "This can't be my grand-daughter". She then poured the water over me. I immediately awoke. I was confused and very tired. I believe that my grandmother came to save me... Maybe the pitch-black man was a witch-familiar or a zombie that came to fetch me. I really don't know where it came from.'

In 1979 the Mashile family assembled to discuss the course of events and decided to take Aaron to a witch-diviner. For this purpose they collected an amount of R1 from all households in the neighbourhood. Upon their return the delegates relayed to a large crowd that the witch-diviner had told them that Aaron kept a snake, which glowed at night and ate the members of his father's second house. When the crowd instructed Aaron to confess, he reportedly said, 'The witch-diviner told me that I got *dihlare* [herbs] from two *dingaka* [healers] to strengthen my headmanship. He said the *dihlare* is horrible and no good. Maybe it changed into a glowing snake.' A fierce argument erupted amongst the crowd. The descendants of Ben's second house were furious and wanted to kill Aaron. But Aaron's former work-mates protected him, saying that the witch-diviner had lied and that Aaron was an innocent victim of malevolent *dingaka*. Eventually they reached a compromise: Aaron would not be killed, but he would be expelled from Kgapa Madi after he had discarded the *dihlare*. Aaron took the crowd to a spot in the corner of his yard where he had allegedly buried the *dihlare*. Men dug a hole of almost a metre deep with picks, spades and shovels, but failed to reveal anything. At this point one of Aaron's half-brothers drew a knife, but others prevented him from stabbing Aaron. Aaron then took the men to his gate, where he started digging by himself. Eventually Aaron produced, what was described to me as, 'beautiful stones sculptured as cats' and 'twigs which seemed like *dihlare*'.

Men then took Aaron to a dam in the Motlasedi river. They forced him to enter the water until it reached waist level and to discard the stones and twigs. The next day Aaron was removed and started to build a home in the open forest near Mapalene. His former neighbour approvingly remarked, 'After Aaron left nobody died here for quite a while. This shows that he was responsible for all the deaths in our settlement.'

In Mapalene, Aaron was still accepted as headman. But in the late 1980s Aaron's new neighbours also started complaining about his presence amongst them. This is after his brother-in-law and own daughter died from tuberculosis. Also, during the course of 1990 three residents of Kgapa Madi committed suicide: a young man shot himself and two adults hanged themselves in their rooms. According to rumours witches had painted tombstones in Mapalene's graveyard to prevent the shadows (*seriti*) of the deceased from troubling them. Aaron – whose responsibility as headman included taking care of the graveyard – was an obvious suspect.

On 4 January 1991 Comrades [ANC Youth League members] convened a meeting at the Mapalene sports ground to discuss the tragic events in their village section. By collecting donations of R20 from amongst the attendants, they raised R4,000 to finance a trip to a witch-diviner. The next day Comrades forced Aaron and 30 other suspects to accompany them in a bus heading for Mbuzini, near Swaziland.

In Mbuzini the witch-diviner forced all suspects to sit in two straight lines with their legs outstretched. Men sat in front, the women behind them, and the Comrades stood in the rear as witnesses. The witch-diviner then beat all those whom he could identify as witches behind their necks with a switch and pulled them by their legs into the shade of a large fig tree. Here six people confessed that they were messengers of witches and the diviner washed them with *dihlare* that would drive them insane if they ever again attempted to practice witchcraft. He then revealed how the nine 'witches' who refused to confess had practised their craft. As a leader of Mapalene's witches, Aaron reportedly kept baboons and turned children into zombies to work in his garden at night. The other witches were alleged to have kept zombies, baboons which killed people and the ape-like *tokolotši* which raped people at night, and to have placed *dihlare* in the footpaths of their victims.

The bus returned to Green Valley on Sunday afternoon and took all witches to the police station where they could be protected from harm. But on Monday, 7 January, ANC leaders asked the station commander to release the witches. Along with those who had been accused of witchcraft in other village sections, the ANC leaders took Mapalene's witches to the Green Valley sports ground, where well over a thousand people had assembled. Jaques Modipane (then MEC for Finance in the Mapumalanga Province) pleaded with the crowd not to kill the witches. 'We don't want any more unnatural deaths', he said, 'but we should not kill the witches. What will happen to their families when they are killed? Their children, who have to attend school, will suffer the most.' Modipane then commanded the witches to fetch their *dihlare* from home and to burn it in front of the crowd. But this measure did not allay the crowd's anger. Some attendants became raucous and tried to assault the witches. Hence the ANC leaders were compelled to return them to the police station for safekeeping. But a large section of the crowd followed the bus and shouted slogans against witchcraft at the police station gates. From here the notorious Mankweng 'riot squad' of the Lebowa Police brutally dispersed them with batons, teargas and rubber bullets.

Aaron returned to his home in Mapalene and died later during the course of the year, possibly from prostate cancer. A comparison of these cases not only illustrates increased anxieties about witchcraft and more violent methods of punishing witches. It also reveals important transformations in the very nature of witchcraft beliefs, in their social contexts and in the political management of witchcraft accusations over this 25-year period. Whereas *ngwa* Mokgope was believed to have worked with the fairly innocuous bush baby, Aaron Mashile and his accomplices were associated with much more fearsome witch-familiars such as snakes, the *tokolotši*, baboons and zombies. In both accusations there were tensions between young wives and their mothers-in-law and between the different houses of polygynous marriages. But in recent years, tensions between neighbours seem to have become more profound. Moreover, witchcraft has become an explosive political issue which seems to be completely out of control. Whilst the local chief had successfully managed the accusation against *ngwa* Mokgope, the accusation against her son, Aaron Mashile, provoked fierce contestation between neighbours, Comrades, ANC leaders and the Lebowa police.

## THEORETICAL CONSIDERATIONS

The present study is primarily ethnographic and historical in orientation. By this I mean that it is mainly an attempt show why witchcraft became such a problematic issue in the South African lowveld and how these changes were lived through by people on the ground via description and analysis of discourses, concrete situations and events. But no ethnographic account is ever 'pure fact'. It may help readers to point out some of the main theoretical concerns that have shaped my understanding of the materials at my disposal. My theoretical framework is eclectic. I seek to blend interpretative and structuralist analysis of witchcraft beliefs, with an elucidation of the subjective experiences of actors, a qualitative sociological investigation of witchcraft accusations and an account of the changing political economic context of beliefs and accusations. Within this rather broad framework, I have three particular concerns: to capture the dynamics of witchcraft, to focus on witchcraft as mystical power and to explore the connections between the social and the symbolic dimensions of witchcraft.

(i) *Capturing the Dynamics of Witchcraft.* My monograph is inspired by anthropological works that treat social and cultural transformations as the central focus of concern (Ardener, 1970; Van Binsbergen, 1981; Packard, 1986; Comaroff and Comaroff, 1993; Geschiere, 1997). These studies transcend the earlier obsession with static, synchronic ethnographic descriptions of witchcraft and diverge from so much functionalist jargon that seems to perceive change as an exceptional aspect of social life. In pursuing this historical line, I am particularly interested in capturing the connections between local patterns of change and wider transformations, and exploring the relations of the unit of my fieldwork with the larger contexts within which it is embedded.

I find Turner's (1967, 1974) processual approach – which elaborates Gluckman's (1940) 'extended case study method' and the concept of 'social drama' – a useful starting point in ensuring a dynamic approach to witchcraft at the micro-level. This approach leads us to put a focal emphasis on social action and captures the complex interplay of different forces in witchcraft accusations. It is perhaps realised most fully in Shore's (1982) detailed account of a Samoan murder mystery. But by now the limitations of Turner's approach are well known. Turner implies, perhaps inadvertently, that the broader social and political economic structures, outside the contexts of drama, are a temporal.

If one wishes to portray the changing nature of witchcraft, a village of the South African lowveld cannot be treated as self-contained. It is vital to recognise the impact of broader forces – the wars of the nineteenth century; Christianisation; labour migration; the creation of native reserves, Bantu Authorities and bantustans; population removals; struggles for national liberation and the South African elections of 1994 – on the local situation. But it is also easy to err in the opposite direction: that is, to see lowveld villagers as the passive victims of external forces. Ortner sounds a perceptive warning. World systems theory, she writes, promotes a capitalist-centred view of the world:

History is often treated as something that arrives, like a ship, from outside the society in question. Thus we do not get the history *of* that society, but the impact of (our) history *on* that society (Ortner, 1984:143).

Ortner argues that as anthropologists we can make a more distinctive contribution by taking the perspective of the 'folks on the shore', rather than by situating ourselves on 'the ship of (capitalist) history' (ibid.:143).

Thus, my aim is not merely to show how villagers reacted to external forces, resisted these forces and accommodated themselves to their impact. I also endeavour to capture how villagers interpreted these forces in terms of their own beliefs, formulating or appropriating new ideas in the process of doing so. I aim to treat people as subjects of their own history.

I identify 1960 as a crucial turning point in my analysis of why witchcraft became such an explosive issue. In this year two hallmarks of apartheid were implemented in Green Valley: agricultural 'betterment' and the Bantu Authorities Act. Betterment involved a complete break with the former settlement pattern in which scattered co-resident agnatic clusters had been the basic units of social organisation. Green Valley's land was divided into clearly demarcated arable and grazing areas, and all households were resettled in compact residential sections. Villagisation facilitated the relocation of numerous additional households, which had been displaced from white-owned farms and from elsewhere, into Green Valley. As a result most households lost the fields that they had previously cultivated and their cattle. Betterment also imposed new forms of intimacy. Whilst people's neighbours had always been their kin, their new neighbours were often complete strangers. Attributions of witchcraft escalated when strangers failed to meet the social obligations of neighbourliness. Moreover, villagisation destroyed the last remnants of subsistence agriculture, forcing even greater reliance on migrant labour. The intense economic uncertainties of migrant labour and new forms of inequality, which were the seedbeds of envy, too, found expression in witchcraft attributions. After 1960 there was a rapid conversion to Christianity and, in the wake of social dislocation, the congregations of Zionist-type churches came to serve as cohesive moral communities. But these churches did not allay suspicions of witchcraft. Instead, they imposed a dualistic cosmology, in which witchcraft was perceived as absolutely evil (replacing earlier ambivalent views).

The implementation of the Bantu Authorities Act of 1958 changed the context of witchcraft accusations. As shown in the case of *ngwa* Mokgope, chiefs previously had the capacity effectively to settle witchcraft accusations in a more or less peaceful manner. But when chiefs became part of Bantu Authorities, they were forced to refrain from intervening against witchcraft. All of this created openings for ever more violent interventions against witches. With the advent of national liberation movements, in 1986, Comrades tried to profile themselves as guardians of the community's morality. Comrades led the struggle against apartheid and took decisive steps to eradicate witchcraft. After 1990, under ANC rule, the Comrades were brought again under adult control and actions witches again became less violent.

(ii) *Witchcraft as Power.* Few classical studies have directly analysed witchcraft in terms of power.[8] Their reluctance to do so possibly stems from the influential Weberian equation of power with social relations of domination and subordination and with political institutions.[9] Unfortunately, this equation may obscure indigenous concepts of power. Weber wrongly assumes a single secular source of power and fails to consider how concepts of power are grounded in cultural resources. As an alternative, Arens and Karp (1989) describe social formations as composed of 'various centres and epicentres of power in dynamic relations with one another' and assert that power 'must be viewed in part as an artefact of the creative faculty of the human imagination' (pp. xii–xiii). They urge anthropologists to explain more carefully what power means, especially with reference to cosmological systems. Their open-ended approach enables a more fruitful investigation of witchcraft as a symbolic formulation of power, derived from extra-human agencies.[10]

Stephen (1987) is among the few scholars who have made progress in this direction. She suggests that in Melanesia 'sorcerers' and 'witches' present 'contrasting images of cosmic power'.[11] Stephen describes sorcerers as dominant persons who deliberately use rituals to impose their will and to mediate cosmic power for both constructive and destructive purposes – to protect, heal, injure or kill. By protecting leaders' monopoly over sorcery through secrets communities sure that their capacity is used for the common good. She characterises witches as socially unimportant persons who harbour totally destructive powers and carry blame for misfortune and death. Because their powers cannot be controlled, they are accused, denounced and punished. Unfortunately, Stephen's (1987) ideal types have limited validity. Studies of Melanesia show that powers cannot neatly be divided by technique – between sorcery as harm through rituals, and witchcraft as harm through an innate capacity.[12]

Despite this, studies of witchcraft in Africa do find resonance in the diverse and contrasting occult powers that she highlights. Geschiere (1997) shows that in Africa witchcraft has both 'accumulative' and 'levelling' aspects. On the one hand it provides indispensable support for the dominant to accumulate greater wealth and influence. On the other hand witchcraft is a weapon of the weak, enabling the poor to level inequalities.

The former notion is most apparent in west Africa, where witchcraft is often seen as complementing the more visible coercive powers of dominant persons. In Cameroon and among the Tiv of Nigeria, living beings that inhabit the body – *evu, djambe* and *tsav* – were deemed to be the principle behind any achievement, endowing people with powers that could be used both constructively and destructively. Their possessors were only denounced once they failed to display benevolence (Ardener, 1970; Geschiere, 1997; Bohannan, 1958).[13] Among the Beng of the Ivory Coast, kings and diviners could use witchcraft to ward off the malignancy of others (Gottlieb, 1989). The Nyakyusa of Tanzania perceived witchcraft as pythons in people's bellies. While they condemned those who used witchcraft for selfish ends, the Nyakyusa revered headmen and chiefs who used their python-power to watch over the country and to drive off evil-doers (Wilson, 1967).

The 'levelling' capacity of witchcraft is more evident in east and southern Africa, where there seems to be greater compartmentalisation between the overt powers of dominant persons and the covert powers of witchcraft. For example, the Azande of Anglo-Egyptian Sudan did not associate witchcraft with Avongara aristocrats, but with the subordinate persons who were deprived, envious and resentful. They deemed these powers to be wholly malevolent (Evans-Pritchard, 1937). Likewise the Zambian Chewa accused relict older women of using witchcraft to prevent fertility, development and progress (Auslander, 1993). The Gisu of Uganda feared the power of cursing of elderly men, who had been impoverished by the inheritance system (Heald, 1986) and Tsonga-speakers in the South African lowveld perceived elderly men who had lost their land and were being neglected by kin as witches (Stadler, 1996).

This monograph aims to show how, through time, the concepts *puso* ('reign', 'govern', 'dominate') and *maatla* ('power' and 'strength') diverged. As in other east and southern African contexts, local people perceived witches as men and women who were relatively subordinate and poor both in terms of money and descendants, but as possessing the extraordinary capacity to cause misfortune. (*Ngwa* Mokgope was an elderly and feeble woman and the formal political influence of her son, Aaron Mashile, had been eclipsed by that of the Comrades.) I also aim to show how relatively more fortunate persons have evoked the imagery of mystical power to legitimise social and political inequalities.

(iii) *The Social and Symbolic Dimensions of Witchcraft.* Another more abstract theoretical concern is to examine the relationship between the social and symbolic determinants of witchcraft accusations. Whilst some sort of combination of these aspects is present in nearly all studies of witchcraft, their relationship is emphasised in two contrasting ways.

Objectivist sociological traditions such as structural functionalism and neo-Marxism, assert (or tacitly assume) the pre-eminence of social structure or of political economy. Studies within this tradition highlight the social contexts of witchcraft beliefs and the instrumentality of witchcraft accusations in social political and economic processes.[14] Such objectivist explanations, often suggestive, are at best partial and can never adequately account for witchcraft beliefs and practices. They slight the exegesis of social actors themselves and de-emphasise the content of beliefs and the ethical ideals and moral orientations that facilitate witchcraft attributions and accusations.[15]

Knauft (1985:351) argues that witchcraft attributions are not passive reflections of strains in the socio-political structure: they are produced by independent complexes of beliefs. Objectivist approaches cannot explain why, in the face of social change, people adopt one set of ideas (e.g., witches) rather than another (e.g., religious revivalism). Why are individuals accused specifically of being witches? Why not of being thieves or political enemies? Moreover, why do onlookers, who are not party to the disputes, accept witchcraft accusations as legitimate? One can only answer these questions by giving the conceptions of actors greater weight and by investigating their logic and symbolism in greater depth. The symbols around which witchcraft beliefs cluster have their own power and influence people even as circumstances change.

A second scholarly tradition encompassing many strands of American culture theory, Levi-Straussian structuralism, interpretative and 'post-modern' anthropology, grants priority to symbolic systems and to the ideological aspects of culture.[16] Historians have, for example, accounted for the rise and decline of witchcraft in early modern Europe in terms of the development of a more unitary and mechanistic view of the world, which undermined the old duality of God and Satan.[17] From within this tradition objective explanations are seen as unattainable and there is an aversion to quantitative behavioural data.

Culturalist approaches too offer an inadequate total explanation of witchcraft. As Heald (1989:4) remarks, the actor's understandings cannot be 'the be all and end all of analysis'. Their most crucial omission is transforming social and political economic contexts that encourage the acceptance of witchcraft beliefs, and exogenous factors such as demographic patterns and ecological aspects. Moreover, analyses of witchcraft that are framed purely in terms of local meanings incorrectly conflate social reality with cultural statements. (For example, Knauft (1985) found an exceptionally high homicide rate among the Gebusi of New Guinea despite their cultural emphasis on 'good company'. This serves as a reminder that one cannot assume the accuracy of folk models.[18]) Emic conceptions often diverge from actual behaviour. Symbolic projections can block social processes from people's awareness and actors can manipulate witchcraft accusations to maximise their own self-interest in ways that contradict what they say or honestly believe (Knauft, 1985:351).

A sufficient understanding of witchcraft demands that we view social action as a whole, rather than treat objective sociological aspects of life and symbolic meanings as mutually exclusive domains of analysis. We need to combine the goals of objectively describing and explaining human affairs, and those of interpreting symbolic meanings (Lett, 1991:324); and place witchcraft simultaneously in the frameworks of social, political and economic structure, and of cosmological and belief system (Packard, 1986; Lawrence, 1987).

This suggestion is not novel. Fortune (1932) and Evans-Pritchard (1937) both show the connections between social organisation and belief systems. Weber (1949) argues that 'causal agency' can only be defined by understanding social life subjectively (in terms of actors' motives) and by supplementing this by documenting actual behavioural patterns. Geertz (1973) proposes that symbolic systems are both *models of* social processes that serve as conceptions of the world, and *models for* action that shape the social order.[19]

My aim is not to resolve the opposition between these scholarly traditions theoretically – as Bourdieu (1990), Giddens (1984) and Ortner's (1984) theories of social practice set out to do – but rather to ascertain the mutual impact of sociological and symbolic factors by means of open-ended empirical enquiry. Here I follow Knauft's (1985) suggestion that we should first frame our analysis in terms of local concepts, beliefs and symbols and then understand these in terms of the lived experience of our informants. The next step is to shift to the objective analysis of social, political economic and demographic factors; rigorously to document concrete behaviour; analyse quantifiable patterns in witchcraft accusations; and to engage in a dialogue with anthropological theory and in critical comparative analysis. By viewing symbolic meanings and sociological patterns in the context that the other provides, Knauft's (1985) method deepens the insights of cultural analysis and facilitates a more nuanced understanding of the instrumentality of witchcraft accusations.

## METHODOLOGICAL CONSIDERATIONS

I conducted fieldwork in Green Valley for intermittent periods from March 1990 until the present. At all times during my fieldwork Eliazaar Mohlala and Kally Shokane – two local teachers – assisted me in identifying research problems, selecting informants, carrying out participant observation and with interpreting information. Because my fieldwork stretched for a period of almost a decade I could directly observe and record many changes in the field. I sought to supplement these observations and to reconstruct events that had occurred prior to my fieldwork by relying upon archival records, earlier ethnographic and historical studies, oral traditions, life histories and the selective memories of my informants.

A central problem in fieldwork was to overcome the resistance of informants to talk about witchcraft. Hammond-Tooke (1981:109) points out that it is a criminal offence, under the Suppression of Witchcraft Amendment Act of 1970, to accuse anyone of practising witchcraft and that such accusations are extremely disruptive (see Appendix C, p. 200). Moreover, we found that some informants also thought that their knowledge of witchcraft might lead us to suspect them of being witches. By means of trail and error we learnt to settle upon the following research techniques.

(i) *Social Surveying*. One of the first tasks we set ourselves was to conduct a social survey of 100 of Green Valley's approximately 2,000 households. We selected an equal number of households in each village section and asked standard questions about household histories, household compositions and details about the health status, income earning and affiliations to churches and other organisations of all household members. Though the sample we assembled was not random, it does provide a basic indication of demographic trends and patterns.

(ii) *Participant Observation*. We collected much information by merely being present where discussions about witchcraft took place. At the Green Valley Primary School teachers often gossiped about village affairs and informed me when they, their kin or neighbours had been bewitched. At funerals, mourners speculated about witchcraft as a possible cause of death and at the services of Zionist-type churches ministers healed the bewitched. We followed up these leads with in-depth interviews.

(iii) *Interviews*. Our interviews about witchcraft were mainly conducted with individuals with whom we were well acquainted. We guaranteed all informants anonymity and promised that pseudonyms would be used in the text. I was surprised to learn how keen many people were to tell us about their experiences as the victims of witchcraft, and of their willingness to reveal the most intimate details of their personal lives. Their motives for divulging such sensitive information was not always obvious, but in some cases they were apparently eager to convince a sceptical outsider about the real dangers of witchcraft. During interviews we tried to let informants speak for themselves. I relied mainly on note taking and seldom used a recorder. There was therefore obviously great variation in the information that I recorded, but in each case we focused on events precipitating the accusation, and on the relations between the victims, accusers and alleged witches.

(iv) *Court Cases*. Disputes between villagers were adjudicated in the chief's *kgoro* (court) on Tuesdays and Fridays and in those of headmen on Sundays. The chief kindly granted us permission to listen and take notes of the proceedings. By regularly attended the *kgoro* we were able to learn about inter-personal conflicts without invading people's privacy. Court cases are public and enable researchers to hear both sides of the dispute. In total we recorded details of 66 disputes, of which ten involved witchcraft. Because the chief was expected to comply with the Suppression of Witchcraft Act, some accused took their accusers to the *kgoro* and details of these incidents were discussed at length. Headmen dealt even more openly with witchcraft and earnestly sought to reconcile the accused with their accusers.

(iv) *Therapeutic Consultations*. *Dingaka* (herbalist-diviners) and Christian healers often treated those who had been bewitched. During February 1992 we recorded details of all the therapeutic consultations of Ketebotse Mogale, an elderly male *ngaka*, and Sebongile Ndlovu, a prophet of the Evangelist Ethiopian Church of Zion. Over this period 132 clients consulted these healers and in 33 cases witchcraft was diagnosed as the underlying cause of misfortune. We investigated all these cases, interviewed the clients about their distress, observed the healers at work and recorded information about their diagnosis and therapies.

(iv) *Reconstructing witch-hunts*. While we learnt of many witch-hunts of the past, four further witch-hunts occurred during fieldwork. These occurred in Green Valley during December 1990 and August 1992, in Arthur's Seat during June 1993 and in Rooiboklaagte during December 1994. Since we only observed a few episodes of these protracted social dramas, we reconstructed what had transpired by interviewing the witch-hunters, witnesses, the accused, political authorities and policemen. We recorded as many different interpretations of each incident as possible.

These tactics enabled us to learn not only about dramatic episodes of witch-hunting, but also about the more commonplace aspects of this phenomenon. New incidents of witchcraft constantly came to our attention and, in total, we collected accounts of 337 different accusations. (See Appendix A for a more in-depth discussion of my fieldwork experiences.)

## ORGANISATION OF THE STUDY

Chapter 2 outlines the historical context of my study and seeks to account for the proliferation of witchcraft accusations with reference to their changing social and cosmological contexts. I argue that during a period of subsistence agriculture people imagined plural sources of misfortune. The metaphysical powers of the ancestors, *dingaka*, witches and the impersonal forces of nature were essentially ambiguous and could each be used in benevolent and malevolent capacities. With villagisation and the transition to a migrant labour economy a phenomenal growth occurred in the membership of Zionist-type churches. Christianisation recast pre-existing mystical powers in a dualistic framework of good and evil, and in this new ecology of belief the witch became the predominant source of malevolence, misfortune and suffering.

Chapters 3 and 4 focus more closely on images of witches as transcending conventional categories of thought. Witches are shown to be subordinate persons in the *motse* ('village' or 'family') who derive their destructive power from their dangerous liaisons with outside forces such as *tlhaga* ('forest') and *makgoweng* ('places of whites'). Witches combine attributes from all these realms: they are *batho* ('people' but also used to denote blacks), keep animals and white persons as familiars, appropriate the attributes of animals, and employ the technologies of whites. These images connote people's desires for sexual passion, wealth and power. With reference to a brief discussion of the South African elections of 1994, I also contemplate the status of whites in local stories of witchcraft.

Chapters 5 and 6 consider the sociology and politics of witchcraft accusations in the domestic domain. Chapter five examines how the distribution of witchcraft accusations reveal tension points in the social structure and how social actors have different capacities to manipulate accusations to their own advantage. Chapter six addresses the often neglected question: why are certain accusations more convincing than others? Through a detailed analysis of five case studies I show the crucial importance of evidence – such as the occurrence of mysterious events and confessions – in attesting to the existence of witchcraft and in establishing the witch's identity.

Chapters 7 and 8 provide a diachronic analysis of the politics of witch-hunting in the public domain. In the 1930s and 40s chiefs mediated in private disputes about witchcraft and organised public witch-hunts in cases of communal misfortune. After the demise of effective chiefly rule, Comrades assumed this role by leading various anti-witchcraft campaigns. I argue that by eradicating witchcraft political actors sought to banish misfortune and to attain legitimacy. In chapter eight I focus on the period after 1990. I show how the recent witch-hunts reveal changing relations of alliance and opposition between different political structures. My analysis points to growing schisms between Comrades, who have been the most vociferous participants in witch-hunting, and ANC leaders who have generally sought to protect the accused.

In the conclusion I contemplate how my research findings can inform the recent debate on resolving the crisis of witch-killings in South Africa.

# 2 SOCIETY, COSMOLOGY AND THE MAKING OF WITCHCRAFT: CONTINUITY AND CHANGE IN THE HISTORY OF GREEN VALLEY, 1864–1995

If escalating fears of bewitchment, a proliferation of witchcraft attributions and accusations, changing witchcraft beliefs and more violent methods of punishing witches can be established, how can they best be explained? This chapter attempts to answer these questions by providing an ambitious historical reconstruction of these changes.

The broad and eclectic perspective that I adopt can best be described as 'ecological'. My use of this term ecology bears little resemblance to the attempt by Harris (1974) to see cultural patterns as an adaptation to their natural environment. Instead, I use the term as a metaphor to denote the complex relationship between witchcraft and the changing social and cultural environments within which it exists. My point of departure is the well-known structural argument that we need to consider items in relation to a wider system or totality, and that items do not carry meaning by themselves in isolation from other items (see Douglas, 1970b; 1973). Whilst acknowledging the importance of locating witchcraft within its political, economic and social environments, or contexts, we need to recognise that witchcraft is more than a protean metaphor for expressing conflicts in social relations. Witchcraft deals with the issues of misfortune and suffering, and is therefore also a component of worldview and religion. Witchcraft must also be understood with reference to alternative formulations of mystical power and competing explanations of misfortune in a constantly shifting 'ecology of belief'.

In reconstructing these changes, I delineate two historical periods. The first period, stretching from 1864 to 1959, was marked by the migration of Northern Sotho and Tsonga-speaking refugees into the area, their social assimilation and desperate struggles to defend their access to land and cultural autonomy. With the passage of the 1913 Land Act, residents became rent tenants who paid taxes to land-holding companies, and later to the South African Native Trust, for cultivation and stock-keeping rights. Subsistence agriculture remained their most valued source of livelihood, but was progressively eroded by drought, population removals and the advent of labour migration. Despite proselytisation by Lutheran and Nazarene missionaries, very few people embraced Christianity. People acknowledged the powers of different metaphysical agencies, including the ancestors (*badimo*), alien spirits, persons such as *dingaka* and witches, and the impersonal forces of nature (*maatla a tlhago*). The ancestors could intervene in the lives of descendants in both benevolent and malevolent ways. While *dingaka* usually healed, and witches perpetrated harm, this distinction was often blurred, for *dingaka* could turn their *dihlare* (potions) to harm others. Though the powers of nature sustained life, the transgression of taboos generated dangerous states of pollution. In this ecology of belief witchcraft was by no means the dominant agency.

The second period is after 1960, when profound social and cosmological transformations occurred. Villagisation destroyed the last remnants of subsistence agriculture, made residents completely reliant on migrant labour and fragmented large domestic units into smaller households. With the introduction of Bantu Authorities and the Bantustan system, chiefship was bureaucratised and lost popular legitimacy. Though missionaries had been active in Green Valley since 1916, Christianisation only had a profound impact after 1960. This is when, in the wake of the dislocations wrought by betterment and Bantu Authorities, numerous villagers converted to Zionist-type churches. Conversion to these churches did not destroy the pre-existing worldview. Rather, villagers recast these agencies in a dualistic framework of good (*botse*) and evil (*bobe*). Christians identified the Holy Spirit as the supreme source of goodness and healing, while they relegated ancestors to a less prominent status, though regarding them still as benevolent protectors. Biblical prohibitions were superimposed on traditional taboos. The new code laid down the rules for moral life and living and was seen as a precondition of health and well-being. Christians associated Satan, witches, alien spirits and *dingaka* with evil and malevolence, but de-emphasised the idea of Satan. In this new ecology of belief witchcraft became the predominant expression of evil. Many villagers contested attempts to recast alien spirits as demons and *dingaka* as wholly destructive. They continued to view these agencies as potentially benevolent.


## AGRICULTURE, ANCESTORS, AND THE AMBIGUITY OF POWER, 1864–1959

The earliest local oral traditions refer to the battle of Moholoholo that occurred between Pulana and Swazi warriors in 1864 (Ziervogel, 1954:107). Following the death of the Pulana chief, Seganyane, the Swazi drove Seganyane's subjects from their homeland at Shakwaneng – near the present-day town of Waterval Boven. Chief Seganyane's three oldest sons (Chichi, Mashilane and Cheou) fled to Sekhukhuneland. However, Maripe, whose father was Seganyane's fourth son, Morage, led his followers into the Acornhoek area. Here Maripe's warriors killed the Bakone chieftainess, Mosala a eja Barama, and the Baroka leader, Marangrang. Maripe incorporated their subjects and ascended mount

Moholoholo. When a Swazi regiment invaded Acornhoek, in 1864, they heard a calf bellowing on top of the mountain and climbed mount Moholoholo, using tree roots to pull themselves up, but Maripe's followers cut the roots and rolled down rocks to crush them. Though many Swazi perished, Maripe's warriors showed no mercy. They descended from the mountain to kill their injured enemies. Only a few Swazi survivors returned to inform their king that his bravest regiment had been defeated.

Descendants of the Pulana spy, Malalathuleng Mokoena, recounted his exploits in detail. Malalathuleng reportedly gained superhuman strength after he slaughtered a bull, which the Swazi had bewitched. Malalathuleng confronted the Swazi regiment by himself. With his hunting-rifle he shot the regimental leader and a Swazi soldier. Malalathuleng also bewitched his enemies. At times he became invisible and laid *sefolo* (a herbal compound) on their paths to cripple them. Beneath the mountain Malalathuleng offered to help a wounded Swazi. But when the enemy stretched out his hand, Malalathuleng severed his arm with a hunting knife. He then made a pipe from the arm-bone, placed *senamane*[1] inside, and blew it to make his enemies tremble.

Stories of the battle capture central historical themes and cosmological concepts. The myths bolstered the claims of Pulana war leaders to chieftainship and validated their claims to land beneath the mountain.[2] Thus, after the battle Maripe established a chiefdom at Maotole, Moletele (another participant) established one at Bedford and Malalathuleng's son established one at Marite. The myths also speak of political incorporation and the people's struggle for autonomy.

In the 1880s, diverse Tsonga-speaking groups fled into the lowveld to escape the Luzo-Gaza wars in Portuguese East Africa (now Mozambique). The first immigrants were Banwalungu who entered the northern lowveld, Hlanganu who settled near Lydenburg and Klaserie, and migrants who crossed the border from the Maputo district to work on the Pilgrim's Rest gold mines.[3] The immigrants who settled in Maripe's chiefdom were readily assimilated, marrying Sotho-speaking spouses, and sending their children to attend Sotho initiation lodges. After the final defeat of king Ngungunyana by the Portuguese, a large group of Shangaans also fled into the lowveld. In 1897, Maripe's successor, Chief Setlhare, welcomed Mpisane Nxumalo, Ngungunyana's uncle (father's brother) and granted him permission to settle in an unoccupied area east of Setlhare. Some Shangaans came to live on the outskirts of Green Valley, under their own headmen.[4] Though the Shangaans were a more insular group, they were never disloyal to the Pulana chiefs.

In an ethnological survey Van Warmelo (1935:105) described the lowveld as unique in its ethnic heterogeneity:

We find today immigrants from all quarters of the compass (save due to the north where there are no people) peaceably living side by side, and the boundaries of tribal influence intersecting and overlapping to an amazing extent.

He noted that of the 1641 taxpayers who paid allegiance to chief Setlhare in 1935, 1,200 were Pulana, 81 Roka, 300 Shangaan and 60 Hlanganu (p. 107).

For many years this part of the lowveld remained free of white settlement, due to the unfavourable climate (in summer the temperature rises above 40°C) and the presence of malaria in the marshier areas. Even during the 'gold rush', mining was confined to Pilgrim's Rest and the Selati river. Only in the late 1880s did Kruger's Republican government survey and sell large tracts of land in the lowveld to speculators and mining companies. Former Afrikaner tenants (*bywoners*) were also granted small 'occupation farms' in exchange for military service (Harries, 1989:91). Encroachment by whites altered the conditions under which Africans held land. Both larger landowners and smaller farmers levied taxes in cash and kind on the African tenants who shared their farms.[5] Being situated beyond the borders of the white-owned farms the Setlhare chiefdom was classified as 'state land'. Kruger's government recognised Setlhare as a 'native chief', in terms of Law 4 of 1885, and allowed him to maintain authority over the citizens of his chiefdom, but his people were, nonetheless, subjected to state-imposed taxes.

After the South African war of 1899 to 1902 the price of land rose and there was a transition from stock to arable farming. Though white farmers experienced an acute labour shortage, this was alleviated with the passage of the 1913 Natives Land Act. By prohibiting Africans from owning land outside Reserves and by imposing fines on landlords who accepted rent in cash or kind, the Act enforced a system of labour tenancy on the farms.[6] Elderly informants, who had been labour tenants, recalled that the household head, or his sons, worked for the white farmer for a period of three months each year, without remuneration. For the remainder of the year they cultivated their own fields and tended their own cattle. Over time, landowners exploited their land more intensely. By the late 1930s irrigation schemes existed on the farms owned by the companies Glens Lydenburg, Hall and Sons, and P.W. Willis, which allowed the cultivation of citrus fruit, cotton, tobacco, wheat and vegetables. As the land available to African tenants decreased, women and children were also obliged to work on the farms. To compensate for their loss of fields and stock, male tenants could work an additional three months for the company for a wage of £5, or periodically engaged in migrant labour.

In terms of the 1913 Land Act the Setlhare chiefdom was declared a 'released area', scheduled for exclusive African occupation. Unlike the situation on the white-owned farms, a system of rent tenancy prevailed inside the released area. In 1929 the African and European Investment Company purchased the farms under chief Setlhare's jurisdiction (Green Valley, Brooklyn, Arthur's Seat, Craigieburn, Dingleydale and Rooiboklaagte).[7] From this point on (until 1948) household heads paid rent to Mr McBride, a company land agent, for residential, cultivation and stock-keeping rights on the farm. (According to an informant, rent was set at 10s for a residential stand, 4s 6d per cow, 1s for dipping and 2s for grazing in 1935.) Movements between the released area and the white-owned farms were strictly monitored and controlled. Labour tenants on the farms were denied access to the released area, and rent tenants in the released area were not permitted to take up residence on the white-owned farms.[8]

Residents of Green Valley were relatively advantaged. The settlement pattern on the farm was one of scattered *metse* (sing. *motse*). A *motse* comprised the homesteads, fields and ancestral graves of a co-resident agnatic cluster. Its inhabitants were typically a grandfather, his sons, their wives, unmarried daughters, children and grandchildren. Fields were as large as the *motse* could cultivate and no stock limitations were imposed. Therefore yields varied according to the productive capacity of the *motse*. Maize was the staple diet, but sorghum, millet, beans, melons, marrows, sweet potatoes and ground nuts were also cultivated. Women planted, hoed, cut thatching grass and raised pigs and chickens. Men uprooted trees, ploughed, built homes and tended to cattle, goats and sheep. Other tasks, such as sorghum threshing, were not gender-specific. In a good year, during the 1930s, larger *motse* harvested up to 90 bags of maize plus 30 bags of sorghum, and kept herds in excess of 150 cattle. Smaller *motse* harvested only twelve bags and kept fewer than ten cattle.

Rural production required co-operation between neighbours. During crucial periods of the agricultural cycle, more labour was needed than even the largest *motse* could supply. For tasks such as hoeing, women held work parties (*matšema*). On these occasions they brewed beer and invited neighbours to work on their fields. Wealthier men loaned out cattle to their neighbours for ploughing. They also placed cattle under the care of their poorer kin (*mafiša*). In return for herding the cattle, their kin used the milk and kept some of the progeny. In times of drought, Green Valley's residents visited Manyeleti and Bedford to ask for maize (*šikila*). Residents of these places were obliged to give a bag of maize to visiting kin and to sell surplus bags to non-kin for £1. They could, in turn, visit Green Valley to ask for maize in bad times.

Though the released areas did serve as labour reserves for the South African mines (Harries, 1989:98), agricultural pursuits were valued more highly than migrant labour. During the 1930s most *metse* adequately met their subsistence requirements from what they themselves produced. By selling produce and stock to traders, they could also afford to pay rent. Wage labour played a secondary role. Men intermittently became migrant labourers solely to purchase clothes. They obtained work-seeking permits from Mr. McBride, travelled to work at Sabie or Pilgrim's Rest on foot, and earned 4s 2d per day.

In the late 1930s, rural producers began to operate under increased pressure. With the aforestation of large tracts of land on the slopes of mount Moholoholo, thousands of Africans were scattered throughout the lowveld.[9] Tenants were also turned off the white-owned farms to make way for cattle and crops.[10] The passage of the 1936 Natives Trust and Land Act accelerated this process. The Act required African tenants to perform six months' labour service, and stated that 'surplus' Africans had to be resettled on land purchased by the South African Native Trust. But since hardly any Trust Land was available in the lowveld at the time, a major crisis developed. Dislocated households illegally moved into the released areas and also into the Kruger National Park. The

Native Affairs Department initially ordered them off the land, but ceased doing so because no alternative places of residence could be identified.[11] The influx of outsiders placed great strain on resources in the released areas. By 1937, vast amounts of land in Green Valley had been cleared and much soil erosion occurred.[12] Moreover, in 1937, 1939 and 1943 plagues of locust, commando worm (*sefenefene*) and drought made agriculture a hazardous enterprise. In 1943, which saw the worst of these droughts, maize surpluses were soon exhausted and people were forced to queue at the general dealer store in Acornhoek to buy rations. The supplies were so limited that there was a stampede by anxious buyers at the store, and a child was trampled to death. Faced with this crisis, large numbers of men signed contracts to work on the Witwatersrand and in Pretoria.[13] For many men labour migrancy henceforth became a career.

During the 1940s and 1950s agricultural production declined to such an extent that it became a mere supplement to migrant wages. In 1948 the South African Native Trust purchased all company farms in the released area. The Setlhare chiefdom now became part of the Bushbuckridge Native Reserve, administered by an Assistant Native Commissioner. Green Valley again served as a reception site for hundreds of displaced households. The Forestry Department continued to evict Africans from their land. White farmers – facing decreased labour requirements due to the mechanisation of production operations – simply issued unwanted Africans with passes and removed them to the Reserve (Harries, 1989:104). Having failed to acquire more land to accommodate the influx of additional households, the Native Affairs Department was compelled to alter the utilisation of land within the Reserve. Between 1952 and 1953 field officers demarcated three residential locations and various arable areas in Green Valley. Whereas households had previously cultivated an average of three morgen of land, they were now allocated only half a morgen for residential purposes and one morgen for agriculture. To ensure the optimal use of land, field officers built a timber depot and dipping tanks, erected fencing, sunk boreholes and sought to limit livestock according to the carrying capacity of the veld.[14] They prosecuted men who ignored the allotments and ploughed their former lands, and arrested women who continued to cultivate along the river beds. Few households could win more than six bags of maize on their reduced fields.[15] In 1951 a foot-and-mouth epizootic further decimated people's cattle herds. Field officers placed Green Valley under quarantine, inoculated all cattle and prohibited stock from entering or leaving the farm. They also burnt the carcasses of dead animals to ensure that nobody ate the meat or used the hides.

Throughout the period of subsistence agriculture, Christianity had little impact in Green Valley. Villagers associated the Christian world view, as propagated by Lutheran and Nazarene missionaries, with subversive external forces and actively resisted conversion. The first missionary in Setlhare was Makata Mashile. As the son of Setlhare's rival for chiefship, Radiye, Makata left the chiefdom for Lydenburg. Here he became a Lutheran and trained as a minister and teacher. Makata was treated with great suspicion when he returned to the chiefdom as a missionary in 1916. Chief Setlhare granted him permission to build a church and two schools, but only on condition that he refrained from involving himself in the affairs of chiefship. At first Makata's only converts were his own kin. They lived as a marginal group, and were stigmatised for their disdain of initiation, polygyny and bridewealth. Makata's son told me that the villagers believed he had been sent by whites. 'People thought the whites would abduct them while they closed their eyes in prayer. Sometimes there was nobody left in church after my father said Amen. Everyone had fled.' Informants criticised Makata for collaborating with the Assistant Native Commissioner, for whom he occasionally acted as interpreter. Yet, despite their refusal to attend church, many villagers enrolled their children at the Lutheran schools. In 1945 Chief Setlhare even donated money to the Lutherans to erect more classrooms.

Four other churches were subsequently founded: a Nazarene Church in 1922, an Apostolic Faith Mission and Zion Christian Church (ZCC) in the 1940s and the New Christ Apostolic Church of Zion in 1957. Nazarene missionaries from the United States erected churches, schools and clinics, and built the Tintswalo hospital in Acornhoek. Yet internal disputes among the missionaries and their condemnation of African traditions undermined their efforts to attract converts.[16] Reverend Mokoena, who worked as a Nazarene Church superintendent from 1942 to 1972, recalled that only a handful of women became church members. The other churches, which were founded by former labour migrants, were no more successful in spreading God's word. Rumours circulated that members of the ZCC were ritual murderers, and few active members of the New Christ Apostolic Church remained after the minister started drinking heavily.

The predominant religious paradigm centred on beliefs in co-existing powers inhering in spiritual agencies, persons and in nature. These metaphysical powers were essentially ambiguous. None wholly represented good or evil in a moral sense: each had both benevolent and malevolent capacities. At times they could bestow health, but at other times they were the source of misfortune. Accordingly, individual conduct was designed to ensure the goodwill of spiritual agencies, to propitiate powerful persons and to the avoidance of any course that might unleash the retributive forces of nature.

(i) *The Ancestors*. Villagers attached great importance to the powers of ancestral spirits, particularly the cognatic ancestors who represented the *motse* as a corporate group (Kiernan, 1982:295). Members of the *motse* conceptualised their relations with paternal ancestors in terms of an ideology of shared blood. Since semen was perceived as white blood, passed down successive generations though sexual intercourse, it was believed the one's body contained the actual blood of one's paternal ancestors.[17] Not only were substances of the ancestors present in one's body: their breath or wind (*moya*) continued to hover around the *motse*.

Cognatic ancestors expressed parental concern for their descendants and guarded their well-being. But if they took offence they could become capricious and punish those who acted contrary to their wishes, or withdraw their protective support, thereby rendering the descendants vulnerable to misfortune. Narratives of Moholoholo and of the battles Tsonga-speakers waged in the nineteenth century highlight the fierce, violent and cruel potential of the ancestors.[18]

Villagers sought to ensure the goodwill and protection of their ancestors by ritual means. After people learnt, through dreams or from *dingaka*, that the ancestors demanded a show of loyalty, or requested gifts, they would acquire various items (old coins, headrests, walking sticks, cloth, *ndumba* [small rondavel-shaped, thatched-roofed, homes] and domestic animals) for them.[19] Chickens, goats and cows were kept for the ancestors and were not slaughtered: they were replaced in the case of natural death.

Invocations (*go phasa*, lit. 'to call') were made to the ancestors when members of a *motse* experienced misfortune, gave birth, harvested the first crops, or returned from work. On these occasions Sotho speakers converged at a shrine (*thokola*) in the centre of their yard, and Tsonga-speakers at the stem of a marula tree. (The tree symbolised genealogical relations: its roots represented the ancestors and its branches the descendants.) Descendants removed their shoes and knelt, facing the direction from where the ancestors came. The *rakgadi* (father's sister) always acted as officiant. She greeted the ancestors, called out their names in order of seniority and said a short invocation, such as, 'Let there be life! Let there be no sickness!' She then spat sorghum beer on the attendants and poured a libation on the shrine, or the tree roots, to cool the ancestors. When migrants returned from work she accompanied them to the shrine and thanked the ancestors for having protected them. The migrant then left a few coins, wrapped in a white cloth, for the ancestors.[20] Migrant labour was regarded as a necessary means to allow a man to meet his obligations to the *motse*, and migrants believed that unless they dedicated part of their earnings to the ancestors their wages could be misused or they might lose their jobs.

Only in times of severe danger did descendants make a blood sacrifice by the graveside of their paternal great-grandfather. At sunrise men slaughtered a cow and spilt its blood at the head of the grave. The father's sister then spat sorghum beer on all those present, and on the grave, recited the family praise poem, and said an invocation. Attendants consumed the meat and beer, but left all bones, unbroken, at the gaveside.

(ii) *Dingaka.* *Dingaka* and witches derived mystical power from sources external to the realm of human settlements. *Dingaka* were guided by their ancestors and alien spirits, while witches worked with animal familiars from the forest. Their powers were generally put to different ends: *dingaka* acted as healers and witches perpetrated harm. Yet these differences were not absolute.

The earliest *dingaka* in Green Valley were Sotho men who were favoured by their ancestors and acquired their skills through a long period of apprenticeship. Amos Inama, a renowned *ngaka*, learnt about the medicinal use of plants from his father and an elderly Pedi herbalist with whom he worked in Germiston. Before treating any client, Amos appealed to the spirit of his paternal great-grandfather for assistance. Male *dingaka*, such as Amos, played a vitally important role as healers, bone-throwing diviners and ritual specialists. During the 1930s the only clinics in the district treated out-patients; and kin carried the desperately ill to the nearest hospital at Pilgrim's Rest on stretchers. This situation did not improve greatly after the construction of the Acornhoek hospital in 1936. (At first the hospital comprised only a single-roomed building.) In the absence of adequate clinical medicine, villagers relied on the therapies provided by *dingaka*. Some *dingaka* specialised in healing insanity, persistent misfortune, somatic complaints, or children's diseases. Others extracted teeth, or stitched deep wounds with sinew from a cow's hind leg. Through the use of divination bones, *dingaka* diagnosed the underlying causes of sickness and prescribed the appropriate rituals. For example, if a woman bore crippled children because she had unknowingly married a distant relative, a *ngaka* could symbolically undo the tie of kinship. He instructed the couple to kneel on either side of their doorstep, and to place a raw goat's liver between them. They were then told to tear the liver apart with their teeth. *Dingaka* placed medicated stones in people's fields to prevent hail and birds from destroying their crops. They also treated sick animals with *dihlare*.

The settlement of Tsonga-speakers in the lowveld saw the advent of a new type of healer who was possessed by alien spirits.[21] The first Tsonga healers were the woman Nkoma We Lwandle ('Cow of the Ocean') and the man Dunga Manzi ('Stirring Water'). These healers were reportedly trained by Nzonzo, a powerful water serpent. Nzonzo was believed to capture people and submerge them in deep rivers. They did not drown, but lived underwater for months, breathing like fish. Only after their kin had slaughtered a cow for Nzonzo would it release its captives. They crawled from the water on their knees and emerged as powerful *dingaka* with an assortment of potent *dihlare*. (This myth resonates with the experience of birth. The foetus, too, lives in fluids inside the womb. See Hirst, 1993.) Nkomo We Lwandle and Dunga Manzi became famous healers and trained numerous women as *dingaka*. Their trainees interpreted persistent pains, infertility and bouts of aggression as signs that alien spirits had entered the bodies of their clients. Three categories of spirits were identified by the languages they spoke: the Malopo, who were Sotho spirits; the Ngoni (derived from the word Nguni), those of Tsonga, Zulu and Swazi ancestors; and the fierce Ndau who came from Musapa in Mozambique.

Spirit possession involved a degree of culpability. The Ngoni spirits of Swazi warriors possessed the descendants of those who killed them at Moholoholo. The Ndau, in turn, possessed the descendants of the Gaza soldiers who had slain them, and taken their wives, in Mozambique.[22] In a ritual, which included drumming, the client danced until she experienced a trance. The healer then exhorted the spirits to speak through the mouth of the afflicted person and to state their demands. The healer also appeased the spirits and persuaded them to assist the person they possessed. Once converted from hostile to benevolent forces, the spirits bestowed the power to heal on their mediums.

After the 1950s, spirit possession became endemic among women. As the erosion of agriculture diminished the importance of women's work, mediumship provided them with a new arena for advancement. Women's association with outside spirits is significant. Allen (1991) argues that in Uganda lineage ancestors are the first resort for moral therapy. But in times of despair, when the inside span of authority can no longer guarantee stability, women, who are unrelated to the lineage ancestors, may be called upon to negotiate with dangerous outside forces. Allen's argument provides valuable comparative insight. Green Valley's women *dingaka* relied on alien spirits to teach them how to diagnose and treat various disorders. The Malopo specialised in healing venereal diseases and sick children; the Ngoni assisted with paralysis of the limbs (*sefolane*) and red spots (*sporiani*); while the Ndau bestowed the powers of clairvoyance and the ability to detect witchcraft.

(iii) *Witchcraft*. In local nomenclature the term witch (*moloi,* pl. *baloi*) denotes a broad conceptual category, referring to persons who had inherited the power and inclination to harm from their mothers, as well as those who deliberately set out to acquire malevolent substances and skills. This difference was fluid and did not correspond to the well-known Azande distinction between 'witches' and 'sorcerers' (Evans-Pritchard, 1937).[23] Like the Azande witches, the power of witches by birth was innate, but unlike the Azande witches, they were conscious of their deeds, learnt how to practice their craft and could use material substances to harm. Those who acquired witchcraft were more akin to Azande sorcerers. They mainly used material substances and were selective in choosing their victims. But should they rub witchcraft substances into their blood, they could become as powerful and reckless as witches by birth.[24]

The activity of witchcraft (*loya*) encompassed poisoning, the use of *sehlare* (pl. *dihlare*) and the deployment of familiars (*dithuri*) and zombies (*ditlotlwane*). Pulana women were widely regarded as the most skilful poisoners. They used the lethal crocodile brain and *sejeso*. Because crocodiles bask in the sun, their brain is considered hot and polluted (*fiša*). Witches inserted small portions of the brain into the food or drink of their victims. After the victim had eaten, or drunk, the witch turned the plate or mug upside down. When they later exposed the inside of the vessel to the sun, the victims would develop stomach cramps and a headache, and his or her brain would crack.[25] *Sejeso* was a mysterious slow poison. Once ingested it transformed into a snail, frog, lizard, or snake that gradually devoured the victim's body from inside.

Witches manufactured *dihlare* from herbs, roots, animal fats and human bodily substances. A type of *sehlare* called *sefolane* was placed on footpaths, entered the body through the soles of the feet and caused paralysis of the legs. *Go kotola* was made from the victim's own nails, urine, faeces, hair, or footprints, and was used to influence his or her behaviour. It could even cause victims to commit suicide. *Šibeka*, made from human blood, was used to drive away rain-bearing clouds. This belief points to the ambiguous meaning of blood. Used by rainmakers, with the approval of the ancestors, blood bestowed fertility upon the soil. In the hands of witches it polluted the earth and prevented rain.[26] Other types of *dihlare* caused friends to fight, cattle to trample their owners and lightning to strike people's homes.

Nearly all witches owned familiars and zombies. Witches commanded their familiars – which included snakes, owls, hyenas, baboons, cats and even lions – to attack their victims. In the 1930s, a notorious witch manufactured lions from clay. Whenever anybody offended him, he sent his 'lions' to kill the person's cattle. Witches allegedly changed their victims into diminutive zombies. They first captured the victim's *seriti* ('shadow' or 'aura'), and then progressively took hold of different parts of his or her body, until they possessed the entire person. Witches deceived the victim's kin by leaving an image of him or her behind. Kin would believe that the victim was dead, but they would, actually, bury the stem of a fern tree that had been given the victim's image. At home, witches employed zombies as servants to do domestic work, herd cattle and work in the fields.

Drawing on the memories of informants, I recorded 27 witchcraft accusations that occurred before 1960. Such a haphazard selection of informants' recollections must be treated with caution, but the small number of cases that were recalled tend to confirm the general impression that such accusations occurred less frequently than in subsequent years. In all cases witchcraft was seen as motivated by feelings of envy, greed and resentment. Thirteen accusations occurred between neighbours, ten between affines and four between cognates. These took place in the contexts of unequal harvests, tensions between women and their daughters-in-law over domestic work, and disputes concerning the inheritance of cattle.

The distinction between *dingaka* and witches was not an absolute opposition between good and evil forces. *Dingaka* could be malevolent. In the 1940s, two *dingaka* were suspected of abducting women and boys who were collecting firewood, and of manufacturing *sehlare* from their body parts. People were so concerned that *dingaka* might cut portions of flesh from corpses that they secretly conducted funerals late at night. It is also significant that eight *dingaka* were among those accused of witchcraft. Similarly, although witchcraft was generally regarded with fear and disapproval, it might be tolerated when the victims deserved punishment. Stories of Moholoholo portray Malalathuleng Mokoena's witchcraft as a legitimate defence against immoral enemies.

*Dingaka baloi* (lit. 'doctor witches') combined the attributes of healers and witches, and were reportedly approached by villagers to bewitch others. Men would, for example, ask them to treat their property and livestock with *tawana*. Should anyone steal these possessions they would become crippled, their eyes would burn and their bodies itch. In retrospect, one man saw the threat of witchcraft as a reason for the low incidence of theft. He remarked, 'In the days of Chief Setlhare the *dingaka baloi* were our policemen.' When a person was bewitched or murdered, his or her kin could also ask a *ngaka moloi* to place *letšwa* on the corpse. *Letšwa* caused the killer to die in a manner similar to that of his or her victim.

In the 1930s, Kgerišhe Monareng, a well-known *ngaka*, was said to have sent lightning that killed a young girl. Previously her mother requested Kgerišhe to strike the person who had stolen her bridewealth money. When

Kgerišhe threw the divination dice he told her that someone from her own house had been responsible. Yet the mother persisted that he should strike the thief. Elders did not condemn Kgerišhe for this.

(iv) *The Powers of Nature.* For villagers the powers of nature were as ambiguous as those of spiritual and human agencies. While these powers were generally recognised as friendly, the transgression of taboos (*diila*) unleased states of pollution and afflictions. As Hammond-Tooke (1981:127) shows, pollution beliefs imposed order on a confusing environment. They highlighted the boundaries between the seasons, nature and culture, life and death, senior and junior, and between different persons. Danger resulted from the entanglement of things that should be kept apart.

Several taboos pertained to agriculture. Should anyone plant *dintlu* (jogo beans) or *mašoke* (pumpkins) during the summer, or fell *phenogela* and *mogamaka* trees, windstorms would blow away the rain-bearing clouds. It was also prohibited to cut *lešako* reeds (used for manufacturing mats) and *bjane* grasses (used for thatching) from the time of sowing until the last crops had been harvested. The presence of wet *lešako* or *bjang* in any *motse* before this time caused drought. As the reeds or grasses dried out, the soil too would become dry. Abortions and the improper burial of a human foetus polluted the earth and prevented the maturation of crops.[27] Sparrows, pangolins and crocodiles were protected species. A dead sparrow attracted swarms of birds to eat the sorghum crops. The blood of a pangolin caused prolonged drought and the skin of a dead crocodile headaches and flu. Chiefs and headmen upheld these prohibitions. They fined transgressors £5 or a cow, and sent guards to remove the unwanted reeds or grasses.

Mystical sanctions protected seniority rules. These rules came into play at the beginning of the planting season. The senior houses in polygynous marriages always had to plant before the junior houses. Mothers delegated the task of sowing to their daughters-in-law, who had to sow in sequence, according to the ages of their husbands. People could only eat the fruits of the harvest after the *go loma* (lit. 'to bite') ritual had been performed. Women first brought beer and crops for the chief to taste. Thereafter they poured libations of beer for the ancestors, and gave pieces of pumpkins and melons to their children. Senior houses tasted before junior houses, and elder siblings before younger ones. Seniority rules were also observed in marriage. Sons were expected to marry in sequence of age, and the wife of the first-born son should always be the first to enter through the gate. Moreover, the oldest son should be the first to leave his parental household and set up a new home. A younger brother could only occupy a new home after his older brother had stayed in the house overnight.

According to local ideas bereaved persons, pregnant women and women who had aborted, were in a dangerous state of *fiša* ('heat' which is extremely polluting, see Hammond-Tooke 1981:122). It was believed that after death a person's *seriti* contaminated anyone who had come into contact with him or her. To avert misfortune, bereaved families observed a week-long period of mourning. During this time they abstained from sexual intercourse, stopped working in the fields and did not touch children. Tsonga-speakers were not allowed to take food, or any other items, from the homes of bereaved families. Widows, who had the most intimate contact with the deceased, observed a year-long mourning period. They wore mourning attire, acted in an introverted manner, used separate utensils, never greeted anyone by shaking hands and did not stay overnight at other people's homes. Widows could only touch children who had been immunised against *fiša* with the *tshepe* root. If a widow walked through any field all relish, pumpkins and melons would dry. At the end of the mourning period elders washed the husband's *seriti* from her body and burnt her mourning attire.

Pregnant women also represented a confusing duality (they were both one and two) and observed the same prohibitions as widows. A woman was expected to give birth at her husband's homestead. Should she deliver at her parental home she would pollute the entire household. In this case she and the child's progenitor had to sprinkle goat's chyme around the yard to cool the home. Miscarriages and abortions caused both the mother and the foetus to be *fiša*. Because the foetus had never seen the outside world, it was *ila* (taboo) to bury it in the sun. A foetus younger than three months was buried in a damp spot by the river side, any foetus older than this inside the homestead. River sand and shade counteracted *fiša*. A mother used her thighs to fill the grave with damp soil. This movement simulated childbirth and restored her fertility.

A final set of prohibitions pertained to sexual intercourse – a potent source of contamination. Because the bodies of spouses regularly exchanged sweat, fluids and *seriti*, sexual intercourse between spouses was deemed to be safe. However, if two men made love to the same woman the essences of their bodies would be transferred to one another, via her, causing impure blood. Incest, as well as sexual intercourse with women who were in mourning, pregnant, men-struating, or who had recently aborted was also strictly prohibited.

The transgression of taboos generated different afflictions. Subversions of the seniority order led to *difeka* (*eka*, lit. 'betray') which caused women in the *motse* to bear crippled children. Children who came into contact with pregnant women, those who had touched corpses, or with men who were polluted by sexual intercourse contracted *makgoma* (verb *kgoma*, 'touch'). They suffered convulsions and a shortness of breath. Transgressions of funeral taboos brought about *mafulara* (verb *fularela*, 'turn one's back on') of which the symptoms were chest pains and profuse coughing. (Informants equated *mafulara* with tuberculosis.) Contact with widows or widowers, and sexual intercourse with women who had recently aborted, generated *lešiši* (lit. 'shudder') – a fatal condition marked by internal bleeding and an inability to urinate. It was also believed that wives who were impregnated by extra-marital lovers bore crippled children, and that contact between men who had slept with the same woman could be fatal. A sick man who was visited by his wife's lover could die. So could anyone who attended the funeral of his wife's lover. This affliction was called *matlolane* (lit. 'jump over').[28]

Since ancestral spirits, human agencies and forces of nature each had malevolent capacities, the prevailing worldview presented various alternative explanations of misfortune. Available evidence suggests that witchcraft beliefs were prominent, but does not indicate that witchcraft was perceived as the predominant source of suffering and death. During the era of subsistence agriculture solidarity between members of the *motse* and co-operation between neighbours were important strategies for survival. In this context the effects of witchcraft accusations were potentially extremely disruptive. It could lead to the permanent severing of relations with kin and neighbours on whom people relied for assistance. Notions of ancestral displeasure and impersonal states of pollution, which were as highly elaborated as witchcraft beliefs, shifted the burden of blame from kin and neighbours, and hence offered a less damaging alternative. Perhaps for reasons of social convenience, illness and death may well have been attributed to the ancestors and nature as readily as they were explained in terms of witchcraft.[29]

## WAGE LABOUR, CHRISTIANITY AND COSMOLOGICAL DUALISM, 1960–1997

The period after 1960 saw important political, economic and social changes that arose from the implementation of agricultural betterment, Bantu Authorities and the Bantustan system. Fundamental cosmological changes also occurred as many residents converted to Christianity.

The reordering of settlement patterns in the 1950s facilitated the influx of additional households. By 1959 Green Valley had a population of 3,480: 2,267 were Northern Sotho, 1,157 Tsonga, 54 Swazi and one Zulu.[30] Officials of the Bantu (formerly 'Native') Trust realised that the ever-growing population had, yet again, outstripped available resources. This concern prompted them to implement a second agricultural betterment scheme. In 1960 all land was redivided into new residential settlements, arable fields and grazing camps. Officers of the Trust relocated all households on to 410 residential stands in eight village sections. For the first time planners recognised that not all villagers could subsist from agriculture. Only some households were therefore allocated arable fields of a morgen in size which could generate an estimated harvest of six bags of maize and an annual income of £67.[31] The other households were expected to earn a living by working at the nearby plantations and timber depot. The household histories that we recorded indicate that very few fields were allocated: only five of 53 sampled households received such allotments. Planners furthermore considered it 'wasteful in the extreme' to let cattle graze on valuable soil and imposed limitations of ten stock per household.[32] Since households could survive neither from agriculture nor plantation work, labour migrancy assumed even greater prominence.

Residents were opposed to betterment, but lacked the capacity for collective protest action. They complied under duress: field officers, reportedly, threatened to burn the homes of those who refused to occupy the new stands. In the village section of Phelindaba household heads were arrested for vacating the stands allotted to them. They claimed, in court, that the stands were infested by termites and uninhabitable. Attempts to impose stock limitations provoked as much bitterness. Field officers took annual stock counts and instructed villagers to sell their surplus cattle to white farmers and the Meat Board at specially arranged auctions, but the auctions drew a feeble attendance after stock owners learnt that cows might fetch as little as R80. Wealthier men hid their cattle or distributed them to relatives, and continued to keep herds in excess of 30 stock.

Relocation drastically redefined the nature of the *motse*, domestic units and neighbourly relations. The *motse* ceased to be a corporate agnatic cluster and became a heterogeneous collection of unrelated households. Given the smaller size of residential stands, large agnatic clusters were fragmented into smaller households, and while parents and uterine brothers were often allocated adjacent stands, they were occasionally dispersed to different village sections. In either case sons achieved greater independence from their fathers. They now paid their own taxes, kept their cattle in separate kraals and their wives cultivated different gardens. Non-kin failed to provide the assistance that people expected from fellow members of the *motse*. In fact, relocations destroyed the networks of reciprocal co-operation that had been built up between neighbours over decades. Work parties entirely disappeared. Many informants described their new neighbours as complete strangers. Reports of cattle and goats destroying neighbours' gardens, strife, theft and even murder now became commonplace. The names given to some village sections allude to the enmities between neighbours. A location where many murders took place was called Kgapa Madi ('scooping blood') and the name of another, Bodlaya Bongolo (Tsonga for 'killing donkeys'), was drawn from an incident in which a man killed a neighbour's donkey that had wandered into his kitchen.

The Bantu Affairs Department encountered difficulties in delimiting the territories over which different chiefs had jurisdiction, and this delayed the implementation of the 1951 Bantu Authorities Act in the Setlhare chiefdom. The Department also failed to persuade Chief Mapalane, who ruled from 1946 to 1956, and his successor, Chief Seganyane II, that Bantu Authorities were politically desirable. After the death of Seganyane II, in 1959, the Bantu Affairs Commissioner appointed Masenyane – the fourth son of Setlhare's first house – as regent. Masenyane collaborated with the Department in introducing Bantu Authorities. Under the new system the Setlhare chiefdom was transformed into a Tribal Authority, and chiefs were made accountable to the Bantu Affairs Commissioner in Bushbuckridge. Chiefs also assumed various unpopular tasks on behalf of government. These included collecting taxes, issuing arable plots, controlling dipping and grazing operations, selecting stock for slaughter and sale, erecting fences and maintaining roads.[33]

Bantu Authorities reflected the South African government's policy of ethnic nationalism, but the Setlhare Tribal Authority initially formed part of the

ethnically heterogeneous Bushbuckridge Native Reserve, which was adminis-
tered by a single Regional Authority. Only after the Promotion of Bantu
Self-Government Act was promulgated in 1959 was the Reserve divided along
ethnic lines. The eastern side, designated as Mhala, was placed under the control
of a Tsonga Regional Authority. In 1962, Mhala was linked with three other
Tsonga-dominated Regional Authorities to the north to form the Mashangana
Territorial Authority. This ethnic grouping became the Gazankulu Legislative
Assembly in 1969, and was designated a 'self-governing' Bantustan in 1973
(Harries 1989:105–6). The western side, in which the Setlhare chiefdom was
situated, was called Mapulaneng, and was controlled by the Mapulana Regional
Authority. In 1973 Mapulaneng became part of the Northern Sotho Bantustan
of Lebowa (BENBO, 1976:16). Elections for a Legislative Assembly in
Lebowa were held in 1973, 1978 and 1983. Candidates promised to return
people's rights to plough along the river-banks and to improve pension
payments. Tensions developed between these ethnically based units and, at
times, the position of Tsonga-speakers resident in Mapulaneng was
precarious.[34] These ethnic structures persisted until the first democratic South
African elections of 1994. Mhala and Mapulaneng were then merged once more
and became part of the Northern Province. Throughout this period there was a
consistent influx of people into Green Valley.

   (i) *Christianisation.* In 1965 there were only four churches and a handful of
Christians in the village. By 1992 most village residents were nominally
Christian: the churches had grown to 26 with an estimated combined total of
5,557 adult members (see Table 2.1, overleaf). But the development of church
membership was uneven. Mission and revivalist churches failed to attract significant followings. In 1992 only 496 (9 per cent) of Green Valley's Christians
belonged to the Nazarene, Wesleyan, Methodist, Lutheran, Roman Catholic
and Dutch Reformed churches; and a further 911 (16 per cent) to the revivalist
Apostolic Faith Mission, Assembly of God, Old Apostolic Church and
Nazarene Revival Crusade. By contrast, what Sundkler (1961:13) calls 'Zionist-
type' churches experienced rapid and spectacular growth. In 1992, 4,150 (75
per cent) of Green Valley's Christians belonged to the ZCC and smaller
Apostolic congregations.

   Ethnographic evidence suggests that the greater attraction of the Zionist-type
churches derived from their 'this worldly' religious emphasis which resonated
with the earlier pre-Christian, cosmology.[35] Mission and revivalist churches
were deeply concerned with the material needs of the poor. Roman Catholic
priests were the most vocal Christian opponents of apartheid, and regularly
assisted impoverished Mozambican refugees with donations of candles, food
and clothes. The Dutch Reformed Church sponsored the most successful
'community projects', including income-generating schemes for women, school
feeding and the building of water tanks and a crèche. But these activities
diverged from their 'other worldly' theological focus on *Modimo*, the distant
God of orthodox Christianity, on moral conduct and transcendent salvation.
The focus of Zionist-type churches on the pragmatic harnessing of the divine

Table 2.1: Green Valley's Churches According to Years Founded and Adult Membership, August 1992

| Year | Name of Church | Church Members | | |
|------|----------------|------|-------|-------|
|      |                | Men  | Women | Total |
| 1922 | Nazarene Church | 10 | 40 | 50 |
| 1940 | Apostolic Faith Mission | 6 | 34 | 40 |
| 1941 | Zion Christian Church | 1,440 | 1,871 | 3,311 |
| 1957 | The New Christ Apostolic Church of Zion in South Africa | 4 | 46 | 50 |
| 1966 | The Republic of South Africa Apostolic Church of Zion | 27 | 114 | 141 |
| 1969 | Westleyan Methodist Church | * | * | 89 |
| 1971 | The Apostolic Republic Church in South Africa | 10 | 50 | 60 |
| 1972 | Nazarene Revival Crusade | * | * | 500 |
| 1972 | African Mission Home Church | * | * | 45 |
| 1974 | Methodist Church | 1 | 6 | 7 |
| 1976 | Jerusalem Ditšhabeng | 3 | 27 | 30 |
| 1976 | Dutch Reformed Church | 15 | 35 | 50 |
| 1976 | Lutheran Church | * | * | 200 |
| 1976 | Roman Catholic Church | * | * | 100 |
| 1978 | Bantu Apostolic Church | * | * | 25 |
| 1979 | The Assembly of God | * | * | 30 |
| 1980 | Jehovah's Witnesses | 6 | 35 | 41 |
| 1980 | The Alpha and Omega Apostolic Church | 10 | 40 | 50 |
| 1982 | Zion Jerusalem Apostolic Church | 5 | 45 | 50 |
| 1985 | The New Ebenaezer Apostolic Church | 5 | 25 | 30 |
| 1986 | Evangelist Ethiopian Apostolic Church of South Africa | 10 | 77 | 87 |
| 1986 | The Old Apostolic Church | * | * | 300 |
| 1987 | The New Assembly Church of Zion in South Africa | 5 | 34 | 39 |
| 1988 | Zion Christian Church (St. Engenas) | 35 | 55 | 90 |
| 1991 | Bopelo Apostolic Church | 12 | 28 | 40 |
| 1992 | Church of the Bright Morning Star | * | * | 103 |
|      | Total | * | * | 5,558 |

NOTE: These figures are based on actual church records or on the personal estimates of church leaders. [*] Indicates the absence of reliable information.

power of the Holy Spirit (*Moya*), the human body and its immediate life worlds addressed the social and psychological effects of political and economic subordination in a more direct fashion.

With Christianisation, different metaphysical agencies and powers were recast in a dualistic framework of good and evil, but for those influenced by Zionist-type churches the emerging Christian dualism was conceived of in distinctively 'this worldly' terms. Zionism constructed a binary opposition between the healing power of the Holy Spirit and the destructive sources of suffering which eclipsed abstract notions of morality, transcendent salvation and sin. Since these conceptions had a profound impact on explanations of misfortune and witchcraft beliefs, it is necessary to consider them in greater detail.

The pivotal role of the Holy Spirit was apparent in the establishment of Zionist-type churches, which were brought to Green Valley by migrants returning from the Witwatersrand. Stories relate how the migrants found relief in the depressing urban environment by joining Apostolic churches, where they experienced the transformative power of the Spirit and were called upon to establish the church at home.

The leadership of Zionist-type churches was based upon a partnership between the preacher, who constituted the group as a collectivity, and the prophet, whose imperative was personal, and who treated the concern of individuals (Kiernan, 1976). The former role was undertaken by a hierarchy of bishops, overseers, ministers (*baruti* lit. 'teachers'), evangelists, deacons, secretaries, treasurers and ushers. These officials, who were ordained by the church, assumed the tasks of preaching, conducting rituals and church organisation. Prophets foretold future events, apportioned responsibility, divined the causes of afflictions and healed sickness. Though ministers sometimes acted as prophets, prophets were more commonly church members who stood outside the church hierarchy. Their gifts derived from an individuated relationship with the Holy Spirit. The Holy Spirit revealed messages to prophets through visions, which only they could see, and voices, which only they could hear. He could also possess them during church services, and speak directly through their mouths (*malele*, glossolalia). The prophet shivered, yawned and snorted, and uttered speeches in strange tongues. Men held all positions of leadership, and Comaroff (1985:240) suggests that they thus reclaimed 'their dominance lost in the degrading subordination of the colonial encounter'. Women acted only as secretaries, ushers and minor prophets.

Despite their subordinate role, women greatly outnumbered men in most churches: sometimes by as many as ten to one. Only in the ZCC, which ritualised masculine values, were men and women represented in more or less equal numbers. This discrepancy can be explained in terms of the capacity of the churches to articulate women's moral interests (Kiernan 1994:79). Local churches upheld Puritan norms, particularly with respect to the uses of money and the sanctity of marriage. Men were prohibited from squandering their earnings on personal enrichment, alcohol, tobacco and gambling, and were enjoined to invest their income in support of their dependants. Many churches also discouraged polygyny and treated adultery as a serious offence.

Zionist-type churches reversed experiences of alienation (Comaroff, 1985:159–94). Zionists symbolically restored the original church and came to serve as moral communities in the wake of the dislocation of cohesive *metse*. Services were held as often as four times per week. Members used kin terms to address each other, and regularly pooled resources. Church leaders managed life crisis rituals and used their influence to settle domestic disputes. Zionist practice also aimed to reconstitute the person in relation to the Holy Spirit, trans-forming the body's depleted physical and social status. Indeed, the vast majority of members joined the churches to find relief from sickness and distress.

Baptism, the wearing of uniforms, dietary prescriptions, and divine healing were central practices in the reconstitution of the body. By the baptism of new church members and the ritual washing (*siwasho*) of those who had been defiled, through immersion in rivers and dams, former identities were dissolved and the convert was reborn in a new life. Church uniforms expressed the spiritual power of their wearers. Ministers and prophets in the Apostolic churches dressed like biblical figures. They grew beards, wore flowing white robes and carried staffs and mitres. Their white robes connoted purity and the activating power of semen. Women members of the Apostolic churches wore blue and green which invoked images of water, freshness and growth. All ZCC members wore a medal of a silver star on strips of black and green cloth. Men's uniforms of khaki cotton and black peaked caps emulated military uniforms, while their white boots evoked the power to stamp evil underfoot. Women's uniforms comprised yellow and green skirts and headscarves. The yellow colour signalled the rays of the sun, light and life.[36] Members of the Zionist-type churches strictly adhered to the dietary prohibitions of Leviticus and were not allowed to eat pork, hare, mopane worm, flying ant or any animal which had died naturally. These prescriptions, and the avoidance of defiling foods, were also signifiers of a reconstructed life.

Healing played a minor role in the other-worldly scheme of mission and revivalist churches. Ministers of these churches usually advised the sick to consult medical doctors, to read James 5, and they prayed to comfort them. In the Zionist-type churches, in contrast, healing was a crucial activity.

Sunday church meetings were marked by personal testimony, the summoning of the Holy Spirit, and by healing rather than formal preaching. In June 1992 I attended a meeting of the Evangelist Ethiopian Apostolic Church, held in the yard of a prophet, Sebongile Ndlovu. Only seven men were present. Minister Mokoena and three evangelists sat behind a table covered with white cloth, while Kally, myself and another visitor sat on chairs towards their left. About 20 women sat in a semi-circle on reed mats. The meeting started with the singing of hymns. Church members then stood up, in turn, to welcome the visitors. The speakers confessed that they were sinners, had forgotten the words of the scriptures, or were not steadfast in their faith, but they thanked the Holy Spirit for His blessings. Minister Mokoena then read from Matthew 13, relaying the parable of the sowing of seeds. He gave only a brief exegesis, saying that the text was really about us and our relations to God. Members of the congregation then commented on the scriptures in the light of their own needs. One remarked, 'There are those who live for God and those who defy Him. If we follow Him, He will protect us and increase our days in the world.' Others alluded to their personal distress. Some said they trembled upon hearing the words of the scripture, or that they were like the seeds that fell on stone. A collection followed, which yielded only R3.61.

The men then knelt and prayed. Women beat drums, rhythmically clapped their hands, and danced in a whirling circle, singing: '*Ntwanano! Ntwanano! Oh Makreste!* [Co-operate! Co-operate! Oh Christians!] The energy generated by the whirling circle facilitated the descent of the Spirit. Minister Mokoena stood in the centre of the circle to channel the spiritual power to the bodies of the sick. As the Holy Spirit entered him he began to tremble and snort. He then held out his staff, sprinkled the sick with holy water and placed his left hand on their heads. As he touched two children, he exclaimed, 'Lord! Heal the little ones from their coughs!' Finally, Minister Mokoena and Sebongile prophesied. Minister Mokoena told a woman that there was illness at her home, and instructed her to pray with him privately. Sebongile warned a visitor that his wife might soon divorce him, and that he might become insane. To avert this, she said, he would have to consult the Bishop for prescriptions.

The practices of Apostolic healers, who treated non-church members at home, resonated with those of *dingaka*. In fact, the parents or grandparents of nearly all healers whom I interviewed had been *dingaka*. As in the case of *dingaka*, their calling was preceded by a bout of illness. The symptoms were also interpreted as spirit possession. But those possessed found relief from Christian healers who exorcised the possessing spirits. During the process of recovery the afflicted person entered into a unique relationship with the Holy Spirit, who bestowed him or her with powers of prophecy and healing. In treating the sick, Apostolic healers worked as mediums of the Holy Spirit that guided them and revealed the causes of sickness, the prognosis and appropriate therapies. As a method of divination Apostolic healers used a multicoloured cord, called *moketwane* (lit. 'chain'). They threw the cord to the ground three times and observed its position to gain insight into the patient's condition. They could also randomly open the Bible at any page to find meanings pertinent to the problem at hand. The complaints brought to Apostolic healers were frequently of a psychological or social nature. They included misfortunes (lost property, unemployment, failing at school), depression, anxiety and paranoia. Certain mild physiological disorders dealt with (such as bodily pains, headaches, weakness, irregular menstruation and constipation) may well have been somatic expressions of personal stress.[37] Prophets only rarely treated severe physiological disorders such as snakebites, epilepsy, asthma, infertility and venereal diseases.

To treat these ailments Apostolic healers prayed for their clients, provided them with counselling, and administered remedies prescribed by the Holy Spirit (*ditaelo* lit. 'instructions'). The most common remedies were cooling with ash, permanganate of potash and holy water; cleansing through enemas and emetics; and strengthening by means of steaming or tying brightly coloured yarn (*dithodi*) around the body. Other medicinal substances included tea, coffee, salt, blue stone, vinegar and methylated spirits. The inorganic nature of the medicines provided a clear contrast with the *dihlare* used by *dingaka* and witches (Hammond-Tooke, 1989:140). Christian medicines had important symbolic properties. This is evident in the manner Paul Marule, a healer of the New Ebenaezer Apostolic Church, treated a woman whose husband, a migrant labourer, had deserted her. To rekindle the migrant's love Paul mixed in a bowl water from behind a river-stone, seawater, soot from the kitchen and soil from the garden. He then soaked the husband's shirt in the mixture and hung it out to dry. Paul also lit candles around his client and prayed for her. Finally, he sprinkled maize seeds around her yard. Paul told me that these items stood for the home, unity and power. The river water had been together for a long time, separated and reunited. Seawater is omnipotent like God: it has power over all the things that live in it. During the correct season, he said, nothing can stop the maize seeds from growing. As they sprout the husband would come home.

Rather than eliminate beliefs in the powers of ancestral spirits, nature, *dingaka* and witches, Christianity reformulated these in dualistic terms.

(ii) *The Ancestors.* Though cognatic ancestors and taboos were no longer a focal concern, both were perceived as constructive sources of well-being. Cognatic ancestors were Christianised to the extent that their fierce capacities were downplayed,[38] while their moral virtues as benevolent protectors were stressed. Prophets claimed that their ancestors acted in a subsidiary capacity to the Holy Spirit and also guided them in their healing activities (cf. West, 1975:179). Ministers acknowledged the power of cognatic ancestors to assist church members and pointed to God's commandment that one should respect and obey one's parents. Yet they always regarded the ancestors as subordinate to God. A catechist, who headed the local Roman Catholic church, formulated these views most concisely:

We blacks are not like other nations who worship idols. We believe in the spirits of our ancestors. When we experience good fortune we thank them. This is not a mistake. Our fault is to place the ancestors on the same level as God. We should elevate God to a higher and holier place.

Sacrifice was deemed sinful because it implied worship of the ancestors rather than God.[39] Church members who conducted *phasa* or *dipheko* rituals could be debarred from leadership positions, suspended, or even excommunicated. Churches devised alternative, Christian, ways of honouring the ancestors. Instead of *dipheko* rituals, Zionist-type churches held all night prayers (*mpogo*) at the homes of distressed individuals. Ministers sprinkled the household members with holy water and asked the congregation to pray loudly that they might be reconciled with their ancestors. Otherwise they encouraged Christians to sprinkle holy water on their ancestral graves.

By the 1990s offerings to cognatic ancestors had greatly declined. This was partly an effect of Christian prohibitions, but also of the declining social importance of these rites. After 'betterment' the agnatic cluster, which had been the social locus of ancestral rituals, ceased to be a co-resident and corporate group. Only a few individuals privately conducted *phasa* rituals in times of crisis. Some were convinced of this need by personal experiences. In 1981, Willias Selepe, who worked on the Klerksdorp mines, dreamt that his grandparents had warned him not to go to work. The next day Willias feigned illness and reported to the clinic. That evening he heard that four of his work mates had died in a rockfall. Upon his return to Green Valley, Willias planted a maroela tree in his yard. Henceforth he would *phasa* at the tree whenever he returned from, or left for, work.

Communal sacrifices hardly ever occurred anymore. Only rarely did wider descent groups converge at their ancestral graves. One exception was the Mashego family society – founded in 1981 to promote solidarity among the Mashego children – which annually slaughtered cows at the foot of mount Moholoholo. Sacrifices were occasionally disguised as 'family meetings'. In 1993, 200 Shokane people were invited to assemble at the village of Wales to recite their genealogy and share the meat of a bull. Those who took part learnt subsequently that the host had actually organised the event in order to gain relief from persistent misfortune.

(iii) *The Powers of Nature*. Beliefs in the powers of nature also became less prominent. Because agriculture was no longer the source of livelihood, actions that caused drought (such as planting crops in the wrong season) inspired less fear. After the introduction of Bantu Authorities, chiefs stopped proclaiming the formal beginning of the ploughing season, performing the rite of the first fruits and punishing the transgression of taboos.

Among Christians, attention shifted to a new set of prohibitions, based on biblical laws (sometimes called *melao ya dikereke*, 'laws of the churches'). These taboos were those stipulated in the ten commandments, the dietary prohibitions of Leviticus, requirements of the Puritan code and any others the Holy Spirit revealed to prophets. Additional taboos, such as the prohibition of blood transfusions by Jehovah's Witnesses, marked the special identity of particular churches. The meaning of Christian taboos differed from those of the past. They enjoined morally good living and were a precondition to empowerment. Adherence to the behavioural code inculcated self-discipline that had the effect of counter-acting subjugation to others in everyday life (Kiernan, 1994:78). Church members who transgressed these prohibitions could be debarred from leadership positions, forced to repent, or were excommunicated. But failure to observe these injunctions did not generate divine retribution, nor mystical afflictions. At worst it impeded healing.

The only traditional taboos publicly recognised by the churches were those pertaining to birth, sex and mourning. Churches required that mothers be secluded with their newly-born infants for a period of up to two months. Church members who were polluted by sexual intercourse were not permitted to touch a prophet's gown because this weakened his power to heal. Churches also supervised funerals; required widows to wear mourning attire of the church; and conducted rituals to cleanse widows at the end of the mourning period. In practice, households privately observed non-Christian taboos with various degrees of commitment. Senior daughters- in-law still sowed before junior ones, children still tasted the first crops in sequence of age, and elder brothers were still expected to be the first to occupy new homes. Villagers also continued to acknowledge the potential dangers of extra-marital sexual liaisons, which had increased greatly with labour migration, but these fears were lessened by the precautions men took against contamination. Men could consult ritual specialists to administer enemas, herbs, holy water or cooling agents to neutralise pollution.

During the 1990s elders were the most inclined to attribute misfortune to the transgression of taboos. Elders claimed that, since the resettlement, villagers had disregarded many taboos, resulting in afflictions. Indeed, some blamed the severe drought of 1992 on the senseless violence in South Africa. Members of the younger generation contested this view, and even denied that murder causes drought. One teacher observed that it rained much more in Natal, the most violence-prone area of South Africa, than in the drought-stricken lowveld. Youngsters were also ignorant of many taboos. Only during the interviews we conducted with elders, did Kally Shokane learn that a man could die if he attended the funeral of his wife's lover.

(iv) *Satan and Other Sources of Evil.* In the local Christian worldview, Satan never achieved great prominence as God's evil counterpart. Ministers hardly ever mentioned Satan in church services and in interviews.[40] The priest of the Old Apostolic Church even disputed Satan's existence. 'You'll never come across any creature named Satan', he said. 'We take Satan to be you or me doing evil things.' On the few occasions that Satan was referred to he was presented as the snake of Eden, an impersonal force which misleads people, or merely as a metaphor for the inclination to perform evil deeds. A leader of the African Home Mission Church explained:

We call it Satan if you go about stealing people's possessions and feel no pity for them. It seems to me that Satan is within people. You can see Satan at work when people necklace others.

Satan's theological marginality arose from the 'this worldly' focus of most churches. Satan represented moral rather than natural evil: he did not directly cause sickness.

Alien spirits, *dingaka* and witches were perceived to be more immediate sources of evil. Ministers and prophets identified the Ndau and Ngoni spirits as malevolent biblical demons. They highlighted the capacity of the spirits to afflict people, to make them ill, to cause men to lose their jobs and women to be infertile. For this reason Christian ritual experts sought to exorcise the spirits from people's bodies through baptism, the sprinkling of holy water and prayer.[41] The Nazarene Revival Crusade conducted a particularly active campaign to eradicate demons. In 1975 a former *ngaka*, whom had converted to the church, demonstrated his new found religious commitment by burning all the items he acquired for the spirits in front of the congregation. For the next five years converts regularly burnt items they had acquired for the spirits, including drums and even live goats at the Green Valley market. The campaign only came to an end in 1980. ZCC leaders complained to ministers of the Nararene Revival Crusade that they had seen former ZCC members, who had converted to the rival church, burn their ZCC uniforms.

(v) *Dingaka*. Relations between Christian leaders and *dingaka*, especially those who worked in association with alien spirits, were extremely tense. Ministers argued that *dingaka* practised witchcraft and exploited their clients, and they prohibited church members from consulting them.[42] Since the 1960s the greater accessibility of clinical medicine and the advent of Christian healing placed *dingaka* under pressure. From being all-purpose ritual specialists, *dingaka* became a less favoured option in the hierarchy of resort (Janzen, 1978).

While conducting the household survey I asked 42 informants about the healers they had consulted. While nearly all preferred biomedicine, most regarded Christian healing as the best alternative; 19 informants regularly participated in healing rites at church and eight had privately consulted prophets. Ten informants had sought remedies from *dingaka*, but many were critical of the outcome of therapy. Joyce Usinga took her son whose body was badly swollen, to three different *dingaka*. Though Joyce spent R400 the boy's affliction grew worse. In retrospect, she remarked, 'They just ate my money.'

*Dingaka* contested this representation of alien spirits as demonic and claimed a legitimate role as healers. Some said that they personally believed in God. Ester Khomane, a renowned *ngaka*, described God as 'the greatest of all ancestors'. She painted crosses inside her *ndumba*, gave her children Christian names and displayed a poster of Da Vinci's painting, *The Last Supper*, in her lounge. For *dingaka* spirit possession was neither amenable to Christian exorcism nor to clinical treatment. During the campaign of the Nazarene Revival Crusade, a minister called two women *dingaka* 'servants of the devil' and commanded them to burn their regalia. Thereafter, both became seriously ill. Only after they left the church and rededicated themselves to the spirits did they regain their health. *Dingaka* insisted that spirits could be rendered helpful, and that the only option was to accommodate them.

The *twa sisa* ritual, held upon the initiation of *dingaka*, dramatised the skills conferred by different spirits. In recent years these rituals became elaborate events and drew in excess of 100 spectators.[43] On the first evening the initiate slept in the same *ndumba* as a goat. In the morning, assistants slaughtered the goat and gave its knee joints to the initiate. She also ate its meat and drank its blood. These proceedings were dedicated to the Malopo who, reportedly, chose the goat because of its ability to find hidden objects. On the second day the initiate was taken to a river in which elders had cast a set of divination bones. After assistants beat drums to evoke the Ngoni spirits, the initiate entered the water and retrieved the bones. She hereby enacted the myth of Nkomo We

Lwandle and Danga Manzi who were trained underwater. The next day the initiate inhaled the smoke of strong *sehlare* that made her fall into a deep sleep. While sleeping the Ngoni spirits communicated with her through dreams. Drums were then beaten again to invoke them. The initiate danced wildly until she experienced a trance. She was then expected to find the goat's gall bladder which her brother had hidden on the instructor's premises. In the final event, called *parula*, the initiate danced to the beat of cowhide drums and became possessed by the Ndau spirits. She dressed in a white cloth and sat on the ground with her legs outstretched. Assistants cut an incision in her tongue and rubbed *sehlare*, called *xirope* in Tsonga, into the wound. *Xirope*, reportedly, enabled her to speak the words of the Ndau.

In daily practice *dingaka* stressed the power of vision that alien spirits bestowed: a vision which enabled them to detect the mystical sources of illness. Attempts by Christian leaders to dissuade Christians from consulting *dingaka* thus had an ironic effect. Villagers continued to perceive *dingaka* as the bearers of ambiguous occult powers. It is precisely because *dingaka* were portrayed as working in alliance with evil spirits, and considered capable of perpetrating harm, that they were deemed to possess the necessary knowledge to reveal and counteract evil. This made *dingaka* an extremely valuable asset.

(vi) *Witchcraft*. In the dualistic Christian worldview witchcraft was seen as the most basic source of affliction (cf. Kiernan, 1984). Only the ministers of mission churches discouraged the belief in witches. For example, a Methodist minister described witchcraft as an illogical superstition. 'If people are sick they're sick, if people are dead they're dead. We must not ask why. It is a matter of God.' Yet their teachings had much less impact than those of the Zionist-type churches that actively perpetuated witchcraft beliefs. In their everyday lives nearly all Christians, even the members of mission churches, acknowledged the existence of witches.

Stories emanating from Green Valley's churches portray an ongoing struggle between Christianity and the sinister power of witchcraft. One story is of an event which, allegedly, happened in the early 1960s. After ZCC prophets warned that the life of a middle-aged man was endangered, the congregation assembled at his home to pray that he might be saved. At dawn the man's son fainted and a snake slithered from the leg of his trousers. ZCC dancers trampled the snake to death, sprinkled the young man with holy water and called his name out loudly. When he recovered, he confessed that he had planned to bewitch his father. From a suitcase in his room he brought two plastic bags. In one bag he kept the snake, in the other *sehlare* with which he aimed to strengthen his fist so that he could beat his father to death. More recent stories relate how familiars fell from people's coats as they entered the gates of the ZCC headquarters at Moria, or how witches caused buses of churchgoers to overturn, or poisoned food at church conferences, or captured patients from the homes of Apostolic healers.

The complex contribution of Christian healers to witchcraft attributions appears from a comparison of the manner in which Sebongile Ndlovu, a middle-aged Apostolic prophet, and Ketebotse Mogale, an elderly *ngaka*, diagnosed the underlying sources of the problems of clients who consulted them in February 1992. While Sebongile emphasised witchcraft, Ketebotse diagnosed most cases of misfortune as due to the transgression of taboos (see Table 2.2, below).

Table 2.2: Diagnosis of the Underlying Causes of Clients' Problems by Sebongile Ndlovu and Ketebotse Mogale, Green Valley, February 1992

| Sources of Misfortune | Ketebotse | Sebongile | Total |
|---|---|---|---|
| Cognatic ancestors | 1 | 5 | 6 |
| Alien spirits | 2 | 6 | 8 |
| Transgression of taboos | 12 | 0 | 12 |
| Witchcraft | 2 | 31 | 33 |
| Only Natural Causes | 8 | 27 | 35 |
| Unknown | 6 | 32 | 38 |
| Total | 31 | 101 | 132 |

Christian healers such as Sebongile accentuated fears of bewitchment. For example, Peter Chiloane consulted an Apostolic prophet after his wife and child ran away from home. Peter merely enquired about their whereabouts, but he was told that his wife and her new lover planned to bewitch him so that they could inherit his pension. Later Peter searched his home and found substances, which seemed like witches' *dihlare*, beneath his mattress and carpet. He became extremely anxious and began to suffer from insomnia. Such revelations were generally taken very seriously. A youngster who was told by a ZCC prophet that his deceased sister had been turned into a zombie and would return home to fetch food, was so scared that he sought alternative accommodation.

Christians did not imagine that witches entered into a pact with Satan.[44] Rather, witches represented an independent source of malevolence, perceived still as persons motivated to harm by envy and resentment. However, in the Christian worldview all forms of witchcraft became wholly evil and intolerable. Even the use of *tawana* and *letšwa* – the *dihlare* directed against thieves and killers – was condemned. For example, in 1994 villagers alleged that a shebeen operator bewitched a boy, who stole R300 from him, with *tawana*. Many were angered when the boy became terminally ill. In 1995 a notorious young man, Tebogo Shai, died tragically in a motor-vehicle accident. One year earlier Tebogo had killed a six-month-old baby while driving his employer's car. Yet, before his funeral, villagers called a meeting to discuss the circumstances surrounding his death. They accused the baby's mother of having bewitched Tebogo with *letšwa* and demanded her eviction.

Despite their emphasis on the evils of witchcraft, the Zionist-type churches did not take the offensive against witches. Prophets readily ascribed misfortune to witchcraft, but were reluctant to name specific persons as witches. Clients were told in great detail how their lives were threatened, how glowing bottles of *dihlare* were placed in their homesteads, or how they were being tormented by witch-familiars; but references to the identity of their assailants were always non-specific.[45] Prophets defended this practice by saying that only those with witchcraft in their blood can pinpoint witches. To find out who had bewitched them villagers drew their own inferences or consulted witch-diviners. Likewise, church leaders did not instigate witch-hunts or the violent punishment of witches. An Apostolic minister explained, 'We abide by God's commandment "Thou shall not kill".'

The predominant Christian response to witchcraft was a defensive one. Ministers excommunicated church members who had witchcraft in their blood and assisted those who confessed to get rid of the witchcraft substances they had bought. Prophets used prescriptions of the Holy Spirit to protect church members against witchcraft and to heal the victims of witchcraft. A young man who suspected witchcraft when his car broke down was told by a prophet to procure black, red and white cloth. To remove all misfortune from his body, the prophet instructed him to tie the black cloth around his waist and leave it in the veld. He was also told to place the red and white cloth beneath his pillow to thank his ancestors for having saved him. Finally he had to purify himself with the blood and eggs of a white chicken.

The fortification of people's homes against witchcraft was an elaborate ritual. After the Sebatane household suffered a spate of deaths, Mr Sebatane asked Sebongile Ndlovu to fortify his home. In a large zinc basin she poured maize meal, sugar, tea, coffee, river-sand, salt, machine-oil, snuff, ash, Jeyes fluid, red pepper, chillies, sulphur, aloe crystals and methylated spirits. She said a short prayer for all household members and sprinkled the basin's contents around their yard. Sebongile explained her choice of some of these substances. The salt, she said, repelled the wild *tokolotši*, while the pepper and chillies blinded other familiars. Jeyes fluid (a strong detergent) neutralised witches' *dihlare*. The aloe crystals – which shine like lightning – immunised the home against thunder bolts. Sebongile also dug several large holes in the yard, which she filled with river-sand, stones and 15 cm long nails. To witches, she said, the sand and stones appeared like rivers they could not cross and the nails prevented familiars from moving underground. In addition she tied yarn cords at the door-posts; fumigated all rooms by burning a mixture of pepper, chillies and sulphur on a spade; and strengthened the Sebatane children with steaming. Finally, Sebongile prayed in front of the gate and asked the Lord to bless the home.

Christianity thus played a crucial role in structuring everyday perceptions of witchcraft. These changes stretched well beyond the confines of the churches. Escalating fears of witchcraft also occurred against the backdrop of villagisation and the change from subsistence agriculture to an economy based on wage labour. Increased tensions among kin and neighbours, and new inequalities, which were seedbeds of envy, favoured personalised conceptions of evil. Moreover, in the more individualistic economic order, in which survival no longer depended upon the solidarity of large domestic groups and neighbourli-

ness, the effects of witchcraft accusations became less disruptive than they had
been in the past.


CONCLUSIONS

This chapter bears out Weber's (1930) contention that in periods of social
transition religious conceptions may be transformed and outlive the social institutions that support them, surviving to confront new situations of life. In Green
Valley the demise of agriculture, increased labour migration and Christianisation did not bring an end to witchcraft beliefs. These transitions rather
contributed to the escalation of witchcraft beliefs. While the necessity of co-
operation between kin and neighbours had inhibited witchcraft attributions
during the period of agriculture, the greater individualism of villagisation
lessened these constraints. The new tensions and inequalities of the migrant
labour economy expressed in witchcraft attributions. With conversion to
Zionist-type churches, marked by a 'this worldly' emphasis on health and a
dualistic cosmology, the malevolence of witches was defined in opposition to
the benevolence of the Holy Spirit and cognatic ancestors. Alternative explanations of misfortune, which invoked the powers of ancestral spirits and nature,
were de-emphasised.

Evidence from Green Valley permits tentative generalisations, which may
explain why the Northern Province has earned a reputation as the 'witchcraft
capital' of South Africa (*New York Times*, 18 September 1994; *The Sunday
Independent*, 16 June 1996; see also Appendix B). Although the intensification
of witchcraft attributions in Green Valley occurred in a broader context of
social, political and economic transitions, these were general to the South
African countryside. Experiences of apartheid, Bantu Authorities, population
removals and agricultural betterment did not differ significantly from other rural
areas (De Wet, 1995). However, the religious changes that took place in this
region were unique and seem to be the crucial difference that may account for
the proliferation of witchcraft.

While significant proselytisation by mission churches – which propagated
'other worldly' salvation and discouraged witchcraft beliefs – had occurred
among the Cape Nguni and Tswana since the 1820s, and the Natal Nguni and
Southern Sotho from the 1840s, it was only in the 1870s that the Berlin and
Swiss missionaries began to establish themselves among Northern Sotho,
Tsonga- and Venda-speakers (Pauw, 1974:416).[46] Among the latter popula-
tions, membership of mission churches remained the lowest in all South
African rural areas, seldom exceeding 40 per cent (Pauw, 1974:421). Among
Northern Sotho, Tsonga- and Swazi-speakers, Zionist-type churches, which
emphasised the evils of witchcraft, took root most strongly. Here the
membership of Zionist churches greatly outnumbered that of their mission
counterparts (Pauw, 1974:422).

These social and cosmological transitions did not merely account for the increased attribution of misfortune to witchcraft. They formed the backdrop for changes in the nature of witchcraft beliefs, the emergence of new ideas about witch-familiars and technologies of witchcraft, as well as new patterns of witchcraft accusations. I explore these themes further in the following four chapters. But this analysis cannot account fully for the emergence of more violent methods of confronting the problem of witchcraft. This requires a discussion of changing political strategies in the management of witchcraft accusations and the eradication of witches. In Chapters 7 and 8, which examine the changing nature of chiefship and the rise of the Comrades movement, I address these matters in more detail.

# 3 WITCHES OF THE LOWVELD AND THEIR FAMILIARS: CONCEPTIONS OF DUALITY, POWER AND DESIRE

Ethnographic studies conducted at different points of time on Northern Sotho and Tsonga-speaking groups of the lowveld have associated witches with a large and varied group of animals. Known as *dithuri* in Northern Sotho, these animals are referred to as witch-familiars in the literature. At the turn of the century Tsonga witches were believed to use nocturnal birds, hippopotami, crocodiles, lions, leopards and even duikers (Junod 1966:506–15). In the 1930s common witch-familiars among the Lobedu were polecats, skunks, snakes, elephants, birds and owls (Krige and Krige, 1965:251). In the 1960s the Pedi associated baboons, wild cats, dogs and bats with witches (Mönnig, 1988:73), whilst the Kgaga singled out ambiguous animals such as genets, mongeese and hyenas as familiars in the mid 1970s (Hammond-Tooke, 1981:99). The persistence of the relationship between witches and familiars through time and place is striking,[1] but the form taken by the relationship was by no means settled. Often the familiar and the witch are represented as distinct beings. For instance, witches may capture, tame and feed familiars. Once tamed, they are trained to carry out the witch's evil wishes. Familiars are sent to steal from victims, attack, injure and kill them. Great intimacy develops between the witch and the familiar; indeed, the familiar can become the witch's lover or child (Krige and Krige, 1965:251). Elsewhere in the texts human and animal identities are shown to merge through a complex series of transformations. Junod (1966:507, 515) writes that Tsonga witches acquired animal-like features such as wings or were transformed into animals. They also changed their victims into leopards, hyenas and snakes. Pedi 'night witches' actually became familiars:

They can transpose themselves into one of their familiars, particularly a baboon, a dog or a bat. They can thus acquire the physical appearance of any animal and go about unhindered to caste a spell upon a person which will cause him to waste away slowly or to go mad (Mönnig, 1988:75).

On the other hand, familiars could become people. The Kgaga did not conceive of familiars as real animals, but believed that they could change shape and metamorphose into human form (Hammond-Tooke, 1981:99).

This chapter considers the symbolic dimensions of the complex relationship between witches and their familiars. Though my aim is not to provide an in-depth account of the various familiars encountered in Green Valley during different historical periods, I do wish to highlight continuities and changes in local discourses. My aim is to focus on the symbolic constitution of only two witch-familiars – the ape-like *tokolotši* and the snake-like *mamlambo* – and to ask why these familiars, in particular, have become dominant symbols of witchcraft in the time-period after 1960.

The chapter draws on a synthesis of etic and emic symbolic interpretations. I argue that, structurally, the meaning of this confusing relationship can only be adequately grasped with reference to local concepts of duality, power and desire. Witches and familiars are shown to constitute a duality in which human and animal identities are different manifestations of a single form. As anomalous beings, witches and familiars stand betwixt-and-between the opposed categories of *motse* (the 'family' or 'village') and *tlhago* ('nature'). They exist simultaneously in the village and the forest, but are not fully part of either realm. Witches are identified with familiars, have the attributes of animals and actually metamorphose into familiars. This duality lies at the heart of the conception of witchcraft as a dangerous, superhuman, power. Because witches combine elements from different realms in a disorderly mixture they transcend the limitations of ordinary humans. Duality also underlies concepts of personhood. The relation between the witch and the familiar resonates with the duality of the person's body and its animal-like instincts and desires. Unlike cultured persons, witches are consumed and dominated by their desires.

Though the structural meaning of witches and familiars has remained fairly constant, there have been important discontinuities in the types of witch-familiars encountered in Green Valley through time. Lions, hyenas, snakes, owls, bush babies, baboons, antelope and wild cats were the most common familiars during the earlier period of subsistence agriculture. Witches frequently sent lions to kill one's cattle and baboons to steal one's crops. Despite increased fears of witchcraft after betterment, informants were adamant that contemporary witches employ fewer familiars. Recent stories of witchcraft no longer mention lions, hyenas, bush babies and antelope, and only occasionally do they refer to owls, baboons and domestic animals. These familiars have been replaced by the *tokolotši* and the *mamlambo*: new witch-familiars believed to have been purchased by local witches from Nguni-speaking *dingaka baloi* on the mines or in KwaZulu/Natal.[2]

I argue that these new familiars were incorporated, and subsequently became dominant, due to their capacity to provide appropriate symbolic comment on transformed situations of life, marked by people's dependence on wage labour. I suggest that the ape-like *tokolotši* symbolises the potential animal-like craving for uninhibited sexual expression. This familiar provokes thought about the separation of spouses and the sexual deprivations that accompany labour migration. The snake-like *mamlambo* objectifies the desire for money in a context of social and economic deprivation, and highlights the destructive social effects brought about by the unrestrained quest for wealth.

My discussion is in two parts. The first explores the structural meaning of witch beliefs and considers the meaning of witches and familiars in relation to other symbols in a larger system.[3] In the second and most substantial part of the chapter I turn to the particular symbolic features of the *tokolotši* and the *mamlambo*, and to emic points of view, and I emphasise the explanations that social actors, themselves, gave for these animals. The ethnographic information I present derives primarily from open-ended interviews with key informants, who were particularly knowledgeable about witch-familiars and freely discussed their theories with me. My information is slightly biased in that men's accounts of the sexual aspects of witchcraft were more detailed than women's accounts. The discussion also draws on 39 instances in which local individuals were accused of keeping either the *tokolotši* or *mamlambo*. These accusations provide an indication of the operational meanings of these familiars.

## NATURE, CULTURE, WITCHES AND FAMILIARS

Through time cosmological ideas in the lowveld have expressed a symbolic opposition between the two broad categories, *motse* and *tlhaga*.[4] Both terms have a wide frame of reference: *motse* refers to the realm of human settlement, and is the public domain of ritual and political action, which is associated with civilisation (*hlabologo*) and culture (*setšo*). *Tlhago* refers to the wild, untamed, realm of nature: it is the domain of vegetation and animals. *Tlhaga* also denotes that which is primordial. This is evident in the phrase *O tlhaga kae?* ('Where do you originate from?') These categories are opposed yet complementary, and have remained very prominent in Green Valley after betterment, expressing a continuing opposition between the local community and the chaos beyond.[5]

The logic expressed by this contrast shapes the perceptions of humans and animals. *Maitshwaro* is the major attribute of personhood that sets people apart from animals. The concept refers to virtuous conduct and character. The phrase *motho yo o na le maitshwaro* literally means 'a person can conduct him/herself well'. It is because people possess *maitshwaro* that they are deemed cultured, responsible, honest and able to control and suppress (*gatelela*) their self-centred desires. Animals lack *maitshwaro*, their behaviour is solely the product of *tlhaga* (nature, but also instinct) and of *duma* (innate desire).[6] Hence, animals are incapable of discipline and constraint, they are governed by their desires for food and sex, which they cannot suppress nor control. As one man explained, 'If an animal sees something it wants, it just runs after it. Animals can't wait. They have food and sex at any time.'

The sets of symbolic oppositions in this classificatory scheme can be summarised as follows:

*MOTSE* (settlement) / *TLHAGO* (nature)
*MOTHO* (person) / *PHOOFOLO* (animal)
*HLABOLOGO* (civilisation) / *LEŠOKA* (wilderness)
*MAITSHWARO* (calculated conduct) / *DUMA* (instinct)

In the lowveld witches and familiars occupy an anomalous position betwixt-and-between the contrasting domains of *motse* and *tlhaga*. These beings exist simultaneously in *motse* and *tlhaga*, but are not fully part of either realm. Witches move across to the animal sphere and cause some animals to move from the animal to the human sphere. Witches are people who reside in the *motse* but they move to the edge of the village by night. They meet under trees at the liminal place where the village borders the bush, to plan their evil deeds.[7]

Many features of witches indicate a symbolic affinity with animals. As babies, witches have the ability to cling to walls like bats. Like nocturnal predators and cats, they are not inhibited by the darkness, and easily move about at night. Like birds, they are capable of flight. Before committing their hideous crimes, witches undress and shed the trappings of culture and civilisation. Despite their nakedness, they feel no shame. Women are subordinate in the male dominated social order of the *motse*, but they may head gatherings of witches.

Familiars are animals in appearance and are primarily located in the realm of *tlhaga*. However, unlike ordinary wild animals, they intrude into human settlements. People nearly always identify the snakes, baboons and owls they encounter in village sections as familiars. Familiars also possess human attributes: unlike wild animals, they have *seriti* ('shadow' or 'aura'). They do not fend for themselves, but are fed like human infants. Familiars are capable of human-like communication: they understand their master's instructions and can even speak. An elderly male informant recounted how, in 1948, people found a cat snared near a river stream. To everyone's surprise the cat called out: '*Hle, ntesetše hle, ke sepele! Ke nyaka go ya gae. Hle, ke sepele, hle!* [Please, let me go, release me! I want to go home! Please, release me!]' After they freed the cat it ran directly towards a man's homestead, but he denied that the cat was his.

The affinity between witches and familiars runs deeper than a mere association or even the shared possession of certain features. In witchcraft human and animal identities are not clearly separate. They appear as different manifestations of a single form. Stories of witches who metamorphose into the shape of their familiars express a confusing duality.[8]

A forestry worker told me a story of a young man who discovered mysterious *dihlare* (potions) at his fiancée's home. She warned him not to use the *dihlare* as it would cause him 'to see miracles'. However, the young man disobeyed and washed his face with the *dihlare* one evening. Suddenly he heard people shouting and found that he was in the midst of witches. Frightened, the man pretended that he too was a witch, and underneath a large tree the witches taught him how to bewitch others. They gave him switches to hold in each hand, and he was instructed to threaten his victims with the right hand, but to beat them with the left. Instead, the young man beat the witches with his right hand and, as he beat them, they died. The next morning many villagers, including the chief's wife, were reported missing. Because the chief was greatly concerned the young man relayed the full story to him. He then escorted the chief and elders to the tree where he had beaten the witches. There they found the witches lying motionless in the shade. The chief pleaded that the young man should revive them. He again held the switches in his hands, threatened with his left, but beat the witches with his right. As he beat them they metamorphosed into baboons, snakes and owls and ran toward the village. Once inside the village, they again changed into human form. The chief praised the young man, but advised him that he should never again visit his fiancée's home.

A teacher told two stories of metamorphosis. At a time when Green Valley was still very bushy, cattle herders regularly saw a duiker in the forest. They often chased it with dogs, but it always disappeared behind the same tree. As they approached the tree an old man appeared and told them he had not seen any duiker. Eventually the herders realised it was the old man himself who had assumed the form of the duiker. The second story is that of a man who awoke at midnight and saw that his wife was no longer in bed. He heard the sound of a sewing machine coming from the room next door. When he went to investigate saw that a large baboon operated the machine. Shaken, he returned to the bedroom. Later he again went to investigate. This time he saw his wife sitting behind the machine. She assured him that he had not seen a baboon: 'It was me', she said. 'You did not see very clearly.'

Duality is crucial to the conception of witchcraft as a form of superhuman power.[9] The superiority and intelligence of witches, as well as their capacity to fly and kill, are aspects of their anomalous positional status betwixt-and-between *motse* and *tlhaga*. As Douglas (1970b) intimates, anomalous phenomena are widely associated with pollution and danger. A condition of impenetrable and destructive power results from the entanglement of spheres normally kept apart. Moreover, by combining attributes from the realms of *motse* and *tlhaga* in a unique configuration, witches transcend human limitations.

Duality and shape-shifting are also intimately related to conceptions of personhood. The duality of person and animal in witchcraft resonates with the duality of a person's visible natural body (*mmele*) and its invisible, libidinal and animal-like desires (*duma*). At times illicit desires are suppressed, at other times they manifest themselves, dominate and consume the body. Rapists, womanisers and promiscuous women who succumb to their desires and violate the proprieties of marriage are described as inhuman (*bo hlola*) and as lacking *maitshwaro*. They and others who behave unacceptably may be called animals. People who turn against their kin are referred to as dogs (*dimpša*). Those who are cunning, dishonest and untrustworthy are called snakes (*dinoga*). In the case of witchcraft such animality is deemed particularly intense. Witches, like animals, completely lack *maitshwaro*. They do not merely succumb to their desires at times, but are totally dominated by their cravings for food, sex, money and revenge. As we have seen, envy (also *duma*) was perceived as the most common motive for witchcraft, and accusations of witchcraft were usually directed against those who were, socially and economically, the most deprived.


## FAMILIARS OF THE LOWVELD AND THEIR SYMBOLISM

Despite the special insights they yield, structural approaches to symbolic inter-pretation have definite limitations. They depend upon the anthropologist's inferences about the implicit and unspoken, but give little weight to the explicit intent of people themselves (Werbner, 1986:155). These interpretations also obscure the ideological implications of symbolism in terms of political power and systems of social control (Morris, 1987:149). Kapferer (1988:4, 43) comments that myths are an integral part of lived experience. Myths provide a framework through which experience achieves significance and find articula-tion through the flow of social action. They motivate action, and gain determinance through the social and political structures and processes of which they are part. His comments are as pertinent to myth as they are to the analysis of familiars as symbolic formulations.

It is therefore essential to complement structural approaches with an analysis of folk interpretations of symbols and to contextualise the emic meanings of witch familiars by considering the manner in which they are evoked in specific instances of witchcraft accusation.

Drawing on folk conceptions, the following discussion investigates the symbolism of the *tokolotši* and the *mamlambo*. These familiars have charac-teristics that set them aside from ordinary animals, and they are comparable to the 'monsters' encountered in Ndembu initiation rites. Turner (1967:106) argues that through the exhibition of the bizarre monsters, complex aspects of life are communicated to initiates, 'Monsters startle neophytes into thinking about objects, persons, relationships, and features of their environment they have hitherto taken for granted.' By combining animal and human form in unique configurations, Ndembu monsters are effective multivocal symbols. The exaggeration of certain features in monsters is particularly thought provoking. Features which 'stand out' are objects of reflection. For instance, a man's head on a lion's body encourages novices to think about lions and brute force.

It is through the configuration of such features that the *tokolotši* and the *mamlambo* objectify the uninhibited, illicit desires for sex and money.


### The Tokolotši *and the Construction of Sexual Desire*

Informants were adamant that Green Valley's witches only began using the *tokolotši* after the population removals of 1960. They speculated that migrants who had worked on the Witwatersrand might have introduced this familiar to the village. Informants said that the *tokolotši* seems like a large baboon (*tšhwene*), but walks on two legs like a human being. 'Like a baboon it is a horrible creature with horrible teeth.' My informants believed that the *tokolotši* had pronounced sexual features and can be either male or female. A teacher explained that the male has an enormous penis which can stretch to any size:

Its penis is like an elastic... Before it enters a home the *tokolotši* will first use its penis to feel if it is safe... The penis will push the gate aside and the *tokolotši* will enter.

The female *tokolotši*, in turn, was said to have huge breasts. Male and female witches were more or less equally prone to use the *tokolotši*. Eight of the eighteen Green Valley residents accused of using this familiar were men and ten were women.

Informants' accounts of the relationship between the witch and the *tokolotši* were both inconsistent and confusing. According to some the identities of the witch and the *tokolotši* remain separate. They thought that witches acquire the familiar from *dingaka baloi* in the form of a root. At home the root changes into a *tokolotši* by its own volition. Alternatively, they said, witches manufacture the *tokolotši* from animal fat, which they use to change domestic animals, such as dogs, into the *tokolotši*. Others were of the opinion that the identities of the witch and the *tokolotši* are inseparable. They said witches smear animal fat on their own bodies to transform themselves into the *tokolotši*.

The idea of duality is expressed by the notion that witches can assume the form of the *tokolotši* and vice versa. Witches are believed to set off at night as *tokolotši* to rape sexually desirable men and women in the neighbourhood. In this form witches are invisible and possess exceptional sexual prowess. One informant argued that witches were more inclined to act themselves in the form of the *tokolotši* than to send it out by itself.

If a witch sends the *tokolotši* to have sex with his neighbour's wife the witch will not enjoy it. The *tokolotši* will. If he wants to fuck his neighbour's wife at night he himself has to change into a familiar – the *tokolotši*.

The *tokolotši* can also assume the witch's image. When witches leave their homes to bewitch others they use strong *sehlare* to lull their human lovers or spouses into a deep sleep. They may also leave a *tokolotši* behind, and it assumes their appearance. I was told of a young man who slept with the daughter of a well-known witch. Making love to her, he felt that she was ice-cold and hairy. When he spoke to her, her voice responded from outside the room. The young man fled, thinking that he had made love to a *tokolotši* that looked like his girlfriend.

Accounts of the end of the relationship between witches and the *tokolotši* are inconsistent. Some informants emphasised a distinctiveness of identities and insisted that the *tokolotši* can kill the witch. If the witch sends it to a fortified home and it repeatedly fails to gain entry, the *tokolotši* may be angered, turn around and attack the witch. Other informants portrayed an essential unity between the witch and the *tokolotši*. They maintained that when the familiar is killed the witch would also die. This is because the witch assumes the form of the familiar, uses the same fat as it does and because there is a mystical interdependence of their identities.

Despite certain similarities, these conceptions of the *tokolotši* in Green Valley during the 1990s differ significantly from the *u-tikoloshe* or *thikoloshe* (in Xhosa) described in ethnographic literature on the Cape Nguni. In the latter accounts the *thikoloshe* usually features as a diminutive hairy, man with an exceptionally large penis. On the basis of her field work in Pondoland during the 1930s, Wilson (Hunter, 1979:275) describes the *thikoloshe* as:

a small hairy being, having the form of a man, but so small that he reaches to a man's knee. He has hair all over his face and coming out of his ears, and his face is squashed up like a baboon. The penis of the male is so long that he carries it over his shoulder, and he has only one buttock.

Though the *thikoloshe* usually lives by itself in some pool of a river, from which it issues to carry out mischievous actions, women *igqwira* (witches) may be accused of having sexual relations with it (Soga, 1931:185, 186; Hunter, 1979:275; Hammond-Tooke, 1962:280–1).

Wilson (1951) relates the Pondo belief in the *thikoloshe*, with its exaggerated sexual characteristics, to women's illicit desires. Among the Pondo, she argues, women's sexual desires tend to be repressed because rules of clan exogamy exclude many potential mates resident in local areas from marriage. She contrasts the Pondo *thikoloshe* to the Nyakyusa idea that pythons exist in the bellies of witches. As Nyakyusa age-villages are not constituted on the basis of kinship, witches are motivated by a lust for meat, not sex. Although this comparison is insightful, it is hard to assess the specific merits of her claim. Hammond-Tooke (1984) shows that Cape Nguni lineages and clans are not, and were not in the past, local groups. Pondo women thus had a wide choice of marriage partners from within their local areas, but it is true that married women could not easily take lovers.

Hammond-Tooke (1974) accounts for the *thikoloshe* in terms of men's perceptions of inter-sexual relations. He maintains that Cape Nguni men are uneasily aware of women's deprivation. As daughters and wives, women are 'perpetual minors'. They may not appear in court, hold political office, be polygynous, take lovers or be disrespectful to any senior man. There is dissonance between this construction of reality and men's suspicion that women are, in fact, more important than they are themselves. Women's fertility is unambiguously located, they dominate the hearth and fields and are 'the sturdy container of lineage interests' (ibid.:131). This contradictory perception of women is associated with guilt. Men imagine that women respond with resentment and cherish negative emotions. By conceptualising the witch in the image of a woman this dissonance is given concrete form. Men view the crux of women's deprivation as sexual because it is here that manhood finds most convenient expression. Women are thus imagined to take daemon lovers to fulfil their sexual needs and to wreak vengeance on men. The most obvious symbol of women's resentment is the compensatory image of the enormous penis of the *thikoloshe*. In this way the witch myth transmutes guilt into 'righteous indignation' and provides an *ex post facto* rationalisation for discrimination (ibid.:132).

Clearly it is inadequate to interpret the *tokolotši* in the lowveld in the 1990s in terms of women's illicit desires or men's perception of women's intolerable position, if only because men are frequently thought to use the familiar.[10] It seems more plausible that the *tokolotši* symbolises illicit sexual desires in a broader sense. This interpretation is supported by the image of the *tokolotši* as a large baboon, the duality between the witch and the familiar and by descriptions of the uses to which it is put.

The ape-like *tokolotši* is an apt symbol for uninhibited sexuality. The meaning of this association derives from the perception of the baboon as sexually promiscuous and as an appropriate human double.[11] In a sense baboons are liminal. Unlike other animals they share many features with people. It is certainly much harder to imagine other animals initiating sexual intercourse with humans. Moreover, baboons display a childish morality. They were considered to be children's peers and were thought to entertain a mystical relationship with them. Any contact with a baboon was seen as endangering a child's health. Adult speakers never spoke the word *tšhwene* ('baboon') in the presence of children, but used the euphemism *selo sa thabeng* ('thing from the mountain'). If a child or a pregnant woman walked on the same path as a baboon, or ate food it had touched, the child or foetus would contract the disease *bagwera ba bana* ('peers of children') and experience convulsions. *Dingaka* used grass from the paths where baboons walk and the skins of baboons and monkeys to heal the disease. The association between baboons and children does not pertain to sexuality *per se*. Of greater significance is that baboons, like children, are not socialised and lack the restraints culture imposes on their wants and desires. The symbolic appropriateness of the baboon as the instigator of unwanted sexual intercourse also derives from the perception that baboons are dangerous, strong and ugly.

Witches were believed to use the *tokolotši* for various purposes. It can guard their homes, steal goods and money from neighbours, and can be kept as a lover. A teacher and a middle-aged taxi owner were rumoured to keep the *tokolotši* for the latter purpose. The teacher's former husband reportedly realised the *tokolotši* lay in bed with his wife when he reached out to touch her, but felt the fur of a hairy creature. He claimed that the *tokolotši* kicked him on the shin and slapped him unconscious. The taxi owner, who consistently refused to marry, allegedly preferred the *tokolotši* as a companion because it brought him wealth. However, its predominant use was to molest, rape and abuse men and women in the neighbourhood.

Unlike moral sex, which takes place for the purpose of procreation, sexual intercourse with the *tokolotši* causes infertility. The *tokolotši* makes women abort or give birth to horrible, deformed, creatures. A young *tokolotši* sometimes sucks milk from the breasts of women, leaving none for their own infants. When it visits men it plays with them in their sleep, sucks their blood, castrates them, or injects them with *sehlare* to make them impotent and sterile.

The very idea of sexual intercourse with the *tokolotši* provoked revulsion and disgust. Women fear that a *tokolotši* had visited them during the night should they feel 'wet' in the morning, or find that their panties have been mysteriously removed, or notice that their husbands lie aside from them, as if they had been pushed away. *Dingaka* tell youngsters who dream of sex and of baboons that the *tokolotši* is troubling them.

Information on the 18 persons accused of using the *tokolotši* supports the idea that this familiar objectifies sexual desire. The victims of such accusations are often sexually promiscuous persons. Lacking *maitshwaro* and having succumbed to their sexual desires, witches exceed the bounds of acceptable conduct. This is shown in Case 3.1, below.

*Case 3.1: The Sexually Promiscuous Neighbour*

One evening in 1993 Andries Mashile, a 23-year-old bank teller in Acornhoek, dreamt of a large baboon. He recalled, 'First the baboon circled my home. Then it entered my room and it ran around my bed. It seemed as if the baboon dug around the garden and in my room. It was a big female and you could see the huge breasts.' As Andries looked at the baboon he tasted bitter herbs in his mouth. 'I also heard my name being called, but I woke up before I could reply. I was dizzy. I listened to hear who was calling. Then I looked through the window, but there was nothing. I could only see shadows.'

The next morning Andries inspected his garden and floor, but could not find any holes. He was very disturbed by the dream and consulted an Apostolic healer that afternoon who told Andries that his neighbours wanted him to marry their daughter. 'The prophet told me that I am in love with a certain girl, but her parents don't like me. He said that the parents of another girl want me to marry their daughter. They send her to me at night in the form of the *tokolotši*. She'll sleep with me, but I won't be aware of it. They have already sent her to me many times.' The prophet also revealed that her mother had given Andries *sehlare* that made him cough.

Andries was convinced by these revelations, because he regularly had wet dreams. He immediately thought that Elizabeth Maatsie, his next-door neighbour who was 19 years old, had visited him at night in the form of the *tokolotši*. This is because her mother had long been suspected of witchcraft and because Elizabeth always behaved strangely in his presence. She never greeted him, but always stared at him. Elizabeth had several lovers and had an abortion two years earlier. Once she was even found naked in someone else's yard. Elizabeth's own household was severely impoverished and desired that she should marry a securely employed young man, such as Andries.

The system of labour migration has clearly had a profound effect on the belief in the *tokolotši*. This familiar became prominent in Green Valley only after the betterment removals of 1960 had enhanced villagers' dependence on wage labour. Migrant labour clearly has a more potent effect in curtailing sexual expression than the 'traditional' proprieties of clan exogamy and polygyny. The system of labour migration, which obliges spouses to live apart from each other for the greatest part of their lives, generates intense fears of marital infidelity. Gordon (1977:224) describes migrancy as a vicious circle:

> The husband suspects the wife of being unfaithful and does not send remittances, whilst the wife justifies acts of unfaithfulness precisely because she does not receive remittances from her husband.

Many accusations stemmed directly from such fears and suspicions. The people who were accused were not migrants, but those who remained in Green Valley. Migrants feared that, in their absence, locally employed men might engage in sexual relations with their wives, and in fact many men did engage in long-term extramarital affairs (*bonyatši*) with their lovers. Migrants regularly accused such men of adultery. Yet it is the elderly and unemployed who were the most vulnerable to being accused of keeping the *tokolotši*. This is because they were considered to be sexually deprived and resentful. Elderly men had lost their sexual vitality. Being unable to support dependants, jobless men tended to be single and not to be desired as husbands. Such men were thought to use the *tokolotši* to compensate for their lack of sexual fulfilment.

Married women, who remained resident with their parents-in-law, while their husbands were at work in the urban areas, faced a unique set of frustrations. They often regarded the attention of elderly and jobless men as an unacceptable nuisance. Case 3.2, below, shows how such experiences could culminate in an accusation of witchcraft.

## *Case 3.2: The Troublesome Father-in-Law*

In 1967 Maggie Segodi married Ripho Moropane and took up residence with her in-laws. Her brother told me, 'The same year we realised something was troubling her.' When Maggie was eight months pregnant she suffered a miscarriage. Though her next pregnancy resulted into the birth of a healthy baby girl, she experienced three further miscarriages. 'She gave birth to such horrible things. The doctors were astonished.'

Whilst Ripho worked in Johannesburg Maggie experienced much distress in the household of her in-laws. In discussion with her siblings, she accused her father-in-law of having used a *tokolotši* to rape and impregnate her. Her brother recalled, 'The old man's behaviour was very peculiar. He was always reserved and quiet. He wore an overcoat and a hat at all times – even in summer. Sometimes at night one could see the old man in the flesh. When Maggie asked him in the mornings, "Why are you troubling me?" he did not reply.'

In 1975 Maggie's siblings rescued her from the Moropane home and returned her to the home of her own parents. There she was treated by a *ngaka* who expelled the *tokolotši* from her body. Maggie subsequently divorced Ripho and remarried. At the home of her new husband she gave birth to a second child who was normal and healthy.

Similar tensions were apparent when villagers accused a 55-year-old man of using the *tokolotši* to rape women at night and to inject men with a syringe to make them impotent. The man had been unemployed for a very long time and had never been married. At a local shebeen (drinking house) he often made unwanted sexual advances to women.

### Witchcraft, Wealth and the Mamlambo

Like the *tokolotši* the *mamlambo* is not indigenous to the lowveld. The first instance of witchcraft that we recorded in which reference was made to the *mamlambo* occurred in 1957. This familiar also seems to have been incorporated into the lowveld from Nguni-speakers via migrant labourers. In local opinion, the first witches who used the *mamlambo* in Green Valley had purchased it from sinister herbalists in Durban.

Witches were said to acquire the *mamlambo* in the form of a root, twig, or as 'something like a fish' contained in a bottle. The root has very peculiar qualities. It seems to be alive. Should one try to cut it, it would jump from one's hands. The root glows at night and casts a mysterious light throughout the home. After some time the root grows into a large snake which is slippery and hairy, has awesome fangs and eyes that shine like diamonds. During the day witches hide the snake in a special trunk or in nearby rivers. The *mamlambo* is also believed to metamorphose into human form. When brought from its place of hiding at night, the snake becomes the witch's supernatural lover. It changes into a white man or a white woman with silver, shiny hair. Moreover, informants believed that the *mamlambo* can assume the witch's own image.

All informants believed that witches keep the *mamlambo* to satisfy their greed and desire for wealth. A local diviner told me, 'Those who have the *mamlambo* are always rich and have many cattle. The *mamlambo* works for them.' Informants suggested that the *mamlambo* predisposes its owners to luck in financial matters or steals the possessions and money of others for them. However, the hedonistic pleasures and wealth derived from the *mamlambo* have great cost. The *mamlambo* was described as greedy, possessive and exceptionally dangerous. No witch can control the *mamlambo* for long. It soon dominates, enslaves and destroys its keeper. It is believed that the *mamlambo* prevents single people from marrying and attacks the spouses of married people.[12] In exchange for the money it brings, the *mamlambo* demands regular sacrifices of chicken, beef and human blood. Should witches fail to satisfy these demands, the *mamlambo* will kill their close relatives.[13] An Apostolic healer elaborated:

The *tokolotši* is better than it [the *mamlambo*]. The *tokolotši* only sleeps with people. The *mamlambo* brings wealth, but it kills people. Every year it demands blood and sacrifice. It needs your next of kin. If you don't feed it with a sacrifice it will turn to you and kill you. It feeds on people and animals.

*Dingaka* and Christian healers performed a special ritual to remove a *mamlambo* from people's homes. They placed the unwanted twig or root firmly inside the goat's anus. The goat was then thrown into a dam to drown, being offered to the *mamlambo* as a surrogate for a human victim.

As in the case of the *tokolotši*, informants believed that both men and women kept the *mamlambo*. They also portrayed the relationship between the witch and this familiar as constituting a duality. The identities of the witch and the *mamlambo* were intertwined in a complex and confusing manner. Witches were deemed capable of transforming themselves into the snake, and it was believed that the snake could assume the witch's image. Moreover, the lives of the witch and the snake were seen as mutually dependent. I was told that if people killed the snake the witch would also die. Some informants assumed that the *mamlambo* lives in the witch's stomach.

The mystical dependence between the witch and the familiar is evident in local interpretations of an incident that occurred in Green Valley during December 1992. In that month a large python slithered across a dust road and approached a village settlement. Observers suspected that the python was a *mamlambo* as there are no bushes in the vicinity where such large snakes can live. Eventually a policeman shot the python with his R4 rifle. A teacher died in the settlement just hours after he killed the snake. Villagers saw the teacher's death as an indication that he was the owner of the *mamlambo*.

Descriptions of the *umamlambo* ('mother of the river' in Xhosa) in earlier ethnographies of the Cape Nguni closely approximate the accounts of my informants. Shape-shifting, sexuality, personal enrichment and human sacrifice are also prominent themes in these accounts. Xhosa-speakers perceived the *mamlambo* as a water-sprite which appeared in the diverse forms of a chain, a goat-skin bag, hide charm, piece of tin and a hoe, and it also assumed the form an unusual snake. With eyes that shine like the lights of a motor-car, the snake had the power to mesmerise people (Soga, 1931:193; Hunter, 1979:286–7; Hammond-Tooke, 1962:285–7; McAllister, 1985). However, unlike in the lowveld, the ethnographies assert that only male witches owned the *mamlambo* and do not mention that witches could transform themselves into the snake. Wilson (1951) writes that men obtained the *mamlambo* from whites on the gold mines and that it becomes a beautiful girl in European dress with which the men made love. The *mamlambo* made such men rich and gave them anything they wished for. Yet the owner of the *mamlambo* must kill his father or mother to appease it. 'There is sure to be death in the family if one is brought home' (ibid.:285).

Even though the Cape Nguni *mamlambo* assumes the form of a beautiful girl, Hammond-Tooke (1974) argues that we cannot explain its symbolic meaning in terms of sexual antagonism. He sees the snake's ability to change shape, form and colour; and its tendency to attack the witch's kin, as more significant. For him, the *mamlambo* is a mediatory construct, mediating between the ideals of kinship loyalty and agnatic and neighbourly harmony; and the actuality of frequent tension between those locked together in bonds of mutual obligation. 'This ambiguity about kinsmen, this cognitive dissonance, is portrayed, and thus objectivised in cultural terms, in the shape (if that is the word!) of beings with ambiguous boundaries' (p. 133).

Unfortunately the capacity of his theory to illuminate ethnographic material from the lowveld is undermined by its failure to posit a specific motive for witchcraft and its failure to consider why the *mamlambo* assumes the particular images of a possessive lover and a dangerous snake. It would be more appropriate to interpret the *mamlambo* as symbolising the illicit desire for wealth. The duality of the witch and the *mamlambo* is similar to the relationship between the person and his or her desires, and the manifestations of the *mamlambo* highlight the dangerous aspects of the uninhibited pursuit of money.

Like Hammond-Tooke, I do not find the sexual hypothesis persuasive. Informants were adamant that when witches purchase the *mamlambo* their desire for sexual passion is secondary to their desire for wealth. Here it is very significant that the lover is described as a white person. In local perceptions whites are associated with status and money rather than sexual passion. Whites are also seen as greedy and dangerous. Junod and Jaques (1939:78) record the well-known Tsonga proverb, '*Mulungu a nga na xaka, xaka ra yena i mali* [White people have no kin/nation, their kin/nation is money].'

The snake also symbolises wealth in a more direct fashion that derives from its association with water. The *mamlambo* is sometimes obtained in a bottle filled with water, and it dwells in rivers. During the bygone era of agricultural self-sufficiency, when villagers depended upon rain for their livelihood, water was the basic source of prosperity. In the contemporary situation water is still seen as a source of fertility and life. Its positive, cooling, qualities are contrasted to the negative attributes of *fiša* (heat) as in drought, fever, pollution and death. Despite these positive connotations, water can be extremely dangerous.[14] People drown in rivers and are struck by the lightning that accompanies rain. Some women considered it taboo to fetch water at night. This is because they believed that water could attract lightning to their homes. In lowveld folklore the snake-like beings *mmamokebe* and *nzonzo* objectify the ambivalent qualities of water. *Mmamokebe*, the dangerous guardian of water, is half-woman, half-snake, and resides in large dams. It is usually peaceful, but may ascend into the dark clouds when provoked. From here it will cause storms to destroy all trees and houses in sight. *Nzonzo* is the water serpent that abducts people and trains them as powerful *dingaka*.

The fact that Botswana's official currency is the *Pula* ('rain') alludes to the shared symbolic attributes of money and water. Money, like water, embodies positive and negative qualities. Money sustains life, but causes tension, strife and bloodshed. The teachings of Zionist-type churches highlight the ambiguity of money. Christians valued the honest acquisition of money, and stated that money should ideally be used to support one's dependants and circulated to those in greatest need. These ideals were dramatised in church collections – called *mogau* ('grace'). Yet money acquired in the absence of hard work and used for personal enrichment was deemed to be extremely dangerous. An Apostolic priest referred to Acts 1 which describes how Judas betrayed Jesus for 30 shekels of silver, purchased a field with his wages of inequity, but eventually committed suicide. Judas' entrails gushed out over the field and it became known as Akel Dada, 'Field of Blood'. *Dingaka* recognised that money could be polluted and therefore 'cooled' the money they earned by sprinkling ash on it.[15]

Snakes too were associated with money. There is a perceptual resemblance between the physical properties of water, coins and snakes. Water shimmers, nickel shines and the scales and eyes of snakes glisten. A ZCC preacher cited Luke 16, which urges us to choose between the righteous path of God and the unrighteous path of Mammon. Mammon, he said refers to money. But added, 'Some people also say it is the snake.' Money dominates people's lives in much the same way as the *mamlambo* enslaves its keeper. The perception that the *mamlambo* feeds on human blood is therefore illuminating.

Tensions over money were the backdrop of many of the 21 cases that I recorded of individuals who were accused of keeping the *mamlambo*. By local standards the accused were of average financial means, but they were considered to be envious of wealthier residents, and particularly eager to attain wealth and positions of influence. One of the accused was a business rival of a wealthy shop owner. Case 3.3 illustrates the tensions evident in their relations.

*Case 3.3: The Café Owner and the* Mamlambo

In the 1950s Joseph Searane, who was born in Green Valley, established the Searane Café on the western outskirts of the village. For two decades the café was the only business in the vicinity. Joseph's prosperity lasted until 1972, the year in which Henry Mokoena, a teacher from Marite, established a second store across the road. Henry's brother – the wealthy owner of a liquor outlet – financed Henry's general dealer store and it was much better stocked than the Searane Café.

Joseph and Henry competed fiercely for customers. The tension between these businessmen came to the fore in soccer matches. Each man owned a soccer team and matches between their sides were characterised by violent conflict. In 1980 a fierce fist-fight erupted after Henry's team lost to that of Joseph. Henry refused to accept the defeat and claimed that Joseph had bewitched his best players.

The businessmen stopped speaking to each other. In 1982 Henry's small van overturned while transporting members of his soccer team and three of the players died in the accident. Henry immediately blamed Joseph for his misfortune. He claimed that Joseph used a *mamlambo* to steal goods from his store and to make his van overturn. After the funeral of his soccer players, Henry and his brother abducted Joseph, threw him into the boot of their car, and took him to a secluded place where they severely assaulted him.

Eight months later robbers shot and wounded Joseph near his home. He was rushed to hospital. To the surprise of his kin, Joseph was reluctant to allow surgeons to operate upon him and remove a bullet lodged in his spine. This, I was told, was because he feared that the surgeons would tamper with his snake. When Joseph died during the operation it was rumoured that the surgeons had indeed killed his snake. Because the snake was a familiar, and hence invisible, the surgeons failed to detect it.

Self-employed individuals who did part-time work in Green Valley were also likely to be suspected of keeping the *mamlambo*. They were *dingaka*, builders, radio repairmen and liquor sellers whose occupations regularly placed them in conflict with other villagers over the payment for their services. For example, during the witch-hunt of 1990, the witch-diviner said a *ngaka* once successfully cured a woman of epilepsy, but because she did not pay him he sent the *mamlambo* to kill her.

Some women who were accused of keeping the *mamlambo* were involved in disputes over money. Conflicts between mothers and daughters-in-law over the remittances of their wage-earning sons feature prominently among these squabbles. Women who derived financial benefits from the deaths of their husbands and kin were also among the accused. This is shown in Case 3.4.

*Case 3.4: The Happy Widow*

Flora Mkhare, a widow who was 65 years old, had long been suspected of practising witchcraft. One of her neighbours remarked that she had inherited the ability to harm from her mother. 'When her mother was still alive the old woman used to say; Oh! People are bewitching one another, but I'm not like that. I only use my power to take people's maize and crops. I don't kill anyone.' Neighbours believed that, motivated by her greed for money, Flora acquired a *mamlambo* and killed her husband and three of her nine children.

During 1974 her husband died in a road accident: riding home from work on his bicycle he collided with his employer's car. Informants suspected that his death was due to witchcraft, as his employer had always been helpful towards him. 'What convinced us was that Mkhare was knocked down by his own *baas*. At the same time that Mkhare left for home, his *baas* took his motor car to go somewhere else and knocked him down. Him and his *baas* [boss] were good friends. They worked nicely together. We think Flora had placed *dihlare* on the road.' When Flora's son told her he wanted to ask a *ngaka* to kill the witch with vengeance magic she, reportedly, became anxious and told him not to do so. Over the next five years Flora's two sons and daughter died. The first son was killed in a motor vehicle accident near Louis Trichardt; the second son, employed as a construction worker, fell from a high building; the daughter died suddenly from a mysterious illness. Shortly after these deaths Flora's daughter-in-law became insane and had to undergo psychiatric treatment.

Flora received compensation for her husband's death, and was granted the pension money of her sons. In addition, she manages the disability pension of her daughter-in-law. Her neighbours were appalled by the fact that Flora sometimes boasts about the sources of her income when she is drunk.

In other cases the financial motive was less apparent, but in three other cases individuals were suspected of keeping the *mamlambo*, following the untimely deaths of several of their kin. (See Case 6.3.)


CONCLUSIONS

Gellner (1973:36–44) points to the limitations of a contextual approach which assumes the rationality of religious beliefs. The *a priori* assumption of all-embracing logical rationality, he argues, may lead us into thinking that there are no beliefs that are contrary to common sense. The approach blinds us to the possibility of examining the role of inconsistent beliefs as a form of social control. A theme of this chapter has been precisely the incomprehensible and somewhat absurd relationship between witches and familiars. It is one of duality in which human and animal identities are both two and one, distinct and indistinct.

Political anthropologists have recognised the role of comparable dualities in conceptions of power. A famous African example is the mystical duality between Shilluk kings and the spirit of *nyikang* (Evans-Pritchard, 1948). Similarly, medieval European kings had two bodies: the Body Natural and the Body Politic consisting of government (Kantorowicz, 1957; Giesey, 1960). The two bodies formed a unity during life, but separated at death. The Body Politic was then transferred to the Body Natural of the next king. The Body Politic was invisible, immortal, devoid of all defects and was constituted for the direction of the people. Its powers removed mortal weakness from the king and ensured the continuity of kingship through successive monarchs. In this way theological formulations pertaining to the duality of the Christ were expropriated to create a 'Christology' of kingship (Kantorowicz, 1957:7).

Just as *nyikang* and the Body Politic were vital to kingship, familiars are central to the power of witchcraft. The duality of the witch and the familiar is symbolic of the division of personhood into higher and lower selves. The higher self is sublimated, cultivated and controlled, but the lower self is culturally undefined and is the source of instinct, life energy, aggression and desire. The lower self is often the focus of fascination. It inspires disgust at one level, but an uncanny and forbidden attraction at another (Friedman, 1991:155).

The theory of familiars does not merely express cultural ideas of power and personhood, but also casts light upon important social transformations in village life. The *tokolotši* and the *mamlambo* emerged in Green Valley in the early 1960s, when the last remnants of subsistence agriculture were destroyed and people became totally dependent on wage labour. The idea of the *tokolotši* with its exaggerated sexual features emerged in the context of labour migration, which heightened suspicions of marital infidelity. The *tokolotši* symbolises the destructive impact of extramarital sexual liaisons. By accusing sexually promiscuous, elderly and unmarried persons of keeping the *tokolotši* more fortunate villagers validate the ideal of sexual propriety. The *mamlambo* highlights the dangers of money. It portrays the selfish lust for wealth as evil, and as leading to infertility and death. Accusations that those who are involved in squabbles over money keep the *mamlambo* dramatise the need for proper restraint in financial matters.

These familiars are certainly not signs of protest. Yet, in so far as they draw attention to structures and processes of deprivation, familiars do constitute a form of implicit cultural critique.[16] The *tokolotši* provokes thought about the sexual repression which accompanies labour migration, whereas the *mamlambo* comments on the differentiation and deprivations that are a keynote of the monetary economy. In this respect the *tokolotši* and the *mamlambo* symbolically delegitimate conventional categories of thought in the political economy of South Africa.

# 4   WITCHCRAFT AND WHITES: FURTHER NOTES ON THE SYMBOLIC CONSTITUTION OF OCCULT POWER

The ethnographic and historical literature on southern Africa depicts a complex relationship between colonialism and witchcraft. The human miseries resulting from colonialism – such as the loss of land, poverty, disease and labour exploitation – are widely documented. It is also well known that witchcraft presents a 'persecutorial' view of misfortune (Taylor, 1992:62): that is, it orientates the sufferer's suspicions towards those with whom he or she has difficult social relations. And yet, while studies recognise that colonialism has generated increased suspicions of witchcraft, they do not show that colonists are identified as witches. Rather, in Zambia, South Africa and in Zimbabwe it is the fellow-colonised who have been accused of witchcraft.[1]

In the Fort Jameson district of Zambia the Chewa were displaced by European farmers, resettled on Native Trust Land and subjected to taxation. The insecurities the Chewa experienced during the 1940s were expressed in the idiom of sorcery. Despite their hostility to Europeans, the Chewa accused poorer members of different matrilineal segments and, to a lesser extent, affines (Marwick, 1965:75). In the 1950s Xhosa-speaking migrants in the South African city, East London, believed witches followed them from the reserves. Yet the migrants who stayed on white people's premises felt safe from witches. The smells of the many chemicals whites keep in their homes were thought to drive away witch familiars (Mayer and Mayer, 1974:165). Different authors assert that the execution of witches reached a zenith during the Zimbabwean war of liberation. Yet this is seen as the result of tensions within peasant communities and not of conflict between peasant communities and the colonial state. Guerrillas and youths reportedly executed conservatives, elders and better-off African farmers (Lan, 1987; Ranger, 1991; Kriger, 1991, 1992).

This chapter investigates the intricate connections between experiences of colonial subjugation and witchcraft beliefs. In contrast to the impression conveyed by the studies I have cited, I aim to demonstrate that colonists do not necessarily fall outside the parameters of witchcraft, and that discourses of witchcraft can present a salient critique of the colonial order. Yet in southern Africa criticisms of colonialism only emerge from a careful analysis of the symbolic dimensions of witchcraft.

People's reluctance to attribute witchcraft to colonists does not stem from the belief that the powers of colonists are non-malevolent and non-mystical. This tendency rather accords with the general emic conception of witchcraft as the power of insiders who are relatively subordinate. Throughout southern Africa witches are imagined to attack their kin and neighbours (Marwick, 1970). It is also conventional wisdom that witches are driven by motives of envy and desire to harm those who are relatively more fortunate than them.[2] Since colonists are wealthy outsiders, their status seems antithetical to the image of the witch. It is inconceivable that colonists should share ties of kinship and neighbourliness with blacks and envy their subordinate and impoverished status.[3]

But exceptions to this trend are possible. Southern African theories of witchcraft emphasise *relative* deprivation. This means that witches are only less fortunate than their victims and that influential persons are plausibly accused of witchcraft when motives of envy are attributed to them. For example, a headman was accused of witchcraft when Comrades replaces Tribal Authorities as the central actors in local politics (see Case 1.2) and a café owner who envied the greater profits of a wealthier business rival (see Case 3.3). Emic theories of witchcraft are also not economically reductionist. Villagers could well conceive of a wealthy man who bewitches a poorer kinsman with a very beautiful wife, and of a barren woman who bewitches her fertile neighbour.

Ethnographic studies of Melanesia which show how narratives of sorcery incorporate symbols of colonial rule (Lattas, 1993) may have important lessons to teach ethnographers of southern Africa.[4] Existing monographs do contain isolated references to beliefs which do, indeed, implicate colonists in witchcraft. For example, Marwick (1965:92) writes that the Chewa condemned the British government of Northern Rhodesia for banning the poison ordeal, used to detect sorcerers in the past. He quotes an informant as saying, 'The Europeans are afraid of being detected themselves if the ordeal is used, for they, too, are the proprietors of sorcery just as they are of whisky.' Marwick (1965:210) also writes that the Chewa attributed supernatural properties to Western medicines and accused Africans employed in hospitals of using strong medicines to kill patients. Such perceptions may well be more general than scholars of witchcraft in southern Africa have acknowledged.

In Green Valley witches were symbolically associated with whites. This association arises from the conception of witches as internal enemies who entertain dangerous liaisons with sources external to the *motse* (Douglas, 1970a:xxxvii). In Chapter 3 we saw how witches transcend the abilities of ordinary African villagers by combining human and animal attributes. But witches can also derive extraordinary power from whites – dominant human outsiders. During the era of apartheid, white employers and government officials were more likely to be perceived as the victims than the perpetrators of witchcraft. Witches were nonetheless imagined to be liminal to the categories *motse* and *makgoweng* ('places of whites') and to appropriate the attributes and technologies of whites. In the months leading up to the South African elections of 1994 important changes occurred in the nature of witchcraft attributions.

Amidst expectations of white disempowerment and black empowerment, rumours circulated that whites were driven by resentment at their inevitable loss of status to poison, and hence bewitch, Africans.

## WHITE DOMINATION AND THE MORAL GEOGRAPHY OF WITCHCRAFT

Residents of Green Valley often spoke about the devastating impact of white domination. There is a common myth that, before his death, Sekhukhune, the famous Pedi paramount chief, saw a vision of ants tormenting his people. An elderly man said in an interview, 'These ants are the *makgowa* [whites] who took our land.' Stories of the past relate how people lost their land to white settlers in the lowveld. Informants blamed whites for the processes whereby they, as the citizens of formerly independent chiefdoms, became labour tenants on farms privately owned by whites, or rent tenants on company-owned farms such as Green Valley. They also cited the implementation of apartheid, the forced removal of people into concentrated villages and stock limitations as further examples of the malevolence of whites. Elders described the role that white agricultural officers played in the reserve as unwanted and very disruptive. Indeed, some blamed the stock losses they incurred, during the cattle epizootic of 1951, on the agricultural officers who injected their cattle with syringes.

People's very general perception of the essential malevolence of whites was reinforced by their formal encounters with white employers, government officials and traders, whom they feared and mistrusted. Villagers believed whites were constantly out to cheat them. Labourers said that farmers paid them starvation wages. Elders complained that white officials deprived them of pension money by entering incorrect birth dates in their identity documents, and women gossiped that a white farmer fraudulently sold donkey's milk as cow's milk in the village. Whites were stereotyped as powerful, wealthy, stubborn, unsociable, racist, devious and cunning. These attitudes are apparent in the informative Northern Sotho and Tsonga names given to white farmers. They include: Hlogokgolo ('big head'), Sehangalashe ('chaser'), Malandele ('pursuer'), Mahebehebe ('gossip') and Malobishe ('dispossessor').

Yet villagers did not speculate a great deal about the nature of the powers that enabled a small minority of whites to dominate a majority of Africans. They assumed that the powers of whites inhered in their visible possession of superior technology, close access to the state and also in invisible, untold, secrets. Such powers were analogous to those of witches. For example, items of technology, such as my word-processor, and mysterious cultural performances, such as the circus, were sometimes explicitly called 'witchcraft'. Ashforth (1996) comments that, as in the case of witchcraft, secrecy lies at the heart of state power.[5]

However, the powers of whites diverged from witchcraft in one crucial respect. Whites were imagined to employ deviousness and malevolence to achieve prosperity and success. This notion was articulated in the occasional insinuation that whites were ritual murderers (*maemae*) – a category distinct from witchcraft. For example, in the 1950s villagers were extremely suspicious of a white garage-owner and his African henchman who drove through Green Valley's streets at night in a car with only one headlight. These men were alledged to have murdered two women – who had disappeared without a trace – for *dihlare*. Such insinuations resurfaced in 1992 when a woman's bloodless corpse was found in Acornhoek. People alleged that she was the victim of a white money-lender from Hoedspruit and local black businessmen who had cut parts from her body and extracted her blood. They believed that the businessmen manufactured *dihlare* from her flesh, which they used to attract customers to their stores, and sold her blood to pharmaceutical companies.[6]

While there is congruence between the status of whites and the status of ritual murderers, whites are thought to be unlike witches. Ritual murderers killed for wealth. Witches were deprived and resentful persons who killed primarily to get even. Villagers thus expressed disbelief when I told them of the European witch-hunts of the past, and of white satanists in Johannesburg. Prior to 1994, only Tumišo Shubane knew that whites, too, could be witches. She learnt this when she worked for an elderly Greek woman in Johannesburg. Tumišo's employer told her that she suffered from persistent backache, and that she had been bewitched by her sister-in-law. The sister-in-law was envious of the employer's sons, who qualified as an engineer and a doctor, and planned to kill the old woman with *sehlare*. Tumišo was very surprised. 'I did not know whites do such things.'

Even those who recognised that there might be witches among whites found it inconceivable that whites would envy and bewitch impoverished Africans. The belief that witches attack only those who reside close to them also made whites unlikely suspects when misfortune befell Africans. The belief is evident in the proverb '*moloi ga a tshele noka* [a witch cannot cross a river]'.

Whites were, however, seen as potential victims of African witchcraft. In one account two African men bewitched their employer – a white shop-owner – after he dismissed them. As a white researcher, who interacted closely with Africans, I was considered to be particularly vulnerable. Indeed, at a church service the minister prophesied that witches planned to make my car overturn. He advised me to fortify my car by placing mercury inside the cubby hole.[7]

To grasp adequately the relationship between white domination and witchcraft, it is necessary to look beyond the sociology of witchcraft and adopt a broader perspective. Such a view needs to encompass the symbolic meanings of witchcraft, and in particular the strategic position that whites, as powerful outsiders, occupy in the 'moral geography' of witchcraft (Auslander, 1993:169–70).

As we have seen in the previous chapter, cosmological views in the lowveld express a generalised opposition between the realms of *motse* and *tlhaga*. Though this dichotomy has remained intact, two additional sets of oppositions have emerged. These are between *motse* and *makgoweng* ('place of the whites') and between *setšo* ('traditions') and *sekgowa* ('ways of the whites'). The contrast between *motse* and *makgoweng* is primarily a spatial one. It resembles the distinction social scientists make between the 'rural periphery' and the 'industrial core' of the southern African political economy (Murray, 1981). *Motse* is a familiar space where people live and socialise. *Makgoweng* is an alien space where people labour for whites and purchase commodities. *Makgoweng* is associated with power, technological innovation, and with danger. Like *tlhaga*, it exists outside the *motse*.

The concepts *setšo* and *sekgowa* are more complex. They do not form a rigid dichotomy, and do not correspond neatly with notions of morality and immorality. Neither does the rhetoric of *setšo* and *sekgowa* necessarily express the collective identity of the dominated *vis-à-vis* the colonial order.[8] As James (1993) shows, this rhetoric is invoked only in specific situations to comment primarily about things which happen within the community. The concepts are idioms through which norms of conduct and generational and gender relations are contested.

*Setšo* can denote both ancient and contemporary practices. The phrase *setšo sa kgale* ('traditions of old') refers to practices such as rainmaking and work parties, which occurred only in the past. When used in this sense *setšo* can invoke an image of the past as a bygone era of prosperity and social harmony in order to lament present-day strife. But this is not always so. Sometimes the past is seen as a harsh time when people lacked material possessions and were cruel.[9] Habitual practices can also be explained as *setšo*. When asked why only women attend certain rituals, informants often replied: 'This is our tradition.' In other instances, *setšo* is used explicitly to foster an image that contemporary practices are continuous with cultural forms of the past.[10] For example, *dingaka* used *setšo* as a rhetorical style to assert their identity with the ancestors. They built *ndhumba* (small round houses) for the ancestors, and decorated these with cowhide-drums, flywhisks and grain baskets. In addition, *dingaka* avoided using items they did not consider to be *setšo*. The ancestors of one *ngaka* forbade her to eat beetroot, jam, canned fish and cooking oil.[11]

Informants did not view the constant introduction of new practices and commodities from *makgoweng* as subversive. Villagers readily sent their children to school, went to hospital, adopted new rituals and used new commodities. Once such items were incorporated they became part of what people did. For example, prior to 1960 adults buried corpses privately at night. Since then public funerals have become commonplace. Yet people seldom called contemporary funerals *sekgowa*. The concept *sekgowa* tended to be used only to refer to new items and practices that seemed ambiguous, or threatened to undermine established interests within the community. By calling a specific practice *sekgowa*, people were, in fact, saying it should not belong in the village. At the same time, they were asserting their own rights. An ANC leader, criticising the lack of co-operation between the Civic Association and the chief, expressed himself in the following words, 'They no longer work according to *setšo*, but according to *sekgowa*. They have been led astray by the *maboer* [Afrikaners].' Men described gender equality as *sekgowa* and as unacceptable to them. Likewise, elders perceived the disrespect young adults displayed toward their parents to be *sekgowa*. A woman who abhorred the youngsters who did not send their parents money from the urban areas, remarked that such youngsters 'live a *sekgowa* lifestyle'.

Witches were perceived as liminal to the opposing domains of *motse* and *makgoweng*. Witches were *batho* (literally people, but also used to denote only Africans) who lived in the *motse*. Yet they derived much of their power from their liaisons with whites and *makgoweng*.

## WHITES AS AN INSTRUMENT AND A METAPHOR FOR WITCHCRAFT

Local discourses expressed the relationship between witches and whites in different ways. This relationship could be direct. Witches were portrayed as using whites as familiars, in much the same way as they used animals. But the relationship could also be metaphorical. Witches could possess the same attributes as whites.

Some stories tell of white familiars as ferocious as the snake and *tokolotši*. In the Hlapa O Ja river, which forms Green Valley's western boundary, is a small dam known as *Lekgowa*. It is commonly believed that familiars hide in the dam and attack passers-by at night. This dam earned its name in the 1940s, when a mysterious white woman was regularly seen sunbathing on the dam wall in the late afternoon. Yet, when people approached, she would dive into the dam and disappear. Villagers believed that the woman caused illness and death. Betty Mathebula, an old woman who was said to have had the facial appearance of a witch, once told her friends she owned the white woman. At first nobody believed her. However, after Betty's death in 1949, the mysterious white woman was not seen again. This added substance to her claim that the white person was her familiar. In the 1970s people again reported seeing a white person at the dam. This time it was a man who walked about carrying a kettle. The man, too, was thought to be someone's familiar.

During the course of my fieldwork, there were occasionally rumours that white familiars had brought about the death of villagers. In 1992 a young woman died mysteriously. People who knew her said she had complained that a white woman pursued her. On the evening of her death, the white woman peeped through her window. In general, dreams of white people were interpreted as omens of great misfortune.

The potential status of whites as familiars is also evident in the idea that the snake-like *mamlambo* assumes the form of a white lover. This representation of a white person who brings wealth, but chases one's spouse from home, bestows infertility and demands sacrifices of human blood is hardly flattering.

The metaphorical relationship between witches and whites is expressed most cogently in the portrayal of witches as masters who keep zombies (*ditlotlwane*, singular *setlotlwane*). Informants' descriptions of zombies broadly resemble the earlier accounts of these entities in ethnographic studies of Tsonga- and Sotho-speakers.[12] Yet, interviewees portrayed zombies as less dangerous and more distinctively human than the ethnographies suggest. They believed that after witches had captured their victims, witches doctored them with strong *sehlare*, cut their tongues, transformed their appearance and thereby changed them into zombies. During the day witches hid their zombies in valleys, or on steep cliffs, but employed them as servants at night.

Narratives of zombies operate like satirical allegory. In this aesthetic genre two disparate levels of meaning are sustained: one the explicit text, the other an implied, underlying, reality which is being satirised. The most obvious allegorical pretext for stories about witches and zombies are master–servant relationships between white employers and black labourers.[13] Allegorical discourses do not take excessive domination for granted, but reframe it and show it in an unconventional light. Its context shifts from the everyday world of common sense to the demonic world of witchcraft. At this meta-social level domination becomes a subject of reflection: witches and zombies provide idioms through which people can view themselves and the power relationships in which they are amassed from without. They enable people to transcend the categories that constrain them, and to recognise them as cultural constructs rather than immutable truths.

The allegorical relationships are evident in numerous idiomatic links. Metaphorically witches possess the same attributes as white employers. By being masters of zombies – like white farm owners and industrialists who command hundreds of black labourers – witches are powerful wielders of authority. It is telling that villagers commonly address whites persons as *baas* or *miessies* (lit. 'boss' or 'madam' in Afrikaans).

Stories of witches and zombies capture the illicit desire to dominate. One tale, as relayed by several informants, tells of an old farm labourer in the Ohrigstad district, who daily had to do strenuous work. He was not paid, and worked merely for the right to reside on the farm. When other workers noticed that the old man refused to work, they complained vehemently to the farmer. The farmer threatened to dismiss the old man unless he, too, weeded the fields. To everyone's surprise the old man promised that he, alone, would weed the fields in a single day. That evening he led a hundred zombies to the field. While he rested under a tree, his zombies did the work. The next morning the old man told the farmer he had completed the task. However, that night the farmer hid in the field and saw what really happened. He was particularly disturbed to see that the witch had turned three white men into zombies. The farmer wanted to shoot him, but the old man fled from the farm with all his zombies. In this story the witch's desire to escape arduous labour and live a life of leisure – indeed, the wish to become like the white farmer – had motivated the old man to acquire zombies.

These discourses also capture the intense fear of being dominated. Nowhere is this more apparent than in the notion that witches employ zombies as servants in a nocturnal 'second world' from where there is no return. In west and central Africa this notion echoes daunting memories of the Atlantic slave trade (MacGaffey, 1968; Austen, 1993; Shaw, 1997). In the South African lowveld they resonate with the experiences of migrant labourers who leave their rural households to earn a living in the alien centres of mining and industry of *makgoweng*.

The mindless tasks of zombies resemble those of unskilled domestic servants and farm labourers. Zombies clean the homes of witches, cook, brew sorghum beer, wash clothes, fetch water with buckets on their heads, collect and chop firewood, build fences, herd cattle, plough, sow, harvest and run errands. One witch was even said to have used zombies to sell fish in his shop. Others allegedly changed their own children into zombies and sent them to work as migrants, so that they could receive the remittances. Zombies were treated harshly. A notorious café owner, who had a fine ear for music, reportedly commanded his zombies to sing as a choir at night. He always stood in front and whipped any zombie who did not sing to his satisfaction. By all accounts zombies were never paid and worked only for maize porridge – the staple diet of black workers.

The unique features of zombies, which set them apart from ordinary persons, exaggerate and caricature some of the less apparent consequences of domination. All zombies were said to be only a metre tall and similar in appearance. Their smallness is suggestive of the diminutive, childlike and sub-ordinate status of black labourers. Their uniformity alludes to the perception that employers treat all labourers alike, rather than as unique persons. Above all zombies are represented as ideal servants who have an endless capacity for hard work. They have no will and display unquestioning obedience to their masters. Witches were said to hypnotise their zombies with strong *dihlare* so that they forgot all events in their previous lives and focused only on the tasks at hand. Moreover, zombies are sexless[14] and, apart from their craving for porridge, have no real human desires. The idea that witches cut the tongues of their zombies is particularly meaningful. Zombies lack the ability to speak, express themselves, or to question, reason with or criticise their masters.

Finally, discourses of zombies reflect upon the helplessness and dependence of dominated persons. Should witches die, their zombies will wander about endlessly in search of porridge. (This alludes to the experience of unemployed persons who appear to be free, but are actually in a hopeless situation.) Being undead, zombies cannot return to their kin. In one story, told by a teacher, a boy's zombie tried to return to his mother when the witch was no longer there to support him. While the dead boy's mother worked in the fields she saw his wandering figure. She then called the police and pleaded with them to kill it. The police, however, removed the zombie to a mental hospital. It is here that the state is presumed to care for many zombies and to shield them from the public. The identification of zombies with inmates of the asylum suggests that, like the insane, zombies are objects rather than active subjects.[15]

The primary point of reference in discourses about witches and zombies is clearly the exploitation of black workers by white bosses. Yet these discourses also provoke reflexive thought about other relations of domination – such as those between wives and their affines. Given the pattern of patrilocal residence elderly women command great authority over the wives of their sons. Like young male migrants, young wives leave their parental households and bear the brunt of unrewarding tasks in their new homes, where they live under the constant surveillance of their mothers-in-law. As in the case of Lesotho, relations between young women and their mothers-in-law were characterised by conflict (Murray, 1981:149–70).

## WITCHES AND THE APPROPRIATION OF *SEKGOWA* TECHNOLOGY

The liminality of the witch *vis-à-vis* the categories *motse* and *makgoweng* is also apparent in the idea that contemporary witches purchase and use *sekgowa* technologies. During the era of subsistence agriculture it was assumed that the power of witchcraft was transmitted by birth. Children sucked witchcraft from their mother's breasts and developed a taste for human flesh while inside the womb. Mothers only taught them to develop their natural abilities. Later in life, the witch child would also inherit its mother's familiars. But as people came to rely on wage earnings witchcraft became a commodity. Villagers imagined that a vibrant secret trade developed in witchcraft substances. Even persons not born as witches could now purchase poisons, *dihlare* and familiars. In recent years those who buy witchcraft have become as numerous, dangerous and powerful as witches by birth whose lust to kill is innate.

As such a perception has emerged that newer forms of witchcraft constantly invade the village from outside. In the same way as witches bring dangerous substances from the forest to wreak havoc in the village, they import a wide variety of familiars and technologies from *makgoweng*. For example, it is believed that witches purchase the *tokolotši* and the *mamlambo* in Durban. The new technologies of witchcraft ranged from insecticides to remote-controlled devices.

(i) *Insecticides and Chemical Poisons*. Fears of poisoning, recognised as one of the oldest types of witchcraft, were still pervasive in the 1990s. But when my informants described specific episodes of poisoning, thy seldom referred to the crocodile brain and *sejeso*. They claimed that witches now used various kinds of *sekgowa* poisons such as insecticides.

Lemoenkloof, a citrus farm where workers regularly sprayed the orchards for worm, was thought to be the major source of insecticides. In 1982 a farm worker called Sidlaye reportedly stole two large canisters of poison and sold this to witches in Green Valley for R3 per teaspoon. At least two villagers are said to have died from Sidlaye's poison: the first a Chiloane boy who drank a poisoned cold drink; the second a Mohobele man who ate poisoned fish. Sidlaye only stopped selling the poison after Mrs. Chiloane avenged her son's death. She reportedly bought poison from Sidlaye and poisoned his own daughter with it. In 1989 Peter Mabuza, another Lemoenkloof employee, allegedly sold 25 litres of poison to three women in Green Valley. One of these women gave poisoned sweets to a Segodi boy. With the assistance of a diviner, the boy's father, Mr Segodi, discovered the poisoner's identity. When he threatened to kill her, she confessed, revealed the names of her accomplices and said she had hidden the remaining poison in an unused pit latrine. Mr. Segodi inspected water from the latrine and found that it was blue in colour. He then reported the three women to the chief, and informed Lemoenkloof's owner that his workers regularly stole poison from his tanks. The farmer promised he would take greater security precautions, and from that time on he personally oversaw the distribution of poison and locked the store room.

Termite poison, soda crystals and brake fluid were also mentioned as poisons that witches imported from *makgoweng*. Some shebeen operators allegedly flushed their glass with brake fluid, causing their customers to become highly intoxicated. This gave them the opportunity to pick their pockets. Certain poisonous chemicals were so mysterious that they could only be described by their effects. They allegedly made skin peel off the victim's mouth and changed porridge so that it became red, brown or blue in colour. Such chemicals were deemed to be as lethal as the crocodile brain.

(ii) *The Night Train*. Before the turn of the century construction was begun on a rail link between Pretoria and Delagoa Bay. This rail line was soon extended from Komatipoort, via Acornhoek, to Pietersburg. Trains running on these tracks transported the first migrant labourers to the Witwatersrand. Only decades later stories emerged of witches' trains (*setimela sa baloi*). An elderly informant told me that during the 1950s his father cleared a site to build a new home. Their neighbour immediately began to quarrel with his father. 'You cannot build here', the neighbour said. 'During the night my train passes through his place. It may destroy your home.' His father did not understand what the man meant, but decided to build elsewhere. An Apostolic healer told me that as a child she heard witches' trains move along the stream beds. She claimed that she and her brother encountered a flying train when they walked home from church one evening in 1961. At a stream they heard a peculiar 'Shiiii' sound above their heads. 'At first we thought it may be birds, but birds do not make such a sound. There was also much steam. I asked my brother "What kind of a thing is this?" It was like a locomotive that blasts cool steam.' They hid behind bushes and only resumed their journey once the noise ceased.

The witches' train was described as 'a very sophisticated familiar'. Witches' trains resembled ordinary trains, but did not travel on rails. They were large, had many coaches, transported hundreds of passengers, and were staffed by personnel dressed in uniforms of the South African Railways. Their passengers, conductors and drivers were purported to be zombies. Witches' trains were hidden during the day, but were used at night to ferry zombies to their workplaces such as the irrigation farms at Dingleydale. 'The zombies work in shifts just like mine workers. While some are transported to work by the train, others are returned to their homes.' Sometimes many witches collectively owned a single train, each using a particular coach for his or her zombies. Witches' trains abducted people who wandered about at night. Should they board, the conductor would ask them 'single or return?' Those who replied 'single' disappeared forever. They were killed, joined the zombies on the train, and were forced to work for the witch. Those who replied 'return' were beaten and thrown from the train at a distant location.

There were many reported encounters with witches' trains between 1978 and 1985. In these years the Pietersburg train transported commuter labourers from villages such as Green Valley and Cottondale at 4am each morning. When some commuters disappeared, only to reappear at mysterious locations, people believed that witches' trains had abducted them. In 1980 Ben Maunye, a young migrant, boarded a train for Witbank and never returned. Two years after Ben disappeared people found the bruised body of a drunkard in the Cottondale forest. The man said he boarded a train, but fell from it. He also claimed that he saw Ben working on the train as a conductor. In 1985 a young woman and her boyfriend walked home from a shebeen (drinking house). Near the river she left her boyfriend and went to urinate in the bush. Herders found her lying in the veld the next day. She was concussed, had sustained severe head injuries and her legs were covered in blood. At home she told her kin that she lost consciousness after someone beat her on the back of her head. Her kin believed that she, too, was a victim of the train. To put an end to these abductions, Cottondale residents asked a witch-diviner to reveal the train owner's identity. The diviner pointed to a retired mine worker who was also a headman. At a public meeting former victims of the train relayed their experiences. Even the headman's sons agreed that their father was guilty. Delegates were then sent to evict the headman from Cottondale.

The morning train service was disestablished in 1985, and commuters have been transported to Hoedspruit by bus since then. Stories of witches' trains became less common, but have not entirely disappeared. Occasionally such trains are sighted in Green Valley. When a housewife stared through her back door one evening she saw a train winding through the bushes. It had coaches and lights, but moved in complete silence. Stories have also circulated of witches' trains that are substantially unlike ordinary trains. Such trains comprise a human chain. The witch acts as the locomotive and walks in front. The zombies act as coaches and walk behind the witch, holding hands as they move. They grab any person whom they meet and drag him or her along.

(iii) *Witch Automobiles*. Stories that witches own automobiles are of recent origin. Although a few wealthier villagers had already owned cars in the 1940s, cars only became a feature of witchcraft in the 1970s. By then buses and combi-taxis had replaced trains as the major form of migrant transportation. In 1972 members of the Phako household regularly saw the headlights of a motor car moving between two village sections and clearly heard its engine running. To their surprise, the car drove through the rough veld where there was no road. It usually descended a hill, crossed a stream, and ascended a second hill. As the car approached their home its headlights faded and the noise of its engine stopped abruptly. A few minutes later they would hear the sound of whistles, similar to those used by *dingaka*. Mr Phako is convinced the car belonged to Skariot Mosoma – an unpopular *ngaka* whom many suspected of being a witch. The reason for his view is that after Skariot was chased from Green Valley, in 1974, on account of witchcraft, the car was not seen again. Skariot was too poor to afford a real car, but drove a witch-car at night.

Witches reportedly manufactured cars from *dihlare* and from the parts of old car wrecks. Such vehicles had peculiar qualities. It was believed that, like familiars, they could change shape. One story tells how a loaf of bread became a combi. The story is of a migrant whose two wives became puzzled by his peculiar pattern of migrancy. He came home very frequently and travelled to Johannesburg with great ease. At times he stayed for weekends, but only left for work on the Monday mornings. The wives found it strange that he always bought a loaf of bread before he departed. To find an answer to these perplexing questions they consulted a *ngaka*. He told them only witchcraft can enable a man to travel so fast, and said their husband changed the loaf of bread into a van. The *ngaka* gave them *sehlare* to smear on his bread the next time he was about to depart. When the wives did this, their husband could not leave for work.

Witches' cars were deadly weapons. At times witches manufactured these cars for the explicit purpose of killing their enemies. As they made the cars they called out the name of their prospective victim. In 1994 Enios and Gerry Mashego, two high school pupils, were sent to buy an 80 kg bag of maize meal. Gerry pushed the wheelbarrow all the way to the shop. When he asked Enios to take over, Enios became scared and fled. Later Gerry found Enios standing underneath a tree. Enios was notably agitated and shouted, 'Go! Buy the maize meal on your own! Don't force me to accompany you!' Gerry was surprised that Enios addressed him in fluent English. Later Enios' family noticed that he displayed signs of insanity. An Apostolic healer told Enios' mother three witches attempted to kill him. As he was about to push the wheelbarrow, they sent an invisible car to knock him down. Fortunately, Enios' ancestors caused him to escape.

(iv) *The Technology of the Flying Witch.* It was common knowledge that witches flew and sent lightning to strike people on the ground. Yet few informants knew precisely how witches fly. Some interviewees thought flying witches appropriated the attributes of birds. A teacher reasoned that witches did not fly as human beings. 'It is not flying in the true sense of flying. People say witches fly when they use the owl. Witches send the owl, or come personally in the form of the owl.' Yeketsang Mohale, who is the only person I know to claim that he actually saw a witch fly, confirmed this view. While Yeketsang worked in Tzaneen during 1966, he was abruptly awakened by the sound of thunder one summer evening. When Yeketsang opened the door of his home and shone his torch he noticed something hanging from his washing line. He described what he saw as follows:

It hung on the line by its feet with its head facing downwards. As I walked nearer I saw it was a human being. Suddenly it fell from the line, but started to fly away like an owl... I saw the man with my own eyes. He was naked and did not have feathers. He used his arms as wings.

Half an hour later the lightning struck a kilometre away from Yeketsang's home, killing three goats.

Other informants thought flying witches also use *sekgowa* technologies. An Apostolic healer interpreted the well-known expression, '*moloi o nya mollo* [a witch farts/excretes fire]' literally. She said powerful flames emerge from the anuses of witches, propelling them through the night sky like human rockets, as they travel about on their malicious errands.[16] The *sekgowa* technologies used by flying witches were also said to include steering wheels, reflectors and aerials. For example, Elias Maluleke's neighbours claimed that he flew around Green Valley at night on a large steering wheel to which he attached feathers that he treated with *sehlare*. A woman heard witches used a reflector, which resembles a car's indicators, to call the other witches when they flew past to join them. Residents the nearby village, Timbabati, described how an aerial protruded from the back of a well-known witch, like a tail, whenever he flew (Stadler, 1994:186).

(v) *Remote-Controlled Sexual Intercourse*. Since the 1970s witches have used *sekgowa* technologies to conduct sexual liaisons. Both male and female witches sent the *tokoloŝi* to rape those whom they desire sexually at night, but male witches now also employ the *mshoshaphanzi* for this purpose in the daytime.[17] A man puts this device in his pocket and approaches the woman. When he rubs it his penis becomes erect and he has intercourse with the woman from a remote distance. The *mshoshaphanzi* will momentarily hypnotise (*go tanyega*) the man's victim so that she responds positively to his advances. The *mshoshaphanzi* enables male witches to have intercourse with any woman, and with several women in succession. People cannot observe this action, but can infer it from the man's facial expressions. A shop-owner once saw a man enter his store, stare at his wife and make peculiar gestures. Believing that the man was using a *mshoshaphanzi*, he lashed the man with a sjambok and chased him from the store. Though informants believed the device was manufactured from parts of the *tokoloŝi*, this idea is clearly modelled on modern technologies from *makgoweng*. Informants compared it to a remote-controlled television switch and an immobiliser for motor cars. A young man explained, 'With an immobiliser you can open your car doors over there when you are standing here. The *mshoshaphanzi* works more or less the same.'

According to local beliefs witches do not employ the *mshoshaphanzi* nearly as frequently as they use the *tokoloŝi*. I recorded only five accounts of men who had been accused of using this device. One of the accused was a teacher. Although he was married, he stayed in the teachers' quarters at school, with his two sons, while his wife worked in Bushbuckridge. His colleagues were surprised that his wife hardly ever visited them and that he so readily accepted this arrangement. They were also appalled when they heard him telling a woman teacher, with whom he did not sleep, that she was no good in bed. Once he detained schoolgirls in the library for no apparent reason. The girls later complained that they felt wet between their legs and claimed he had used the *mshoshaphanzi* to molest them. When the principal learnt of this, he summoned the man to his office and threatened him with expulsion. Woman teachers had become very wary of him. Whenever he stared at them, they frantically stabbed with pens in the air in front of their legs to ward off the *mshoshaphanzi*.

Not all new technologies were called *sekgowa* and were associated with witchcraft. Great selectivity was obviously involved. The items witches used were those that seemed the most alien, ambiguous and threatening. Like animals which invaded the village from the forest, these technologies were 'matter out of place' (Douglas, 1970b:5). Only in witchcraft narratives were impoverished people represented as the powerful owners of whites, servants, trains and automobiles. The liminality of the witch, *vis-à-vis* the village and *makgoweng*, was also apparent in the anomalous images of insecticides in people's food, trains and automobiles which run where there are no rails or roads, flames coming from a person's anus and the remote controlled penis.

The items involved are apt symbols of power, wealth, domination and danger. Insecticides are highly ambiguous. Whilst informants recognised that the use of insecticides enabled citrus orchards on white-owned farms to be more productive than village gardens, they were acutely aware of the dangers of insecticides, and did not use these in the village. Trains, automobiles, planes and the *mshoshaphanzi* connote the power of mobility, but also convey the profound dangers of speed and the unregulated movement of persons and objects. Trains are objects of fascination because they symbolise the connections between the village and *makgoweng*. Indeed, the train journey was integral to the subordination of black labourers who were compelled by economic necessity to leave their rural homesteads for *makgoweng*. Train journeys were arduous experiences. A man who worked at a textile factory in Johannesburg during the 1950s recalled that migrants had to board new trains several times along the way. These trains were always overcrowded and migrants were frequently robbed. But of far greater concern was that trains separated fathers and sons from their dependants, sometimes forever.[18] Like trains, automobiles link people to *makgoweng*. As symbols of status they gave people great mobility: but the highways are profoundly dangerous and automobile accidents were a very common cause of death. The *mshoshapanzi* portrays uninhibited, amoral and uncontrolled male sexuality.[19]

## THE 1994 ELECTION AND THE WITCHCRAFT OF WHITES

The South African general elections of April 1994, which formally brought about the end of white minority rule, had a direct impact on local perceptions of witchcraft. In the months preceding the elections villagers anticipated a reversal of fortunes. Like many other South Africans they anticipated a 'world turned upside down', marked by immediate and complete social integration, black empowerment and white disempowerment (Babcock, 1978). In the context of these expectations pre-existing notions of witchcraft changed. In these months whites were no longer seen only as a source from which African witches derived their power: witchcraft was also directly attributed to whites.

Villagers perceived an ANC victory was a foregone conclusion. By 1994 the ANC was the only effectively organised political party in the Mhala and Mapulaneng areas. The ANC enjoyed overwhelming support. ANC election meetings were regularly held and Green Valley's electricity poles and marula trees were decorated with colourful ANC posters promising 'Rights for Women' as well as 'Jobs, Peace and Freedom'. Even the elders who resented the unscrupulous behaviour of the local Comrades, supported Nelson Mandela and intended to vote for the ANC. Locally the ANC had hardly any political rivals. Prospective voters strongly rejected Bantustan-based political parties. Widespread corruption in Lebowa stigmatised the United People's Party. The organisation of Gazankulu's Ximoko Progressive Party, which some Tsonga-speakers supported in the past, was in complete disarray. Before the election Mr E.E. Nxumalo resigned as Ximoko's leader and joined the ANC. At a mass meeting in Thulamahashe he called on Gazankulu's teachers and civil servants to do likewise. The PAC, National Party and Democratic Party had little support. In fact, those who did not support the ANC were pensioners and church leaders who had decided not to vote.

Informants were very ambivalent about the elections, however. Some clearly had utopian expectations of the benefits an ANC victory would bring. Unemployed men expected that it would be much easier for them to find jobs. Employees expected wage increases, women that water supplies would improve and teachers that more schools would be built. An ANC activist who is also a school principal remarked that many pupils believed the South African situation would improve overnight. 'The youth have very high expectations. They think there will be free education, housing and jobs. These things may come after five years, but the youth think they will come immediately after the elections.'

There were also feelings of cautious optimism, pessimism and extreme fear that violence would erupt on the election days. An insurance salesman told me many of his clients cancelled their policies. Wealthier women stockpiled large quantities of non-perishable foodstuffs. A manager at Acornhoek's largest supermarket reported sales of unprecedented amounts of canned food and gas cookers. While only two gas cookers had been sold in the previous six months, customers purchased 48 cookers in the week before the election. Doris Nyathi, the wife of a school principal, bought large quantities of wood, gas, candles, sugar, maize meal, flour, tinned food and washing powder. She did so after she saw white women stockpiling on television. Poorer housewives also wished to stockpile, but did not have enough money to do so.

Television broadcasts of exceptionally violent episodes – such as the Shell House shootings in Johannesburg and the Mmabatho revolt – captured the public imagination and inspired fear. There were also reports that right-wingers from ESCOM would cut off all electricity and attack blacks in the darkness. In an interview one man said the new government would not meet people's aspirations. He was scared that, as in the case of Mmabatho, the youth could go on the rampage and loot stores. What informants feared most, however, were reprisals by aggrieved whites. People were acutely aware that lowveld whites dreaded the elections. The defeat of the National Party and of General Viljoen's Freedom Front, which most whites supported, was as imminent as an ANC victory. Informants also believed whites would lose a great deal under an ANC government. They said the ANC's envisaged programme of land redistribution, and Peter Mokaba's slogan, 'Kill the farmer! Kill the boer!' could prompt whites to resort to violence.[20]

Local events gave substance to these perceptions. As the election date approached, many villagers reported that whites became increasingly resentful of them. At the Green Valley market vendors told me the white farmers, from whom they bought fruit and vegetables, suddenly became unco-operative. Emily Machate regularly bought mangoes, bananas, maize and sweet potatoes from Mahebehebe – a white man who owned a farm north of Hoedspruit. In March Mahebehebe told her he no longer wished to sell anything to blacks and that she should rather buy these goods from Nelson Mandela. Emily was very surprised: 'Mahebehebe was always friendly, but he has changed. Today he insults and beats people. Mahebehebe has become nasty and rude. The whites despise us because we support Mandela.'

Early in 1994, members of the right-wing AWB had attacked commuters on the roads north of Green Valley. On 17 April the local ANC Youth League hired two buses for members to attend an election rally in Pietersburg. At Jongmanspruit ten rifle-wielding AWB men waved for the buses to stop. When the first bus raced past, the men opened fire. Bullets ripped apart a rear tyre of the bus. The second bus stopped, and the AWB men forced its 90 passengers to alight, kneel alongside the road and raise their hands. The AWB men searched the bus for weapons and told the youths they had trespassed on *volkstaat* territory.[21] Non-ANC members were also attacked. In April armed white men stopped ZCC pilgrims travelling in a small van from Moria to Green Valley. They drew pistols and instructed the occupants to alight and lie down on their stomachs. Only after the pilgrims pleaded with the white men were they allowed to go. Reverend Sekgobela, who drove the van, identified one of the men as the son of his former employer. The Reverend asked the young man why he had stopped them, but he did not reply. At the request of the ANC, police started patrolling the roads north of Green Valley, but rumours persisted that mysterious lights were seen at the Klaserie bridge and that taxis were shot at. These incidents generated confusion and anxiety. Villagers not only feared physical revenge. Some were scared white farmers would refuse to sell their produce after the elections.

Against the backdrop of these perceptions rumours arose that whites sought to bewitch blacks. These rumours were novel. Yet the rapidity with which they spread throughout the lowveld shows how plausible they were in the new political context that had emerged. Musambachime (1988:203) argues that captivating rumours arise in times of insecurity. 'Rumours are believed or passed on because they express concern(s) or fear(s) of the population in a manner which is comprehensible to them within their particular context.' From being dominant outsiders, whites were becoming dominated insiders who envied blacks. Villagers were well aware that the AWB did not perpetrate violence from a position of strength. Instead, they saw the attacks as a sign of just how desperate the AWB were. Of all types of witchcraft, poisoning seemed the most appropriate to whites. White farmers recognised poisoning, possessed unlimited supplies of insecticides and chemicals, and regularly supplied villagers with food.

The witchcraft rumours of 1994 were modelled on an earlier scare that arose after people discovered peculiar tablets in the maize meal that was sold during the drought of 1992. Some people alleged that these were birth control tablets manufacturing companies had placed in the maize meal to cause impotence among men and sterility among women. Others disputed this interpretation, saying that the tablets merely prevented fermentation. These sinister attempts to reduce the black population were not described as witchcraft.

An incident that occurred early in March ignited the rumours of 1994. A white man sold quarter-loaves of bread with mango relish (*achaar*) for only 20c at several schools. Pupils and teachers at the schools in Landela and Edinburgh developed food poisoning after they ate the bread. Wildly exaggerated reports of the incident soon spread throughout the lowveld. In Green Valley, I heard, 20 children were poisoned by whites and admitted to the Matikwane hospital. (A nursing sister at the hospital could not confirm this.) People who heard this story became petrified of anyone distributing food in the villages. When a black employee of the Albany bakery arrived at a high school in Ludlow to deliver bread scholars claimed that whites had hired him to poison them. They tied the man to a chair with ropes and called a health inspector to determine if the bread was toxic. Only when the bread was shown to be harmless the man was released. A few days later a member of the Allendale school committee saw whites dumping milk containers in the veld, near a water hole for cattle. He told colleagues they poisoned the milk and placed it where herders would find it.

Politicians actively perpetuated the rumour that started in the schools. On 13 March a young man drank home-brewed beer in Green Valley and started vomiting severely. That evening he was taken to hospital, but was certified dead upon arrival. At his funeral Mr Sithole, a well-known politician from Cottondale, delivered a fiery oration. (Mr Sithole was a prominent member of the Ximoko Progressive Party and the Gazankulu Legislative Assembly, but now supported the ANC.) Mr Sithole said that whites from Hoedspruit had actually poisoned the young man, and warned that these whites planned to reduce the number of Africans to ensure that fewer votes were cast for the ANC. He furthermore asserted that, by issuing Africans with dangerous weapons to kill each other, the South African government assisted the farmers in their clandestine activities. Mr Sithole spoke of the attacks on commuters and pleaded that people should not use the northern roads nor accept food from 'generous' whites. Many believed a neighbour poisoned the young man and branded Mr Sithole as an opportunist. Yet his oration heightened people's fears.

During March and April, ANC election candidates and organisers addressed a series of meetings attended by teachers, Civic Associations and ordinary villagers. They warned people that whites would employ any devious method to defeat the ANC. In the Blyde district farmers allegedly misinformed workers about voting and taught them to draw crosses next to the symbol of the party they disliked. The ANC officials also said whites would use tactics similar to those employed by the Democratic Turnhalle Alliance (DTA) in the Namibian elections of 1990. The DTA allegedly doctored food with invisible election ink and delivered these to South West Africa People's Organisation (SWAPO) strongholds. When people's hands were scanned under ultra-violet rays at the polling stations it showed that they had already voted. In this way SWAPO lost many votes. Likewise, the food whites delivered in the lowveld could be stained with election ink.[22] Furthermore, the ANC officials cautioned people against accepting bread, mango relish and T-shirts from whites. It was likely that the food would be poisoned and the T-shirts doctored with chemicals.[23]

A clerk of the Setlhare chief and Comrades also alerted people to this danger. On 25 March the clerk overheard a telephone conversation between a school inspector and a nurse. They spoke of children who were poisoned in Bushbuckridge. The clerk was so shaken that she telephoned all principals in the area and asked them to dissuade pupils from accepting food from whites. Early in April Comrades told high school pupils in Green Valley that whites had distributed poisoned bread in Acornhoek, as well as fruit, vegetables and coins that contained election ink. One morning in April Comrades drove through the streets of Shatale and announced, over loud-hailers, that the AWB had poisoned Shatale's water tanks.

In April Mosotho – a generous white farmer who spoke northern Sotho very fluently – was accused of witchcraft. Since 1991 Mosotho's labourers had delivered under-grade potatoes to the ZCC and Roman Catholic churches in Acornhoek. They did this on the request of church leaders. But before the election, the labourers started distributing potatoes from the lorry at the Tintswalo hospital. Young men confronted the labourers and told them the potatoes were smeared with poison and election ink. The labourers denied this, saying that they, and even Mosotho himself, were card-carrying ANC members. Hence they had no reason to 'wipe out' their Comrades.

These rumours were widely accepted as truthful. Some ANC supporters refrained from eating fruit, vegetables and jam during the elections. Yet informants described the witchcraft of whites as a very recent phenomenon which accompanied the elections. During an interview a housewife explained:

'We have lived with whites all along. We were oppressed, but we were never bewitched. The olden whites hated us, harassed us, and beat us. But the recent whites are poisoning us. This is because of politics.'

The belief was thus intimately connected with the vision of an inverted social order in which whites are dominated by blacks. It is significant that ANC officials were among the rumour's most vociferous proponents. As the most likely beneficiaries in a post-apartheid South Africa, they feared the witchcraft of whites the most intensely.

The volatile nature of these rumours, which disappeared as quickly as they started, should be emphasised. People's worst fears were not realised. Throughout the lowveld the elections proceeded without the occurrence of any major incidents of violence. On 27 April, AWB members tried to set up roadblocks to prevent blacks from voting in Hoedspruit, but were dispersed by a contingent of the South African Defence Force. It soon became known that the ANC had won an overwhelming victory.[24] However, villagers realised whites would not be impoverished overnight. White farmers have not been deprived of their land. In addition, the demise of the former Bantustan bureaucracies brought about many new commercial opportunities. Within months of the elections, whites set up many flourishing businesses in Acornhoek. In the context of a new South Africa, which is rather more familiar than people expected, whites would continue to be perceived as dominant outsiders who are unlike witches. By December 1994 people had only vague memories of pre-election rumours. Some have even begun to doubt whether whites really poisoned blacks. A ZCC Reverend ate the potatoes Mosotho delivered to his church every day and said nothing had ever happened to him. 'Some people wanted to destroy the image of whites in the new South Africa. This was election fever.'

## CONCLUSIONS

The case of witchcraft shows the great complexities involved in studying the 'consciousness of colonisation' (Comaroff and Comaroff, 1992b:236). Narratives of witchcraft present a complex symbolic discourse on domination and power – a discourse that the concept 'resistance' cannot adequately describe or illuminate. Here I recall Worsley's (1957) misguided attempt to explain the advent of the John Frum movement on the Tanna Island of Melanesia, during which islanders anticipated the arrival of cargo, as 'the first stirring of anti-colonial nationalism'. The movement broke out in 1940 when only one district agent and four white merchants were present on the island (Jarvie, 1963:129).

I have sought to demonstrate that 'resistance' was not apparent in the sociology of witchcraft accusations. Through time the evil power of witchcraft has been attributed to relatively deprived insiders. Harsh experiences of apartheid in the lowveld did not lead to the belief that whites were witches. As dominant outsiders, whites were more likely to be victims of the witchcraft of blacks. In fact, it was only during the South African elections of 1994, which signalled an end to apartheid and the demise of white domination, that witchcraft was attributed to whites. Rumours of the witchcraft of whites were a product of political turmoil in which villagers anticipated 'a world turned upside down'. There are historical parallels to this phenomenon in the ethnographic literature on central Africa. MacGaffey (1968) describes 1960, the year in which the Congo attained independence, as a time of great excitement. He notes that there were expectations that Congolese would occupy the homes of Europeans and be endowed with unlimited wealth. 'Europeans were frequently referred to as witches. A white man with a lantern was said to go about stealing people's souls' (ibid.:175).

Yet, despite the fact that whites were seldom deemed to be witches a careful deconstruction of narratives of witchcraft points to the symbolic affinity between witches and whites. Through internal enemies, witches liaise with the places of whites and appropriate the attributes of whites. Witches were portrayed as masters with servants and as using *sekgowa* technologies that were inaccessible to ordinary villagers. The images of witches and zombies bring to mind the miserable consequences of domination. Moreover, witchcraft beliefs reflect on the subversive potential of the capitalist economy, and on the destructive effects of *sekgowa* technologies such as insecticides, trains, automobiles and planes. But like the cargo cultists of Melanesia, villagers of the lowveld did not merely resent the cultural forms, commodities and the power of dominant social groups. These were also objects of envy and desire. Through narratives of witchcraft, villagers did not seek to reject, or overcome, the domination and technological power of whites. Rather, villagers recast these in their own terms.

# 5 WITCHES, COGNATES, AFFINES AND NEIGHBOURS: THE CHANGING DISTRIBUTION OF WITCHCRAFT ACCUSATIONS

This chapter turns to explore the incidence of witchcraft accusations in the domestic domain and, more generally, it sketches a sociology of witchcraft accusations in Green Valley. The established starting point for such an enquiry is Marwick's (1965, 1970) theory that witchcraft accusations are a social 'strain-gauge', which indicate tension points in the social structure, and that the drama of accusation initiates a process of restructuring social relationships.

Marwick (1965) contends that among the Chewa sorcery accusations reformulated problematic social relations that were not susceptible to juridical processes. He found that 60 per cent of sorcery accusations occurred within the matrilineage. As the matrilineage grew beyond the size that its resources could sustain, tensions over inheritance and succession became apparent. The leaders of different matrilineal segments then jockeyed for position and often attempted to discredit their rivals by accusing them of sorcery. In retrospective accounts, sorcery justified segmentation. It served as an idiom for initiating processes of fission, enabled the accusers to break off redundant social relations and to discard unwanted obligations. Marwick (1965) notes that sorcery accusations were absent in the case of conjugal relations, because hostilities between spouses were expressed and redressed by alternative means. The Chewa could attribute misfortunes at home to the transgression of taboos, and the courts, which readily granted divorce, could easily dismantle conjugal relations.

Recognising the multidimensionality of witchcraft, this chapter aims to reformulate Marwick's sociological theory of a 'strain-gauge' in terms of local structures of domination and conceptions of power. At a general level, evidence from Green Valley does bear out Marwick's contention that the distribution of witchcraft accusations, between persons standing in various relationships, reveals tension points in the social structure. To realise this insight, he highlights the importance of recording information about the alleged witch, the supposed victim, and the accuser. Marwick (1970:286) asserts that the relationship between the alleged witch and the accuser 'provides a more accurate indication of the tensions involved'. The relationship between the alleged witch and the victim deals more with the 'realm of informant's beliefs' (ibid.:285).

But friction does not always, nor even usually, lead to witchcraft accusations.[1] Something else must be added to the explanation. Marwick does not do justice to the extent to which witchcraft accusations refer to specific cosmological ideas and to concepts of the witch as a category and a person (Knauft, 1985:3). Marwick also neglects the connections between mystical beliefs and social power. He fails to explore sufficiently how claims of witchcraft are grounded in structures of domination, may be shaped by political agendas and can perpetuate the subordination of certain categories of persons. For example, McLeod (1972) shows that by possessing the prestigious *benge* poison oracle – which alone provided authoritative proof of the existence of witchcraft – Azande aristocrats could reinforce their dominance over commoners and Azande men over women. In this chapter I aim to show how the distribution of witchcraft accusations provides an indication of the different capacities of social actors to manipulate these beliefs within the contexts of local frameworks of meaning.

In Green Valley, ideas about the inheritance of witchcraft were too nuanced to inhibit witchcraft accusations. (Some but not all children of a witch inherited witchcraft from their mothers, and anyone could purchase witchcraft substances.) The supposition that witchcraft operated in situations of intimacy and relative deprivation had a more profound impact on accusational patterns. As we have seen, villagers imagined that witches were driven by envy and jealousy (both *lehufa*), and by desire (*duma*) to harm relatively more fortunate persons who reside close to them. Only when these motives could be invoked were accusations of witchcraft plausible. For example, though villagers resented whites, their resentment only culminated in attributions of poisoning during the elections of 1994, when it seemed that whites were being deprived of political power, and would be forced to integrate socially with blacks.

Before and after 1960, witchcraft accusations occurred most frequently in personal relationships that were close, competitive and marked by social inequality. Because cognatic relations were co-operative, cognates seldom accused each other of witchcraft. The relations constituted by marriage were competitive, however, and parents often made witchcraft accusations against their daughters-in-law, husbands against their wives and the senior houses in polygynous marriages against junior houses. Yet most witchcraft accusations occurred between neighbours, because disparities in wealth was most apparent in the case of neighbours, and perceptions of these inequalities generated intense fears that envious neighbours would resort to witchcraft. Therefore, the distribution of witchcraft accusations in Green Valley does not offer a gauge of social tension *per se*, but rather of the specific problems that arise from per-ceptions of social inequality.

THE DISTRIBUTION OF WITCHCRAFT ACCUSATIONS, 1943–1960

From the selective memories of informants I recorded 27 witchcraft accusa-tions that occurred before 1960. Though this small number of cases are by no means a representative sample, they do allude to the different forms of co-operation and sorts of tensions that were characteristic of the local agricultural economy of this period. Four accusations (15 per cent) occurred between cognates, ten (37 per cent) between people related by ties of marriage and 13 (48 per cent) between non-kin.

The relatively few accusations between cognates is partly attributable to the nature of the *motse* as a co-resident agnatic cluster which co-operated in culti-vation and herding. An ideology of common blood propagated solidarity between patrilineal descendants, and sacrifices to the ancestors explicitly dramatised such unity. The blood of the sacrificial animal, which was poured onto the ancestral grave, served as a symbolic reminder of the ties of blood that bound descendants. Matrikin were also very important. By severing the relations between cognates, witchcraft accusations could disrupt these forms of co-operation and endanger the integrity of the *motse* as a production unit. Some allegations of witchcraft between brothers occurred against the backdrop of tensions resulting from primogeniture, when the oldest son inherited the bulk of his father's estate and cattle. (See Case 1.1.) Moreover, when cross-cousin marriage was common among Sotho-speakers, strife between spouses could generate tensions between other cognates.

The relations between affines and between the different houses of polygynous marriages were more conducive to strife. In the 1940s and 1950s arranged marriages were common. Ten of the 17 informants who married during this period recalled that their parents had chosen spouses for them. Some migrants recalled that upon their return from work they discovered that their parents had married wives for them in their absence. Even those who chose their own spouses had to obtain their parents' approval before they could marry. An integral aspect of arranged marriages was that parents assisted their sons in paying bridewealth. Bridewealth was standardised: Sotho families demanded ten heads of cattle for their daughters and Shangaan families twelve. Though these demands were substantial, households with large herds of cattle could easily afford bridewealth. Poorer families could negotiate to pay an initial deposit, which enabled the bride to move to their home, and to pay the out-standing bridewealth subsequently. They could also negotiate to pay bridewealth in cash. (A man who worked in Pilgrim's Rest mines only completed his bridewealth payments of £40 after the birth of his fourth child.) Only in exceptional cases did men incur bridewealth debts.

Residential rules were strictly patrilocal. Apart from the women who married Mozambican migrants, young adults tended to marry local people whom their parents knew. (Sotho-speakers frequently married their cross-cousins.) Weddings enacted a bride's journey from her natal homestead to the homestead of her husband's parents (Stadler, 1994:142–50). Thereafter, the newly married wife lived with her husband's parents and worked exceptionally hard for them. Even before dawn, she was expected to fetch water and firewood, stamp maize, prepare food and sweep the yard. This was because her in-laws washed and ate soon after they woke, and because they did not want her to spread dust when they received visitors. For the remainder of the day, she worked in their fields, gathered relish, cooked, ground sorghum, brewed beer, cleaned the home, washed clothes, smeared the floors with cow-dung, fetched more water and firewood and stamped more maize. Her in-laws seldom assisted her with any of these tasks. At all times she had to display subservience towards them. A wife was not allowed to eat chicken, and had to obtain the permission of her in-laws before she could use household items. In addition, a wife's husband would send remittances to his parents.

Despite residing with her in-laws, a wife still belonged to her father's descent group. She was often addressed by her maiden surname. For example, she could be called *Ngwa* ('from') Mashego, and not Mrs Machate. A wife's ambiguous status was expressed by the metaphors of the head and body. A Tsonga proverb states, '*U hakelela miri hayi nhloko* ['You buy the body not the head'].' Bridewealth only signalled the transfer of a woman's body: her head remained the property of her own kin. A husband was not permitted to beat his wife on the head, and when a wife's corpse was carried to the grave, her agnates carried the head-end of the coffin and her affines the body-end. After marriage, a wife could, periodically, visit her agnates. Her agnates could also visit their son-in-law to *xirwalo* ('bring beer' in Tsonga). During these visits they brought food, drinks and a chicken or goat. The son-in-law had to estimate the value of these 'gifts' and pay them the cash equivalent. *Xirwalo* enabled the wife's agnates to enquire about the well being of their daughter and grandchildren. Only after the husband's younger brothers had married could the couple set up their own homestead. Now, the wife worked solely for her husband and received his remittances. Yet both agnatic and affinal relations continued to be important.

The extent to which ties of marriage were embedded in wider social relations is clearly apparent from the distribution of witchcraft accusations. While not a single accusation occurred between spouses, seven were made against affines. Wives accused authoritarian mothers-in-law of keeping snakes and zombies and of killing their own grandchildren to feed these familiars, and accused sisters-in-law of being envious witches. Older women, in turn, accused unco-operative daughters-in-law of poisoning their husbands with love potion (*moratišo*) and blamed her natal group of bewitching their affines.

In three cases different houses of polygynous marriages accused each other of witchcraft. Two men accused their half-brothers of bewitching the children of neighbours, and another accused his half-brother of being so envious of his hardworking oxen and beautiful wife that he sent lightning to strike them. For many men, Chief Setlhare, the founder of their chiefdom, was the ideal masculine model. Chief Setlhare kept hundreds of cattle, married twelve wives and left more than 60 children. But, even in the past, women did not idealise polygynous marriages. These accusations occurred in the context of enmities between co-wives and of formally prescribed inequalities in their rank and status. A man's first wife was usually his senior wife. However, if a man married his cross-cousin she would assume the senior rank, and his first wife would be demoted. In either case the senior wife would be called *mosadi tsong* (chief wife) by the junior wives and *mma mogolo* (big mother) by their children. She seldom did domestic work. If a husband built a home for one of his junior wives, his senior wife should stay there, sleep in the bed and sweep the floors before the junior wife could take up residence. If a man's junior wife died, while his senior wife was still alive, he was prohibited from wearing mourning clothes. (This would have suggested that he was a widower.) When a husband returned from work, he should first visit his senior wife and present her with gifts. The senior wife's children and daughters-in-law also took precedence. During initiation, her sons walked in front of their half-brothers. Her daughters-in-law had to be the first to sow, harvest and taste the crops (*go loma*). Any breach of these rules was thought to afflict women of the *motse* with *difeka*, causing them to bear crippled children.

Despite the emphasis on good neighbourliness and on co-operation by neighbours in agricultural pursuits, most accusations of witchcraft were made between non-kin: five occurred between neighbours and eight between rival ritual specialists. Whilst the residential pattern in Green Valley was one of scattered *metse,* there was hardly any conflict over land. Fields were as large as household labour could cultivate and did not encroach upon each other. The most serious squabbles between neighbours were those between individual men that arose from drunkenness or disputes over lovers. Such fights were settled through a ritual called *go tshware lana* ('to reconcile'). Disputing parties each bought a chicken, cooked the birds on a common fire and shared the meat. The neighbours who were accused of witchcraft generally failed to reciprocate kindness and social support, and were envious, resentful and less fortunate persons. For example, in 1947, when Grace Chiloane became seriously ill, she blamed her neighbours of venting their anger by poisoning her because she had refused their son's marriage proposal. Four years earlier a dancer collapsed and died at the feast that was held to celebrate the return of initiates from the lodge. His hosts accused their neighbour, an impoverished old women standing at their gate, of having bewitched him. Previously they had refused her, when she begged them for food and clothes.

The witchcraft accusations between ritual specialists were so common precisely because the realm of cosmology and healing were marked by such fierce competition between rival religious paradigms and healers. ZCC prophets accused non-Christians and *dingaka* of keeping zombies and snakes at their homes. Initiation masters blamed other, less successful, initiation masters for the illnesses of initiates. Furthermore, the chief's official rainmakers attributed their inability to make rain to the misdeeds of envious *dingaka* who had laid *šibeka* in the veld to drive away the rain-bearing clouds. (In Chapter 7 I discuss these accusations in greater depth.)

## THE DISTRIBUTION OF WITCHCRAFT ACCUSATIONS, 1960–1995

During my period of fieldwork we gathered information on 310 witchcraft attributions that occurred between 1960 and 1995. These permit a far more detailed examination of the social tensions expressed in witchcraft accusations. We could record the accused–accuser relationships in 291 of the attributions, the accused–victim relationships in 279 and the victim–accuser relationships in 293. Nineteen attributions did not result in the naming of a witch. Some informants had diagnosed their misfortunes as being due to witchcraft, but did not find out who had bewitched them. In seven cases individuals were pointed out as witches, but it was not specified whom they had bewitched. Sometimes answers to questions about the identity of a witch were vague statements, such as, 'her own relatives' or 'neighbours'.

Table 5.1 shows the distribution of witchcraft accusations by the accused-accuser relationships. In 6 per cent of the accusations, the accused and accusers were cognates, in 42 per cent they were relatives by marriage and in 53 per cent they were non-kin. These figures correlate fairly closely with the accused–victim relationships, as indicated in Table 5.2. In 29 per cent of the accusations the accused and their supposed victims were relatives by marriage and in 47 per cent they were non-kin. The greatest discrepancy pertains to the involvement of cognates in witchcraft. While cognates seldom accused each other of witchcraft, others often identified cognates as the agents of witch attacks on kin (24 per cent of the cases). This discrepancy indicates that cognatic relations were co-operative. These accusations were very damning precisely because cognates were expected to care for each other. For example, an informant told me that Nomsa Letsele had bewitched her own son. In 1978, her son, a construction worker, fell from the third storey of a building, and Nomsa received his pension money. Later I learnt that the son dearly loved his mother, and that Nomsa's co-wife, who despised her, had made the accusation.

Table 5.3 shows the victim–accuser relationships. If we discount the cases where the victim was also the accuser, the concern that cognates (expressed towards) each other's well-being was strikingly apparent: 61 per cent of the accusations were made by the victim's cognates. Non-kin (such as neighbours, the Comrades and co-workers) acted on behalf of the victim in 27 per cent of the cases. Relatives by marriage were the least supportive. Only in 12 per cent of the cases did individuals accuse others of bewitching their spouses, affines or those related to them by polygynous marriages.

These trends are further illuminated by Table 5.4, which shows the relationships between plaintiffs and defendants in cases brought before the *kgoro* (courts) of the chief and headmen: 50 per cent of the disputes were between non-kin, 45 per cent between relatives by marriage and only 5 per cent between cognates. Disputes thus tended to occur in precisely those relations that were prone to witchcraft accusations.[2] However, the disputes between non-kin tended to be of a less serious nature than those between relatives by marriage. The former concerned insults and squabbles over loud music, the ownership of a cow, premarital pregnancies and the non-payment of debts amounting to R100. The disputes between spouses and affines concerned divorce, physical assault, inheritance and bridewealth debts amounting to R1,000.

Table 5.1: The Relationship between those Accused of Witchcraft and their Accuser(s), Green Valley, 1960–1995

| Relationship | N | % | Relationship | N | % |
|---|---|---|---|---|---|
| COGNATES | | | RELATED BY POLYGYNOUS MARRIAGE | | |
| Grandparent | 1 | | co-wife | 5 | |
| Parent | 4 | | co-wife's brother | 1 | |
| Child | 2 | | half siblings | 17 | |
| Sibling | 5 | | sister's co-wife | 1 | |
| Father's brother | 2 | | mother's co-wife | 3 | |
| mother's brother | 1 | | mother's half-sister | 4 | |
| sibling's child | 2 | | grandmother's co-wife | 1 | |
| cross-cousin | 1 | | Total: | 32 | 11 |
| Total: | 18 | 6 | NON-KIN | | |
| AFFINES | | | Neighbours | 85 | |
| husband's parent | 5 | | shebeen operator/client | 7 | |
| husband's sibling | 3 | | fellow drinkers | 3 | |
| husband's sibling's child | 1 | | political rival | 1 | |
| daughter's husband | 3 | | elders/Comrades | 14 | |
| daughter's husband's parent | 5 | | business rival | 4 | |
| sister's husband | 5 | | co-worker | 7 | |
| sister's husband's mother | 1 | | husband's co-worker/wife | 2 | |
| son's wife | 6 | | fellow church member | 3 | |
| brother's wife | 14 | | teacher/scholars | 1 | |
| brother's wife's parent | 3 | | soccer rival | 3 | |
| son's wife's parent | 4 | | thief/victim | 1 | |
| wife's parent | 7 | | lover | 3 | |
| wife's sibling | 1 | | lover's kin | 9 | |
| father's sibling's spouse | 4 | | lover's other lover | 2 | |
| grandfather's brother's wife | 1 | | spouse's lover | 4 | |
| 'related by marriage' (unspecified) | 3 | | former wife/husband's new wife | 1 | |
| SPOUSES | | | healer/client | 2 | |
| Total: | 66 | 23 | rival initiation master | 1 | |
| Husband | 9 | | | | |
| Wife | 13 | | Total: | 153 | 53 |
| Total: | 22 | 8 | | | |
| | | | TOTAL | 291 | |

\* percentages of sub-totals have been rounded up.

Quantitative evidence thus shows a significant, but uneven, correlation between witchcraft accusations and social structural tensions. Cognates were the most supportive, the least likely to be involved in disputes and the least likely to accuse each other of witchcraft. Relatives by marriage seldom came to each other's defence, were often involved in serious disputes and often accused each other of witchcraft. Non-kin sometimes defended each other and were less likely to be involved in serious disputes than relatives by marriage. Yet witchcraft accusations occurred most frequently between non-kin. I shall explore these trends in greater depth in the sections below.

Table 5.2: The Relationship between those Accused of Witchcraft and their Assumed Victims, Green Valley, 1960–1995

| Relationship | N % | Relationship | N % |
|---|---|---|---|
| COGNATES |  | RELATED BY POLYGYNOUS MARRIAGE |  |
| father's brother | 4 | Co-wife | 3 |
| mother's brother | 1 | co-wife's child/grandchild | 3 |
| sibling | 6 | sister's co-wife | 1 |
| parallel-cousin(FBS) | 2 | sister's co-wife's son/grandson | 3 |
| cross-cousin (FZS, MBS) | 4 | husband's mother's co-wife | 1 |
| child | 30 | mother's co-wife | 1 |
| sibling's child | 8 | half-siblings | 4 |
| grandchild | 10 | mother's co-wife's great | |
| great grandchild | 1 | grandchild | 1 |
| Total: | 66 24 | Total: | 17 6 |
| AFFINES |  | NON-KIN |  |
| husband's parent | 8 | neighbour | 82 |
| husband's sibling | 4 | shebeen operator/client | 6 |
| husband's brother's wife | 2 | fellow drinker | 2 |
| husband's sibling's child | 2 | political rival | 3 |
| stepchild | 3 | business rival | 4 |
| daughter's husband | 2 | healer/client | 4 |
| daughter's husband's parent | 2 | rival initiation master | 1 |
| daughter's husband's sister | 1 | teacher/scholars | 1 |
| brother's wife | 3 | fellow scholar | 1 |
| son's wife | 9 | soccer rival | 3 |
| son's wife's parent | 2 | thief/victim | 1 |
| son's stepchild | 1 | lover | 4 |
| wife's brother's son | 1 | lover's kin | 13 |
| wife's brother's son's wife | 1 | lover's other lover | 3 |
| unspecified | 2 | spouse's lover | 1 |
| Total: | 43 15 | former wife/husband's new wife | 1 |
| SPOUSES |  | Total: | 130 47 |
| husband | 16 | TOTAL | 279 |
| wife | 7 |  |  |
| Total: | 23 8 |  |  |

## THE CO-OPERATIVE RELATIONS BETWEEN COGNATES

*Tšhwene ge ere 'Hoo!' e tshepile lewa.*
(When the baboon says 'Hoo' it relies on the cliff.)

In the period after 1960, an appeal to cognatic kinship remained the most effective way of gaining social support. Betterment altered the nature of cognatic relations. The constituent units of large cognatic clusters were dispersed to different residential stands, and the material basis of domestic

Table 5.3: The Relationship between the Assumed Victims of Witchcraft and their Accuser(s), Green Valley, 1960–1995

| RELATIONSHIP | N | % |
|---|---|---|
| SELF | 82 | 28 |
| COGNATES | | |
| grandparent | 3 | |
| parent | 66 | |
| mother's brother | 2 | |
| father's brother | 6 | |
| sibling | 18 | |
| cross-cousin | 2 | |
| child | 14 | |
| brother's son | 2 | |
| sister's son | 1 | |
| 'own relatives' | 14 | |
| Total: | 128 | 44 |
| AFFINES | | |
| husband's mother | 2 | |
| daughter's husband's mother | 1 | |
| Total: | 3 | 1 |
| SPOUSES | | |
| husband | 11 | |
| wife | 5 | |
| Total: | 16 | 5 |
| RELATED BY POLYGYNOUS MARRIAGE | | |
| mother's half-brother | 3 | |
| half-brother | 1 | |
| husband's half-brother | 1 | |
| grandson of co-wife | 1 | |
| Total: | 6 | 2 |
| NON-KIN | | |
| neighour | 30 | |
| Comrades | 19 | |
| colleague | 3 | |
| fellow student | 2 | |
| fellow church member | 1 | |
| lover | 1 | |
| soccer player/club manager | 1 | |
| fellow drinker | 1 | |
| Total: | 58 | 20 |
| TOTAL | 293 | 100 |

Table 5.4: The Relationship between Plaintiffs and Defendants in Cases
Brought Before *kgoro* of the Setlhare Chief and Headmen, Green Valley,
1991–1995

| RELATIONSHIP | N | % |
|---|---|---|
| COGNATES | | |
| brother | 1 | |
| brother's daughter | 1 | |
| father's father's brother's daughter | 1 | |
| Total: | 3 | 5 |
| AFFINES | | |
| husband's mother | 1 | |
| husband's siblings | 1 | |
| mother/stepson | 1 | |
| daughter's husband | 2 | |
| daughter's husband's mother | 1 | |
| son's wife | 3 | |
| son's wife's mother | 1 | |
| wife's brother | 1 | |
| unspecified | 1 | |
| Total: | 12 | 18 |
| SPOUSES | | |
| wife | 14 | |
| husband | 4 | |
| Total: | 18 | 27 |
| NON-KIN | | |
| neighbour | 21 | |
| trader/customer | 2 | |
| mechanic/customer | 1 | |
| *ngaka*/client | 2 | |
| husband's lover | 2 | |
| daughter's husband's lover | 1 | |
| daughter's lover | 2 | |
| colleagues | 1 | |
| commoner/headman | 1 | |
| Total: | 33 | 50 |
| TOTAL | 66 | 100 |

co-operation was undermined. Since households were deprived of their fields,
income was now generated solely by individual wage earners, outside the
group. Since betterment, kinship has operated situationally. Support networks
now included only those close relatives with whom people could establish and

maintain relationships. The value of common descent was still assumed, however, and so people relied more on cognates than on strangers.[3] Solidarity between cognates was ritualised during weddings and funerals, and was evident in the formation of family burial societies. There had also been a shift from jural (as in property holding rights) to moral obligations. Strong moral ties bound individuals with their grandparents, parents, siblings, cousins, uncles and aunts. However, different obligations attached to each of these relationships, which affected the prevalence of witchcraft accusations.

(i) *Grandparents and Grandchildren.* Elders were often suspected of witchcraft. Here Heald's (1986) analysis of deviant motivations among the Gisu is illuminating. She argues that the Gisu saw the capacity to engage in witchcraft as an attribute of age. Elders are powerful, owing to increased wisdom and the control of certain types of knowledge. Yet their power is not that of active adulthood, which slips away into infertility and infirmity (ibid.:75).[4] Nonetheless, only one man in my sample accused his grandparent of witchcraft. In this case the accused was a maternal grandfather, who had deserted the accuser's grandmother.

The mutual relations between grandchildren and grandparents were close and affectionate. Informants described children, who were cared for by their grandparents, as spoilt because they were never punished. As members of alternate generations, children and grandparents were expected to tolerate each other's jokes, and these jokes were often sexual. Grandmothers 'smelt' the penises of their grandsons, and grandchildren, in turn, fondled their breasts.[5] Permitted disrespect stems from the recognition that the statuses of the elderly, and the very young, are equivalent. Like elders, children are asexual and dependent (Stadler, 1994:89). No economic obligations were attached to this relationship: grandchildren were not expected to support their grandparents, and they did not inherit from them.

Enmities were exceptional, and occurred only between grandparents and older grandchildren. Ntsako Mkansi complained to me that, whenever she received her pension, her older grandchildren always demanded pocket money from her. Sylvia Namane found it difficult when her three grandchildren were sent to stay at her home. The two elder girls misbehaved and Sylvia sent them back to their mother. 'They had no respect. At night young men visited them and they made so much noise that I could not sleep.' Yet Sylvia still cared for her grandson, a high school pupil, because he had not yet started with his 'adolescent trouble'.

(ii) *Parents and Children.* Relations between children and parents were less egalitarian and more reserved. Children were obliged to obey their parents, and could not expect them to tolerate their jokes. Relationships between father and child were particularly formal. One could not speak to a father about sexual matters, and had to approach him through an intermediary when making requests. Parents were obliged to protect their children, and to support them financially in their childhood years. Once children became wage earners, it was their duty to care for their parents. Very few people shunned these obligations.

Indeed, every single elderly person in the household sample derived some kind of support from his or her children.

Tensions surfaced when dependent children demanded greater financial and social support from their parents. In 1988, a schoolboy stole R800 from his father. His father found out, and beat him severely with a stick. In 1990 a 14-year-old boy committed suicide, after his stepfather beat him. Neighbours recalled that the previous evening the boy's mother was drunk, and that he said that she was unfit to be his mother. But these tensions were not expressed in witchcraft attributions: informants deemed dependent children to be too immature to practice witchcraft.

Witchcraft accusations only occurred once parents became the dependants of their children. In four cases married wage-earning sons accused parents, to whom they failed to give money, of witchcraft. During 1993, Tshepo Maile's wife threatened to divorce him because he was impotent. The couple consulted a *ngaka*, who revealed that Tshepo's mother, a widow, resented him because he had failed to take care of her. The *ngaka* also said that Tshepo's mother sent a *tokolotši* at night to molest him, and to make him weak, so that he was unable to have sex with his wife. Later Tshepo built his mother a new home, to pacify her. Circumstantial evidence was decisive in the other witchcraft accusations between children and parents. Olga Ndluli had heard the rumours, circulating among neighbours, that her father kept a *mamlambo*, but she disregarded these. However, one afternoon Olga saw a large snake slithering across their dining room floor. When Olga informed her father, he disputed the snake's existence, and pleaded with her not to tell others about the snake. Only after her father's death, three years later, did Olga tell friends about her experience.

(iii) *Uterine Siblings.* Sibling groups are characterised by internal solidarity and equivalence (Radcliffe-Brown, 1965:65). Villagers treated uterine siblings as social equals, and perceived sibling rivalry as scandalous. Upon his retirement, in 1994, Sello Theko bought five cows, but within only three months all his cows were stolen. A *ngaka* then told Sello that his brother had stolen the cattle. Sello's brother was furious when he learnt of these insinuations, and assaulted one of Sello's friends. When Sello reported his brother to the chief's *kgoro*, the chief said that their dispute was so serious that it had to be heard behind closed doors.

After 1960 inheritance rules changed. As in other South African rural areas, land shortage and diminished agricultural returns resulted in a system of ulti-mogeniture (James, 1988). While older sons left their parental homestead, the younger son inherited the residential stand, home, fields and most cattle from his parents. This did not amount to preferential treatment of the youngest brother, but saddled him and his wife with the arduous responsibility of caring for his aged parents by sending regular remittances, and by working in their gardens (James, 1988). Ultimogeniture lessened disputes over inheritance. Labour migrancy also facilitated sibling solidarity. In the absence of wage-earning parents, sibling groups remained together, and developed close bonds. When the sons later became labour migrants, they often secured work from the same employer. In the contemporary period, seniority between siblings was only apparent in ritual contexts. Brothers were expected to marry in sequence of age; and the wife of the oldest brother should always be the first to sow and harvest.

Responsibility towards one's siblings was evident in the continued practice of sibling adoption. After their marriage, elderly women gave the husband's youngest sibling to the newly married couple. For the rest of their married life, they cared for the child. The wife washed his clothes, and her husband supplied him with money for education. For example, when my research assistant, Kally Shokane, studied for his BA degree, his elder brother, a truck driver, paid his tuition fees. Kally, in turn, paid the fees of his younger brother, who studied Information Science. The equivalence between uterine siblings was apparent in the respectful manner in which brothers treated their sisters. One man said that a sister is actually senior to her brothers:

Even if she is younger than me, she is *thakangwaga* [first born]. She does not have authority in her own house, but in the homes of her brothers she is the senior. Her sons always walk in front of my sons at the initiation lodge. *Difeka* can come if you do not accept her seniority.

Only five witchcraft accusations occurred between uterine siblings. One accusation expressed conflicts over the inheritance of cattle. In the other cases there was circumstantial evidence for witchcraft, *dingaka* persuaded people that their siblings were witches and people sided with their spouses against their siblings. In 1966, a *ngaka* told Casius Zwane that his sisters had bewitched his wife. Casius accepted this diagnosis because his sisters had quarrelled with his wife, and because of circumstances surrounding her death. (She was pregnant, had suffered from fever and experienced hallucinations.) Casius took revenge by killing his sisters' cattle, and his sisters sent their sons to assault him. Casius later moved away to another village.

(iv) *Children, Uncles and Aunts.* Adults were obliged to assist with the socialisation of their siblings' children. A father's sister was called *rakgadi*, his elder brother *ramogolo* and his younger brother *rangwane*.[6] As 'female father', the *rakgadi* was expected to listen to the problems of her brother's children, advise them about marriage, visit them when they were ill, invoke the ancestors on their behalf and assist his daughters when they gave birth.[7] The *ramogolo* and *rangwane* also had to be informed of the well-being of their brother's children. It was their duty to discipline the children, assist them and supervise their funerals. If their brother died, they had to divide his estate among his dependants. In his absence, they could also negotiate bridewealth payments. If the *ramogolo* or *rangwane* died without leaving progeny, their brother's children could inherit from them.

A mother's bother was called *malome* and her sisters *mmamogolo* or *mmangwane*.[8] The *malome* acted as a 'male mother' and guardian of his sister's children.[9] If his sister died, and her husband's family was unable to care for her children, it was his duty to adopt them. He also listened to their problems, assumed responsibility for their initiation, advised the boys about sex, saw that no foul play was involved when they died and assisted in carrying their coffins. If the *malome* died without progeny, his sister's children could inherit from him, sharing with his brother's children. The *mmamogolo* and *mmangwane* had to be present when their sister's children were born, assist in the *ntšha ngwana* ritual during which they are brought from the home, and had to be kept informed of the major events in their lives.

As cross-cousin marriages diminished, strife between children and their *malome* or *rakgadi* lessened. The five witchcraft accusations that I recorded between children and the siblings of their parents do not indicate regular tensions. Some accusations were incidental. For example, Willy Moleme was convinced that his *ramogolo*, a *ngaka*, practised witchcraft. When Willy walked past the home of his *ramogolo*, late one evening, a large snake appeared from nowhere, and stared at him. The next day, Willy's *ramogolo*, reportedly, told him, 'My son. Don't walk about at night! Where shall I play when you walk about?'

(v) *Cousins*. Parallel-cousins (i.e., the children of one's father's brother or mother's sister) were classificatory siblings, who were called *ngwanešo* or *kgaetšedi*. (The same terms applied to uterine siblings.[10]) Cross-cousins (i.e., the children of one's mother's brother or father's sister) were called *motswala* (a term with no sex or age distinctions). The difference between parallel- and cross-cousins was pronounced among Sotho-speakers, who were permitted, and encouraged, to marry their cross-cousins (unlike Shangaans).

Relations between cousins were devoid of specific obligations, but were very co-operative. During stick fighting, cousins were not permitted to be opponents. Cross-cousins tolerated disrespect. Once a sturdy man stopped his van, alighted, and showed his fist to Eliazaar. In an angry tone, he said, 'You donkey! You witch!' Eliazaar merely laughed. He later told me the man was his cross-cousin. 'Our cousins are like toys. We play with them.' Villagers believed that physical contact between cross-cousins of the opposite sex could cure the ailments – *madi a magolo* (big blood) and *seše manyane* (twitchy eyes). To cure a boy of *madi a magolo*, he undressed, and was washed with a cloth soaked in his cross-cousin's urine. To cure a girl of *seše manyane*, her cross-cousin rubbed his penis against her eye.

Strife and witchcraft accusations between cousins were uncommon. Like many other villagers, Skariot Mosoma's cousins were convinced that he was a witch (see Case 7.2, pp. 144–5). They even recalled that he joked with them about witchcraft. (He taught them witches' songs, and demonstrated how witches dance.) Yet they did not fear that Skariot would bewitch them. 'He was our cousin and he protected us. He said that he always pleaded for us at the witches' meetings, and told the other witches not to kill us.' Conflict over the inheritance of cattle formed the backdrop to the only recorded witchcraft accusation between cousins. After Eric Tlou died, in 1974, his sister's son, Selios Mapaile, received the bulk of his herd of 80 cattle. Eric's son was furious and claimed that Selios had bewitched his father so that he could inherit the cattle.

Loyalty between cognates transcended the occasional enmities that arose among them. Brothers and sons sometimes joined together to avenge a person's death, and agnates were usually the first to defend and protect a person, whom others had accused of witchcraft.

## AFFINAL RELATIONS AND WITCHCRAFT

*Mosadi ke tšhwene. O lewa mabogo.*
(A woman is a baboon. We eat her hands.)

While cognatic relations remained co-operative despite the traumas of betterment, the relations between relatives by marriage were exceptionally disharmonious. Bridewealth debts and the ambiguous status of wives in the homes of their husbands' parents regularly provoked conflict.

From the 1950s, the nature of bridewealth and marriage changed drastically. Herds were greatly diminished by the cattle epizootic of 1950, by stock limitations, by reduced grazing areas and by cattle theft. Consequently, parents could no longer assist their sons with bridewealth cattle. Sons now paid their own bridewealth in cash. Moreover, the value of bridewealth was no longer standardised, but varied according to the bride's educational qualifications. In the 1980s, one man asked R480 for his oldest daughter, who was uneducated, and R1,400 for his youngest daughter, who had a matric.[11] For young men bridewealth became a serious burden. Most paid over a protracted period of time, incurring considerable debts. Only three weddings were held in Green Valley during 1990. This indicates how few men had paid up their bridewealth, and shows how expensive weddings had become. (Rodney Mathibela took 14 years to pay off his wife's bridewealth of R1,500, and he then paid an additional R2,000 for his wedding ceremony.[12])

As Stadler (1994) has shown, high bridewealth discouraged hasty marriages and enabled daughters to continue residing in their natal households. It also ensured that a wife retained recourse to the protection of her agnates, even after she had moved to the home of her in-laws. Since bridewealth was hardly ever considered paid up, her husband's parents seldom achieved complete authority over her, and her status was constantly in dispute. The threat of desertion was always a powerful tool in domestic negotiations.

Because sons were expected to pay bridewealth themselves, they were entitled to choose their own wives. Through time arranged marriages disappeared, and cross-cousin marriages became uncommon. Sotho men argued that if they took their cross-cousins as wives, and failed to pay bridewealth promptly, they would incur the wrath of their own kin. As such, a man's wife was likely to be a stranger to his parents and the possibility of conflict increased. Many elders complained that the wives of their sons were lazy, insubordinate and cooked only for their own husbands and children. One story relayed how a blind woman asked her daughter-in-law to cook tripe, but the daughter-in-law threw nappies into the pot, smeared gravy on them, and dished these up. The story may well be apocryphal, but highlights perceptions of extreme disrespect. Elders resented the economic independence of their daughters-in-law. They said that in recent years sons sent money to their wives, rather than their parents. The agnates of deceased men found it particularly disconcerting that the widows of these men inherited their estates. Three disputes which were brought before the chief's *kgoro* concerned inheritance.[13]

There were 66 witchcraft accusations between affines. In 21 instances, members of the wife's agnatic group accused members of the husband's agnatic group. Many of these accusations were motivated by a deep concern for the well being of the newly married wife and her children at the home of her in-laws. A wife's parents-in-law were convenient scapegoats for any misfortune that she, and her children, suffered. Parents-in-law possessed ample motives for witchcraft: they resented insubordination by their daughter-in-law, and were envious of the fact that she received the bulk of their son's remittances.

The experiences of Jackson Shai show the intensity of such suspicions. Jackson's daughter began to display symptoms of insanity shortly after she married Ivy Moreku's son. A month later, an ostrich kicked Jackson on the farm where he worked, and he suffered an internal haemorrhage. Jackson claimed that because Ivy was furious when her son divorced his first wife to marry Jackson's daughter, she sent the ostrich to attack him. Only three sons-in-law were accused of witchcraft. All these men had notorious reputations as witches. In 1988, Alfred Nobela's parents-in-law claimed that he poisoned their daughter. Alfred was a storeowner, who had an extramarital affair with his shop assistant. Previously his mother had been evicted from Green Valley for keeping familiars. These accusations were uncommon because the status of a son-in-law as a wage earner was contrary to the image of a deprived witch.

The accusations that young wives made against their affines arose out of domestic squabbles. One evening Lesedi's son screamed in his sleep, 'I don't want to herd goats.' Lesedi suspected that her brother-in-law had tried to turn her son into a zombie. He was a *ngaka*, and he had complained that his own sons never herded his goats. Sometimes accusations against parents-in-law served to legitimise desertion. In 1989, Abelang Molimi returned to her parents after she quarrelled with her mother-in-law. She told her father that her mother-in-law had kept a *mamlambo* hidden inside a trunk, and said that a *tokolotši* had attacked her at the home of her affines.

Husbands and their agnates made 45 witchcraft accusations against members of the wife's agnatic group. In 21 of these cases they directly accused daughters- and sisters-in-law. As a co-resident household member the daughter-in-law was strategically placed to bewitch her affines. She could poison the food that she cooked, and could treat the clothes that she washed with *dihlare*. As a member of another descent group, who was treated as a servant, a daughter-in-law was often suspected of disloyalty. Moreover, an accusation of witchcraft against a daughter-in-law would not necessarily disrupt the solidarity of her husband's agnatic group. These factors are apparent in the case of Morris Khomane, who became fatally ill in 1986. (He had diarrhoea and vomited blood.) Morris' mother accused his younger brother's wife, Lucia Mohlolo, of having poisoned him. She said that, before his death, Lucia had given him *mageu* (light beer) to drink, which contained portions of a crocodile brain. Lucia was always sulky, and regularly complained that her own husband did not support her as well as Morris had supported his wife. Lucia, allegedly, poisoned Morris so that his wife, too, could suffer. The accusations against the wives of fellow household members might be interpreted as bids to terminate stressful relationships, and to remind men that their primary obligations lay with their agnates rather than with their spouses.

When the agnates of a deceased man accused his widow of witchcraft, they undermined her claims to inheritance. If she was evicted, the agnates of her husband could inherit his estate. Case 5.1, below, shows the potential instrumental motivations for such accusations.

### Case 5.1: Affines, Inheritance and Witchcraft

In 1993, Danson Maoko, an ESCOM employee, worked on a high-voltage electricity pylon and was tragically electrocuted. Danson's father, Jan, believed that witchcraft was involved because Danson had, mysteriously, ignored his supervisors' instructions and touched a live wire. Jan claimed that Danson's wife,

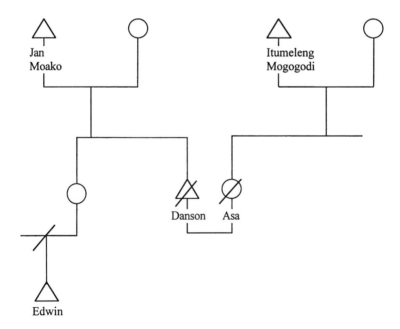

Figure 5.1: The Domestic Situation of Asa Mogogodi

Asa, and his father-in-law, Itumeleng Mogogodi, had sent familiars to put him in a forgetful state. After Danson's funeral, Jan took hold of Danson's van and gave it to his daughter's son, Edwin. Being dispossessed of her rightful inheritance, Asa experienced great stress in the household of her parents-in-law. Two months later she committed suicide. Villagers found Asa hanging, by her headscarf, from the branch of a small tree.

In October 1993, a witch-diviner revealed that both Itumeleng and Jan were witches: Itumeleng had bewitched his son-in-law, Danson; and Jan used *sehlare* to make his daughter-in-law, Asa, commit suicide. Since then the two families had not spoken to each other. Danson's agnates retained his possessions and were, subsequently, granted his pension.

The witchcraft accusations that were made against the wife's agnatic relatives expressed feelings of discontent about interference in household affairs by overbearing affines. Kopano Sedibe found it disconcerting that his son regularly dodged school to look after the cattle of his wife's brother, Tlabego Mokoena. When his son suddenly became ill, in 1982, Kopano claimed that Tlabego tried to transform the boy into a zombie. Kopano told me that he had often seen Tlabego in the veld on a bicycle, conveying a bag of maize meal, and alleged that Tlabego went to the veld to feed his familiars. These accusations served notice on his affines to keep their distance, and, indeed, redefined the boundaries between affines and agnates. Other accusations brought tensions over bridewealth debts to the foreground. After Tumelo Mogale collided with another vehicle, he told his friends that he suspected that his mother-in-law, to whom he had still owed much bridewealth, of witchcraft.


SPOUSES AND ILLICIT LOVERS AS WITCHES

*Monna ke selepe. O lala a a dimilwe.*
(A man is an axe. He can be borrowed.)


One of the most significant changes in the distribution of witchcraft accusations was the proliferation of accusations between spouses since 1960. On 22 occasions individuals accused their spouses of witchcraft; on four, their spouses' lovers; on one occasion, the spouse of a lover; and on another, a divorcee accused her former husband's new wife.

Though nearly all adults were married (see Table 5.5), very few had realised their aspirations to a harmonious marital life. As in other southern African rural areas, marital strife was extremely pervasive in Green Valley.[14] Conjugal bonds had become increasingly frail: 62 (27 per cent) of the 227 marriages that I recorded had ended in divorce.[15] This problem was most acute among the younger generation.

The formal, inflexible, nature of conjugal bonds contributed to marital disharmony. Conjugal relations were not egalitarian, rested upon clearly opposed gender roles, and involved very specific obligations. Notions of economic activity, sexuality, procreation and the socialisation of children were all implicated and these were sensitive and important matters (Niehaus, 1994).

Husbands were the primary breadwinners and the work of their wives was largely confined to child-rearing and housekeeping. This is because wage-earning opportunities were largely restricted to men: 88 percent of the economically active husbands in the household sample were employed, and only 17 per cent of the economically active wives (see Table 5.6). The status of husbands as wage earners enabled them to dominate their wives. Wives displayed obedience and respect by clasping their arms when they shook hands; by sitting on mats rather than chairs; and by speaking softly in men's company. Husbands bluntly refused to help their wives with any domestic work. On one occasion I asked a woman to teach me how to stamp maize, but her husband told her not to do so. 'Men who stamp maize are idiots.'

Table 5.5: The Marital Status of Adults in Sampled Households by Gender, Green Valley, 1991–1992

| Marital status | Men | Women | Total |
|---|---|---|---|
| Married | 112 | 121 | 233 |
| Remarried | 8 | 2 | 10 |
| Widowed | 13 | 39 | 52 |
| Single | 32 | 13 | 45 |
| Divorced | 21 | 18 | 39 |
| TOTAL | 186 | 193 | 379 |

Table 5.6: The Employment Status of Adults in Sampled Households by Gender and Marital Status, Green Valley, 1991–1992

| Employment Status | Men | | | Women | | | All Adults |
|---|---|---|---|---|---|---|---|
| | M | NM | T | M | NM | T | |
| Pensioner | 30 | 4 | 34 | 28 | 27 | 55 | 89 |
| Employed locally | 24 | 6 | 30 | 13 | 13 | 26 | 56 |
| Commuters | 23 | 3 | 26 | 1 | 6 | 7 | 33 |
| Migrant labourers | 36 | 21 | 57 | 2 | 8 | 10 | 67 |
| Not working | 11 | 19 | 30 | 78 | 24 | 102 | 132 |
| TOTAL | 124 | 53 | 177 | 122 | 78 | 200 | 377 |

Note: M – married, NM – not married, T – total

The failure of persons to fulfil their obligations as spouses generated much conflict. Wives nearly always complained that their husbands provided inadequate money, and readily deserted consistently unemployed men.

Husbands, on the other hand, complained when their wives failed to maintain order at home or spent money unwisely, and they normally divorced women who failed to bear children. In extreme cases, desperate childless women faked pregnancy, and attempted to steal the babies of others. But childbirth *per se* was no guarantee of a durable marriage. A divorced woman told me, 'Men despise women who can't bear children. But even if you bear ten children your husband may still leave you for a childless woman.'

The practice of *bonyatsi* was the foremost threat to conjugal harmony. In Green Valley *bonyatsi* was a normal, but morally non-normative, practice. Unlike prostitution (*bofebe*), it denotes a long-term extramarital liaison. Men provided intermittent amounts of money to their paramours, but these were not directly negotiated for sex.[16] Labour migration contributed greatly towards *bonyatsi*, but does not account for the pervasiveness of this practise. Locally employed men and the wives of non-migrants also engaged in *bonyatsi* and some migrants kept *dinyatsi* (paramours) in Green Valley.

Men and women engaged in *bonyatsi* for different reasons. Men argued that they were inclined to be polygynous, but that financial constraints prevented them from marrying many wives. They compensated for this by keeping *dinyatsi* (Spiegel, 1991). If other women could not share a man, they could at least borrow him for a while. Men also regarded extramarital sex as very passionate.[17] Women kept *dinyatsi* for economic reasons. Kotzé (1986:26) writes, of another lowveld village: 'To men, multiple sexual relations are a national sport; to women it is the primary source with which to ensure their and their children's survival in the face of male dominance.'

Unlike among the Chewa, tensions between spouses were seldom expressed in allegations about the transgression of taboos. Men certainly feared that sexual intercourse with extramarital lovers, and with women in a state of *fiša*, could lead to various afflictions, to the birth of crippled children, venereal diseases and to AIDS. Indeed, they took precautions against these dangers. Midway through the initiation ritual, male initiates were given beer to drink containing a powder that was made from the foreskins of all initiates. It was believed that this made the initiates immune to each other, so that they would not be affected if they slept with the same woman. Men also used condoms and relied on the prescriptions of *dingaka* and Christian healers to circumvent illness.[18] As a final resort a husband who had sex with his *nyatsi* before he impregnated his wife, could confess and perform the *alafela* ritual. When the couple had sex for the first time after the child's birth, the husband rubbed his semen against the child's head, and the wife twice pushed the child through her legs.

In a context where divorce was frowned upon and only reluctantly granted by the chief's *kgoro*, witchcraft accusations between spouses justified separations. It is important to recognise the different inclinations of husbands and wives to instigate separations, and also the manner in which notions of gender informed witchcraft accusations.

Nine wives accused their husbands of witchcraft. A wife could only afford to separate from her husband if she, herself, was a wage-earner, or if her agnates were willing to support her, or if she found another man to marry.[19] Because a wife inherited from her husband, it was in her interest to remain married for as long as she could tolerate it. In addition, a wife could not readily attribute motives for witchcraft to her husband, who was the dominant partner in the conjugal relationship. Husbands were more likely to vent their anger in overt than in mystical ways. Men divorced wives who failed to bear children, beat wives who squandered money, or complained too much, and sometimes violently assaulted the *dinyatsi* of their wives. Indeed, one man threatened to behead his wife and her six children with an axe, and chased them from his home, after they complained that he neglected them. Men also withheld money from their wives. Morati Mohlatswa, a migrant labourer, discovered that his wife had been impregnated by her *nyatsi*. For almost a decade now Morati has slept at his sister's home whenever he visits Green Valley, sent money to his sister from work and asked his sister to purchase food for his children.

In only four cases did wives claim that they, themselves, were victims of their husbands' witchcraft. Some of these accusations were made under duress. Richard Nkari was enraged when he discovered that his wife, Mercia, had an extramarital affair. When his neighbours told him that his dog had killed their goose, Richard killed the dog and threw its carcass down the pit latrine. Mercia saw the trail of blood, and fled to her brother's home. She told her brother that she feared Richard might bewitch her. At night, Mercia said, it felt as if she slept with a wild *tokolotši*. These accusations were not readily accepted as truthful.

In the other cases the husbands' assumed victims were their own kin, and the *dinyatši* of their wives. Faith Mathonsi took her insane son to the ZCC prophets in Moria. For three months the prophets unsuccessfully tried to cure him. Faith's husband repeatedly refused to come to Moria when he was asked to do so. At home, Faith told her neighbours that her husband had bewitched his son, because the son demanded cattle from him. Husbands were sometimes suspected of using *ku balo* – a type of *sehlare* – to bewitch the *dinyatsi* of their wives. *Ku balo* allegedly caused unfaithful wives and their lovers to get stuck together like dogs while copulating.[20] It could also cause the lover to be struck by a snake, to become impotent, or to be found out. In 1989, the son of a prosperous businessman died while he had sex with Virginia Mnisi, the wife of a Mozambican refugee. Virginia accused her envious husband of having used *ku balo* to kill her *nyatsi*.

The inclination of wives to remain married was apparent in the three witchcraft accusations that they made against the *dinyatsi* of their husbands. These accusations expressed resentment against the women who stole their husbands and were bids for reconciliation. Benson Ngobeni had an affair with his next-door neighbour, a widow, and supported her financially. When Benson's wife became ill, she said the widow wanted to kill her. A *ngaka* supported her claim, and Benson terminated his illicit love affair.

Thirteen men accused their wives of witchcraft. Husbands could separate from their wives without experiencing a loss of income, and generally found it easy to attribute motives for witchcraft to their wives. Husbands were aware that wives resented being dominated and deprived of remittances. In addition, a wife was strategically placed to bewitch her husband. Only she washed his bedding and clothes. In the hands of witches these items, which contain a man's *seriti* and body dirt, were deadly weapons. Witches can, for example, manufacture *sejeso* from a man's body dirt. A wife can also poison her husband's food. One man highlighted this fear, saying, 'In our culture a man does not just die. We blame his wife.'

Wives seldom vented their anger overtly. Violence was not a viable option. Martha Phokane lost her temper when she saw her husband buying clothes for his *nyatsi*, and attacked him in public: but her husband withheld all remittances from her for the next three months. Some wives reported their husbands to the *kgoro* of the chief and headmen. (Wives were the plaintiffs in 14 of the 18 marital disputes that I listened to.) But this was a cumbersome means of gaining justice: many cases were dismissed because of insufficient evidence, husbands failed to appear, or disclaimed responsibility on the grounds that they were not legally married. When husbands were found guilty of misconduct, they were usually fined an amount of R300: R50 was deducted for court fees and R250 went to the wife.

Women frequently consulted *dingaka* and Christian healers about their marital problems. Of the 101 clients who consulted Sebongile Ndlovu, an Apostolic healer, during the course of February 1992, 24 were women who wished to marry the correct husband, bear children, or reunite with their husbands. Sebongile's therapies ranged from prayer and counselling, to the use of *ditaelo* ('prescriptions' from the Holy Spirit) such as holy water, strong coffee, eggs, steam and woollen cords. Men could easily misconstrue the attempts to heal ruptured social relations as witchcraft. One of Sebongile's clients told her that she feared others might kill her husband because he often became very aggressive. To immunise her husband against this danger, Sebongile stabbed his shirt and sprinkled seawater on it. Should the husband have found out about the consultation, or seen her operations, he could well have suspected witchcraft.

In ten cases husbands who felt that they were secretly being manipulated, claimed that they were the victims of their wives' witchcraft. Bokosi Mathebula told me that his former wife kept a *nyatsi* at home while he worked in Tembisa. He alleged that she used *sehlare* to make him send money often, but come home seldom. These stories also contrast the physical violence of husbands with the mystical powers of their wives. Mandla Sibuyi beat his wife when he discovered that she had committed adultery. As Mandla sat at their dining room table, the next day, a snake bit him on his leg. His sons searched the entire home, but could not find the snake. Believing that his wife had bewitched him, Mandla left for Johannesburg.

Husbands also justified separating from their wives by claiming that their wives had bewitched others. After Calson Mathole found a new lover, he chased his wife from home. His wife's parents wanted to discuss the situation with him, but Calson's neighbours told them that he had accused her of causing death. The neighbours, however, did not know to whose death Calson referred.

## POLYGYNY AND RELATIONS BETWEEN CO-WIVES

*Monna ke lepai. Re a apolelana.*
(A man is a blanket. We share him.)

By the 1990s very few men were polygynists. Of the 120 husbands in the household sample, twelve were married to two wives, one husband to three, and another to seven wives.[21] Polygynists were generally older and wealthier men. Some recalled that their parents had owned many cattle and could easily afford to provide enough bridewealth for them to marry more than one wife. The other polygynists were businessmen or held steady jobs. Polai Matsane could marry seven wives because he once owned a butchery and two general dealer stores.

Discontent between co-wives was generated less by differentials of rank than by envy about unequal provision, and in some cases by the inability of polygynists to provide adequately for many dependants. When co-wives had their own fields, husbands could easily provide them with life's necessities. But this was not possible in present-day circumstances. Many women found it ridiculous that men could even contemplate marrying more than one wife. Because competition for a husband's affection was most intense when co-wives lived on the same residential stand, most polygynists built their wives' homes in different village sections.

Wives dreaded the prospect of sharing a husband. Sometimes a wife's refusal to allow her husband to marry a second wife was the pretext for divorce. But being a co-wife in a polygynous marriage was preferable to being single: co-wives were at least still entitled to some financial support from their husbands. After Khensani Matukane's husband married two more wives, he could only provide her with a bag of maize meal each month. To support her children, Khensani was compelled to take up work as a child-minder. Junior wives faced even greater difficulties. Before marriage, their husbands would promise to take good care of them, but these promises were seldom fulfilled. Husbands usually continued residing with their first wives, and tended to have less respect for their junior wives.

Suspicions of witchcraft arose from enmities between co-wives. Women constantly feared that their dissatisfied co-wives could resort to witchcraft. A *ngaka* said that she thought polygyny ought to be outlawed, because it frequently leads to witchcraft. 'When a man marries two wives problems will immediately start. If one of his wives gets angry she won't tell him, but she'll ask others for advice. These people will give her *dihlare*.' Witchcraft allegations were most acute when co-wives contested the estate of their deceased husband.

The members of junior houses made 17 witchcraft accusations against those of senior houses. But this does not indicate a clear pattern. Circumstantial evidence led Aaron Mashile's half brothers to accuse him of witchcraft on no fewer than 13 occasions (see Case 1.2). The other cases show that senior wives were sometimes thought to have bewitched the junior wives who undermined their status. This was evident in the case of Tšhabi Sekgobela, who shared a home with her senior co-wife. The senior wife resented Tšhabi because she was barren and Tšhabi had given birth to three healthy children. She often swore at Tšhabi for having 'stolen' her husband. When Tšhabi's leg became lame, she accused her co-wife of witchcraft. 'She even warned me she would buy *dihlare* to bewitch me.'

The 15 accusations made against members of the junior houses were sociologically more telling. As intruders who occupied a subordinate status, junior wives were thought most likely to deploy *dihlare* and familiars to advance their own interests. The tensions which precipitate witchcraft accusations could be very subtle. In 1983, Edson Masiye returned from the initiation lodge. A spectacular party was held to celebrate his return, and he was presented with numerous gifts. A month later, Edson died of tuberculosis. Edson's mother claimed that her junior co-wife had placed *dihlare* on his gifts. She allegedly resented the fact that the party, which was held for her own son, who returned from the same initiation lodge, was a less jolly occasion.


## NEIGHBOURS, TENSIONS AND SOCIAL INEQUALITY

*Uga celi nhlobo na Bembe e tele.*
(Tsonga, Lit. Do not dig a well while the Limpopo is full.)
(Fig. Do not trust outsiders while you have relatives.)


Villagisation and the removal of hundreds of displaced households into Green Valley broke up the networks of reciprocal co-operation that had been built up between neighbouring households over the decades. Since 1990 these processes generated increased tensions and disputes and escalating accusations of witchcraft between neighbours.

One might have expected that competition over the allocation of residential stands would have featured prominently in narratives of witchcraft, but this was not borne out by my research. Only in four accusations was competition for land mentioned. In 1994, Baiketile Malatsi and Nononi Mqiba fought over the right to cultivate some vacant land. Baiketile and Nononi brought their dispute to the chief's *kgoro*, which gave judgement in favour of Nononi. A few months later Nononi bought curtains in Johannesburg. As she entered the shop, she fainted and suffered from total amnesia when she came to. The Indian shopowner found Nonini's identity documents, and arranged for a taxi to take her home. Nononi's fellow household members suspected that Baiketile had bewitched her.

More prominent were the disputes arising from premarital love affairs, and the tensions between neighbours and shebeen operators. Like *bonyatsi*, premarital love affairs were a source of extreme conflict. Young men engaged in many love affairs, and often refused to marry, or to pay bridewealth, after they had impregnated their girlfriends (Stadler, 1994:94–8). As the progenitors of illegitimate children, they could negotiate to pay a fine, called *go hlaola* (to select), to free them from all further obligations. (This fine was usually set at half the value of bridewealth.) But young men even regarded *go hlaola* as excessive. Their refusal to support their girlfriends led to backstreet abortions and infanticide.[22]

Young men sometimes justified terminating their love affairs by accusing their girlfriends, or agnates of their girlfriends, of witchcraft. Some also claimed that the mothers of their former girlfriends bewitched them, because they had rejected their daughters. Competition between lovers also led to witchcraft accusations. At the funeral of Daisy Hlongwana, a 19-year-old-woman, mourners alleged that she was the victim of witchcraft. The previous year, Daisy had visited her boyfriend and found him with another woman, and a fierce argument erupted. When Daisy returned, her panties were missing. Shortly thereafter, Daisy experienced *ngopa* (excessive menstrual flow) and had two successive strokes. The mourners said that her boyfriend's other lover had bewitched Daisy's panties.

Premarital pregnancies might also generate bitter conflict between the families of the youngsters involved. In December 1992, Sofi Langa, an unmarried mother, died in hospital due to pregnancy complications. Her grandmother blamed her boyfriend, Moses Shokane, for her death. Moses became extremely depressed. On the evening of Sofi's night vigil, he hung himself, leaving a suicide note, which read:

*Bageso, e yang polokong yo Sofi. Le se naganele ba gobo yena. Ga se bona ba mpolailego. Ke ipolaile nna, ka baka la gore, ka rata Sofi kudu kudu. Ka ntle gage ga ke na bokamoso.*
[My family, please attend Sofi's funeral. Do not blame her family. They are not responsible for my death. I have killed myself because I love Sofi very much. Without her there is no future for me.]

Sofi's grandmother died from asthma 14 months later. Her kin accused Moses' mother of using *sporiani*, a very potent *sehlare*, to avenge his death.

The ten witchcraft accusations that were made against shebeen operators and against clients of shebeens expressed discontent over the selling of liquor as a money-making enterprise.[23] Shebeens were perceived to be sites of immorality. Their operators contravened the prohibition on the consumption of liquor by many churches, enticed labourers into squandering their hard-earned salaries and deprived dependents of remittances. Shebeens were also associated with alcoholism, adultery and fighting. Men often slept at one shebeen, which was frequented by loose women and prostitutes. In December, 1994, a schoolboy was stabbed to death on the premises of another shebeen operator, who served children liquor. At 12pm, on 21 January 1995, a man offered two young women a ride to Green Valley from an Acornhoek shebeen. When he did not stop at the intersection, the young women realised that he was trying to abduct them and jumped from his van. One woman broke her neck as she hit the tarmac. Many villagers blamed the shebeen operator for her death.

I heard many allegations that shebeen operators used witchcraft to boost their profits. Some, allegedly, poisoned the liquor they sold. This made their customers very drunk, and enabled the shebeen operators to pick their pockets. Others used *dihlare* to cause their customers to forget their change – even if their paid with R50 notes. One notorious woman was said to have used a *tokolotši* to call men to buy at her shebeen, and to molest them when they slept. Fellow drinkers were also accused of poisoning. Harry Usinga died shortly after friends brought him home from a shebeen, one evening in 1976. His wife was furious and shouted that nothing had been wrong with him when he left home. She claimed that Harry's enemies had injected a fatal poison into his can of beer, while he visited the toilet. These accusations signalled a warning that shebeens are dangerous. A woman ZCC member told me, 'The only way to prevent poisoning is to stop drinking and to attend church.'

But the tensions over plots, love affairs and shebeens amount to only a fraction of the witchcraft accusations that occurred between neighbours. In many cases no direct conflict was apparent between the accusers and the accused. The vast majority of witchcraft accusations between neighbours were, rather, informed by perceptions of social inequality, and by the occurrence of strange and peculiar events.

In Green Valley social inequality was most apparent between neighbours. Wealth, health and good fortune was not distributed equally or equitably. Some households were conspicuously successful: their men earned good wages, their women gave birth to healthy children, their youngsters passed at school, they lived in well-built homes, and could afford luxuries such as television sets, telephones, furniture and motor cars. Other households were much less successful: their members experienced prolonged periods of unemployment, suffered ill health, did poorly at school, lived in shanties and struggled to make ends meet. For villagers these inequalities, which were fertile breeding grounds for feelings of envy and resentment, could easily lead to witchcraft.

From the perspective of the accusers, the practice of witchcraft had levelling implications (Geschiere, 1997). Witches were seen to be against progress and prosperity. Some witches were assumed to kill their neighbours because they wanted to see their families suffer as they did themselves. Other witches were presented as thieves who stole maize meal and money from their neighbours' homes with the aid of invisible familiars.

Villagers believed that any sign of success could motivate witchcraft attacks from envious neighbours. For example, soon after Hitekane Manzini, a well-known *ngaka*, started building a new home, with money supplied by her daughter, her clientele dwindled. Later Hitekane uncovered a plastic bag, containing *dihlare*, at her gate. She told me that her next-door neighbours had buried the *dihlare* to drive away her clients. Similarly, when Florence Nokeri took her ill child to a *ngaka*, she was told that a noise at her home had attracted the attention of her neighbours. Florence asked the *ngaka* whether it could be a music system that her husband had recently purchased. The *ngaka* replied affirmatively. 'Yes. This can make such a sound. Be careful! Your neighbours are on your heels!'

Educated young men, who held well-paid jobs, considered themselves to be particularly vulnerable to their neighbours' witchcraft. Ruben Malatsi hired a taxi to transport family members and friends to his graduation ceremony in Pietersburg. To celebrate the occasion he bought a cake with his name inscribed on it. While they were in Pietersburg, one of his neighbours demanded to see the cake. Ruben's sister believed that the neighbour wanted to poison the cake, because none of her children had matriculated, and refused her permission. The neighbour reacted in the most peculiar manner. She took off her blouse and shoes and walked home. Ruben's sister also believed that the neighbour's familiars were pestering her. Young men perceived such attacks as unjustified and complained that neighbours overestimated their wealth.

Suspicions against neighbours were often so intense that the mere invasion of private, domestic, space by uninvited guests was sufficient to produce witchcraft accusations. Fatios Malope, a lecturer at the Mapulaneng College of Education told me that when he installed electricity at his home, an elderly woman entered his gate. Without greeting anyone, she went to sit on his verandah. Fatios called three of his neighbours, and asked them whether they could identify the stranger. One neighbour called him aside, and told him, 'Around here this lady is known for evil deeds.' Fatios then threatened to kill her, but the old woman did not react. She only spoke after he sprinkled holy water on her. 'What did I do wrong?', she asked. She then got up and left. The lecturer was convinced that the old woman sought to bewitch the members of his household. Though she appeared to be drunk, he could not smell any liquor on her. He also discounted the possibility that she might have been insane. 'Why was there such a difference in her behaviour after I sprinkled the holy water on her?'

Strange, and unexpected, behaviour by neighbours could also lead to witchcraft accusations, in the absence of any conflict between the accuser and the accused. Strangeness included a close affinity with animals. Bolayi Malope refused to sell one of his oxen, and it eventually died of old age. Neighbours offered to assist him to skin the ox, but Bolayi told them to mind their own business. Only late that evening did he skin the animal himself. Rumours soon emerged that the ox had no intestines, and that Bolayi had hidden familiars inside the ox. Friday Silinda was accused of witchcraft after neighbours saw a mongoose standing on his fowl-run and Tom Phokane because he regularly worked at home until 2am.

Other individuals invited witchcraft accusations through morally reprehensible behaviour. They included Bafedile Mohlatswa, who did not mourn her grandmother's death, and Olda Chiloane, who once asked a child whether he could identify a man 'sleeping' by the roadside. (The man was actually deceased.) Ritual specialists, who were exceptionally secretive, and employed extraordinary therapies, were also considered by neighbours to be akin to witches. In 1963, villagers stoned a baboon to death. To the surprise of many, a *ngaka* arrived, cut out parts from the baboon's carcass and took these home. Rumours soon emerged that the baboon was actually his familiar, and that he cut the parts so that he could revive it. In the 1990s, a Malawian immigrant, who practised as an Islamic healer and sold the most peculiar ointments, was also suspected of being a witch.

In addition tensions between business rivals, co-workers, soccer teams, church members and ritual specialists were also pronounced. Poorer business-men and envious co-workers were occasionally accused of witchcraft. Lodrick Malebe, the owner of a general dealer store, regularly found that his goods were missing. Because none of the store's burglar protection had been broken, Lodrick believed that his neighbour, the owner of a small shop, had sent familiars to steal his goods at night. Lodrick did not confront his neighbour, but paid a *ngaka* to fortify his store against witchcraft. Though the relations between co-workers tended to be co-operative, workers who suffered misfor-tunes after they had received wage increases might suspect witchcraft. However, witchcraft accusations between co-workers were more likely to occur in urban workplaces.

Competition was extremely fierce within, and between Green Valley's seven soccer clubs. Club owners often placed bets of up to R500 on their teams, and players admitted that their teams employed *dingaka*, and used *dihlare*, to enhance their chances of success. Soccer rivalries gave rise to many witchcraft accusations. Cedric Dibakwane enjoyed enormous success as the manager of United, but many of his players complained that Cedric had exploited them. When several players left United for other clubs, and sustained mysterious injuries, they accused Cedric of witchcraft.

In the period after 1960 witchcraft accusations between rival ritual special-ists, such as initiation masters, *dingaka*, ministers of religion and Christian healers has persisted. Kgerišhe Thibela, a successful and wealthy initiation master, became very suspicious when the son of Polai Mohlala, a less successful initiation master, came to be initiated at his lodge. (Initiation masters are expected to initiate their own children.) When the boy returned to his father one night, Kgerišhe accused Polai of having sent his son to bewitch his initiates. Church members sometimes accused *dingaka* of witchcraft, and vice versa. For example, a ZCC deacon told me that Skariot Mosoma, a *ngaka* who had been expelled from Green Valley for witchcraft, always hated the ZCC. He alleged that one of Skariot's victims was the driver of a van transporting ZCC pilgrims to Moria. The leaders of established churches also branded some heretics as witches. It was widely rumoured that the minister of a new church, which had seceded from the ZCC, kept a snake to heal, and to enrich, the members of his congregation. Moreover, clients believed the ritual specialists, whom they felt had exploited them, had used their esoteric knowledge for destructive purposes.

Some healers were accused of bewitching their clients when they were supposed to fortify their homes; of prescribing herbs that turned into familiars and bottles of *dihlare* that exploded.[24]

## CONCLUSIONS

After he had listened to several informants recall specific episodes of witchcraft accusations, Kally Shokane remarked, 'Witchcraft means many different things to many different people.' Kally's comment aptly describe the diverse nature of witchcraft accusations: a diversity that cannot be accounted for by single-strand theories about 'social stress' and the 'resolution of redundant relationships'.

As we have seen, villagers attributed blame for the misfortunes they suffered to aggrieved parents whom they failed to support and to in-laws to whom they owed bridewealth debts. Witchcraft accusations also expressed resentment against persons who had inherited, or attained positions of status at the expense of others. In the case of affines and spouses, witchcraft accusations can plausibly be interpreted as bids to terminate stressful relationships, to justify separation, to deprive wives of inheritance and to warn overbearing parents in-law to keep their distance. But witchcraft accusations might also be part of a strategy of reconciliation. This can be seen in those cases in which wives who wished to retain the affection of their husbands made witchcraft accusations against the lovers and co-wives of their husbands. The witchcraft accusations that occurred between non-kin were sometimes informed by competition for land, clients, wage increases and status in soccer clubs and in the churches. They were also an attempt to allocate less fortunate villagers with blame for misfortune, to patrol household boundaries, impose moral standards and to explain the occurrence of strange and unexpected behaviour.

Despite the great variety of these meanings and purposes, certain generalisations may none the less be made about the distribution of witchcraft accusations. Through time narratives of witchcraft increasingly present a complex discourse on social inequality, deprivation and envy. Witchcraft accusations clustered in personal relations that were marked by the existence of various forms of inequality. In the vast majority of cases relatively privileged villagers accused those who were relatively disadvantaged of witchcraft. Subordinate persons rarely had the capacity to use witchcraft accusations as a means to challenge social inequality.

Anthropologists working in other social and cultural contexts have pointed out that the theory of witchcraft has levelling implications. Evans-Pritchard (1937) argued that among the Azande fears of witchcraft promoted charitable behaviour. Similarly, Geschiere (1997) has shown that, in the Cameroon, witchcraft was perceived as an attack on inequality, and that this led members of the new state elites to redistribute their wealth. At a more subjective level, Bercovitch (1989) argues that, like the notion of conscience and guilt, witchcraft confronts individuals with the moral significance of their actions.

He maintains that among the Nalumin of Papua New Guinea the theory of witchcraft reveals the wrongs individuals have done, and the failure of communities to act according to their own ideals. 'The witch', Bercovitch writes:

reminds people of how they have wronged others. But the witch reminds people that they have done wrong in a manner different from how conscience is said to work: as an internal threat of vengeance rather than an internal sense of guilt. (Bercovitch, 1989:155)

Similar observations might be made with reference to Green Valley, but here the levelling implications of witchcraft were perhaps less significant than the support given to the relatively privileged. Witchcraft accusations were used as a means to defend, protect and reinforce social inequality. By defining the desires of those who have been deprived as illegitimate and evil, witchcraft accusations legitimate success. As Fisiy and Geschiere (1991:253) observe, witchcraft accusations offer special opportunities to defend oneself against the levelling pressures of needy kin and neighbours.

# 6 'A WITCH HAS NO HORN': SOCIAL TENSIONS IN THE SUBJECTIVE REALITY OF WITCHCRAFT

Having explored the structural distribution of witchcraft accusations, this chapter asks why certain accusations are more plausible than others? To achieve this goal our analysis needs to go beyond demonstrating how, at a general level, the distribution of witchcraft accusations, between persons standing in various relationships, reveal tension points in the social structure. We cannot merely assume, like some students of witchcraft, that tense social relations, in themselves, are the prime determinants of the identity of both the accuser(s) and the accused. For example, Macfarlane (1970) argues that in sixteenth-century England witchcraft accusations arose from quarrels over gifts and loans, rather than strange events.

Although there was sometimes an emphasis on the strangeness of an event, for instance when a woman's body was sometimes covered with lice which 'were long, and lean, and not like other lice', strangeness, in itself, was not enough to produce a suspicion of witchcraft. (Macfarlane, 1970:296)

This assumption is reductionist and instrumentalist.[1] Witchcraft is seen as an idiom of social relations and processes, and questions of evidence are deemed to be peripheral. It is either assumed that proof is impossible, or alternatively, that tension is the only proof of witchcraft. Boddy's (1989, 1994) critical comments on attempts to explain mystical beliefs, such as those in Zār spirits, in terms of cross-gender competition, illuminates the limitations of this approach. She acknowledges that in some cases spirit possession may well be motivated by status considerations, but argues that one cannot explain away mystical beliefs in their entirety by merely documenting their instrumental potential. For Boddy (1989:6, 139) the argument about social conflict is unidimensional and oversimplifies matters: it underestimates the faculty of mystical entities in people's life-worlds, detracts from the polysemy, richness and subtlety of beliefs and does not do justice to the way in which they may alter people's conception of their experiences. However important these factors are to our informants, they are implicitly deemed incidental when the investigator's focus is on social-structural conflict.[2]

This chapter critically re-examines the relationship between social tensions and witchcraft. It goes beyond merely sketching the social context of witchcraft accusations to focus on the views that social actors had of their own situations, and on how individuals subjectively inferred the existence of witchcraft and the identity of alleged witches. I intend to show how witchcraft provides individuals with a discourse to conceptualise and articulate otherwise incomprehensible and inexpressible experiences. Emic understandings are essential as they motivate, guide and justify action. For believers, who perceive the existence of witches as a reality, questions of evidence are crucial and complex. As Geertz (1973:90) reminds us, religious conceptions are only accepted if they are constantly justified, clothed in an 'aura of factuality' and seem 'uniquely realistic'.[3] Residents of Green Valley were extremely sceptical when I told them of the theory that prior social tensions are expressed in witchcraft accusations. My informants insisted that, on the contrary, it is witchcraft that generates tensions. Some elders drew my attention to the Northern Sotho proverb '*Moloi ga a na lenaka* [A witch has no horn].' The proverb, they said, means that a witch's identity is never obvious and cautions people not to accuse their enemies of witchcraft.

The chapter is divided into two parts. The first considers the ontological status of witchcraft in local knowledge. I argue that the perception of witchcraft as a transcendent reality protects the belief against disproof. I show that people perceive the occurrence of mysterious events as manifestations of occult powers. In these situations circumstantial evidence, revelations through divination and dreams, and confessions attested to the reality of witchcraft. Part two provides a detailed analysis of five case studies, and critically scrutinises the role of social tensions relative to other types of evidence. I argue that social tensions were neither a sufficient, nor even a necessary, condition for witchcraft accusations. Villagers did perceive a conflictual relationship between the victim and the accused, prior to the advent of misfortune, as a motive for witchcraft. Therefore tensions were part of the wider framework of evidence they used to justify particular accusations. But villagers believed that witches often struck without motive.

## WITCHCRAFT AND THE RELATIVITY OF REALITY

Overing (1985) argues that the positivist preoccupation with defining 'what is true' in terms of verifiable observation obscures the authorising processes through which truth is created, 'what truth means' in other situations and alternative conceptions of reality. Her message is that reality is culturally constituted and relative.[4]

These insights are very pertinent to witchcraft. Villagers of the lowveld perceived reality as dualistic. They did not merely acknowledge the existence of a visual, empirical, realm of ordinary humans, but also a realm of transcendent realities. Like the Holy Spirit and the ancestors, witches were real and present everywhere, but invisible. This conception can be illuminated by the metaphor of a one-way mirror – witches can see other people, but people cannot see them.

By day witches were ordinary people who might even appear to be sociable, friendly, kind and hospitable. However, at night, when everyone else slept, witches committed malicious deeds. Even then witches were thought to be invisible as they moved about, or to assume the shape of their familiars. Witch-familiars were hidden in trunks, in rivers, or in dams during the daytime. At night familiars also travelled in disguise. An Apostolic healer is the only person I know who claims to have seen the *tokolotši*. She recounted that she observed it one evening, but was quick to point out that when she saw the *tokolotši* it had assumed the form of a dog. Similarly, there were no eyewitness accounts of witches' trains. Individuals who had boarded these trains were said to disappear forever or, if found, to suffer from total amnesia.

The belief in the transcendence of witchcraft has important implications for evidential value. Evans-Pritchard (1937) drew a crucial distinction between the totality of witch beliefs at a conceptual level and their invocation in specific situations. Transcendence immunises the totality of witch beliefs against disproof, and evidence is less important at this level. Here Kuhn's (1962) notion of the paradigm is an appropriate analogy. Like the central premises of paradigms in the human sciences – such as the subconscious, class conflict or social structure – the key assumptions of witch beliefs escape critical scrutiny.[5] However, in the context of specific situations, such as unexpected deaths, proof of witchcraft becomes vital. Then evidence which supports the system of witch beliefs is evaluated more rigorously (Gluckman, 1960:102–8). But even in these situations suspicions about witchcraft and the identity of those responsible cannot be verified through direct observation. Different kinds of evidence are required.

The occurrence of perplexing and mysterious incidents of misfortune that ran counter to the predicted, or predictable, flow of life usually generated the first suspicions that malevolent occult powers were operative.[6] A school principal justified his belief in the reality of witchcraft by recalling a very strange event. Three weeks previously, the prop shaft of a mobile truck had broken and smashed through the windscreen of the car following it. The prop shaft flew past the driver, hit the passenger in the rear seat and severed the head from his body. Such events, the principal said, cannot possibly occur naturally. Other non-normal events cited as evidence for witchcraft were not as dramatic. Samson Nyathi told me that he had repeatedly encountered problems with his car. One morning he found dents on his car's bonnet. To him it seemed as if something had walked on the bonnet at night. The next evening the car's alarm went off repeatedly. Samson inspected the car, but found nothing wrong. He later heard dogs whining outside. The next week Samson was involved in a car crash. A panel-beater repaired the damage to his car, but soon a pack of dogs savaged and damaged the car's grill. Samson found this incomprehensible and thought someone had bewitched him.

Various kinds of circumstantial evidence also attested to the reality of witchcraft. For informants, the display of envy and resentment was related to witchcraft rather as a motive is related to crime. This is evident in the allocation of blame for the death of Tom Malope. In 1989 Tom won a motor van in a competition organised by Radio Tsonga. Whilst driving his new van he swerved to avoid colliding with cattle. The van overturned and Tom died instantly. Relatives suspected his sister of witchcraft, because she complained to them that she, too, had entered the competition but had not won a prize, and said that she envied Tom.

Likewise, verbal statements were incriminating evidence. An elderly man recalled that in the 1950s he drank *marula* beer with a group of his friends. Before leaving the circle of beer drinkers, Betwell Radebe jokingly said, 'I can make anything happen.' Minutes later the weather changed. A whirlwind blew sand into the men's beer and lightning struck nearby. When Betwell returned he asked the men, 'Did you see me?' The beer drinkers were convinced that Betwell had sent the lightning. The identity of witches was also inferred from the appearance of baboons and snakes in people's yards, the discovery of naked people in the village, the anomalous appearance of people in graveyards, excessive secrecy and from people's intimacy with other well-known witches.

Confessions, and revelations through divination and dreams, were the most authoritative evidence of witchcraft. A teacher mentioned a schoolboy's confession as the reason for his belief in witchcraft. When he asked the boy why he slept in class, the boy replied, 'I did not sleep last night. My mother made me feed her things at the river.' Likewise, the revelations of *dingaka* and prophets furnished substantial proof of witchcraft. After his sister's funeral, Nareswana Ramphiri consulted a Zionist prophet, who said witches had changed his sister into a zombie. Nareswana told me, 'I believe this because I am a full member of the church.' The acceptance of such revelations was based on the belief that *dingaka* and prophets had special access to hidden truths. Because of their relationship with the ancestors or the Holy Spirit, they were seen as mediators between the empirical and non-empirical realms.[7] Dreams, too, were thought capable of revealing transcendent truths. For example, Milton Machate interpreted his dream of a snake that bit his children as a forewarning that someone was going to bewitch them.

## CASE STUDIES ON SOCIAL TENSIONS AND EVIDENCE FOR WITCHCRAFT

The above-mentioned examples of the use of evidence in the construction of witchcraft have merely been illustrative. If the argument is to be pushed further, specific examples of witchcraft accusations must be examined in greater depth.

Turner (1967) has argued that in the study of witchcraft it is insufficient merely to illustrate some or other structural feature, such as which particular relatives are being accused. He insists that witchcraft accusations are the product of a complex interplay of processes and forces that demand a dynamic treatment. To probe what the significant variables are in particular situations, and how they are combined, Turner advocates use of the extended case study method. Witchcraft accusations should be examined within the context of their field of action. Account should be taken of structural principles, processes of change and of 'cultural facts, such as beliefs, symbols, values, moral rules, and legal concepts,... in so far as these constitute determinable influences inclining persons and groups to action'(Turner, 1967:118).

Though my analysis falls short of meeting these extensive demands, I have tried to follow Turner's suggestions as closely as possible. In each of the five cases below I have sought to present detailed information about the field situation. Attention is focused on the social relations, and on the rivalries and alliances between the victims, accusers and the alleged witches (Marwick, 1970). These cases are fairly representative of witchcraft accusations that occurred during fieldwork, and the criteria for their selection has been their potential to illuminate the different types of evidence used in the construction of witchcraft. Case 6.1 highlights the way in which accusations are justified even where social tensions are involved. Cases 6.2 and 6.3 show the social effects of labelling and illustrate the manner in which individuals may be blamed for many misfortunes. Cases 6.4 and 6.5, which highlight the importance of confessions and rumours respectively, show how accusations can occur in the virtual absence of social conflict.

### Case 6.1: Lebo Mnisi: Illness, Marital Strife and Dreams

On Friday 15 January 1991, Gladys Mnisi told me that her mother was ill. I expressed concern, as I was well acquainted with Mrs Lebo Mnisi. A 52-year-old *ngaka*, she was among my best informants. She was extrovert and intelligent, and had taught me a great deal about her practice. Three days later I visited her. By then her condition had greatly improved. She was keen to tell of her illness as it involved witchcraft and the ancestors – topics we had previously discussed.

Lebo said that she became feverish the previous Thursday. That night she dreamt that a zombie approached her, shouting, 'Because you've seen me you'll die!' Lebo then pushed the zombie into a room in which many men were seated. Believing that the men would beat the zombie, she tried to lock the door from outside. However, the zombie escaped and continued to pursue her. Lebo was perplexed by the dream. She recognised the zombie that tormented her as that of Maureen Nyathi, a woman who had died long ago. Lebo became convinced that the dream was a premonition of witchcraft. On the Friday morning she saw, in a vision, that her husband's former lover had tried to bewitch her by smearing *sehlare* on him. As a result of her dream, Lebo believed that if she touched her husband she would get fatally ill.

Lebo's interpretation of the dream was informed by marital tensions she had experienced throughout her adult life. She previously resided in Thulamahashe, but moved to Green Valley with her three children after her first husband abandoned them. In Green Valley she married Freddy, who worked as a migrant labourer in Johannesburg. After 1987 Freddy seldom came home. He informed her that in Johannesburg he lived with another woman whom he planned to marry as his second wife. When Lebo learnt of his extramarital love affair, she was certain he, too, would desert her. But in 1990 her marital relationship improved dramatically. Freddy was transferred to Witbank, jilted his lover and rededicated himself to his wife. Since then he has visited Green Valley every fortnight.

When Freddy arrived at home on Friday afternoon, Lebo told him of her fears. They decided to consult a *ngaka* in Witbank the next morning. However, on Friday night Lebo dreamt that she fought with her husband and heard a voice saying she would die on the way to Witbank. At midnight Lebo awoke, complaining of heart palpitations. Freddy and Gladys gave her white *sehlare* to drink. Lebo told them Magidane (a Ngoni spirit) had revealed to her the dangers she faced through dreams. Magidane also told her that Freddy should wash himself with *sehlare*. He did as instructed. On Saturday the couple consulted a local *ngaka*. He confirmed that a woman had tried to bewitch Lebo and revealed that there were tensions between Lebo and Freddy's respective ancestors. The *ngaka* instructed them to conduct a ritual to calm the ancestors. They performed the ritual after they arrived home. Lebo soon recovered.

Lebo's experiences show the inter-relatedness of social tensions and witchcraft. A tense spousal relation was the pretext of the accusation, and it was predictable that she would blame her husband's envious lover. Lebo's expression of distress resonates with the tactical use of spirit possession by marginalised persons. Lewis (1971) has shown, for example, how women can employ ecstatic possession as a strategy to achieve consideration and respect. Possession, he argues, affords women an opportunity to insinuate their demands without jeopardising men's dominant position (ibid.: 79, 86). Yet the case shows more than a mere attempt to resolve tensions. Lebo used convincing evidence to justify her accusation. She only accused her husband's lover once she became ill, dreamt of a zombie, saw the witch's identity in a vision and had this confirmed by another *ngaka*. For Lebo the reality of witchcraft was indeed relevant.

*Case 6.2: Sarafina Maatsie: Deviance and the Tenacity of the Witch Label*

From the time that the Maatsie household relocated to Green Valley from Craigieburn in 1970, neighbours regarded them as strange. There were rumours that Sarafina Maatsie's maternal grandmother had struck people with lightning in Craigieburn. Neighbours were surprised to learn that the family had changed their surname from Nyathi (Tsonga) to Maatsie (Northern Sotho). Some thought they must be trying to hide some former shame.

The household was regarded as deviant. One index of this was the troubled marital histories of Sarafina's children. By 1993 Thabo, the oldest Maatsie son, was 35 years old and had been divorced five times. His first, second and fourth wives separated from him after they quarrelled with his mother, and his third wife left after Thabo's sisters assaulted her. Thabo divorced his fifth wife after she cheated on him with other men. Thabo had built a house for his new girlfriend in another village section and had not brought her to live with his mother. Mrs Maatsie's other children had had similar problems. Simon was married, but his wife deserted him after she became ill. Rebecca was married and had a child, but when her husband became unemployed she left for Germiston and married another man without her first husband's knowledge. Daniel was married, but his wife had left him and returned to her parents. He lived with his mother because he was unemployed. Elizabeth, who was 18 years old in 1993, had had an abortion. Roselina still lived at her mother's home although she is married and pregnant.

Sarafina was first publicly accused of witchcraft in 1978. The accusation stemmed from tensions between her and Thabo's first wife. When she noticed that Thabo's wife had not become pregnant within the first three years of their marriage, she reportedly said, 'This chicken does not lay eggs.' Thabo's wife complained to the next door neighbour, Mrs Sekgobela, that Sarafina had insulted her. Mrs Sekgobela told her that, like her grandmother, Sarafina was a witch. Sarafina later blamed Mrs Sekgobela for Thabo's divorce. The Maatsie and Sekgobela families met to resolve the dispute, but failed to reconcile the two women. When Mrs Sekgobela became ill she blamed Sarafina. When Sarafina's youngest child died in 1983, she in turn accused Mrs Sekgobela of witchcraft. Neighbours unanimously sided with Mrs Sekgobela. Many were convinced that Sarafina practised witchcraft and argued that Thabo's wives had left him because they became aware that 'abnormal things' happened in the home.

Mysterious occurrences were cited to support this view. Once, children playing in Sarafina's yard saw a snake slithering from her home to bask in the sun. A child told her parents that the snake wore beads. Employees of the Acornhoek bakery, who delivered bread to nearby shops in the early morning hours, claimed that they had seen 'small people' filling buckets with water at the tap in front of Sarafina's home.[8] They told others that the small people were really zombies who brewed sorghum beer for her. The evidence most suggestive of witchcraft was that a shop owner found Rebecca walking naked in front of his store at 5am. He was so furious that he threatened to shoot her, but his wife restrained him.

Sarafina had become very unpopular at the market where she sold fruit and vegetables. Other vendors told me they suspect that she stole primus stoves and used *dihlare* to attract customers. In 1988 Izaac, who was responsible for locking and unlocking the market stalls each day, died without displaying any prior signs of illness. When Sarafina became the new market overseer, it was alleged that she had bewitched Izaac and turned him into a zombie.

One man actually confessed that Sarafina was his accomplice in witchcraft. This happened in 1990, when Comrades took those whom they suspected of witchcraft to a witch-diviner in Mbuzini. The man who was pointed out as a witch was threatened with violence to make him reveal his accomplices. He immediately put forward her name. Sarafina disputed the accusation and phoned her son Thabo, who worked as a railway policeman in Johannesburg at the time, to ask him to come home to protect her. Thabo complied and only returned to Johannesburg again once her life was no loger in danger.

During fieldwork we interviewed several of Sarafina's immediate neighbours. They blamed her for a wide variety of the misfortunes that they had personally experienced.

(i) Mrs Ndlovu had suspected Sarafina of witchcraft since she had seen her walking naked in her yard one morning. She thought Sarafina's witchcraft had been the cause of her daughter's heart disease and her son's motor vehicle accident. Sarafina was allegedly envious of the fact that all the Ndlovu children had passed their matriculation examinations. Mrs Ndlovu was, however, of the opinion that Mrs Sekgobela did not kill the youngest Maatsie child. When the child was still a foetus, Mrs Ndlovu dreamt it climbed from its mother's womb. The foetus then walked to Mrs Ndlovu's gate, where a dog had dug out red *sehlare*. The foetus ate the *sehlare* and then returned to its mother's womb. Mrs Ndlovu said the child died shortly after birth because it ate the *sehlare* its mother buried at the gate.

Mrs Ndlovu also believed that in 1991 Sarafina bewitched her own husband, who died in Johannesburg, to obtain his pension. She alleged that prior to his death Sarafina had poured *sehlare* into the washing powder with which Rebecca washed his clothes. Sarafina's sons were reportedly furious at their father's death and Daniel even beat his mother with a stick. Mrs Ndlovu claimed that late one evening she saw Mr Maatsie's ghost. When Mrs Ndlovu heard drums being beaten at the Maatsie home, a week later, she thought the family had hired a *ngaka* to expel the ghost.

(ii) Milton Machate, a teacher, complained vehemently about Sarafina. During 1993 the Machate household was struck by an inexplicable series of misfortunes. In March Milton's wife developed boils on her legs. A prophet told her the boils were caused by *sefolane*. In April his daughter complained that she felt something moving in her ear. Nurses examined her, but found nothing wrong. However, a prophet said that witches had sent worms to bite her ear and wanted to turn her into a zombie. Over the Easter weekend Michael, Milton's younger brother, who studies in Pietersburg, visited home. The very same day that Michael returned, he was hospitalised with an inflamed appendix. A prophet told Michael that his neighbours in Green Valley, who were envious that he was at University, had bewitched him. In May Milton went to Dingley-dale by car to visit a colleague. As he returned, he experienced a mysterious blackout, 'The next thing I remember is walking bare footed on the road. As I looked around I saw that my car was in flames.' Milton arrived at home late that evening. The next morning Sarafina told Milton's mother that she had heard of the accident, and asked if Milton was alive. 'Where the hell did they get the information from?', Milton asked me. He believes that Sarafina bewitched him because he did not marry her daughter, Rebecca.

(iii) During the course of December 1992 Stanley Mokatswa, a young policeman, experienced two successive accidents while he pursued suspects in police vehicles. Consequently the station commander opened a docket against Stanley for reckless driving. An Apostolic prophet told Stanley that an envious woman had bewitched him so that he could get impatient behind the steering wheel. The prophet did not name the witch, but said that she lives three homes away. (Sarafina lives three homes away from him.) Stanley is convinced that Sarafina vented her anger against him because he regularly bought groceries and furniture for his mother while her own sons did not.

In this case the manner in which tensions are related to witchcraft is by no means obvious. Sarafina was definitely despised by her daughters-in-law and by other fruit vendors. Yet it was Sarafina's neighbours who were her prime accusers. Their strained relations with her followed, rather than preceded, suspicions of witchcraft. (The quarrel between Mrs Sekgobela and Sarafina only erupted after Mrs Sekgobela told Thabo's wife that Sarafina was a witch.) Mrs Ndlovu, Milton Machate and Stanley Mokatswa did not compete with Sarafina for scarce resources. They avoided her at all costs because of their perceptions of strange events in her household. For a variety of reasons they were more fortunate than Sarafina, and regarded her envy as a sufficient motive for witchcraft. The revelations of their dreams, and of *dingaka* and prophets reinforced their beliefs that she was a witch. What is most telling about this case is that Sarafina was blamed for witchcraft on at least 15 different occasions. These attributions were interrelated. Neighbours regularly spoke to each other about Sarafina, and she had become a convenient scapegoat for their misfortunes. This points to the tenacity of the 'labelling' effect, a term for what might otherwise be described as giving a dog a bad name and hanging it. When a witch lives next-door it is very likely that sickness and motor vehicle accidents will be blamed on witchcraft.[9] This effect is captured by the Northern Sotho proverb '*Phiri ya feta nku ya timela. Re re ke phiri* [If a hyena walks past and a sheep goes missing. We blame the hyena].'

*Case 6.3: Sam Makola: Genealogy and Mysterious Deaths*

In 1952 Sam Makola, a 13-year-old boy, became ill after being circumcised at an initiation lodge. Sam's wound healed very slowly. He was feverish, suffered from diarrhoea and was confused. One evening Sam cried bitterly, saying that his mother, Edna, was calling him to go home. The initiation master was surprised since women are strictly forbidden to visit initiation lodges and nobody had seen his mother in the vicinity. When Sam's condition deteriorated, a *ngaka* was summoned to determine the cause of his illness. The *ngaka* examined Sam, and the following afternoon the *ngaka* addressed the parents of all initiates at a clearing outside the lodge. In an angry tone he exclaimed that Sam's mother was responsible for his condition. At night, he alleged, Edna had sneaked into the lodge to fetch her son and forced him to milk cows at home.

The *ngaka* then gave Sam herbs to drink. Informants recalled that the herbs made Sam excrete and that a worm-like creature protruded from his anus.

Most onlookers were convinced of Edna Mokola's guilt. She had already been suspected of witchcraft, two years previously, following the death of her sister-in-law. Some adults believed that Edna came to the lodge in an invisible form, and took Sam home, leaving only his image behind. Others thought that Sam himself flew home. Upon his return, they said, he was trapped by an anti-witchcraft serum that the initiation master had planted in the lodge. An assistant of the initiation master told me the worm-like creature was really a witch familiar. 'It looked like a tapeworm (*dibokwana*), but it was something strange. It had no head.' After the local headman heard of the incident he summoned a *pitšo* (gathering). Here he furiously reprimanded everyone that an initiation lodge is not a place where witches should play.

Sam Mokola recovered from his illness. As a young man he left to work in Johannesburg. Only much later did he return to Green Valley and start working at the Air Force base in Hoedspruit. By 1990 Sam had been twice divorced, and lived with a third woman in a home which he, himself, built. Though elders remembered the incident in Sam's childhood, it was only in 1991, when Sam was 52 years old, that he was publicly accused of witchcraft.

The accusation was sparked by many incomprehensible deaths in the Mokola family. In 1978 Sam's father passed away after a long bout of illness. In the early 1980s his sisters Doreen and Ester died, while Doreen had previously lost two of her children shortly after their births. One morning in 1985 Sam's mother bid him farewell as he set off for work. She died at 10 am the very same day.

Three years later Sam's youngest sister, Rachel, who had long suffered from illness, separated from her husband and moved into Sam's home with her three children. From here she underwent training as a *ngaka*. Once Rachel had completed her apprenticeship, Sam slaughtered an ox to welcome her home. For a while it seemed as if Rachel's health had improved. But on 15 June 1991 she again complained of stomach cramps and fell down dead as she made her way toward the outdoors pit-latrine. Sam immediately informed his neighbours when he discovered Rachel's corpse. Because no rigor mortis had set in they suspected that a witch might have captured Rachel's body, leaving only an image behind. Throughout the night a *ngaka* attempted to retrieve Rachel from the witch. She beat drums, burnt animal fats and herbs, and ran through the veld blowing a whistle. Yet it soon became clear that Rachel could not be saved.

The next morning Sam's younger brother, Moses, told friends that Sam had bewitched Rachel and promised to take revenge. (Moses had long been angry because Sam had not invited him to Rachel's reception party.) On 19 June Moses walked to work. As he reached the outskirts of Green Valley he collapsed. Two teachers came to his assistance and rushed him to hospital, but he was certified dead upon arrival.

Rachel and Moses Mokola were buried on Saturday 26 June. The atmosphere at their funeral was extremely tense. The master of ceremonies rushed through the proceedings and a Zionist priest gave a very short sermon. His message was simply that God promised eternal life to the righteous, but would cast out all evil doers. Sam was notably anxious and was surrounded by men whom he had asked to protect him. During the funeral Rachel's oldest son, Calvin, conversed with fellow members of the ANC Youth League. Late that afternoon Calvin knifed Sam. Sam spent the night in hospital, where he was treated for neck wounds. Upon his release, he found that his home had been burnt to the ground. Informants had anticipated the attack. They were convinced that Sam practised witchcraft, kept a *mamlambo* and had killed his relatives to feed it human flesh. Sam subsequently relocated to Hoedspruit.

It is doubtful that prior social tensions account for the accusation of witchcraft against Sam Makola. It is certainly true that Sam quarrelled with his brother before the death of their sister and even thereafter. Yet, contrary evidence can also be found. One of Sam's neighbours, who was convinced that both Sam and his mother, Edna, were witches, dispelled any notion that they were visibly troublesome. He recalled that Edna had once invited him to eat at her home whenever he was hungry. About Sam he remarked, 'To his family members he was always very, very, friendly. He pretended to be very, very, good.' It may seem that there were political tensions between Sam (an employee of the South African Air Force) and Calvin (a member of the ANC Youth League). But this was not so. At the time Sam, like many other Air Force employees, supported the ANC-affiliated trade union, NEHAWU. Moreover, political tensions were never mentioned in any of the interviews that we conducted. In the case of Sam Makola circumstantial evidence was clearly most decisive in producing an accusation of witchcraft. Primary among these is the correlation between Sam's return to Green Valley and the deaths of his family members, and also Moses' mysterious death immediately after he had threatened to kill Sam. Sam's genealogy and his mother's dubious reputation for practising witchcraft also gave the accusation against him an aura of factuality.

## Case 6.4: Albert Nziane: Dreams and Self-Confession

Albert Nziane firmly believed that he kept a *mamlambo*. He readily confessed this to kin, neighbours, the Civic Association, my research assistants and to me. Albert's belief stemmed from complex personal experiences. Though 35 years old, he had never held a stable job. Instead, he repaired radios and worked as a builder on a part-time basis. Albert lived alone in a two-roomed house, was single, and had never engaged in heterosexual relations. Many people were greatly concerned about Albert's predicament. His next-door neighbour told me, 'It is very bad to live like him. He does not even have a girlfriend. Women sometimes visit him, but they only talk. Then they leave.' Some thought Albert was somewhat mentally retarded. Others insisted that he was of average intelligence. The latter was certainly my impression.

Albert remarked that his misfortunes started from childhood. After his mother's death in 1969 *nzonzo* spirits started to torment him. He claimed that the spirits tried to drown him: while swimming in a river with other boys, he got stuck in the river sand and only emerged after a prolonged struggle. Since then, Albert has feared water. 'Today I cannot even look at water. To me water seems like a shiny mirror.' Albert claimed that the spirits would only allow him to marry once he has been initiated as a *ngaka*. But this was too expensive. 'I can propose to any woman, but she'll reject me.' From our discussions it emerged that, as a youngster, the white school principal for whom Albert worked as a gardener had sexually abused him. The school principal regularly forced Albert to accompany him to a nearby dam, to undress and to masturbate him. Albert also blamed the principal for not being married. 'He taught me to produce pleasure by myself. This had a bad influence on me. Today I feel no need to have sex with women.'[10]

In 1992 Albert repaired the radio of a Malawian *ngaka*. When the *ngaka* came to fetch the radio, he asked whether Albert wanted to marry. Albert replied in the affirmative. The *ngaka* then gave Albert a matchbox containing roots, which he said was a love potion (*moratišo*). Albert claimed he could not understand the *ngaka*'s instructions properly because he spoke a Malawian language. 'I just pretended to listen and took the roots under duress.' At home Albert hid the roots inside an old gramophone. Soon he realised that they affected him in mysterious ways. 'My relations with people immediately became bad. Those who passed my home insulted me for no reason. I also became aggressive toward them. I could not understand what was happening.' Within a month Albert began to experience nightmares. He once dreamt that a blue snake emerged from a hole in a log and slithered towards his aunt. Albert screamed to warn her, but she could not hear him. The snake then came directly toward him. Albert awoke at 3 am, his body drenched in sweat. The next evening he dreamt that a white woman was seated on his bed and that he simultaneously experienced convulsions. His head knocked against the woman, but she did not say a word. Albert awoke and went to sleep in the kitchen.

The next morning he consulted a local *ngaka* about his nightmares. After she inspected the roots, she told Albert to break and discard them, because they were really snakes. Albert complied, but remained sceptical. He observed that the broken roots remained green. Moreover, as he threw away the roots he imagined hearing a woman's voice. In a mocking tone, she said, 'This man is throwing his wife [away].' Albert looked around, but saw nobody. For the next two nights Albert slept peacefully. However, on the third night he was again beset by fear, noticed a strange green light floating in his room and became feverish. He rushed to the *ngaka*'s home to ask her about the light. She gave him *sehlare* to burn so that he could sleep peacefully, yet the light reappeared beneath his table and bed. Some evenings Albert was so scared that he slept at the *ngaka*'s home. Even here, he saw the mysterious light that, he said, caused him to dream of a snake. In addition, his whole body started itching for some unknown reason.

Eventually, Albert paid his father's brother (*ramogolo*) – who is also a *ngaka* – R100 to fortify his home against the snake and to cure his aches. The *ngaka*'s brothers were furious when he informed them that Albert possessed a *mamlambo*. They feared Albert might have to sacrifice one of them to the snake. When they confronted Albert, he took them to the place where he originally discarded the roots. Because they found nothing there, they became restless and asked Albert to accompany them to the Malawian *ngaka*. But they found only the *ngaka*'s wife at home. Albert's uncles then reported the matter to the Civic Association. A leader of the Association told me that they tried their 'level best' to help Albert. They, too, went to the Malawian *ngaka*'s home, but found that he had moved to live with his second wife in Thulamahashe.

In December 1993 Albert believed that the snake still pestered him. 'There is no way of getting rid of it. Many nights, I dream that I'm sleeping with other men's wives.' He was, none the less, grateful that his *ramogolo* had neutralised the snake's power. 'That is why I have not seen the real snake. It only troubles me in my dreams.' Albert criticised the Civic Association for failing to evict the Malawian. He complained that he still suffered from fever, felt 'things' moving inside his body and youngsters mocked him about his 'madam' throughout the village. Yet by now, Albert said, he had grown used to suffering.

The case of Albert Nziane cannot be explained in terms of prior tensions between the accusers and the accused. In fact, Albert's confession that he kept a *mamlambo* amounted to a self-accusation. The cultural fantasies of the *mamlambo* and witchcraft provided him with a language through which he could articulate his mysterious dreams of snakes and white women, and his perceptions of strange lights. He could not comprehend nor express these experiences in any other way.

Albert's interpretations of his experiences occurred against the backdrop of personal distress, loneliness, paranoia, insomnia and sexual anxieties.[11] But what makes psychological sense often makes sociological nonsense. Although those who confess to witchcraft often seek to redefine that nature of witch-beliefs, and thereby lessen their crime, this seldom has the desired effect. For instance, among the Azande, accusers did not share the view of confessors that witchcraft was unconscious. They perceived it as a conscious activity (Evans-Pritchard, 1937:58). Through confession Albert laid himself open to the possibility of retribution. Albert's uncles did not totally endorse his perception of himself as the victim of a *ngaka*. For them, both Albert and the *ngaka* were equally at fault.

*Case 6.5: Harry Chiloane: Rumours of Resurrection*

On 19 October 1992 Harry Chiloane, a young man from Buffelshoek, died in a motor car accident in Benoni. Nobody who attended Harry's funeral in Buffelshoek had noticed anything suspicious. However, in 1993 a schoolboy told me that Harry was still alive and had visited his mother. He said Harry lived at the home of a *ngaka*, but would return permanently to his mother on Saturday 28 February. At the time the story seemed so bizarre to me that I saw no need to make further enquiries. Yet I soon became aware that the story was extremely widespread. At two schools and at the market I heard people saying that Harry would miraculously return from the dead.

On 23 February my field assistants and I drove to Buffelshoek to investigate. Here we met Elphas Shai – a friend of one of my assistants. Elphas had heard the story from Harry's *malome* (mother's brother). A *ngaka* apparently promised Harry's mother, Rohniah, that he would ensure Harry's safe return if Rohniah paid her R3,000. Elphas believed that the *ngaka* had deceived Rohniah to deprive her of her hard-earned cash, and predicted that many people would be disappointed.

One of my field assistants asked me to drive to the home of his aunt, Sina Mashego, Rohniah's close friend and neighbour, and we asked her to introduce us to Rohniah. Sina advised us against this. She said Rohniah was concerned about the rumours that were flying about and did not want to speak about Harry to outsiders. Sina was, none the less, willing to tell us the entire story. She visits Rohniah daily and was well informed of all the details.

Sina told us that Rohniah was badly shaken by Harry's death, which was more mysterious than it appeared to outsiders. At the time a furniture company employed Harry as a truck driver. In Benoni a traffic officer instructed Harry to stop and to pull off the road. The officer inspected the truck and found the rear indicator light to be defective. Harry got out and walked to the rear of the truck, and gave the information needed by the traffic officer to write out a ticket. While they were talking, the driver of an oncoming truck lost control of his vehicle and collided with the stationary truck, killing Harry. Rohniah could not comprehend many aspects of the story as it was relayed by the traffic officer in his report to the furniture company. What she found puzzling was why the driver of the oncoming vehicle lost control, and why Harry could not get out of the truck's way, as the officer had done. She also failed to understand why Harry's body did not burn when both of the trucks exploded into flames. Rohniah suspected that witches had turned Harry into a zombie.

Rohniah told Sina of many uncanny experiences at home since Harry's funeral, which had led her to believe that her son had visited her. At first she could feel his *seriti* (shadow or aura) at home, but ignored it. One evening she heard Harry's voice saying, 'Mother! Please feed me!' Rohniah was shocked and sat in the kitchen until late. At 9pm the kitchen lights suddenly went off. She was convinced that it was Harry who had switched off the lights. Since then Rohniah regularly heard Harry's voice saying *'Thobela'* (greetings) at 4 pm – the time he usually came home from work while he was still alive. Each evening Rohniah prepared porridge and tea for her son and left these on the kitchen table. Each morning the food would be eaten. Rohniah became convinced that Harry was not really dead. She did not believe these experiences were of a ghost because ghosts can neither speak nor eat. I put it to Sina that I had learnt that there are three components to a person – *mmele* ('body'), *seriti* ('shadow') and *moya* ('breath') – and asked which of these had returned. She was not sure, but was convinced that it was more than the mere *seriti*. 'It greets, eats porridge, washes its hands and pours out the water.' Yet, Sina said nobody had actually seen Harry's figure.

Rohniah eventually consulted a *ngaka*. The *ngaka* claimed witches had captured Harry and were trying to turn him into a zombie. At his funeral, she said, people had not buried Harry, but the stem of a banana tree. The *ngaka* also said that she had spoken to Harry, who told her of many deceased people who are kept by witches to plough their plots at night. Some lived by sucking the blood of living people. Others, like Harry, had not been completely transformed into zombies and still collected food from home. On a second occasion the *ngaka* told Rohniah that another diviner had found Harry and was busy healing him at her home. She promised Rohniah that Harry would be cured and returned to her on Saturday 28 February if she paid an amount of R3,000. Rohniah was convinced the *ngaka* spoke the truth. She even took off her mourning clothes and had began preparing a reception party for Harry.

It is unclear whether Rohniah actually accused anyone of witchcraft. However, on Tuesday 24 February Lethabo Mohale heard from friends that a *ngaka* had said that her mother had bewitched Harry. Lethabo became furious. She stood at the gate shouting insults at Rohniah – her neighbour and affine. Lethabo even threatened to take Rohniah to a witch-diviner. Rohniah then reported Lethabo to the chief's court for cursing at a bereaved family. The chief heard the case, but did not pass a judgement.

On Saturday 28 February about 300 people waited in vain for Harry's return at the Chiloane home. Rohniah remained indoors and cried bitterly throughout the day. I first met Rohniah on 17 July 1993. She now blamed the entire episode on rumours, saying that there were many who still believed Harry to be alive. On one occasion some people came from Bushbuckridge and opened the door to look for Harry. Some claimed to have seen him at a birthday party. Others told her they saw him repairing her roof. 'People laugh at me, but I feel pain', she said.

Rohniah's experiences again underline the complexity of witchcraft beliefs and accusations. More intensive investigations may well yield greater insights into the relationship between Rohniah and Lethabo, her neighbour, but such an exercise may be futile. Even if their relationship is shown to have been one of sustained conflict, such conflict would not account for her previous expectation that Harry would return from the world of the dead. The precise evidence for her belief that witches had captured Harry is hard to pin down. The mysterious circumstances of his death, the manner in which she imagined hearing his voice, the disappearance of the food she left for him and also divinatory revelations seem to have been crucial. The possibility that Rohniah had experienced auditory hallucinations cannot be excluded. As a great deal of comparative literature has shown, maternal reactions to child death often include hallucinated or dreamed visitations from the deceased (Raphael, 1983). The case also highlights the role of rumours in the construction of witchcraft. Rumour transformed Rohniah's belief that she heard a voice into firm proof for witchcraft. Throughout the wider area people heard that she had actually seen

her Harry. (This is similar to the incident in Case 6.2, where rumours transformed the 'small people', seen by drivers of the Acornhoek bakery, into
zombies.) Like paradigm and label, the distorting effects of rumours bestows
witchcraft with an aura of factuality.[12]


CONCLUSIONS

This chapter has cautioned against the sociological determinism evident in the
*a priori* assumption that social conflict alone is sufficient to determine, or
enable us to predict, whom the accuser(s) and those accused of witchcraft would
be. Moreover, we have seen that social tensions alone seldom aroused the initial
suspicions of witchcraft.

The anthropological perception of witchcraft as an idiom of social relations
may well obscure rather than illuminate the role of interpersonal conflict in the
actual witchcraft accusations that we recorded. Villagers clearly distinguished
between social tensions in general and the types of tensions that they associated
with witchcraft. In Green Valley individuals were regularly accused of being
rapists, adulterers, thieves, sell-outs, arrogant or unbearable persons. Witchcraft
does not refer to these visible actions, but denotes mystical deeds, motivated by
envy, malice and resentment. These emotions were part of complex webs of
evidence that believers and accusers used to construct, and to reconstruct, the
reality of witchcraft in specific situations. They were no more important than
the occurrence of unexpected and painful events, strange verbal statements,
confessions, social and genealogical ties to other known witches, deviance,
nakedness, the anomalous appearance of wild animals near homes, dreams,
divinatory revelations and the uncritical acceptance of rumours.

In the cases examined certain patterns occur with great regularity. One
pattern is the prominent manner in which the paradigms, labels and rumours
structure the interpretation of perceptions. Another is the emphasis on
divinatory revelations and dreams in narratives of witchcraft. Divination and
dreams were the most appropriate source of information in the verification of
transcendent realities. They are related to events in the transcendent realm in the
same way as direct observations are related to events in the empirical realm.

Peek (1991) provides important clues to why this should be so. He argues
that divinatory consultations are motivated by an intense desire to know the
real reasons for the occurrence of events. Diviners are resorted to in times of
crisis when there is 'no sufficient body of knowledge available to enable people
to cope in practical terms with the hazards of life' (ibid.:194). In these
situations, Peek suggests, diviners generate a temporary shift to a contrary, non-
rational, non-normal (perhaps paranormal is a better word) mode of cognition.[13]
This enables people to acquire information which is not normally accessible.
Because the language of divination is cryptic and ambiguous all revelations
have to be translated and discussed. During the dialogue between the diviner
and client there is a transference and counter-transference of information.

Known facts are scrutinised in the light of a different perspective and old elements are reorganised into new arrangements (ibid.:202). In Green Valley, divinatory consultations were certainly the moments when people reviewed known observations in the light of the witchcraft paradigm.

Fisiy and Geschiere (1990) highlight the crucial role of divination in the construction of witchcraft. They point out that since Cameroon's independence state courts have convicted witches on the basis of testimony provided by 'witch-doctors'. In Green Valley similar alliances were not apparent between ritual specialists and the sate. It is precisely because diviners and Christian prophets stood independent from sectional interests that villagers appreciated them as a source of extra-social revelatory knowledge.[14]

Peek's insights can be applied just as fruitfully to dreams. From the cases presented it is clear that villagers did not dismiss dream experiences as irrelevant to their everyday lives. As in divinatory consultations, cognitive processes are shifted to a non-rational, paranormal mode during the state of dreaming. Dreams too are believed to provide people with a glimpse of transcendent realities.[15] Dreams contained cryptic images that were translated and discussed, leading people to evaluate known observations in the light of a new paradigm. In this manner dreams played a major role in the construction of witchcraft. It is no coincidence that Wilson (1951) described the witch as the 'standardised nightmare' of society. In Green Valley, images of small people, large apes, snakes and white women featured as prominently in dreams as they did in narratives of witchcraft.

But dreams were not the only sleep-related experiences that provide an experiential base for local theories of witchcraft. Albert Nziani, Rhoniah Chiloane and Andries Mashile insisted that their perceptions of white women, strange lights, voices and apes were not dreams. These occurred while they were fully conscious and aware of their surroundings. Such perceptions were most likely to have been visual and auditory hallucinations that arose from a common syndrome called 'sleep paralysis' in biomedical literature. Sleep paralysis occurs as a transition between sleep and wakefulness and is characterised by an inability to perform voluntary movements, vivid hypnagogic hallucinations, exhaustion, anxiety and sweating.[16] Like dreams, the experience of hallucinations initiate and sustain witchcraft beliefs.[17]

In the study of witchcraft it is imperative that we pay close attention to the details of people's narratives. It is essential to recognise the emic status of witchcraft as a reality, and to acknowledge the importance of circumstantial evidence and paranormal modes of cognition. These cannot merely be swept under the rug of 'social tensions'. As Evans-Pritchard (1937) argued many years ago: the social does not determine the ideational. He attributed central causality to ideational systems, and recognised the mutually conditioning impact of these dimensions of life. This insight remains pertinent to the contemporary situations.

# 7 WITCH-HUNTING AND POLITICAL LEGITIMACY: CHIEFS, COMRADES AND THE ELIMINATION OF EVIL, 1930–1989

Over the past two decades, press reports have highlighted the involvement of prominent political actors in several episodes of witch-hunting, particularly in the former Bantustan of Lebowa. In December 1983, chieftainess Ramaredi Chuene, sister of the late Dr Phatudi (Lebowa's former chief Minister), and 227 citizens of her chiefdom near Lebowakgomo were charged with stoning a Mrs Nkhuna to death. Previously, 18 *dingaka* had accused Mrs Nkhuna of sending lightning that struck a hut (*Rand Daily Mail*, 24 April 1984). During 1986, in the wake of what the press described as a 'civil war' between the Sekhukhuneland Youth Organisation and security forces, police uncovered 43 'necklaced' bodies in three Sekhukhuneland villages. The dead were allegedly victims of a campaign to eliminate collaborators and witches (*Sunday Times*, 20 April 1986). In June 1987 two members of the Lebowa Legislative Assembly were acquitted on charges of 'terrorism' after they had allegedly called for the elimination of tribal rule and witchcraft. These charges related to events around Bushbuckridge, where 36 suspected witches were killed (SAIRR, 1988:907).

The subject of this chapter and the following one is the politics of witch-hunting. As in Chapter 2, my approach is diachronic. Through the use of archival records, life histories, the selective memories of informants and oral traditions, I aim to reconstruct changes that have occurred in the politics of witch-hunting between 1930 and 1989. In the following chapter I shall examine the political history of witchcraft after the unbanning of the ANC in 1990. My analysis of witch-hunting departs from much of the anthropological theories that treat witch-hunting as a covert attempt to mystify subordinates or to intimidate political opponents. I insist that the political significance of witch-hunting arises directly from the conception of witchcraft as mystical power and from the attempts of ordinary villagers to deal with undeserved misfortune. However, given this long-established, deeply held set of beliefs, political actors from neo-traditional chiefs to radical Comrades have found it politically convenient to assist in the identification and punishment of witches.

## WITCHCRAFT AND POLITICS IN ANTHROPOLOGICAL THEORY

There is a considerable literature, by anthropologists and historians, on the role of witch-hunting campaigns in a variety of political struggles. For some, anti-witchcraft cults are a trick played by the ruling class to mystify the poor. For example, Harris (1974) argued that the European witch-craze of the sixteenth and seventeenth centuries was an attempt by the nobility and clergy to persuade the poor that their troubles were caused by imaginary witches, rather than by real powerful and wealthy people. 'The principal result of the witch-hunt system', he wrote, 'was that the poor came to believe they were victimised by devils instead of princes and popes' (ibid.:247). In consequence, the poor did not confront 'the ecclesiastical and secular establishment with demands for the redistribution of wealth and levelling of rank' (ibid.:239).

Other analysts have viewed witch-hunting as an attempt to intimidate or disable political opponents. Mitchell (1956) and Marwick (1965) noted that accusations of witchcraft accompanied competition for headmanship. Steadman (1985) proposed that the aim of Hewa witch-hunters in Papua New Guinea is to generate fear. The public punishment of witches, he argued, communicates the accusers' willingness to use violence to dispose of any competitors who threaten their interests. Steadman observed that Hewa witch-hunters killed members of nearby flooring and roofing groups against whom they bore grievances. The punishment of witches may thus represent a test of power between corporate groups, establishing or sustaining a balance of fear. However, influential men were not killed as witches, but rather weak, vulnerable individuals residing with them. (Killing strong men, or those likely to be defended by them, was extremely dangerous.) Steadman also argued that expressing the competition in the idiom of witchcraft had certain advantages. The accusations are not verifiable and are therefore appropriate 'where the reality of the crime is irrelevant' (ibid.:112). Moreover, the accusation could later be dropped if there was a possibility of future co-operation.

More recently witchcraft beliefs have been seen as a form of protest and resistance for the weak. Rowlands and Warnier (1988) and Geschiere (1997) view witchcraft as lying at the heart of political processes in Cameroon. In a one-party system, where village communities lack the capacity to express political dissent, witchcraft constitutes a 'popular mode of political action' and is a reaction against the offensive behaviour of elites. In Cameroon, power, wealth and success are viewed ambiguously, as reflecting the possession of occult powers. Should villagers experience misfortune, they may accuse powerful and wealthy persons of witchcraft, or may actually threaten to use witchcraft against them. This set of beliefs thus place members of the urban political elite with connections with a village of origin under considerable pressure to act benevolently and to redistribute resources. They are 'expected to put their positions in the state apparatus or party to good use, to provide their villages with roads, a school, a dispensary, etc. and their kin with salaried jobs' (Rowlands and Warnier, 1988:130).

The relationship between witchcraft and political processes are, however, often very complex and defy attempts to contain them in single-strand theories. So, for example, Harris' (1974) and Steadman's (1985) formulations exhibit the familiar defects of objectivist and instrumental approaches. Neither author can satisfactorily account for the fact that witchcraft accusations seemed to be so persuasive. Harris fails to show how the poor came to accept a belief that apparently went so strongly against their interests. Steadman (1985) questions explanations of witch-killing which 'assume that the killers believe in witches, even although the accuracy of such assumptions cannot be verified' (ibid.:112), yet he argues that among the Hewa the 'idiom of witchcraft' can be used to mobilise wide support for the killing of 'innocent' individuals, even those who may be distant relatives of some killers and their supporters (ibid.:116).[1] Such theories de-emphasise the existential dimensions of witchcraft (Cohen, 1979).

An adequate account of witch-hunting in Green Valley should ideally take cognisance of the status of witchcraft as a personalised conception of malevolent power, which enables people to explain, diagnose and compensate for unmerited misfortune. Krige (1947:8) provides some useful clues to the political potential of witch beliefs when he writes:

since evil operates through the medium of human beings it can also be brought under human control. The parts assigned to the characters, the witch and the sorcerer, presupposes a just world, ordered and coherent, in which evil is not merely outlawed, but can be overcome by man-made techniques. In the results men feel secure and the moral order is upheld.

If witch beliefs are taken seriously, in their own terms, it is possible to see witch-hunting as a creative attempt to eliminate evil. This represents an opportunity for political actors. By co-operating in the management of misfortune, political actors can potentially tap a potent source of political legitimacy. Although they cannot undo the crime of witchcraft they can protect the innocent from future harm by neutralising the witch. Evans-Pritchard (1937) writing of the Azande, and Wilson (1967), writing on the Nyakyusa, pursued this line of argument. Evans-Pritchard showed how the Avongara's king and princes' authority was backed by their use of prestigious poison oracles, to which commoners appealed for the final verdict in cases of witchcraft. Wilson describes Nyakyusa chiefs as 'leaders in the war by night against witchcraft' (ibid.:96). As custodians of morality the chiefs legitimately used their 'python power' to detect evil, to defend villagers from witchcraft and to punish wrongdoers. (There is little indication that they accused their political rivals of witchcraft.)

These possibilities are most fully realised at times of economic or political crisis, when the whole world seems to be threatened (Richards, 1935). Willis (1970), in his overview of central African witch-cleansing cults, suggests that these cults promise to 'inaugurate the millennium, the age of bliss... in which pain, disease, untimely death, violence and strife, war and hunger will be unknown' (ibid.:133).

CHIEFLY INTERVENTIONS IN WITCHCRAFT, 1930–1955

Fields (1982:527) argues that in pre-colonial Africa witchcraft was a crime. But for colonial rulers witchcraft was a superstition and the African judges and executioners of witches became murderers. Late in the nineteenth century and onwards, the British colonial administrations in South Africa passed a series of laws that prohibited witchcraft accusations as well as threats and attempts to practice witchcraft.[2] These laws expressed the ideals of the civilising mission that demanded no compromise with witchcraft. Indeed, the colonial authorities perceived any belief or practice pertaining to witchcraft as 'primitive', baseless, repugnant and even diabolical. These beliefs had to be repressed by law and eliminated through the spread of Western civilisation.

Fields (1982) acknowledges that in practice the manner in which colonial states dealt with witchcraft often contradicted the ideals of the civilising mission. Colonial regimes could not afford large scale policing to rule solely by force. Nor was their sufficient commonality between the rulers and the ruled that would have allowed the exercise of legitimate authority. As such, order could only be sustained through the maintenance of African authorities, redeployment of African institutions and the preservation of indigenous culture (ibid.:569).[3]

Whilst the South African government might well have had sufficient coercive capacities to enforce the anti-witchcraft legislation, its segregationist policies ostensibly ensured African self-government. As in the case of British indirect rule, the South African government reserved land for exclusive African occupation, allowed chiefs to rule on a daily basis and to enforce 'native law and custom'.

Abel Erasmus, Native Affairs Commissioner of the *Zuid-Afrikaanche Republiek*, recognised that – as the son of Maripe Mashile who led the Pulana to defeat Swazi invaders in the battle of Moholoholo – Setlhare had built up a very large following. He thus appointed Setlhare as chief in terms of Law 4 of 1885 (probably during the Anglo-Boer War). In 1914 Setlhare and a few of his loyal supporters left for Europe to participate in the First World War. King George IV presented him with a rifle in recognition for his services.[4] Setlhare was one of only four Pulana chiefs granted civil jurisdiction by government in terms of Act 38 of 1927. As such, the state recognised decisions reached in his *kgoro* as binding on the parties involved unless they appealed to the Native Commissioner.[5] After his death in 1945, Mabelane succeeded his father Setlhare.

Elderly informants portrayed the times of Setlhare and Mabelane as a golden era of stability, law and custom. However, according to members of the royal family, the early period of Setlhare's reign was marked by intense conflict over the chiefship. They said that since Maripe's father, Morage, was merely the fourth son of the Pulana chief Seganyane, his descendants had a weak genealogical claim to chiefship (see Figure 7.1 overleaf). It was only because Seganyane's eldest sons – Chichi, Mashilane and Cheou – sought refuge in

Sekhukhuneland, that Maripe became the leader of the Pulana in their war
against the Swazi, proclaiming himself as chief after his decisive victory. Rivals
also disputed the assumption that Setlhare was Maripe's son. According to
some, Setlhare was born from an illicit sexual relationship between Maripe's
youngest wife and his oldest son. When Maripe learnt of this he chased his son
from his realm and made the young Setlhare his heir.[6] Although the 'real facts'
will possibly never be known, it is clear that Setlhare faced a severe crisis in
legitimacy when he became chief.

Setlhare, however, successfully entrenched his claim. By participating in the
First World War, Setlhare won support from the new South African
government. Upon his return from Europe, he changed his surname from
Mashile to Chiloane. (This name derives from the word *chilo* – a grinding stone
– and means 'conqueror'.) He then set about establishing a new genealogy for
the chieftaincy. Setlhare also actively sought to ensure the loyalty of his subjects
throughout his reign.

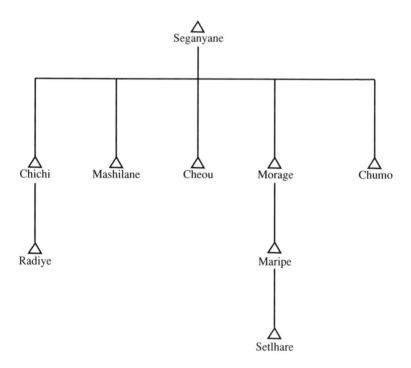

Figure 7.1 The Genealogy of Setlhare's Predecessors

However, in 1919 Chichi's oldest son, Radiye, did attempt to depose
Setlhare. Radiye arrived from Sekhukhuneland with many followers and set up
camp at the Motlasedi river. When Setlhare failed to reach an agreement with

Radiye, he asked the Shangaan chief, Mpisane, for assistance. Armed with spears and knobkerries, Mpisane's warriors attacked Radiye and his men, captured their cattle and destroyed their shelters. Radiye escaped into the Moholoholo mountains. He later negotiated with the Native Commissioner in Sabie, but could not persuade the Commissioner to install him as chief. Radiye's descendants eventually returned to Setlhare's chiefdom, where they lived as subordinate members of the royal family and devoted their energies to the Lutheran church.

After Chief Setlhare's death in 1945, the Native Affairs Commissioner recognised Setlhare's son, Mabelane, as 'the Pulana chief with the greatest following'. The Commissioner felt compelled to confirm his appointment, although he described him as a quarrelsome and uneducated man, who often drank too much.[7] Since Mabelane lacked Setlhare's personal charisma, his legitimacy depended upon the extent to which he could emulate the precedents that his father had established. Prior to 1955 the interventions of chiefs in the eradication of witchcraft were part and parcel of the strategies they used to mobilise support.

Setlhare and Jon Mabelane Chiloane mediated very effectively in disputes that arose from witchcraft accusations, and were occasionally the central actors in the organisation of witch-hunts. Under their reign, chiefly rule conformed to what Sansom (1974a:137–47) described as the Western pattern, characteristic of the South African inland plateau, in which administrative functions and resource regulation were centralised under chiefly authority. Chiefs heard disputes in their *kgoro* and directly controlled access to the means of production by allocating land to households. They also controlled agricultural activity. Nobody could plough until chiefs announced the beginning of the season, and villagers could begin to bring in the harvest only after the chiefs had performed the rite of the first fruits. The chiefs also enforced a number of taboos pertaining to the planting of crops, and forbade villagers from ploughing after lightning had struck or death had occurred.

Chiefs Setlhare and Mabelane created multiple alliances with the families of commoners through their strategic choice of wives and headmen. Most of Setlhare's twelve wives, and all of Mabelane's three wives, were commoners, drawn from influential families. The chiefs also tended to appoint the fathers of their wives as headmen, rather than members of the royal family. To ensure the loyalty of the youth, Setlhare established a Pulana initiation lodge and officiated as the initiation master. *Ngwa* Inama, Setlhare's principal wife, officiated at the initiation of girls.

Informants recalled that Chief Setlhare never attended the rituals of his subjects, but sent his right-hand man to represent him. He always sat behind the *kgoro*. His councillors would listen to the cases, convey the relevant information to him and would again relay his judgements. Some accounted for Setlhare's reluctance to appear in public in terms of his intense fear of witchcraft. He always employed a taster as a precaution against poisoning. The taster even accompanied him on his ventures during the First World War.

Sansom (1974b:260) argues that the power of Western chiefs was immanent in the system of allocating resources, and chiefly rituals did not invest chiefs with semi-divine characteristics (Kertzer, 1988:46–54). Rather that emphasising the role of the chief himself, rituals constructed and reconstructed the *mošate* as the political centre.[8] Rituals aimed, for example, at ridding the land of commando-worm (*sefenefene*), making rain and punishing witches, were organised from the *mošate*. They involved popular participation and confirmed the moral identity of the chiefdom.

Chiefs summoned herbalists to the *mošate* when commando-worm invaded Green Valley's fields. Herbalists cleansed the land by sprinkling medicines at the corners of all fields and burning grass from each field in a bonfire. Thereafter headmen assembled about 100 pre-pubertal children, to the *mošate*, and issued them with bottles containing ash and commando-worm. At daybreak, the children emptied the bottles into the Motlasedi river and shouted, 'Worms! Worms! Go back to Phalaborwa.' Informants did not doubt the rite's efficacy.

*Ngwa* Photo, a *ngaka* and relative of the famous rain-queen Modjadji (Krige and Krige, 1965), was the first rainmaker in the chiefdom. She reportedly arrived in Green Valley during a time of famine, and became chief Maripe's official rainmaker after she had successfully made rain. Her sons and grandsons subsequently inherited her position. Elderly informants recounted that Chief Setlhare and Chief Mabelane organised these rituals annually. In August, before the first spring rains were expected, headmen collected donations from all citizens of the chiefdom, and sent delegates to fetch rain *sehlare* from Queen Modjadji. Upon their return they handed the *sehlare* to the rainmaker, who mixed it in an earthen bowl with unknown substances. The rainmaker then made invocations to the ancestors of the local chiefs and of Queen Modjadji. The next day she gave children *sehlare* and led them to sleep overnight at the Motlasedi river. The children also placed leaves of the *mmilo* tree (medlar) on the borders of the chiefdom. Elderly informants claimed that it always rained within hours after the children had returned from the river.

These rituals conveyed the impression that life itself depended on the *mošate*. Yet even the most optimistic informants conceded that drought regularly occurred. In these situations witchcraft was invoked as a 'secondary elaboration' (Evans-Pritchard, 1937), excusing the *mošate* for the failure to make rain.[9] Supporters of the chiefs sometimes accused *dingaka*, who were envious of the official rainmakers, of having used *šibeka* to drive away the rain clouds. They allegedly did this in the hope that villagers would pay them to remove their *sehlare*.

*Ngwa* Photo blamed witches for the drought of 1939. On her advice, Chief Setlhare summoned several *dingaka* to the *mošate*. The *dingaka* sniffed out Polai Molobela, a middle-aged farm worker and herbalist, as the culprit. Polai, who lived in a shanty on the northern outskirts of Green Valley, had previously been expelled from the neighbouring Moletele chiefdom for using *šibeka*. An old man recounted that many villagers resented his presence in Setlhare's area:

We all knew Polai as a witch. Even the children. If he entered your home and you refused him beer your beer lost its colour and became tasteless. If you quarrelled with him and you walked away you'd find a baboon a few metres away. Even in broad daylight... He was full of tricks, but never killed anybody.

The accusation was popularly approved. At Chief Setlhare's *kgoro*, Polai was threatened with death unless he confessed and revealed his *sehlare*. Polai reportedly took the witch-hunters to an isolated place and showed them a broom hanging from a tree. Underneath the tree were pieces of clay pot with distinctive marks. Informants believed that as the broom swung it chased away the rain clouds. They recalled that all grass, shrubs and bush around the tree were dry. Polai was tied to a tree stump and a huge fire built around him. This, I was told, was 'to make him feel the heat he caused us to endure'. The *sehlare* found at Polai's home was also burnt in the fire. Setlhare released Polai only when he pleaded for mercy, but expelled him from the chiefdom.

In 1941, locusts invaded Green Valley's maize fields, very little rain fell and commando-worm destroyed the remaining crops. In response to this crisis, Setlhare organised a team of men to search the village for *sebeka*. The witch-hunters returned with Kagišo Madibe whom, they said, had placed a goatskin, smeared with human blood, near the river. Kagišo was one of Green Valley's wealthiest men. He had seven wives, cultivated large maize fields and practised as an initiation master and a *ngaka*. Although Kagišo's son was married to *Ngwa* Photo's daughter, tensions had developed between him and the rainmaker. Kagišo had fortified people's fields against commando-worm and birds and claimed that he too could make rain. Kagišo was punished in the same way as Polai, but was not expelled from Green Valley.

The year 1954 was the last time a Green Valley resident was accused of preventing rain. He was Thomas Segodi, also a *ngaka* and initiation master, who was apprehended by Chief Mapalane's headman. Prior to this another initiation master had accused Thomas of bewitching his initiate. Chief Mabelane found Thomas guilty of having stolen *dihlare* from *Ngwa* Photo's sons, sending lightning and preventing rain. Mapalane's guards punished Thomas harshly when he initially refused to confess. He sustained severe blisters from the fire they built around him, and was released only after he admitted guilt and promised never again to lay *sebeka*.

Polai Molobela, Kagišo Madibe and Thomas Segodi were not political opponents of the chiefs, nor were they associated with political rivals. Kagišo and Thomas were rivals of the chief's rainmaker, who had also identified them as witches, so they may well have been victims of the intrigues at the court. However, they also served to represent a threat to the subsistence base of all villagers. Polai and Kagišo were both immigrants from Phalaborwa, and to some extent the accusations mirror the perception of Phalaborwa as a hot, dry and impoverished area where beggars, thieves and witches lived.[10]

Setlhare and Mabelane also mediated when commoners accused each other of witchcraft. In direct contravention to government policy, the chiefs encouraged household heads to report suspected witches to the *kgoro*. (The Native Affairs Department required that chiefs implement the colonial anti-witchcraft laws, in terms of which it is a criminal offence to accuse someone of witchcraft.) Setlhare resented interference by government in his right to dispose of cases among his subjects. When appeals were made against his decisions, he consistently refused to supply the Native Commissioner with reasons for his judgements. On 26 August 1941 the Assistant Commissioner summoned Setlhare and his headmen to discuss the issue, but they did not attended the scheduled meeting.[11] Consequently the Governor General revoked Setlhare's civil jurisdiction. This measure did not affect the chief's prestige in the least. Setlhare continued to adjudicate on disputes submitted to him and was relieved not to be worried by the clerk of the court. The only difference was that dissatisfied litigants could not appeal against his decisions, but had to commence proceedings *de novo* in the magistrate's court.[12] Only late in Mabelane's reign was civil jurisdiction restored to him.[13] Throughout this period the chiefs fully exploited their judicial autonomy and dealt with witchcraft accusations in the manner they deemed fit.

When they heard a witchcraft case, the chiefs required both the accuser and the accused to deposit a stake of up to five cattle for safekeeping at the *mošate*. The chief and each party then elected representatives to accompany the accused to a witch-diviner in Phunda Malia, near Venda. (They walked the entire distance, 200 kilometres each way.) One *ngaka* explained that only the witch-diviners of Phundu Malia, who are still held in awe throughout the lowveld, were deemed competent enough to 'sniff out' witches.[14] Because the witch-diviners feared that relatives of the accused could retaliate, they were only prepared to point out witches with the chief's consent. If the diviner pronounced the accused to be a witch, he would cut holes into the accused's clothes and shave his hair in a rough manner. The accuser would then collect the cattle from the *mošate*. If the accused was found not guilty, the accused blew a goat's horn upon entering the village to proclaim his innocence, and would be awarded the cattle in compensation for having been wrongfully accused.

In as many as eight of the 17 witchcraft accusations I recorded that were made prior to 1956, the accused sought the assistance of chiefs. Four of the accused were taken to Phundu Malia. Two were proclaimed not guilty and two were identified as witches. One informant recalled that after a neighbour accused his *malome* (mother's brother) of witchcraft, Chief Setlhare gave the parties permission to consult a witch-diviner. A week later, his *malome* returned from Phundu Malia and blew a goat's horn to show that he had been absolved. Others who were found guilty of witchcraft in Phundu Malia had to forfeit between three and five cows (see Case 1.1). Those who bewitched individuals were not punished as violently as the rainstoppers who threatened the entire community. Their humiliation and the compensation that they paid in cattle was generally deemed to be sufficient.[15] One elder remarked, 'In the past witches were not killed. Their punishment was to be exposed.'

As the power of witchcraft was viewed more ambivalently than in the contemporary period, no action was taken against the suspect if the victim of witchcraft had engaged in anti-social behaviour. It might be felt that the victim had earned the retaliation. In 1951, ten years after Chief Setlhare punished Kagišo Madibe for rain stopping, Kagišo's grandson drowned. The boy's father, Exom Madibe, suspected that Kagišo had sent familiars to kill his child. Exom was furious and asked his father-in-law to bewitch Kagišo. His father-in-law commanded Exom to fetch Kagišo's urine and bewitched it. Shortly afterwards, Kagišo became unable to urinate and died. In this case vengeance magic was seen as a just form of punishment for witchcraft.

The legitimacy achieved by Setlhare and Mabelane was as much the product of ritual action as it was of their control over land. Their actions against witches were an important ritual strategy to retain authority. It dramatised their capacity to punish the perpetrators of misfortune, and to assist those who sought compensation for the crimes that had been committed against them by witches. Despite this, witches won the final battle. Although Setlhare was said to have been more than a hundred years old when he died, members of the royal family suspected that he was bewitched. Before his death he displayed the classical symptoms of *sefolane*. (Setlhare's leg was paralysed.) Many also suspect that witches caused Mabelane's death, at the age of 55.

## BANTU AUTHORITIES, RELOCATION AND WITCHCRAFT, 1956–1986

In the 30 tumultuous years that followed Mabelane's death, the autonomy and power of chiefship was greatly eroded. Chiefs no longer had the capacity to oppose witchcraft and began to dissociate themselves from witch-hunting. The form of witchcraft accusation, the control of witches and the very conception of a witch now changed radically.

The power of chiefs was undermined by the impact of wider structural processes and by local accidents of chiefly succession. Following the implementation of the Bantu Authorities Act of 1951, the Setlhare chiefdom was transformed in 1959 into a Tribal Authority, and chiefship became bureaucratised. Setlhare's chiefs were no longer accountable solely to their subjects, but also to a Bantu Affairs Commissioner, magistrate and to a Regional Authority in Bushbuckridge.[16] In terms of the Bantu Authorities Act, white agricultural officers of the South African Bantu Trust assumed a more prominent role than chiefs in allocating land, conserving soil and in regulating agricultural activities. Chiefs were obliged merely to assist the agricultural officers with planning their area for betterment and with its division into residential, arable and grazing land.

The chiefs of this period also lacked the charisma of their predecessors. Elders described Elson Seganyane II, who was installed as chief in 1956, as a chief who scorned Setlhare's traditions, never summoned rainmakers to the *mošate*, *sjambokked* people at his *kgoro* and was an alcoholic. Seganyane's guard told

me, 'He always roamed around as if he was insane. The Commissioner told me
to look after him like a herdboy. Once I even had to handcuff him.'

When Seganyane II passed away in 1959, his heir, Nkotobona, was a toddler
and the Bantu Affairs Commissioner appointed Phineas Masenyane Chiloane
– the fourth son of Setlhare's first house – to deputise as a regent. Masenyane's
appointment suited the aims of the South African government. In a letter to his
political superiors, the Commissioner commended Masenyane for being pro-
government and supportive of the Bantu Authorities. He also describes
Masenyane as quiet and unassuming man of good character, who should do
well with good councillors. Yet, in the same letter, the Commissioner expressed
dismay that the Setlhare chiefdom had lost prestige and standing.[17] With
Masenyane's collaboration, the Commissioner set up the Setlhare Tribal
Authority, implemented a 'betterment' plan and even took control of the
chiefdom's finances of £2,000.[18] Members of the royal family recalled these
years with sadness. They told me that, as a young man, Masenyane had been
brain-damaged in a rockfall in the mines. In 1962 he could no longer speak
properly and had to step down as acting chief.

Josia Senone – the eldest son of Setlhare's third house – replaced Masenyane.
Senone's widow said he lacked the power of a proper chief and was greatly
constrained by the Commissioner, who even appointed headmen on his behalf.
Throughout his reign, Senone faced great opposition from members of the royal
family. After a dispute with his brothers over the subdivision of residential sites,
he relinquished his position and left Green Valley, returning upon the insistence
of the Commissioner, but only after his brothers had apologised to him.
Loyanang Chiloane, another of Setlhare's sons, also challenged Senone. As a
youngster Loyanang had burnt down the Lutheran school, but had been excused
on grounds of insanity. He had later worked as a migrant in Pretoria. On his
return, he had established an Apostolic church in Brooklyn and claimed that he
was the rightful chief. Many people, including Senone's right-hand-man,
supported him. Loyanang eventually committed suicide.

German Sitondane, Seganyane's younger brother, ruled from 1969 until
1989. German was baptised by the ZCC, but he soon lost his way. He became
a chronic alcoholic and a very ineffectual chief. In 1984, during one of
German's prolonged drinking bouts, a councillor took over as acting chief. Only
when the magistrate discovered that the councillor had accepted bribes for residential stands did he reinstate German as chief. Yet German did gain some
support by turning a blind eye to many official regulations. The owner of a
small store described him as 'a man among men'. 'Chief German never had a
grudge against anybody. Many people set up businesses without a licence, but
he never troubled them. He never collected any money from us.'

Whilst the power of chiefs declined, there was a general increase in social
tensions within and between households. Villagisation not only altered the composition of domestic units, but also had a profound effect on gender and
generational relations. It placed women in a powerless and precarious position.
Through working in the fields, women had made the most important contribu-

tion to household diets, but after relocation they came to rely, almost completely, upon the remittances of migrant men. In the absence of migrant fathers, mothers and grandparents found it hard to discipline children. Boys no longer herded cattle and were free to attend school more regularly. This enhanced children's status *vis-à-vis* their illiterate parents. The ties between chiefs and the youth – which were so prominent in initiation, rainmaking and in the cleansing of fields from worm – were also severed. Setlhare was the last chief to act as an initiation master. Subsequently, all the initiation masters were commoners. Since the 1960s generational relations have been characterised by 'cohort dissonance'.[19] Green Valley's youth have little insight into events which shaped the lives of elders, but they are confronted by a range of new problems which their parents had not experienced.

In the context of villagisation and the dualistic worldview propagated by Zionist-type churches, fears of bewitchment intensified and attributions of witchcraft escalated. Certainly the pattern of accusations altered. In the new social and ideological context, witches were no longer seen to threaten the subsistence base of the community. Indeed, informants suggested that all the rainstopping *dihlare* disappeared during the removals. Witchcraft was now seen as directed solely against individuals. It was also believed that witches adopted new familiars and technologies, and even vengeance magic came to be viewed as unacceptable and as evil.

Despite this increase, chiefs very seldom intervened when villagers accused each other of witchcraft. With the introduction of Bantu Authorities, chiefs were placed under the constant surveillance of the Commissioners. The Commissioners compelled chiefs to abide by the provisions of the new Suppression of Witchcraft Act No. 3 of 1957. This Act consolidated the earlier anti-witchcraft laws into unified legislation for the whole country. In terms of the Act anyone who indicates another person as being a witch, or attempts to practice witchcraft, can be fined up to R2,000, imprisoned for up to ten years and/or whipped up to ten strokes. If a person accused of witchcraft was killed, the perpetrator could be jailed for up to 20 years. A second category of offenders are persons who approach 'witch-doctors' to 'smell out' others as witches, advise others how to bewitch, supply them with 'the pretended means of witchcraft' or attempt to put into operation processes which are calculated to injure other people or things. They can be sentenced to a fine not exceeding R500 and/or imprisoned for a period not exceeding ten years. Even those who claim to possess the powers of divination can be fined R200 or imprisoned for two years.[20] (See Appendix C.)

In only 13 (10 per cent) of the 127 recorded witchcraft accusations that occurred between 1956 and 1986 did chiefs, councillors, or headmen defy the Commissioners and give people permission to consult a witch-diviner. Seganyane II sometimes sent his driver to take accusers and accused to a witch-diviner in Giyani. On one occasion, for example, a headman's wife was found guilty of practising witchcraft, and Seganyane II forced her to compensate her victim's family with two cows. Then, after an unfortunate incident in 1959, chiefs were no longer able officially to support witch-hunting. Before the burial of Seganyane II, his councillors had called a *pitšo* to discuss the circumstances surrounding his death. At the meeting it was alleged that the chief's body showed burn marks and that he had been bewitched. Men apprehended William Lekoba, a *ngaka*, and took him to a witch-diviner at Phunda Malia. The diviner pronounced William guilty of prescribing a herbal concoction which had turned the chief into an alcoholic, made him insane and eventually killed him. Upon William's return an angry crowd confronted him. When William tried to defend himself with an axe, the crowd stoned him to death. In response to this incident the Commissioner banned all *pitšo* and prohibited visits to the witch-diviners.

Later Chief German and a few headmen had the courage to defy these regulations. In 1969 an employee of the Setlhare Tribal Authority lost two of his children and suspected that his maternal grandfather was responsible. The two men privately placed a stake with Chief German and procured a letter of authorisation from him to go to a witch-diviner in Giyani. Five years later an influential family of Botshabelo complained to the chief that their neighbour kept zombies. Others also claimed that he sent baboons to steal their maize meal. Chief German instructed the local headman to collect donations of R1.50 from all households. This money was used to send ten delegates and the suspect to Giyani. Because the witch-diviner confirmed that the suspect was a witch, the chief asked his driver to remove him to Islington. These events were both exceptional and presumably happened without the Commissioner's knowledge.

The vast majority of families could not secure the assistance of chiefs to gain compensation for the crimes that had been committed against them by witches. To many it seemed that the chiefs were more inclined to support the perpetrators than the victims of witchcraft. For instance, in 1975 Maggie Segodi fled from the home of her husband, Ripho Moropane, because she was convinced that her father-in-law had sent a *tokolotši* to rape her (see Case 3.2). Ripho and his father then laid a charge of desertion against Maggie at the *kgoro* of the Kgapa Madi headman. Although her family explained fully what had happened, the headman judged that they had to refund all bridewealth and pay an additional R200 to compensate Ripho's family.

Sansom (1972) has argued that witchcraft accusations, in the full sense of public denunciation, hardly ever occurred in the Mekgwang area of Sekhukhuneland during the 1960s. He accounts for this in terms of the difficulties of mobilising public support, rather than the absence of witchcraft beliefs. In accusing others of witchcraft, individuals put themselves at risk. In Green Valley many families faced a similar dilemma. Without the support of chiefs and headmen, whom they felt had betrayed them, villagers such as Maggie Segodi saw themselves as the powerless victims of evil forces. They could not confront the suspected witches by themselves. In fear of their lives, many villagers relocated to safer locations and joined Zionist-type churches. These churches, which experienced a dramatic increase in membership throughout this period, have made a concerted attempt to heal the bewitched and fortify homes against witchcraft (see Chapter 2).

Although Sansom (1972) correctly highlights the difficulty of mobilising support against witches, it would be erroneous to suppose that this was impossible. In Green Valley – apparently in contrast to the situation Sansom portrays in Mekgwang – many families were able to take revenge for the deaths of their kin. This occurred in as many as 21 of the 127 recorded cases of witchcraft accusations. In these situations the accusers deemed the nature of witchcraft horrific, and they were certain of the witch's identity (see Appendix D).

Cases 7.1 and 7.2 show some of the dynamics of witch- hunting during the period from 1956 to 1986.

*Case 7.1: The Killing of a Poisoner*[21]

During the 1970s, Abel Dilebo was employed as a migrant worker at ISCOR – the parastatal iron and steel manufacturer – in Pretoria. His wife, Lisbeth, was in her thirties, unemployed, and afflicted with a protruding goitre. A neighbour described her as 'good natured', but suggested that she might have experienced tensions with her husband. 'All the time she went about the village with other women. She was not even at home when her husband arrived from Pretoria. I think she was unfaithful to him.'

In 1977, Abel came home for Christmas. Two days after his arrival, he called his neighbour to the fence and told her someone had poisoned his tea. Abel spilt some of the tea from his cup onto the grass, and even though the tea was cold it destroyed the grass where it fell. When Abel saw this he exclaimed, 'This may be the last time you see me alive.' The neighbour's husband then rushed Abel to hospital in his van. At 10 am the next morning, Abel passed away. His relatives were convinced that Lisbeth poisoned him. At the hospital, nurses reportedly handed his mother a note, which read:

*Mmane. Ka Labobedi mosadi waka o ntsheletše tšhefu. Ngaka e mpotšhitšě bjalo. Ga go na e mongwe ke yene mosadi waka yeo a mpolailego.*
[Mother. On Tuesday night my wife poisoned me. The doctor told me it was poison. There is no person besides my wife who killed me.]

(Abel was illiterate, and people said the nurses wrote the letter on his instructions.)

During the week-long mourning period, Abel's relatives met on several occasions and plotted to kill Lisbeth. Only one relative disagreed. She argued that during their marriage Abel had always supported his wife well and said that without a husband Lisbeth would starve to death. Therefore she would not have killed her husband. Lisbeth stayed indoors throughout the entire period of mourning, and refused to eat any of the food her mother-in-law prepared. Neighbours advised Lisbeth's mother to rescue her and hide her in a safe place, but the old woman did not believe that her daughter was under threat.

At the funeral Abel's sister made a demonstration. When the minister asked the widow to put soil into her husband's gave, the dead man's sister pulled the blanket from Lisbeth's head and threw it into the grave. As she did this, she shouted, 'Today you look like a bride in a wedding dress! Who are you going to marry?' Hereby she insinuated that Lisbeth looked forward to marrying a new husband. Abel's sister then beat Lisbeth. When Lisbeth fell, Abel's brothers beat her with shovels and asked her to show them the poison. Lisbeth agreed to do so, but her attackers did not relent. They pushed aside those who sought to protect the woman and began casting stones at her. After a prolonged struggle, Lisbeth's relatives removed her from the gaveyard, but they were too late. Lisbeth died a few minutes later.

Lisbeth's sister had run from the graveyard to call the Acornhoek police, but their arrival was delayed for many hours. At Abel's home, the police interrogated some of the onlookers, slapped Abel's aunt and arrested his four brothers. All four men were imprisoned, for periods varying from three to four years. After the tragic deaths of Abel and Lisbeth, Abel's parents raised their children in Zoeknog. Neighbours did not approve of Lisbeth's killing, but were convinced she had poisoned Abel to get his ISCOR pension.

## Case 7.2: Assaulting a Witch[22]

The residents of Botshabelo had long suspected Skariot Mosoma of practising witchcraft. An elderly *ngaka*, his behaviour seemed strange and rude. He lived his life in absolute secrecy and never attended funerals. Even next-door neighbours did not know his wife's maiden name.

One night in 1966, a boy reported hearing strange winds, followed by footsteps on the roof. The footsteps sounded like those of a cat, but of a much larger creature. Once he dreamt that baboons approached his family home. The baboons fought each other in front of the gate and then entered the yard. Another evening he screamed and told his father that something had grabbed and slapped him. After this incident the boy became seriously ill. The illness persisted for months, but he recovered after being treated by an Apostolic healer. In September 1968 his elder brother died in a motor vehicle accident near Nelspruit. The death seemed unnatural, as none of the other passengers was injured. The deceased had suffered no external injuries and his body remained warm. His *malome* thought a witch had captured him as a zombie. When he consulted a witch-diviner in Giyani he was told that a tall, bald-headed man was responsible for the death of his nephew. Skariot Mosoma matched the diviner's description, the *malome* planned to confront him, but the boy's father prevented him from doing so.

In 1973 lightning struck and killed four people in Botshabelo. Local residents suspected that Skariot, the cousin of one of the deceased, had sent the lightning. Skariot owed his cousin money and had quarrelled with him prior to his death. It was rumoured that after the incident Skariot had told a relative that he did not deliberately kill the young man, but the latter had stood in his way when he flew through the air.

In 1975, a 70-year-old woman and her husband died in mysterious circumstances. Prior to her death, she dreamt that her daughter-in-law had strangled her. Five months later her husband collapsed and died while he was inspecting the banana trees in his garden. Their sons secretly visited a witch-diviner in Giyani after the funeral, and he told them that a bald-headed man and his woman helper had bewitched the deceased. Later they arranged a second journey to the diviner, accompanied by representatives of four influential families of Botshabelo. Skariot and the daughter-in-law of the elderly couple were asked to accompany the party as witnesses. The diviner identified Skariot as the leader of Botshabelo's witches, and the daughter-in-law as his accomplice. He said they used owls, baboons and snakes as familiars.

On their return to Botshabelo, the daughter-in-law escaped, but Skariot was assaulted and left for dead. Relatives later took him to hospital, where he allegedly told a friend that he managed to survive only because the wings of his invisible owl had shielded him from the blows. While Skariot was in hospital, young men searched his home for evidence of witchcraft, and under his bed they found calabashes and herbs, but they were unsure whether these were used to harm or to heal people. They also found a piece of meat in his kitchen, which they suspected was the arm of a monkey or of a child. The men then burnt Skariot's home. Police later arrested three men between the ages of 25 and 30 in connection with the incident. When he was discharged from hospital, Skariot fled to Bushbuckridge.

Even without the assistance of chiefs and headmen, Abel Dilebo's relatives were able to organise for revenge when they gathered in the emotionally laden atmosphere of his funeral. In the case of Skariot Mosoma, suspicions built up over many years, and eventually he was publicly accused. It is significant that the four families who took Skariot to the diviner were all associated with the ZCC. Their common church-membership provided the basis for mutual support. In the absence of institutionalised means of gaining compensation for witchcraft, they accusers deployed exceptionally violent forms of punishment. In other instances people accused of witchcraft were attacked with axes, strangled, beaten, set alight with petrol, or even shot. The homes of the accused were also destroyed and they were expelled from Green Valley. Such violence was partially legitimised by the belief that witches were not fully human and possessed animal-like attributes.

Cases 7.1 and 7.2 highlight the divergence between the popular sentiments of villagers and the attitudes of government. Every action against witchcraft by villagers provoked counter-reactions from the authorities. Not only were villagers denied permission to consult witch-diviners, but the witch-hunters were imprisoned. After the death of their brother in 1978, men planted a flag in Petrus Nokeri's yard to warn him that he was suspected of witchcraft. The police rushed to Petrus' assistance and arrested five of the men. Such incidents generated the perception that the authorities sided with witches. During an interview, an elderly man described this situation as intolerable.

There were witches in the past, but they played around at night and did not kill people. Then the chiefs were in control and the witches feared them. Now it seemed to us that the magistrates and the Commissioners protected the witches. Because the witches knew that they were being protected they would continue bewitching people as they pleased.


COMRADES AND WITCHES, 1986–1990

In the 1980s, national liberation movements and the Comrades occupied the political void left by the erosion of chiefship. The eradication of witchcraft was a major public issue during this extraordinary period of political mobilisation.

In recounting the history of opposition to apartheid, Elphas Mogale, a former ANC senator, described the Setlhare area as 'politically dormant for a long time'. This is because mission schools failed to enlighten people about oppression, few migrants joined trade unions and local people generally despised the lifestyle of politicised urban areas. No counterpart to the Sebatak-gomo migrants' association of Sekhukhuneland (Delius, 1989) had, for instance, emerged in the lowveld to resist the imposition of Bantu Authorities and 'betterment'. Political mobilisation was sporadic. In the 1950s the brothers Matsikitsane and Segopela Mashile joined the ANC and led tenant struggles against the use of child labour by the Hall & Sons farming enterprise.[23] With the banning of the ANC they were jailed on charges of 'sabotage'. Released in 1963, they were banished to the Transkei and the Ciskei respectively (Ritchken, 1995:290). Political activists such as Philip Chiloane and Johnstone Mlambo, who arrived in the lowveld during the 1970s, failed to build significant support bases. After he spent twelve years on Robben Island, Philip Chiloane was employed at the magistrate's office in Bushbuckridge and campaigned against the Bantustans. In 1978, he was killed by a letter bomb. Johnstone Mlambo, former deputy president of the PAC, regularly visited Green Valley, but soon went into exile in Tanzania. During the 1976 uprising a few students fled from Soweto to complete their schooling in Green Valley, but their message of black consciousness had hardly any impact on the local youth.

This situation changed in the 1980s. A number of ANC underground networks became operative in the area.[24] The Mashile brothers returned to Acornhoek, and were both elected to the Lebowa Legislative Assembly. By making ministers accountable for bureaucratic inefficiencies, and by taking local issues to the highest authorities, they effectively used their prominent positions to further popular causes (Ritchken, 1995:299–301). After the formation of the United Democratic Front (UDF), political activity spread rapidly throughout Lebowa (see Delius, 1990, 1996; Lodge and Nasson, 1991; Van Kessel, 1993; Ritchken, 1995). Mapulaneng too became the scene of widespread protest. In Shatale, the Mashile brothers and teachers from the Witwatersrand assisted in establishing several UDF structures – the Mapulaneng Crisis Committee, Shatale Youth Congress, a teachers' association and student representative councils.

In April 1986 the Mashile brothers and the Mapulaneng Crisis Committee convened a mass meeting in Green Valley to discuss local problems. At the meeting, a Setlhare Crisis Committee and Brooklyn Youth Organisation were launched. Twelve adults were elected to the committee. (They were a telephone exchange operator, truck driver, migrant labourer, bank teller, two Hoedspruit employees and six teachers.) The Setlhare Crisis Committee proved unable to survive police repression and met on only three occasions. By May, all its active members had been detained.[25] The Brooklyn Youth Organisation was more resilient and attracted a very large following among young men. They organised from schools and held meetings late at night. Such youths, known as Comrades, were now in the forefront of political struggle. One young man recalled, 'Before 1986 youngsters played soccer and stabbed each other, but now we started mobilising the masses.'

The political prominence of young men in the region mirrored developments throughout South Africa at the time. Bundy (1987) describes the political education of students in the 1980s as spectacularly rapid nation-wide. He explains this in terms of a number of interrelated processes. Foremost were accelerated growth in the numbers of children and young adults and a substantial expansion in African schooling, despite its glaring defects. In the context of the South African economic crisis, there was mounting unemployment among the young. High-school leavers, he writes, 'have been thrust in the labour market at precisely the moment that it is contracting...'(Bundy, 1987:312). The impact of unemployment and potential unemployability was a spur to radicalism.

Similar processes were apparent in Lebowa. As a consequence of labour migration, 72 per cent of Lebowa's *de facto* population were under the age of 20 in 1985 (DBSA, 1988:127). From 1980 to 1986 the number of secondary school students in Lebowa more than doubled. Yet the quality of education was desperately poor and school children had few prospects. This is indicated by the low, and declining, pass rates for matric exams. In 1984 the pass rate was 57 per cent, in 1986 42 per cent and in 1989 only 34 per cent (DBSA, 1988:61; SAIRR, 1988:165, 1989:514).[26]

Like the youth movements of Cape Town and Sekhukhuneland that have been described by Bundy (1987) and Delius (1996), the involvement of the Brooklyn Youth Organisation in local educational issues provided the framework for wider forms of community action. Initial campaigns focused on the schools. Through a series of class boycotts, students demanded an end to the payment of R80 'school building fees' and called for the introduction of student representative councils, free books and an end to corporal punishment. Although several students were arrested, principals conceded many of their demands. In other campaigns they confronted white businesses and the Tribal Authorities, which they perceived as exploitative. In 1986, Comrades organised a stay-away on May Day and launched a boycott of a Bushbuckridge super-market. They laid concrete slabs in the streets to force workers to stay at home and confiscated consumer goods. In 1987 the Brooklyn Youth Organisation called upon villagers not to pay annual site taxes (R1), service rents (R15, for water and graveyard maintenance) and stock levies (85c per head large stock, 40c per head small stock) to the Tribal Authorities. By now the activities of the Tribal Authorities had almost ground to a halt.

The actions of the youth, who played a pivotal role throughout the protest, were definitely inspired by a strong sense of 'generational consciousness' (Bundy, 1987). In interviews conducted during the 1990s Comrades often described elders as politically ignorant and uneducated. One activist remarked, 'Elders have old-fashioned ideas and are scared of the whites. They think they [whites] are God.' Yet the label of a 'youth revolt' (Van Kessel, 1993:596) obscures many crucial dimensions of these dramatic events.[27] First, the label fails to capture the gendered nature of political activism. The Brooklyn Youth Organisation was dominated by a masculine ethos that valued fearless bravery. One informant pointed out the similarity between men's initiation and partici-pation in the struggle. 'There you become a man. When you are from the initiation you won't reveal any secrets when the police capture you because you have already experienced torture.' Very few young women actively par-ticipated in the organisation. This, men said, was because they feared confronting the police.[28] Second, the label 'youth revolt' downplays the extent to which many adults tacitly supported the Comrades. The Comrades did attack institutions controlled by adults, but selected their targets very carefully. Facing economic hardship, many adults resented paying school building fees and Tribal Authority taxes. There were also consistent rumours that local shop-owners were really behind the boycotts of white-owned businesses. Such support was often covert, and was not necessarily expressed in formal political alliances between student and worker organisations.

The Comrades did not merely confront exploitation. Many campaigns of the Brooklyn Youth Organisation were aimed explicitly at gaining legitimacy among adults. By fiercely opposing the notorious *psyanga* youth gang, the Comrades gained considerable moral credibility.[29] *Psyanga* carried out a reign of terror from Cottondale. In Acornhoek, they wrung the necks of chickens, destroyed groceries and kidnapped and raped women. *Psyanga* also burnt a furniture store in Green Valley. Comrades *sjambokked* several *psyanga* members and burnt their homes. Moreover, the Comrades negotiated with a nearby saw mill to provide safe transport for its employees and formed squads to escort commuters home at night. They regularly organised marches to the Acornhoek police station to demand the more effective provision of piped water and roads, and the installation of electricity. In 1989 more than 10,000 people participated in such a march. Catholic priests walked in front of the procession, and adult women marched along carrying empty water canisters.

The Comrades came to play an important role in the politics of public morality. To some extent their actions resembled those of the rural Welsh youth groups described by Peters (1972). Welsh youths exhibited seemingly anti-social behaviour such as removing gates, cutting shapes in cornfields and thrusting hens down chimneys. However, Peters does not regard such acts as anti-social. Rather, he sees them as condemning the pride of immoral individuals. Many adults tacitly approve of the youth. They are regarded as teaching those who display arrogance, or engage in inappropriate sexual relations, a lesson. Peters suggests that criticism of such individuals in fact originates with adults. Institutions controlled by adults such as law, religion and kinship lack flexibility in dealing with such ambiguous social relations. Institutionally, adults are unable to control, for instance, associations between local girls and stranger men, or to punish adultery. By delegating the responsibility of moral control to youths the adult community is able to maintain its integrity. Adults also sustain anonymity by ascribing such actions to 'the young' rather than to specific individuals. Youths are jurally minors, with a limited sense of externality. 'Their ignorance or immaturity gives the youth group the irresponsible freedom to act; maturity traps adults into the measured responsibility of inaction' (Peters, 1972:135).

Comrades also intervened in the morally ambiguous field of witchcraft, and dedicated themselves to the complete eradication of evil.[30] Throughout Lebowa, youths engaged in witch-hunting (Delius, 1990:26; Van Kessel, 1993:608–11). Between April and May 1986, Comrades attacked more than 150 suspected witches in Mapulaneng, killing at least 36 (SAIRR, 1988:907). Most of these killings occurred in Casteel and Brooklyn. In Casteel, Comrades burnt to death three witches. In Brooklyn, Comrades killed an Apostolic minister, and *sjambokked* to death three women pensioners who allegedly kept zombies (Ritchken, 1995:366). In Buffelshoek, Comrades executed a shebeen-owner whom had been charged at the chief's *kgoro* for having bewitched children, although the chief had found him not guilty.

Evidence from Green Valley suggests that although young men led the witch-hunts, adults made the initial accusations of witchcraft as in the past. Violent methods of punishing witches had also been entrenched since the 1970s. What had changed was the identity of the witch-hunters. In a context where chiefs no longer assisted the bewitched, and the police arrested those who took justice into their own hands, only the Comrades were willing to act decisively against witches. The Comrades were motivated by a concern to remove the sources of people's misfortune. By delegating this responsibility to the youth, adults could sustain anonymity and preserve their moral integrity.

In 1986, the Comrades called a series of meetings and asked adult men to name those whom they suspected of being witches. Of the meetings in Brooklyn, which were presumably attended by many Green Valley residents, Ritchken (1995:367) writes: 'The most enthusiastic accusers were the older, unemployed men. They would refer to previous occasions when witches were identified, but the witch would then bribe the chief or the *induna* [headman] and remain in the community.' The names that were popularly approved were recorded on a list and disciplinary teams were formed to punish the witches.

In Green Valley, Comrades set alight two homes and stoned a woman to death. Adam Ngobeni, their first victim, was a *ngaka* who had arrived in Bodlaya Bongolo from Ohrigstad during 1973. Adam initially attracted many customers, but his clientele dwindled when it was rumoured that he sold witchcraft substances. After his brother's daughter suffered a miscarriage and died, many suspected that Adam might have bewitched her. A neighbour, who heard eerie noises emanating from Adam's yard at night, told me that he believed Adam kept zombies. In April 1986 an elderly man and a few Comrades came to inform Adam that the *dihlare* he sold had killed a child in Kgapa Madi. Adam, reportedly, said he could not be blamed for what customers did with the potent herbs they bought from him. Late that evening Comrades smashed the windows of Adam's home and threw a home-made petrol bomb inside. The bomb failed to ignite, however. The next morning, Adam and his fellow household members fled to Cottondale with all their possessions. That afternoon, the Comrades demolished his home.

Adults were also the first to suspect that Rufus Mosoma and Nana Selepe, the next victims of the Comrades, were witches. Diviners had identified Rufus (Skariot's brother, see Case 7.2) as a witch on two previous occasions. Although Rufus had been initiated as a *ngaka*, he founded a very peculiar church, with only two members, who would say prayers at the river each evening. In 1973 Rufus was blamed for the death of a man who had suffered a heart attack. A diviner revealed that his church meetings were really assemblies of witches. When Rufus' grandson died, ten years later, another diviner said Rufus' familiars killed him. In 1984 youngsters saw a monkey in a tree nearby a shop, threw stones at it and followed the monkey until it disappeared at Nana Selepe's home. The next year the child of Nana's next-door neighbours died from measles and was buried behind their home. When Nana later drove her cattle through their yard, the cattle desecrated the child's grave. The neighbours said they saw Nana scooping soil from the child's grave with her hands and accused her of witchcraft. Nana's family met with her neighbours, but they failed to resolve the dispute.

Late one evening in April 1986, about 15 Comrades came to Rufus Mosoma's home. Rufus heard their voices and escaped through the window. When the Comrades forced open the door they found only his wife in the bedroom. She was drunk. They grabbed her by the arms, dragged her outside and set the home alight. The Comrades then left for Nana Selepe's home. Here they smashed open the door and found only Nana and her daughter inside. (Two of her sons worked in Johannesburg. The third lived in another section of Green Valley.) The Comrades dragged the two women outside and then proceeded to stone Nana to death with large bricks. As soon as they left, Nana's daughter ran to her brother's home to inform him of what had happened. They reported the incident to the police, but the daughter failed to identify any of the assailants. Because the Comrades warned people not to attend the funeral of any witch, very few people attended Nana's burial. Her family relocated to

Khiyelane, but relations between them and their former neighbours have remained extremely tense.

Even soccer players turned to the Comrades when they feared that their former club chairman, Edward Maile, had bewitched them. Upon being dismissed from his post Edward had, reportedly, threatened them, saying, 'Be careful the next time you play.' In the matches that followed many players were injured, and their ball mysteriously disappeared at a soccer practice. A *ngaka* informed some of the players that Edward had bewitched them and had stolen the ball. Moreover, a close friend of Edward's son reported having seen the ball underneath Edward's bed. Being too scared to confront Edward, the players reported him to the Comrades. That evening the Comrades threw what was described to me as a 'hand grenade' through Edward's window, but the device did not explode.

Comrades conducted witch-hunts in Tsakane and Mapalene. In Tsakane there had been a number of sad incidents in the course of 1988: some youngsters went insane, a man committed suicide and four middle-aged members of a family died in mysterious circumstances. Comrades collected donations from villagers, rounded up suspects, and took them to a witch-diviner. Youths destroyed the homes of those identified as witches by the diviner and planned to kill them, but the police intervened. In 1989, Mapalene's youths consulted a witch-diviner after a man had been poisoned. The Comrades then summoned a meeting and played a cassette recording of the diviner's voice that blamed a particular man and woman for his death. Both were heavily *sjambokked*. Police arrested three men in connection with the incident. Two were released later, but the third was imprisoned for a period of 18 months.

The Comrades certainly demonstrated their capacity to deal decisively with witches. Since they were often a third party – unrelated to either the assumed victims or witches – they could sustain anonymity and often escaped police detection. In only one of the five cases that I described did the police arrest the attackers. The Comrades were thus a very valuable resource for those who sought revenge against witchcraft. This becomes even clearer if we compare these cases with the few cases that villagers referred to the Tribal Authorities. After Mr Segodi's son died of suspected poisoning in 1989, he obtained the consent of the headman to visit a witch-diviner in Giyani. Upon his return, Mr Segodi accused three women of poisoning. When he threatened one woman, she confessed to the crimes. A week later, Mr Segodi's home was burnt. His children clearly identified the three women as the arsonists and Mr Segodi reported them to Chief German's *kgoro*, but he dismissed the case on the grounds of insufficient evidence.

None of the victims of these witch-hunts was associated with the Tribal Authority or with other political enemies of the Comrades. The witch-hunts did, however, articulate generational tensions (see Appendix E). While many of the assumed victims of witchcraft were young, all the accused were elderly (although Kganetši Mamba, the youngest, was only in her forties).

The Brooklyn Youth Organisation did not achieve unqualified legitimacy among adults. At best, they evoked a mixed response. Many adults, in particular male migrants, were grateful to the Comrades. They commended their courage and commented positively upon the disappearance of the *psyanga* gang and upon the reductions in school fees and in taxes. Others distrusted and resented the Comrades. Bundy (1987) points to youth militancy, a political perspective of immediatism, and a naive underestimation of the state's resources as likely reasons for the failure of the Cape Town youth movement to establish a common political cause with their parents. These factors were certainly applicable to the Brooklyn Youth Organisation.

But the criticisms that adults levelled at the Comrades did not have to do with their broader political strategy. What adults feared most was that the actions of Green Valley's youth presented a direct challenge to their authority.[31] Through their control of the student representative council, the Brooklyn Youth Organisation had effectively taken over the running of the Maripe High School. In one confrontation scholars accused the principal of embezzling funds and chased him from the school. In another they attacked a teacher, whom they accused of being a 'sell-out', and kicked him unconscious. Youths also challenged parents' control over the discipline, sexuality and spiritual lives of their children. The Brooklyn Youth Organisation disciplined unruly youngsters in people's courts. They also ordered young women to attend night meetings, where many were made pregnant with the excuse of 'operation production', which aimed to replace those who had been killed in the struggle.[32] Youths also interrupted night vigils and instructed the mourners to sing 'freedom songs'. When organising marches, *sjambok*-wielding youths often went from house to house and forced adults to attend the protests.

Many adults, although not opposed witch-hunting *per se*, criticised the manner in which the Comrades intervened. Adults thought they used improper methods to identify witches, since they seldom consulted witch-diviners. Many did not believe that Nana Selepe had bewitched her neighbour's child. According to an alternative theory, the child died from *makgoma* and her own father was to blame. When she was ill her father came to visit her from Johannesburg, where he worked as a migrant, and gave her a sip of his cold drink. Informants said that, since he had been *fiša* from having sexual inter-course with his pregnant wife, he should have avoided all contact with her. Given the arbitrary methods of witch-identification, diviners and elders feared that they might become the victims of witch-hunts. A *ngaka* recalled that, during the witch-hunts, 'My trainees all got rid of their medicines and joined the churches'. An elderly woman told me, 'I'm scared of those who go around singing at night. We always feel threatened by the Comrades. Years ago members of our family could sleep outside when it was hot. Now we can't. I'm even afraid of you.' The very severe punishments were also criticised. Unlike the violence of witches, the violence of the witch-hunters is visible. Elders saw the Comrades as over-zealous in their attempts to banish witchcraft. They told me Comrades would disrupt funerals and ask mourners not to eat meat because this would encourage neighbours to bewitch one another. As Foucault (1986:9) observed of torture as a European spectacle, the punishment enforced against witches offset the crime itself, making the tortured an object of pity.

On 25 November 1989, the Sofasonke (meaning 'We die Together') Civic Union was established at a public meeting in Brooklyn.[33] Sofasonke's agenda was to oppose the Comrades politically, and to re-impose the authority of adults. Sofasonke's constituency was drawn from among those to whom the Comrades presented the greatest threat. Teachers, parents (mostly mothers), the family members of those who had been accused as witches and a few headmen attended the meeting. Two high school principals, Chief German's head councillor and a Nazarine minister were elected to Sofasonke's executive committee. The sphere of Sofasonke's operations rapidly extended to Green Valley, and the Mapelene and Phelindaba sections became known as Sofasonke strongholds.

Sofasonke soon went on the offensive. On 26 November, a group of about 800 Sofasonke supporters, most of whom were women, burnt the homes of seven prominent Comrades. Armed Sofasonke groups patrolled the village at night, ensuring that there were no youth on the streets (Ritchken 1995:414). Since no arrests were made, and Sofasonke was allowed to meet openly during the national state of emergency, many informants believed the police supported Sofasonke.[34] Late in December, Sofasonke launched another attack. They burnt five homes in Green Valley, belonging to families who gave refuge to youth leaders, destroyed Sekgopela Mashile's home in Buffelshoek and fired gunshots at Matsikitsane Mashile's car. On the morning of 26 December, women found the van of Matsikitsane's burial society standing next to the Green Valley timber yard. Outside lay Mathews Thibela's corpse and Benson Mashile who had sustained bullet wounds in his thigh. Villagers assumed Sofasonke had murdered them. Both men were associated with the Comrades. (Mathews was Matsikitsane's driver, Benson his nephew.) Again the police made no arrests.

On 28 January 1990, Nelson Ramodike, Lebowa's Chief Minister, with representatives of the South African Council of Churches and of the UDF, met Sofasonke and Comrade leaders in an attempt to end the violence. The next day Ramodike made an urgent appeal for peace at the Maripe High School. Yet that very night several houses and cattle were burnt and a Comrade leader was seriously injured. The Comrades retaliated by burning the homes of the chairman and vice-chairman of Sofasonke. The next day they attacked Sofasonke's chairman, the principal of a school in Brooklyn, and necklaced him. Over the Easter weekend, Sofasonke members butchered a 15-year-old schoolgirl, the sister of a Comrade leader. This time a riot squad of the Lebowa police arresting 20 Comrades and five Sofasonke members. Only now did the violence subside.

Within months, the Sofasonke Civic Union had disintegrated. It is significant that none of those killed in the battle between Sofasonke and the Comrades was identified as witches. Comrades distinguished between witches and their opponents, whom they termed *ipimpi* ('sell-outs'). The political label of *ipimpi* is very loaded and, in itself, justifies violent action. It does not require a reformulation in mystical terms. Sofasonke remained an elusive organisation which did not have the wholehearted support of adults. Adults feared that Sofasonke endangered the lives of their children. An elderly man adequately summarised feelings when he remarked, 'It has been much worse since Sofasonke has been around. They said they were better than the Comrades, but they also killed people.'

## CONCLUSIONS

Clearly many – perhaps most – people in Green Valley took witchcraft very seriously. The reality of such beliefs, as an intellectual attempt to explain, manage and compensate for undeserved misfortune, cannot lightly be dismissed as an idiom that masks ulterior motives, and is aimed at intimidating political opponents. On the contrary, witch-hunting must be understood in the first place as an attempt to eliminate misfortune. Those who support and organise action against witches therefore perform a valuable social service, and attain political legitimacy.

Despite important changes in the forms of witch-beliefs and in patterns of witchcraft accusation, there have been remarkable continuities in its political implications over time. From 1930 to 1957, witches were perceived as threatening the livelihood of the entire Green Valley community. In this context, witch-hunts, which were aimed at restoring fertility to the land, reaffirmed the solidarity of villagers, and constituted the *mošate* as political centre of the chiefdom. Impoverished *dingaka*, blamed for using *šibeka*, were not necessarily or even usually associated with the political opponents of the Setlhare chiefs. In the post-relocation years, witches were perceived to threaten individuals and individual households. From 1986, Comrades exploited public perceptions that the South African government protected witches. They gave powerless individuals the necessary public support to accuse neighbours and kin as witches, and although many elderly people felt intimidated by the Comrades, it can be argued that this was a consequence of, rather than a motivating factor for, witch-hunting. In making accusations youths sought the public co-operation of village adults, and followed the consensual identification of individuals as witches. It is notable that members of Sofasonke were killed not as witches, but as political opponents.

Heald (1989) has shown that similar vigilante groups, engaged in the eradication of witches and thieves among the Bugisu of Uganda during the 1960s, relied on the widest basis of public support. In the context of a power vacuum at the local level, these groups are seen as enabling the Bugisu to come to terms with a life situation of anarchy and lawlessness. The anti-witchcraft movements that occurred in Green Valley were more akin to the 'witch-finding' movements that have been reported in Uganda, and in Sakumaland in Tanzania (Heald, 1989; Bukurura, 1994; Mesaki, 1994) than to the 'witch-cleansing' cults that have been described in central Africa (Richards, 1935; Marwick, 1950; Douglas, 1963; Willis, 1968, 1970; Auslander, 1993; Green, 1994, 1997).[35] As in Uganda and in Sakumaland, individual witches were sought out and severely dealt with. In central Africa, in contrast, witch cleansing involved the collective consumption of anti-witchcraft serum, to counter witchcraft in those who harboured it, and to protect those who did not. Willis (1970:131) sees a sense of social renewal as a general outcome of witch cleansing. 'Supposedly, a new and morally regenerated life then begins for everyone.' Witch-finding certainly involves greater ambiguity, contestation and violence than witch-cleansing. Yet witch-finding was merely a different technique of eradicating evil.

The political pay-off that follows from instigating a witch-finding movement can only be understood when it is appreciated that it is directed against evil itself and not merely against political opponents. These movements set up a moral opposition between the witch-hunter and forces of evil, and associate its leaders with a struggle against the perennial human problems of death and misfortune, which are a more compelling force in motivating people to action than purely political obligations. People are more likely to be active participants in a hunt for those whom they hold responsible for endangering their harvest, or for the death of their child, than to recite praise poems to a chief or to celebrate May Day. Finally, because they pose a general threat to the community rather than to any particular section of it, all sorts of people can combine to act against them. Many different actors, with diverse beliefs, can identify themselves with witch-hunting.

# 8 THE ANC'S DILEMMA: THE SYMBOLIC POLITICS OF FOUR WITCH-HUNTS IN THE 1990s[1]

The unbanning of the ANC in February 1990, precipitated major political changes. The ANC was transformed into a government-in-waiting and became the dominant partner in South Africa's government in April 1994. In rural areas of the north, where it had been associated with rebellious youths, the ANC broadened its support base. Van Kessel (1993:612) aptly comments, 'Many of the adversaries of the youth activists of the 1980s now see ANC membership as an insurance policy for the future.' Bantustan leaders were won over to the ANC camp to prevent them from subverting the struggle, and through the formation of Contralesa chiefs were harnessed for the progressive cause.[2] School principals, teachers and businessmen took control of many ANC branches, and youth activism was confined to the ANC Youth League. 'There are signs that the youth, after being hailed as 'shock troops of the revolution', now feels cast aside and marginalised' (ibid.:613).

These processes were very apparent in the Setlhare chiefdom. The intense conflict that prevailed between the Comrades and their opponents in the 1980s gave way to a situation characterised by pluralistic political structures.[3] Adults assumed control of local ANC branches, of ANC Women's Leagues and Civic Associations (civics), chiefship was reconstituted and the political influence of the Comrades diminished. In the new context that emerged, each of the political structures have special constituencies, but are aligned to the ANC. Though relations between these structures have been competitive and tense at times, there have also been moments of co-operation. Most villagers have not seen these structures as opposed, but have come to regard them as complementary resources which they can utilise situationally. A woman can, for instance appeal to ANC leaders for information about national politics, ask Comrades to apprehend stock thieves, inform the Civic that a tap is without water, divorce her husband at the chief's *kgoro* and ask the local headman to allocate her a new residential site. She would not perceive these actions as contradictory.[4]

With the unbanning of the ANC, the issue of witchcraft again posed a major political dilemma. Previously political activists could afford to take an unambiguous stance against witchcraft. As we have seen, the Comrades attacked witches in an attempt to root out evil and perform a valuable service. They

156

deemed chiefs, who took no action against witchcraft, and the police, who arrested only witch-hunters, to be 'enemies of the people'. Yet haphazard methods of witch-finding, and brutal forms of punishment, eroded their legitimacy among adults. Since 1990 the ANC national executive has strictly forbidden ANC members from acting against witches. Van Kessel (1993:611) writes, 'With hindsight, the leading activists saw the witch-burnings as a serious mistake, which diverted the struggle from the real enemy.' The ANC-led provincial government of the Northern Province has fiercely opposed witch-hunting. Seth Nthai, Member of the Executive Council (MEC) for Safety and Security, soon announced drastic steps 'to stamp out the barbaric killings' (*Weekend Argus*, 18/19 March 1995). Nevertheless, the victims of witchcraft have continued to seek the support of local ANC officials in having witches expelled.

An investigation of the politics of witch-hunting in the 1990s is a task of great analytical complexity. Earlier studies of central African witch-cleansing cults may well illuminate the aims of witch-hunters in the lowveld.[5] But the contention of these studies, that anti-witchcraft movements create cohesion within communities, fails to capture the contestation and terror which characterises witch-hunting in the lowveld.[6] Given the pluralistic political structures of Setlhare, it would also be inappropriate to view these witch-hunts as rituals that bolster and legitimate, or challenge and delegitimate, a single centre of power.[7] While this approach may well be appropriate to the earlier witch-hunts, the contemporary situation is more complex. The witch-hunts of the 1990s are multifaceted social dramas, bearing a variety of meanings for different constituencies, within which political actors compete for influence.[8]

Moreover, political actors are subject to different sets of constraints. Local ANC officials are caught in a Catch-22 situation. They fear that, like the chiefs who were compelled to implement the unpopular Suppression of Witchcraft Act, they could earn a reputation of siding with witches and lose support among villagers. But if they accede to the popular demand to act against witches, they risk being condemned by the ANC national executive to whom they are accountable.

This chapter outlines the political changes that occurred in Green Valley, and in the wider Setlhare area, after 1990. I then examine the processes of political contestation and risk as these were manifested in four episodes of witch-hunting: the Green Valley witch-hunts of December 1990 and August 1992, and the expulsion of witches from Authur's Seat in October 1993 and Rooiboklaagte in November 1994.[9] I argue that these witch-hunts dramatise growing schisms between Comrades and ANC officials. Comrades have been the most vociferous participants and have acted in consonance with popular interests, seeking to overcome their political marginality. ANC officials have, somewhat reluctantly, complied with the national executive's instructions to refrain from involving themselves or to protect the accused. By assuming greater responsibility for the managing witchcraft accusations, the Setlhare chief has claimed a legitimate role in the new political dispensation. My analysis of the Rooiboklaagte witch-hunt suggests that, in future, novel political alliances may well emerge between Comrades and chiefs.


TOWARDS PLURALISTIC POLITICAL STRUCTURES, 1990–1995

In 1990, ANC structures mushroomed throughout the lowveld. A regional ANC office was established in Nelspruit and a zonal office in Acornhoek. As soon as enough membership cards had been sold in a particular area, its residents could apply at the regional office to form an ANC branch and elect a committee of twelve members. In this manner ANC branches were constituted in the Mapalene, Tsakane, Kgapa Madi and Khiyelane sections of Green Valley. These local branches fall directly under the regional office in Nelspruit. (The zonal office merely supplies them with information.) Other ANC structures also emerged. Former members of the Brooklyn Youth Organisation set up six Youth League branches in Green Valley. Women, who were previously excluded from formal political participation, joined the Women's League in large numbers. By 1991, seven branches of the Women's League had registered. Mapalene, the largest branch, had 221 members and met every fortnight. Its leader told me they sought to 'uplift the lifestyle of women', assist rape victims and prevent the police from arresting women beer sellers.

At a meeting in Manyeleti, early in 1990, civics were launched in the lowveld. Two civics were founded in Green Valley: one in Mapalene, the other in Bodlaya Bongolo. Most Civic members are adults. (Two Hoedspruit employees, three housewives and three unemployed men were elected as the office bearers of the Mapalene civic. A night watchman was the chair of the Bodlaya Bongolo Civic and the additional members were pensioners, housewives and a teacher.) Many villagers equate Civics with the ANC, but civics claim that they represent a broader constituency and deal with 'community' rather than 'political' issues. Civics focused on the provision of water, electricity and roads. They have also mediated in disputes between villagers. Yet, poor attendance at meetings by office bearers has impeded the efficiency of the civics.

With the establishment of multiple ANC and civic structures, youth activism diminished. Since 1991, Comrades no longer held weekly meetings at the sports grounds. Green Valley's Youth Leagues also began to act independently of Brooklyn's Comrades. In 1992, local pupils effectively challenged the control that Brooklyn's youths exercised over the student representative council at the Maripe High School. During the 'back-to-school' campaign, the council established a disciplinary committee. The committee had to ensure that pupils attended classes, arrived on time and wore uniforms. When the committee lashed two boys with *sjamboks*, pupils from Green Valley pelted stones at them. Pupils forced Brooklyn's Comrades to disband the disciplinary committee and to resign from the council. They also decided that, in future, only the principal would administer corporal punishment.

The regional office and new ANC leadership curbed excessive militancy. After serving five years on Robben Island as a political prisoner, Elphas Mogale was released and became the most prominent ANC leader in Setlhare. An experienced and articulate activist, Mogale has consistently favoured negotiation over confrontation. ANC and Civic militants suffered a major setback in 1992. In response to complaints by workers at the Hoedspruit Air Force base that they were not provided with transport and were being underpaid, the Civic members asked the NEHAWU to intervene. NEHAWU failed to win any concessions and called on workers to stage a 'sit-in'. In response the Air Force summarily discharged about 600 strikers. Those who lost their work were furious with the Air Force, but many also believe that the civics and NEHAWU used the wrong strategy.

On many other occasions, the ANC and Civics successfully advanced popular causes. By regularly submitting memoranda to the police station they alerted government to peoples' need for water and electricity. Comrades installed new water pipes and apprehended stock thieves. In 1993, the ANC organised a consumer boycott to protest against the assassination of Chris Hani, the leader of the South African Communist Party. With the civics they also negotiated to ensure that as many local people as possible would be employed at the new Acornhoek shopping complex. In 1994, local branches ran a very successful campaign for the South African elections. They kept villagers informed of ANC policies, organised identity documents and transported voters to the polls. (See chapter four.) After the ANC's victory Elphas Mogale was appointed to the South African senate.[10]

Following Chief German's death in November 1989, chiefship was in a state of crisis. Three sections of Green Valley were without headmen and the boycott of local taxes was still stringently enforced. The royal family named Nkotobona, a former social work student, as German's successor. However, political activists described Nkotobona as 'illegitimate' and 'weak', and feared reactionary councillors might mislead him. On the evening of 16 May 1991 unidentified gunmen fired 26 rounds at the former leader of the Brooklyn Youth Organisation, wounding him in the arm. Comrades assumed that Nkotobona had sent the gunmen and burnt his home. They also attacked his councillor, alleged that he was a Sofasonke agent and kicked out eight of his teeth. Sittings of the chief's *kgoro* were suspended and a contingent of soldiers was sent to guard Nkotobona.

Different views of chiefship emerged within the ANC. Most of the Comrades, whom I interviewed, denounced chiefs as undemocratic. The Youth League of Budlaya Bongolo urged household heads not to make any donations for Nkotobona's installation as chief. However, senior ANC leaders, such as Elphas Mogale, argued that by opposing chiefs the ANC would alienate elders.[11] Mogale envisaged a local government comprising both elected officials and chiefs. He took the view that chiefs should serve as *ex officio* members and participate in decision-making, but should not vote. Civic leaders also expressed a desire to co-operate with the chief.

Late in 1991, there were signs that Nkotobona had gained acceptance among those who fell outside the ANC structures. For the first time in five years, Setlhare's residents paid stock taxes at the chief's offices. When it became apparent that the lowveld would experience drought, church leaders assembled at his home to pray for rain. In February 1992 Nkotobona joined the ZCC and was baptised in Moria. In this manner he secured support from a very large and well-organised constituency. ZCC members now openly supported the chief and conducted all night prayers at his home.

Nkotobona's appeal to tradition and his allegiance to the ZCC were evident during his installation as chief. At 7am on 21 March, the royal family gathered beside the graves of Maripe and Setlhare. After they had slaughtered a beast, Nkotobona's *rakgadi* introduced him to his ancestors. She loudly proclaimed, 'Here is the one who shall rule! He shall guard your throne! Hold him well!' She then gave him Setlhare's lion skin and walking stick. On 27 March, Nelson Ramodike and the Lebowa cabinet formally installed Nkotobona as chief. A leopard skin was draped over his shoulders, the Chiloane praise poem recited in his honour, and he was presented with a ZCC walking stick blessed by Bishop Lekganyane. Women's dance groups and ZCC brass bands gave impressive displays. Although the ritual was well attended, ANC members were conspicuous by their absence.

After Nkotobona's installation, the *mošate* was re-established as a political centre. Nkotobona appointed new headmen and made the ZCC leader's brother, a former trade unionist, his councillor. Again headmen began to speak at all funerals, to listen to disputes and to refer all problematic cases to the chief's *kgoro*. The chief's offices became the weekly venue for a clinic and the monthly venue for pension distributions. Local ANC branches also reluctantly began to accept Nkotobona. On 17 May 16 ANC delegates met with him to complain that the police disrupted their meetings. Nkotobona denied that he sent the police, and informed the delegates that as a member of Contralesa he had met Nelson Mandela and empathised with the ANC. The chief promised that his representatives would attend their meetings to protect them from police harassment. The delegates apologised for those who burnt his home, saying this had occurred due to an unfortunate misunderstanding.[12]

Despite continuing tensions between the ANC, Civics and the chief, there have been instances of mutual co-operation. At his *kgoro* the chief has fined people for moving into Green Valley without informing the Civics, and has asked ANC leaders to provide authoritative testimony. He has also invited Civic leaders to speak at the installation of new headmen. Headmen have even referred cases to the Comrades. In 1993 a woman reported her stepson to the headman of Phelindaba for insulting her. But he advised her and her husband to report the boy to the Comrades. The civics have, in turn, invited the chief's representatives to attend their meetings, and have referred divorce cases to the *kgoro*. In June 1993, Comrades collected donations of R2 from households in Tsakane, handed over the money to the chief and asked him to arrange for the

Lebowa Department of Works to sink new bore holes. One of the Comrades said they did this because, 'the chief has power with Lebowa'.

Such co-operation stems from the recognition that the chief also has the capacity to advance popular causes. For instance, in 1993 a crisis arose when Lebowa proposed to establish a township near Acornhoek. They first approached Moletele's chief, but he said they should rather build the township in Green Valley. Moletele's chief sent delegates at night to mobilise support for this idea in Green Valley. Villagers complained to Nkotobona that they would be unable to afford township rents. Nkotobona then called a *pitšo* and criticised the Moletele chief. He proposed that the township be built in Acornhoek. The ANC and Civics supported this proposal.

These political changes have had a fundamental impact on witch-hunting. During the 1980s the victims of witchcraft, and even those accused, could turn only to the Comrades for support. In the new political context they have wider options, for they may seek to mobilise the support of the various ANC structures, the civics or the chief. The witch-hunts of the 1990s are thus complex ritual dramas that reveal changing alliances and competition between political actors, as well as illuminating their capacity to influence the outcome of local events.

THE GREEN VALLEY WITCH-HUNTS, CHRISTMAS 1990

In the last week of July 1990 Green Valley was shaken by nine deaths. Six young men, including three members of a soccer team, died in car accidents. An elderly man committed suicide and people found a woman's corpse outside her home with stab-wounds. On Saturday 4 August, five funerals were conducted at Kgapa Madi. As mourners left the graveyard, a leader of the ANC Youth League announced, over a loud-hailer:

If five people die every week, more than twenty will die in a month. If things go on like this we'll all die. You yourself may be next. The priests should pray to God to stop these deaths. But if these deaths are man-made the ministers should pray that the witches must stop... The witches think they are safe because I told my Comrades to stop burning them.

Some mourners shouted: '*Tsamayang baloi!*' (Away witches!) Others quickly made their way home.

In December, the largest witch-hunt in Green Valley's history commenced. Over a period of two weeks 34 people were identified as witches in four village sections. The scale of the witch-hunt dramatically linked scattered individual concerns, co-ordinated the actions of local groupings and gave them a distinctive public flavour. Comrades were the most prominent witch-hunters, but many adults assisted them. A Youth League member told me that the 'community' (*badudi*) had called most of the meetings. 'They just needed the help of the Comrades – their sons.' But the witch-hunts soon became the subject of political contestation. Following instruction from the regional office, ANC leaders prevented Comrades from harming the accused.

(i) *Kgapa Madi*. Residents of Kgapa Madi, where one of the deceased soccer players lived, collected donations of R2 from households and consulted a witch-diviner in Giyani to determine the cause of his death. However, the diviner refused to assist them. Suspicions of witchcraft heightened when women found the corpse of a 14-year-old Comrade hanging from a tree by a noose made from his own shirtsleeves. On 20 December a meeting was held, R2,000 collected and delegates were sent to a witch-diviner in Mbuzini, near Swaziland. The diviner informed them that the young man had been bewitched by his own relatives, but said he required R2,000 more to sniff out the witches. A traffic official arranged for additional collections to be taken. The Comrades and other witch-hunters then took 30 suspects to Mbuzini in two small vans.

When the vans returned, two days later, residents were told that the witch-diviner had identified seven witches. Zacharias Ripanga, the soccer player's *malome*, was accused of laying *sefolo* on the road to make his car crash. Elia Lubisi, who was furious when the soccer player divorced her daughter, had assisted him. Godfrey Mnisi and his wife, Tinyiko, were said to have caused his stepson to commit suicide. (The young man was known to have been disre-spectful to his stepfather.) Three other Kgapa Madi residents (Jeremy Rabothata, Precious Siwele and Mafaneseni Malebe) were 'sniffed-out' as keepers of zombies. The Comrades instructed all the accused to climb on top of the vans, to confess to the crowd and to say who had helped them bewitch their victims. Some swore at the crowd. Others were more co-operative and identified six additional witches.

After the meeting, Comrades searched the homes of the accused for evidence of witchcraft. Youths dug beneath Jeremy's coal stove, where they imagined he kept zombies, but found only a piece of decayed meat. Jeremy's refusal to eat the meat indicated that it was really human flesh. Thereafter they proceeded to demolish the homes of witches and to evict them. Some fellow household members of the accused even supported these acts. Precious Siwele's husband asked the Comrades not to demolish his house, as it did not belong to his wife, and vowed to chase her away. They consequently demolished her room only. In other cases, kin desperately sought to protect accused persons and asked ANC leaders to halt the demolitions. ANC officials arrived from Nelspruit and persuaded Kgapa Madi's Comrades not to take any further action. With the exception of four witches, who fled to Phalaborwa, all the accused had returned to Kgapa Madi by January 1991.

(ii) *Khiyelane*. On 18 November a schoolboy died while he was being trans-ported to the Garankuwa hospital by ambulance. Previously he had suffered from headaches, vomited and lost his appetite. Because the boy had said that other people did not want him to eat, his parents suspected witchcraft. A month later a migrant returned to Khiyelane with his Christmas bonus, but drank at a local shebeen before going home. The next morning he was found in a fruit store, naked and confused. His salary, savings book and identity document were missing; he could not recall what had happened.

The migrants' son told fellow Comrades about the incident, and they met to discuss the problem of witchcraft. After intensive investigations, they called on Khiyelane residents to assemble on an open stretch of land. The Comrades had found a bottle of termite poison and brake fluid at the home of Njojo Makone and his wife, Kabi. They alleged that the couple had poisoned the migrant's beer and robbed him. Afisi Ralifeta was accused of bewitching the schoolboy, her husband's nephew. She had behaved very strangely at the night vigil and, reportedly, woke the boy's father after the funeral to tell him, 'Don't worry. Your son is well where he is.' At the meeting, Afisi's own son confirmed that she was a witch and said she had caused his father to desert their family. The Comrades also said Madira Mogakane kept a snake. In 1988, her grandson had killed another youngster in a fist fight and neighbours had alleged that she had doctored his fists with *sehlare*.

Armed policemen arrived while the witches were being *sjambokked* and dispersed the Comrades. Njojo and Kabi Makone sought refuge at a Civic leader's home, and Madira fled to Gazankulu. The next morning witch-hunters loaded Afisi's possessions on to a truck and removed her to Violetbank.

(iii) *Tsakane*. On Christmas day a five-year-old boy from Tsakane disappeared. All next day residents searched for the child, without success. Towards evening a meeting was called at the Tsakane sports ground and it was decided to consult the witch-diviner at Mbuzini. He would be asked to identify the witches who plagued Tsakane. Donations of R20 were collected from residents.

The boy's parents suspected that Stefina Morale, a shebeen operator, and her white boyfriend, had kidnapped the child. On Thursday 27 December, Stefina and many other suspects were forced to board the bus. When the bus returned at 9pm on Sunday, the delegates informed people of the diviner's revelations. They said that Stefina was a ritual murderer and that seven suspects practised witchcraft. Kgalipa Lubisi was presented as the leaders of Tsakane's witches. He allegedly rode a white horse at night and had killed his lover's husband. His accomplices were accused of keeping familiars, sending a *tokolotši* to rape young women, killing their relatives, disrupting meetings of the Civic and of stupefying the late Chief German by burying a baboon skull under his gate. The Comrades removed Tsakane's accused witches to the police station. Here they were detained until 7 January, when they were brought to the Green Valley sports ground together with the nine residents of the Mapalene village section who had also been accused of witchcraft (see Case 1.2).

On Monday 7 January, ANC officials asked the station commander to hand over Tsakane and Mapalene's witches to them, and assured him that they would protect the witches. They took the accused from the police station to the sports ground, where well over a thousand people had gathered to see the witches. Even senior members of the ANC regional office were present. Jaques Modipane, an activist from Brooklyn who was the MEC for Finance in the Mpumalanga provincial government, pleaded with the crowd not to harm the witches and instructed the accused to burn their *dihlare* in public. Although the suspected witches did this, the crowd became so antagonistic that the ANC officials had to transport them back to the police station by bus. Youths followed the bus on foot, gathered outside the gates and shouted for the witches to come out. Eventually a riot squad of the Lebowa police violently dispersed them.

To understand the political implications of these events, we need to scrutinise the different roles played by Comrades and ANC officials more closely. Through their participation in the witch-hunts, Comrades who were marginal within the ranks of the ANC demonstrated their political capacity to fellow villagers. By allocating blame for unmerited misfortune, publicising personal affairs and by seeking to expunge evil they claimed a legitimate role in creating a sphere of public morality. As junior members of the Youth League unknown outside Green Valley, individual Comrades were not constrained by the demands of the ANC national executive.

An analysis of the process by which witches were identified, and, indeed of the identity of the accused shows that the Comrades did not manipulate the witch-hunt in a cynical attempt to eliminate (or to intimidate) their political opponents. Unlike the witch-hunts of the 1980s, the procedures adopted by the Comrades to identify witches seemed convincing and fair. According to different observers Comrades did not secretly communicate with the witch-diviner.[13] He also sniffed out only a few of the many suspects they brought to him. The observers did not fear that the diviner had identified the wrong witches. They were more concerned that some witches may have washed themselves with powerful herbs to escape detection.

Standard ritual sequences were followed in Mbuzini to reveal the witches of Kgapa Madi, Tsakane and Mapalene. The procedures were modelled on earlier methods employed by witch-diviners. The visitors from Green Valley arrived in Mbuzini late at night or early in the morning. Before entering the witch-diviner's premises guards asked them to remove their shoes and headgear and to hand over any weapons, marking the premises as a sacred ritual space.[14] The visitors who arrived at night slept in corrugated-iron buildings.

In the morning men and women were ordered to stand, in sequence of age, in two parallel lines. The arrangement of people according to gender and age – the principal axes of social life – was important to the ritual. The lines create a 'moral map' and impose symbolic order on a world that has run amok.[15] In their lines the visitors walked to four small corrugated-iron rooms. Here the diviner met them, demanded the money they had collected and 'cooled' the notes with ash.[16] About ten *mathwasane* (apprentice diviners) then appeared, wearing costumes of baboon and antelope hide. They divided the visitors into four groups and led each to a particular room. Once inside, the *mathwasane* revealed what had happened in Green Valley and pointed out witches from among the suspects. They spoke cryptically, saying only that the witches were killers who kept familiars.

The suspects were then led to the centre of a clearing, and told to sit down with their legs outstretched. (The same position is assumed when diviners sniff out familiars from the bodies of their clients during the *ku femba* ritual.) Men sat in front, women in the middle and the Comrades stood at the rear. On the edges were statues of oxen and lions, in front a large fig tree with tatters of old clothes hanging from its branches. Here the *mathwasane* beat large cowhide drums to invoke the witch-diviner's spirits. When the witch-diviner arrived he appeared frightening and danced like a wild beast. He was adorned in leopard skins and ostrich feathers, and wore whistles and a dried vulture's heart around his neck. In his right hand was a switch made from wildebeest and hyena hair, in his left a spear and sjambok. The diviner's costume was integral to his performance. He invoked the attributes of predators and scavengers to combat the beastly power of witchcraft. The diviner was said to 'sniff' (*dupa*), rather than 'see' (*bona*), the witches. He derived this power from the hair of the wildebeest and hyena, and from the vulture's heart. The wildebeest migrates vast distances and is exposed to different kinds of *moya* ('wind', but also spirit).[17] Hyenas and vultures possess uncanny powers of detection. 'A vulture', I was told, 'can come all the way from Skukuza to devour a carcass in Green Valley.'

The diviner bypassed those who were innocent, but beat those who were guilty of witchcraft at the back of the neck with a switch. (Hereby he confirmed the *matwasane*'s revelations.) The diviner then dragged all the witches, whom he had identified in this manner, toward the fig tree by their feet. Here he revealed their crimes and commanded them to confess. Observers described the confessions as the most convincing part of the witch-finding ordeal. The diviner treated the witches from Kgapa Madi and Tsakane who confessed as harshly as those who did not. However, he washed the six of the 15 witches from Mapalene who confessed with *dihlare* and absolved them from any further blame.

The diviner then proceeded to kill the witches symbolically. He beat them behind the neck with a switch, cut crosses into their hair, commanded them to undress and smeared their bodies with black oil. By using the switch in this manner, the diviner emulated witches who use hyena tails to put their victims to sleep.[18] Lowvelders consider the back of the neck as the body's most vulnerable part and associate it with death. Oxen are stabbed in the back of the neck when slaughtered. Moreover, it is seen as an omen of mourning to place one's hand behind the neck when seated. The haircut is an essential part of funeral rites. At night close relatives of the deceased shave the corpse's hair and place this in the coffin.[19] Corpses are buried naked and wrapped only in white linen.[20] By smearing the witches with black oil, the diviner tainted them with the colour of decay and death.[21] Finally, he *sjambokked* the witches and chased them back to the bus.

The characteristics of the accused conformed to local stereotypes of witches (see Appendix F). The accused were generally elderly and of an insecure occupational status. Only Nelson Silinda (a road construction worker) and Tinyiku Mabuza (a domestic) were regular wage earners. The others were jobless, received pensions, or engaged in casual labour such as building, carpentry, fruit-selling and shebeen organisation. Like the elderly, the under- and unemployed are seen to be envious and to deviate from ideal model of adulthood, which requires financial independence. Kin and neighbours had long suspected many of the accused of practising witchcraft. The family members of some had died shortly before the witch-hunts. Sindondana Nkwalini resided in Kgapa Madi, but had remarried and moved to Tsakane after the death of his wife and daughter. Six of the 32 accused were *dingaka*. This concurs with the well-established perception that *dingaka* are likely to practise witchcraft.

Comrades condemned the accused for transgressing general moral percepts, rather than for being political enemies. The accused had different political affiliations. Aaron Mashile was a headman, and Stefina Morale a leader of the ANC Women's League and Civic. Sipho Mashego, a former chiefly councillor, was accused of bewitching the late Chief German. Despite the insistence of informants that one cannot infer a witch's identity from observed behaviour, according to gossip many of the accused had behaved in anti-social ways. Some were described as drunkards who used vulgar language, others as idle gossips. Sarafina Maatsie had once threatened other fruit sellers that she would call her son (a policeman) to arrest them. The police had previously arrested Njojo and Kabi Makone on charges of stock theft. Adeline Moleme had insulted a school principal and called his teachers *dagga* (cannabis) smokers. Isiah Baloyi had been expelled from an Apostolic church, Kgalipa Lubisi was a well-known adulterer and four of the accused worked as shebeen operators.

ANC and Civic leaders had much greater public visibility than the Comrades and their performance was judged not only by villagers, but also by the regional office. Their participation in the witch-hunts therefore entailed considerable risks. ANC officials accordingly sought to negotiate a balance between the conflicting demands of their constituents and those of their political superiors. Like the Comrades, they desired that witchcraft should be brought to an end. A leader of the Women's League said, on radio, that she did not believe in witches. But she later told me that this statement did not reflect her real views. 'I only said that to prevent havoc.' For this reason the ANC and civic leaders only partially complied with the directives of their political superiors. They did not halt the witch-hunts, nor prevent Comrades from visiting the witch-diviner, but rather sought to minimise the terror of witch-hunting. The leaders could not countenance the killing or expulsion of witches. A prominent ANC branch member told me that such actions would trigger harsh police retaliation, and anger the ANC's national executive. Local ANC leaders perceived the exposure of witches, the punitive ordeals of the diviner and the burning of *dihlare* as sufficient. For them Comrades could exercise a legitimate role in the politics of public morality only under adult control. Unchecked by the ANC, the youth would certainly have expelled the witches, allowing no hope of return.

Most villagers supported the witch-hunt and were glad that there were no killings. Yet many criticised the local ANC leadership for aligning themselves with the police. A young teacher, who 'lost all confidence in the ANC', argued that they protected the witches only because Stefina Morale and her son were ANC members. Some Comrades described the ANC as misguided and said that mild forms of punishment would not deter born witches.

## THE EXPULSION OF MALULEKE, AUGUST 1992

Chief Nkotobona played no role during the 1990 witch-hunts. Yet his absence did not, in any way, undermine the ritual's prestige (see Perry and Perry, 1991). It was rather a sign of the crisis in chiefship at the time. Neither the victims of witchcraft, nor those accused, bothered to seek the assistance of the newly-appointed chief. He simply had too little political clout.

This situation changed after Nkotobona forged an alliance with the ZCC and was formally installed as chief. When sittings of the chief's *kgoro* recommenced, some of the first cases it heard arose from the witch-hunts of 1990. On 17 July 1992, Lerato Matlala, an elderly woman, reported Tintswalo Mhawule to the *kgoro* for having assaulted her. The *kgoro* heard that, while the two women were drinking beer, Lerato had called Tintswalo a witch. Tintswalo was furious and dragged Lerato to the police station, but the police merely laughed at the drunk women. Men of the *kgoro* blamed both women. They reprimanded Tintswalo for having beaten Lerato, but the prosecutor also said Lerato had acted irresponsibly. 'The chief's heart bleeds because you speak of witchcraft. You're creating a fire that will take people's lives.' No fines were imposed.

From 1992 on, it became common for people accused of witchcraft to report their accusers to headmen or the chief. As many as ten of the 66 recorded disputes brought before the *kgoro* between 1992 and 1994 concerned witchcraft. The plaintiffs sought to exploit the chief's firm stance against witchcraft accusations. For example, in February 1993, Dennis Mokanatla testified that Lethabo Motsoane had despatched relatives to his home one evening. Armed with axes, they accused him of witchcraft and threatened to kill him. Lethabo confessed that she had sent her relatives, but said she had done so with good reason. In 1992, two of her sons had died and during the period of mourning Dennis had told her brother that the boys had deserved to die because they were hooligans. The chief fined Lethabo R300 for character denigration.

Following the 1990 witch-hunts, local ANC leaders convened a series of meetings to persuade ANC supporters and the Comrades to accept those accused of witchcraft back into Green Valley. Subsequently ANC branches and the Civics became extremely reluctant to mediate in disputes concerning witchcraft. When this was unavoidable they, like the chief, tended to support the accused. After a woman became critically ill during childbirth, her husband accused their next-door neighbour, Zandile Buthelezi, of having thrown *sehlare* into their house. He threatened the old woman that he would behead her with an axe. Zandile resorted to the civic, because she still owed the *kgoro* money. The Civic merely told the young man to calm down.

The Civics and ANC branches did not oppose the chief's involvement in such disputes, observing that there was a historical precedent for chiefs to manage witchcraft accusations. Moreover, the officials were relieved that they did not have to side with the accused, at the cost of some popularity. It therefore suited them to transfer the responsibility for action to the chief.

Chief Nkotobona exploited the political space that he was granted and through his involvement in the management of witchcraft accusations, he claimed a legitimate role in the changing political situation. Indeed, there were signs that, in certain instances, the chief was prepared to uphold the interests of the accusers. Although Granny Chuene accused her daughter-in-law, Lita, of witchcraft, men of the *kgoro* fined Lita. They did so because Lita was cheeky and insulted her mother-in-law. The most significant of these interventions was in August 1992, when Chief Nkotobona complied with the popular demand of Green Valley residents to remove Elias Maluleke and his stepson from Green Valley.

In 1988, Elias Maluleke moved from Arthur's Seat and settled in the Mapalene section of Green Valley. Here he took up residence with a divorcee, who had four children from her previous marriage, and secured employment as a guard of the late Chief German Sentotane. Though Elias was not a regular churchgoer, he said the opening and closing prayers at the chief's *kgoro*.

Green Valley's residents soon became suspicious of Elias. They did not know why he had moved from Arthur's Seat, and found it curious that Elias, despite his Tsonga surname, could not understand a word of the language. Indeed, some speculated that Elias might have changed his name to disguise the crimes he had committed elsewhere. Others commented on the strangeness of his garden. There was a water hole that reportedly sheltered a large toad, tortoise and snake. They also criticised Elias for having planted *lešako* reeds, since the presence of wet *lešako* in any village is believed to cause drought.

However, it was the behaviour of Elias' eleven-year-old stepson, Daniel, that provoked most concern. Teachers told me Daniel was absent-minded and frequently dodged classes. Once a teacher found him sitting by himself underneath a tree, and asked him why he did not attend class. Daniel merely replied, 'I'm scared of the snake.' At other times Daniel was even found wandering about in adjacent villages. Eventually the headmaster asked Elias to take Daniel to a psychologist. Elias did not comply, and Daniel became a primary school dropout.

Josh Shubane, another guard of the chief, first accused Elias of witchcraft. But since Josh drank heavily, nobody took him seriously. However, during the witch-hunt of December 1990, Elias was one of the eight Mapalene residents identified as witches. The witch-diviner proclaimed that Elias kept zombies and had used baboons and a snake to bewitch his neighbours. Henceforth Elias became known as *Legotlo* (rat). (A rat, I was told, is harmless by day, but perpetrates evil at night.) Children were now scared to walk past his home.

At 5am on 19 August 1992, when Grace Khoza left her home to fetch water, she saw Daniel in her backyard. He was naked and had defecated in her kitchen. Grace rushed to the ANC Women's League to complain that Elias had sent his stepson to steal her maize. On their advice she phoned the police. At 7 am Elias arrived at her home, dressed Daniel and gave him herbs to drink. Minutes later the police questioned Grace, Elias and Daniel. As the police left, women pleaded with them to evict Elias. That afternoon the ANC Women's League discussed the situation with the chief. He promised that he would consult his councillors, but urged the women meanwhile not to harass Elias and Daniel. That evening an apostolic prophet and two young men confronted Elias' wife, demanded to know his whereabouts and assaulted her. The police promptly arrested the three men.

Two days later, at 4am, Lebo Shai's children woke her. They told Lebo they had felt something tugging at their blankets. As Lebo lit a candle in their room she saw Daniel's face. Again Daniel was naked and had defecated behind the door. Lebo then locked Daniel in the room, blew a whistle and called her neighbours. She told the leader of the local ANC Women's League that she had found a 'horrible witch' in her home. The two women then phoned the police. When the commanding officer of the Acornhoek police station arrived, just after sunrise, Lebo relayed what had transpired and said Daniel had taken clothes, money and a bus ticket from her wardrobe. The officer inspected the room, spoke to Daniel and then left saying, 'I'll ask the chief to evict Maluleke.' By 10 am a very !arge crowd had assembled at Lebo's home to inquire about the strange events.

Later the police officer informed the chief that Elias' safety could no longer be guaranteed, and suggested that he be removed to a patch of land, behind the police station, where many others who had been evicted on account of witchcraft were accommodated. That afternoon the Maluleke household and their belongings were transported by truck to the police station. A large group of women followed the truck chanting:

*Maluleke o apara jeans! Maluleke ga a apole overall bošego le mosegare!'*
['Maluleke wears jeans! Maluleke does not take off his overall night and day!']

The words insinuate that Elias hid witchcraft substances in his overalls. At the station the women demanded the release of the three men, who had assaulted Mrs Maluleke.

Informants were unanimous that Elias had sent his stepson to steal people's possessions at night. Elias' next-door neighbour told me that he had noticed a steering wheel and chicken-feathers in Elias' yard. He said Elias washed the children with *sehlare* (medicine), tied feathers around their waists and flew with them on the steering wheel. On 19 August, he alleged, Daniel was sent to steal maize meal from Grace's home to feed his stepfather's zombies. On 21 August, he said, the child lost his feathers in flight and fell near Lebo's house.

THE NEW LINES WITCH-HUNT, OCTOBER 1993

In 1993 a crisis arose in New Lines, a section of the village Arthur's Seat. Early in October, two brothers died from fever. Comrades collected R35 from each household to consult the witch-diviner in Mbuzini. Their departure was delayed, however, by the occurrence of further deaths. An elderly man died from unknown causes and a young boy drowned. People found the boy with only his feet in the river and thought a *mamlambo* had killed him. On Friday 22 October, residents of New Lines met to finalise the arrangements for their journey.

Again local ANC leaders transferred the responsibility for action to Chief Nkotobona. First, Comrades from Brooklyn disrupted the meeting at New Lines and proclaimed that the ANC had banned all witch-hunts. Soon after the Comrades from Brooklyn departed, Chief Nkotobona arrived in New Lines with members of the Lebowa police. Those assembled asked the chief to issue them with a letter of consent to visit the witch-diviner. But the chief said that he was not allowed to issue such a letter, and demanded that New Lines' residents hand over the money that they had collected to consult the witch-diviner. The residents refused and insisted that their journey would proceed as planned – even without the letter.

That evening Comrades of New Lines forced about 50 elders, whom they suspected of witchcraft, to board the bus for Mbuzini. Only seven Comrades accompanied the suspects on the bus. The driver first stopped at the home of a ZCC Reverend and asked him to bless the journey. The Reverend prayed for everyone and sprinkled holy water on the bus. They arrived in Mbuzini at 8 am

Though the witch-diviner and *matwasane* followed roughly the same procedures as they had during Green Valley's witch-hunts, their performance was less convincing. Impartial observers questioned the authenticity of their revelations.[22] First only the Comrades alighted to meet the diviner. During this time they, presumably, conferred with him and handed him a list of those whom they wanted him to point out. After the suspects formed two lines the diviner demanded R5,000. The Comrades paid only R3,000, but he accepted this amount. Observers found his generosity very peculiar. One informant speculated that the Comrades had visited the diviner on an earlier occasion and paid him a deposit of R2,000. 'Why did he not ask them to turn back?'[23]

The *mathwasane* then divided the visitors into four groups and led each into a zinc room. Here they described, in great detail, the deaths that occurred in New Lines and how the people were bewitched. They also pointed out the culprits from among the suspects. One informant was impressed by their revelations, and recalled all the incidents they spoke of. She later learnt that the *mathwasane* in the other rooms said exactly the same. Sceptics accounted for the congruence between the stories of different *mathwasane* by saying that the Comrades informed them what happened. There were further discrepancies at the clearing. The *mathwasane* asked the accused for their names, recorded these in a booklet and gave the booklet to the diviner. Sceptics also observed foul play when the diviner sniffed the witches. A young man, reportedly, asked him, 'What about the one who killed my mother?' He then asked the young man to fetch the culprit from among the suspects and also dragged her towards the fig tree.

Underneath the tree the diviner accused eight people of witchcraft – seven men and one woman (see Appendix G). He alleged that Itumeleng Magogodi sent familiars to kill his son-in-law, and accused Jan Maoko of having bewitched his daughter-in-law. Joseph Moeketsi, an Apostolic priest, allegedly kept a *mamlambo* near the river. It assumed the form of a person, killed two boys and sucked their blood. Kgomotso Chiloane sent rats and cockroaches to steal maize meal from his neighbours. Piet Nkadimeng kept a cat skin in a trunk and revived the cat at night to guard his home. Boy Dube, an initiation master, struck his mother's house with lightning. Thato Mohlala was accused of having bewitched his *malome*'s family and Prudence Maluleke of killing her affines.

Contrary to the normal procedure, those accused were given no opportunity to defend themselves, or to confess. They protested, but the diviner told them to keep quiet and proceeded to punish them. One informant only seemed to be certain that all the accused were guilty, and she told me that she believed the confessions were unnecessary. 'Witches are like thieves. They only agree when they are caught in the act.' She also mentioned that the witches ran incredibly fast after the diviner *sjambokked* them – some elders even outran the middle-aged ones. She accounted for this anomaly by suggesting they ran with the speed of their familiars.

Those accused were not allowed to clothe themselves during the return journey. (Thato Mohlala was completely naked, Joseph Moeketsi wore only a jacket and Jan Maoko a pair of trousers.) When the driver stopped to change a tyre at Malelane, Prudence Maluleke's affines assaulted her, but she escaped and fled into town. The driver refused to drive any further if anyone else was harmed. Only with great difficulty did the Comrades regain control. They apprehended Prudence in town, moved the accused to the back of the bus and formed a protective barrier between them and the other passengers.

The driver arrived in Setlhare at 1 am on Sunday. Fearing that the witches would be killed, he drove straight to Chief Nkotobona's residence. For the remainder of the night people slept in the bus. After sunrise Chief Nkotobona and the police escorted the bus to a primary school in New Lines. Here a large crowd gathered to see the witches. The police and local ANC leaders first made them sit in a semi-circle and then called on the witches to alight. An ANC leader asked the crowd what should be done. They demanded the immediate eviction of all witches from New Lines. The police then escorted all of the accused to the police station and collected their possessions in New Lines. They stayed at the police station for four days, but then started erecting shanties behind the police station, where others who had been evicted from the villages for witchcraft resided.

Members of the households of the accused were outraged by what had happened. Jan Maoko's grandson, a soldier, attended the witch-finding ritual in Mbuzini and when Jan was pointed out as a witch, he protested vehemently. He fetched Jan from the police station and subsequently protected him in New Lines.

The experiences of Prudence Maluleke, who sought the assistance of her family and Arthur Seat's headman, reveals much of the political dynamics of the witch-hunt. It thus merits more detailed consideration.

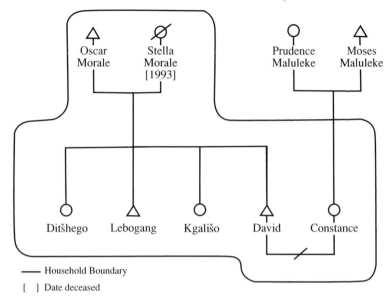

Figure 8.1 The Domestic Situation of Prudence Maluleke

The accusation against Prudence stemmed from tensions that arose after her daughter, Constance, married David Morale. Shortly after her marriage, Constance told neighbours that her sisters-in-law (Ditšhego and Kgališo) had had abortions. When Constance's in-laws learnt of her gossip, they turned against her. Once Lebogang even claimed that Constance had poisoned their maize meal. The situation became intolerable. Eventually the Morale and Maluleke families met, resolved their differences and were reconciled, but the peace proved to be fragile. After Stella Morale's death, early in 1993, Constance was again suspected of witchcraft and returned to her parental household under duress. By most accounts David's family actively collaborated with the Comrades and encouraged the witch-diviner to point out Prudence as one of the witches. In Mbuzini the diviner said that Prudence had given Constance poison and told her to kill Stella. Prudence's brothers were convinced that she was not guilty, fetched her from the police station and brought her home. In New Lines they reported the Morale family to the headman for having wrongfully accused Prudence of witchcraft.

After prolonged negotiations, both families agreed to settle the dispute by consulting a second witch-diviner in the north. For this, the headman gained the chief's permission. The chief's councillor took Prudence, a guard and representatives of the headman and of both families to the north in his van. Eventually the party located an appropriate witch-diviner at Minga. The diviner said he could see, from his bones, that an old woman had recently passed away.

Before her death she was in great pain, but she was not bewitched. She died from *sesepedi* ('boils') which are natural. The representatives of the Morale family now asked him, explicitly, whether there was a witch among the visitors. The diviner again threw his bones, touched Prudence on the shoulder and said, 'You suspect this person! You also think her daughter is a witch! But I say she is not!' All the representatives agreed that the diviner had demonstrated his competence. Upon their return, the headman held a public meeting in New Lines and declared that Prudence had been found not guilty. Oscar Morale commented, 'We no longer trust anybody. The witch-diviners say this and that. Today she is a witch. Tomorrow she is not. One cannot know who the witch is.'

On 5 October, Prudence laid a charge against the Morale family at Chief Nkotobona's *kgoro*. Oscar Morale testified that they had indeed 'put the flag' on Prudence (*go hlomela sefoka*, to accuse her of witchcraft). The headman of New Lines said he had given the families permission to consult a diviner and that the diviner had found Prudence not guilty. A leader of New Lines' Comrades also gave evidence. He agreed that the diviner had absolved Prudence, but remarked that he would not condone any fines imposed by the chief. The prosecutor criticised the Comrade leader for having changed his statement and reprimanded another Comrade for taking notes in the *kgoro*. Chief Nkotobona fined the Morale family R4,000. (This was to cover fees of the *kgoro*, expenses incurred during the journey and compensation for Prudence.) The chief also asked the headman to hold a meeting in New Lines and to instruct the residents to accept Prudence back into the village. The headman expressed a fear that he might be killed at the meeting, and the chief promised that he would deal with this sensitive issue himself.

Pandemonium erupted outside the *kgoro*. A Comrade shouted, 'This is no court. This is shit! It must be closed!' He also said that he did not want to see Prudence in New Lines. David Morale shouted that Prudence might be innocent, but that his wife, Constance, definitely practised witchcraft. Prudence's brothers threatened to beat David. Prudence eventually returned to her home in New Lines, but, as far as I could ascertain, the Morale family had not paid the fine.

In November I interviewed Boy Dube and Thabo Mohlala in the witches' location. They dismissed the witch-diviner of Mbuzini as a fraud, saying he was not the diviner who had officiated during the 1990 witch-hunts, but his son. In 1991 people who were cheated by the old diviner killed him. The men claimed the Comrades had victimised them. Boy said that his nephew had engineered the accusation against him. Thabo blamed his *malome*. Some time ago, he had built his *malome* a five-roomed house, but his *malome* did not pay him. All desperately wished to return to New Lines, and hoped that Prudence had set a precedent for this, but they were unsure whether their safety could be guaranteed. 'The chief must assist us. He must show his power.'

During the witch-hunt of New Lines local Comrades had again intervened decisively on the behalf of the assumed victims of witchcraft, but even when viewed in the most favourable light, the legitimacy of their intervention was

questionable. Their success was undermined by the perception that irregulari-
ties had occurred during the witch-finding ritual. The Comrades of New Lines
had also acted without the support of other ANC-aligned structures. In fact,
Brooklyn's Comrades had opposed their visit to the witch-diviner. A striking
aspect of the witch-hunt was the very low profile that ANC and Civic leaders
maintained throughout the unfolding of the events. They distanced themselves
from the victims, and from those accused of witchcraft. Only after the witches
were pointed out did an ANC leader address residents of New Lines, but he did
so in the company of police officers and the chief. By intervening on behalf of
the accused, the Setlhare chief and his headmen played a role comparable to
that of ANC officials during the Green Valley witch-hunts of 1990. The chief
protected the accused from harm, the headman of New Lines subverted the
authority of the Comrades by staging a convincing counter-ritual to prove
Prudence's innocence, and the chief's councillors belittled the Comrades who
gave evidence at the *kgoro*. The Setlhare local government exploited divisions
among the ANC structures, stood up to the Comrades and demonstrated that,
in certain contexts, those accused of witchcraft and their kin might constitute a
constituency of some political significance.

As the South African elections of April 1994 approached, Chief Nkotobona
began to play a more active part in the management of witchcraft accusations,
and ANC and civic officials referred more cases to the chief and his headman.
No longer did the chief limit himself to imposing fines on the accusers. As in
the witch-hunt of New Lines, the chief and headmen sometimes sought to
resolve disputes about witchcraft by referring the parties concerned to witch-
diviners, seeking to demonstrate that they were not indifferent to the problem
of witchcraft.

## THE ROOIBOKLAAGTE WITCH-HUNT, NOVEMBER 1994

Shortly after the ANC's victory in the South African elections of 1994, Seth
Nthai, the newly appointed MEC for Safety and Security in the Northern
Province, addressed a public gathering at Thulamahashe. He said that he was
horrified by witch-killings and he strongly condemned witch-hunting. Nthai
called on the Acornhoek police to arrest anybody who accused others of
witchcraft. He also issued a firm warning. Should the Acornhoek police fail in
their duty, he would take disciplinary measures and send police from elsewhere
to arrest the witch-hunters. Those who attended the meeting gained the
impression that the new government would be as unsympathetic to the victims
of witchcraft as the previous regime had been. In fact, Nthai suggested that the
ANC would compel the police to oppose witch-hunting even more fiercely than
in the past.

Local events reinforced this perception. In January 1994, I attended the
funeral of Caroline Mloto, a young woman from Phelindaba. A sad and solemn
atmosphere prevailed. Caroline was one of only four Maripe High School

students who had recently attained a university exemption in her matric exams. At the time of her death she was pregnant and complained of painful legs. At the funeral I heard mourners saying Caroline had died from *sefolane*. Some even whispered the name of the woman whom they suspected of witchcraft. Contrary to the normal procedure, the headman gave a leader of Phelindaba's Comrades a chance to speak at the graveside. In a determined voice, he said:

Today I speak on behalf of the ANC Youth League. Three youngsters died in Phelindaba during 1993. Now it is 1994 and we are again burying a youngster. Each time there is death in Phelindaba it is the death of a youngster. This is disheartening. Do you remember 1986? Then we were against such things and our parents were even against us. They said we were not mature enough to speak of witches and chased us from our homes. Then we stayed in the bushes. Today we are again prepared to live in the bushes and eat wild fruit and berries. Everyone should listen to what we say. We cannot tolerate the death of youngsters. Blessed are those whose hands are clean! Woe to those whose hands are stained with blood!

The chief's councillor then addressed the mourners. He voiced similar sentiments: 'The death of youngsters makes me feel aggrieved. Why do youngsters die so often? Here we elders stand. We do not die. The former speaker is correct. Take heed. Today I see the smoke of a glowing log.'[24] The next Saturday three more people were buried in the Phelindaba graveyard – an adult woman, a boy and a toddler. On the Sunday, the Comrades called a meeting and demanded that delegates be sent to a witch-diviner. However, Elphas Mogale persuaded the youth that the ANC could not afford to get involved in witch-hunting. This episode conveyed the impression that, on the issue of witchcraft, the position of the Comrades may well diverge more sharply from that of senior ANC officials than from the chief, but it remained uncertain whether the Comrades would actually collaborate with the chief to expel witches.

That question was answered in Rooiboklaagte, where a spate of misfortunes had occurred in 1993. A mother and her baby died tragically in a motor car accident, and two boys drowned. In response to these deaths, villagers established a witch-hunt committee, to which they elected several Comrades and a few adults. The committee collected R10 from each household and sent delegates to a witch-diviner in Phunda Malia. Two days later the delegates returned, asked for more money and again left for Phunda Malia. The diviner did not identify any witches, but gave them *šita baloyi*, a type of *sehlare* which would 'eat' anyone who attempted witchcraft. After the village was fortified with the anti-witchcraft serum, there were no more tragic deaths for a while.

Late in 1994 I was told, 'Things went from bad to worse.' A nine-year-old boy drowned and thieves shot two adult villagers. On 15 December, a single lightning bolt struck five homes in the most peculiar manner. It injured a teenager in the first home, injured a toddler in the second, struck a young man in the third and smashed down the walls of the last two homes. The next day the witch-hunt committee reported the incident to Rooiboklaagte's headman. Although he was infirm and very ill at the time, the headman convened a meeting to discuss the lightning. People requested him to issue them with a letter of consent to visit a witch-diviner. The headman replied that he could write a letter only when two families accused each other of witchcraft – not when the whole community was involved. This, he said, could lead to killings. Yet he suggested that people should choose two delegates to speak to Chief Nkotobona. While attending the *kgoro* on 17 December, I saw the chief speaking to the headman and the delegates. I could not hear what they said, but saw that the young men were dissatisfied when they left. Apparently the chief also refused to write a letter.

On 18 December the delegates reported back to the villagers. People complained that the anti-witchcraft serum was no longer effective and enquired whether the committee had spent all the money previously donated. The committee reported that they still had a bank balance of R2,000. Once the financial matters were sorted out, representatives were elected to return to Phunda Malia. In Phunda Malia the witch-diviner recalled having told them, in 1993, that he would not charge them if they still encountered problems and returned to him within three months. But the time had expired. He also demanded a letter from the chief. The delegates then consulted another diviner in Tzaneen. For only R800 he revealed that their headman was ill, lightning had struck and that four witches were plaguing the village. He cryptically described their features and said one man used a walking stick.

In Rooiboklaagte the delegates relayed, as precisely as they could, what the diviner had told them. After prolonged discussions people decided that Lucky Mohulane, Lot Mandlazi, Izaac Ngwenyama and Saul Mathonzi – all local men previously suspected of witchcraft – matched the profiles of the witches he described. Lucky was an obvious choice. When his girlfriend terminated their love affair in 1976, he told her, '*Ke tla go bona* [I'll see you].' She died the following month. In 1993, when Lucky's nephew was crippled by an accident, Lucky confessed to having purchased a root from a *ngaka moloi*. At a *dipheko* ritual he discarded the root and slaughtered a cow and four chickens for family members. In December 1994, the lightning struck Lucky's brother's home and Lucky was evasive when his brother called him. Lot had been expelled from Craigieburn for practising witchcraft and came to live in Rooiboklaagte during 1989. When Lot became an eminent Apostolic healer, rumours emerged that he bewitched people so he could cure them. After the lightning struck, people saw a trail of maize meal running from the home of a businessman to Lot's place. Some thought Lot used the lightning to steal his maize meal. Lot also limped, matching the diviner's description. Izaac and Saul had very unfavourable reputations. While Izaac resided in Green Valley he allegedly poisoned his mother because she quarrelled with his wife. Neighbours believed Izaac kept zombies. This was because he owned several well-kept gardens, but nobody was ever seen to weed these. Moreover, Izaac had told women to bring him all the wood- beetles they could find. (According to local belief *sefolane* is manufactured from these beetles.) Saul, a *ngaka*, was also suspected of keeping zombies. Youngsters forcefully apprehended the four men, brought them to the meeting and asked them to confess. The men denied being witches and said any witch-diviner would confirm this.

The next day the committee took the four men to chief Nkotobona. When they announced that they intended to revisit the witch-diviner, the chief agreed to send along his guard to see that no harm was done. The diviner proclaimed all four men guilty. He revealed that Lucky kept a *tokolotši*, Lot sent lightning and that Izaac and Saul kept zombies. The diviner also said there were other witches in Rooiboklaagte – a man and several women. One of these women allegedly kept a *tokolotši* and tied a horn around her waist to rape other women. At a feedback meeting the committee relayed what the diviner had said. When the witches were asked to confess, only Lucky stood and remarked, 'I have been sniffed, but what about the women?' Fierce arguments then erupted and during the ensuing confusion the accused fled from the meeting. With his fellow household members, Saul moved to a village adjacent to the Kruger National Park.

Although Rooiboklaagte's headman was very ill by then, he tried to protect the accused and announced that he would fine anyone R4,000 who even spoke of witchcraft. On 30 December, the headman passed away. The very next evening Comrades went to the homes of the accused and instructed them to move. At Lot's home they encountered fierce resistance. Betty Mashiloane, who was visiting Lot at the time, pointed a revolver at the Comrades and said, 'Lot is not a witch! You must go!' On Sunday 1 January 1995, the committee, nonetheless, removed the accused to the police station. They carried Lot, a cripple, all the way. The police pitched tents on the lawn at the station to accommodate the men. That afternoon the police arrested four witch-hunters and locked them up in the cells. (One of those arrested was the headman's son.)

Most villagers supported the evictions and were infuriated by the arrests of the witch-hunters. On 2 January, approximately 200 protesters marched from Rooiboklaagte to the police station. Here they sang freedom songs and demanded that the men be released. However, since it was a public holiday, the station commander was not present. On 4 January the protesters reassembled. This time the station commander negotiated with their leaders. He insisted that the magistrate would only release the men if R300 was paid for each in bail money. For this purpose, the witch-hunt committee drew some of their savings from the bank and collected donations of R5 among protesters. At 1pm they paid the station commander R1,200. At 7 pm the men were released and a jubilant crowd returned to Rooiboklaagte.

Villagers still feared that there were witches in Rooiboklaagte. Betty Mashiloane, who had threatened the Comrades with a revolver, was widely suspected of being the woman who kept a *tokolotši*. Stories circulated that, long ago, she had bewitched her brother after he inherited all the cattle of their parents. As a woman minister, Betty had built an Apostolic church by herself. She had also never given birth. Informants claimed this was because her *tokolotši* ate the foetuses of her children. It was also rumoured that Maphela Phako, an Apostolic prophet, dispensed *dihlare* that turned into snakes and caused men to lose their work. Tsakane Chiloane reportedly used a monkey to kill her husband, her daughter-in-law and her newly born triplets. Cinderella Shupe and Lucas Masilela were said to be the other witches. Cinderella was a *ngaka*, who had arrived in Rooiboklaagte four months previously, whereas Lucas reportedly bewitched his girlfriend's child after she had left him for another man.

On 5 January, the committee convened another meeting and decided to transport Betty and Lucas to the police station. However, when four men arrived with the witches in a small van, they too were arrested. (One of them was Chief Nkotobona's guard.) Angered by the arrests, the committee turned to the local civic and the ANC's Reconstruction and Development Programme (RDP) Forum for assistance. Both structures refused to help. A member of the RDP Forum asked me, 'How can we help them if we know nothing of their constitution?' Again the committee collected donations of R5 from households, and a businessman donated R500 to meet the shortfall. When the committee paid bail for the four men, they reportedly told the station commander, 'We did not hurt the witches and cried to the government for help. But you arrest our people.' The station commander summoned Chief Nkotobona to the police station to discuss the situation, but in protest against the arrest of his guard, the chief refused to attend the meeting.[25]

With the exception of Lot, who relocated to White River, and Cinderella, who fled to Green Valley, all the accused returned to Rooiboklaagte. Police warned that anyone who troubled the witches would be arrested. Izaac's wife later complained to the civic that Comrades sang songs in the streets at night and threatened some of the accused. At her request, the civic met with the accused and the witch-hunt committee. Izaac's wife said she could not identify the Comrades, who forced open her door, because they turned their backs toward her. The Civic asked the accused and the committee members to forgive one another.

The Rooiboklaagte witch-hunt was much more widely supported than the witch-hunt of New Lines. The biographies of the accused conformed to the stereotypical characteristics of witches (see Appendix H). They were elderly and poor. Their ages varied from 50 to 65 years. Lucky, Saul and Maphela were unemployed; Lucas, Tsakane and Lot were pensioners; Izaac cultivated gardens and Betty ran a tuck shop. The accusations also express common fears beginning with the widespread suspicion that healers exploited people and used their esoteric knowledge for destructive purposes. Nearly all the accused worked as ritual specialists. Izaac, Saul and Cinderella were *dingaka*; Lot and Lucas were prominent church members; and Betty and Maphela Apostolic were healers. Further, the unregulated arrival of newcomers placed pressure on the village's fragile resources. Only Lucky and Betty were natives of Roooiboklaagte. The other accused had all recently immigrated: Lot came from Wales, Izaac and Cinderella from Green Valley, Saul and Tsakane from Arthur's Seat, and Lucas from Marite. Some had arrived as recently as in 1994. In an interview Comrades directly highlighted this concern by saying, 'Our headman was always too polite. He just took in anybody from the outside without investigating their prior deeds.' It is significant that Apostolic churches facilitated the arrival of newcomers and enabled them to achieve status within the community.

The accusations also expressed the fear that standards of morality were being threatened. Like the agony columns of a magazine, biographies of the accused contain stories of domestic squabbles, divorce and extramarital affairs. Lucky was twice divorced, drank hard liquor and was a malicious gossip. Izaac divorced his first wife, took another man's wife and frequently quarrelled with his stepdaughters. Saul's wife deserted him after she found out about his extramarital affairs. Lot, Lucas and Betty's husband seduced other men's wives. The women who were accused had also behaved offensively. Cinderella was not on speaking terms with her daughter-in-law. Tsakane's daughters had all separated from their husbands. In a sense, the accusations redefined acceptable gender roles. Lucky and Saul both lived alone with their young stepchildren. Betty, who was accused of lesbianism, behaved assertively like a man. She was childless, worked as a builder, chased her mother-in-law from home and slapped her husband.

The witch-hunt of Rooiboklaagte points to the formation of a new set of political alliances and oppositions. As in the past, Comrades led the popular anti-witchcraft movement. Yet, despite the use of freedom songs characteristic of 1986, they acted under the banner of a special witch-hunt committee and not the ANC Youth League. As the events unfolded, a novel form of co-operation developed between the Comrades and the chief. The witch-hunters actively sought Chief Nkotobona's assistance and he, in turn, sent his guard to accompany them to the witch-diviner. The arrest of the chief's guard and of the headman's son by the police also provided grounds for an identity of interest between the Comrades and chiefship.

ANC and Civic leaders were able neither to redefine the nature of the witch-hunt, nor to refer the responsibility for protecting the accused to the chief. As local representatives of the new government they were invariably associated with the arrests of the witch-hunters. They were disconcerted by this role. Although the leaders whom I interviewed condemned witch-killings, they felt that the new government should allow people to consult diviners in cases of witchcraft. The head of Rooiboklaagte's RDP Forum argued that even socio-economic improvements would not eliminate witchcraft. 'A poor man who is a witch', he said, 'will not stop practising witchcraft when he becomes wealthy.' 'Witchcraft is in his blood.' He, and other leaders, advocated a return to the traditional system. Families who accuse each other of witchcraft, he said, should place bets at the *mošate*. If the witch is proven guilty he should be fined, admonished and ordered to burn his *dihlare*, or be expelled from the community. As in the past, he argued, the rest of the community should not get involved. Likewise, the deputy chairperson of a Green Valley civic remarked, 'Mass mobilisation around witchcraft can only result in killings.'

Even junior policemen questioned their role during the witch-hunt. Some criticised the station commander and said they were no longer content to care for the witches. Stories have emerged that baboons come from the witches' village to steal food from the police station. Policemen also commented on the strange behaviour of Rooiboklaagte's witches. During their first evening at the police station the accused slept outside on the lawn because their tents were too hot. The next morning the lawn was mysteriously covered in water. There were even rumours that Lot flew from the police station. One informant recounted that Lot sang the very peculiar song:

*Nna ba ka sa nkgone. Dilo tse ke hlwa ke di bona. Ka se tšhwenye ke basemanyane.*
[They cannot outdo me. I usually see such things. Small boys won't trouble me.]

On a few occasions Lot disappeared and was seen on the Acornhoek road, at the Mahleve dam and in a shop at Green Valley. He allegedly flew to these destinations to demonstrate his power. One evening, a policeman accused Lot of jumping on top of his car, denting the bonnet and of smashing the windscreen. On the morning of his departure from the station, Lot asked the chefs to make him tea, but he disappeared before the water had boiled.

Residents of Rooiboklaagte remained unconvinced that the witch-hunters had succeeded in ridding the village of witchcraft. Nowhere was this more apparent than in the tragic execution of Magodi Thabane on 24 June 1996, merely 18 months after the arrests of the witch-hunters. Whilst discussing the eviction of witches, several informants asked, 'What about Magodi Thabane?' They were most surprised that Magodi, a 60-year-old truck driver at the Department of Malaria Control, had not been identified as one of Rooiboklaagte's witches. Many villagers suspected that Magodi had bewitched his brother, Elijah, and Elijah's three sons. These men had all died mysteriously in the 1980s. Elijah and his second son complained of headaches and the other sons died in motor vehicle accidents. In May 1995, shortly before the witch-hunt, Magodi's nephew, his nephew's wife and child were also killed in a motor vehicle accident. One informant remarked, 'We were so surprised. Three people died, but the car was not damaged beyond repair.' He continued, 'Magodi's co-workers also complained that he was a witch. They said that whenever he is not on good terms with you, you'll die.' One of Magodi's sons even accused his father of sleeping with his wife in the form of a *tokolotši* and moved from Rooiboklaagte to another village. My informants speculated that people did not take Magodi to the witch-diviner because they were afraid of him.

On Wednesday morning, 24 June 1996, Magodi started the truck to collect workers from their homes. But only about 100 metres from home two armed men stopped the truck and confronted Magodi. Magodi alighted from the driver's seat and fled, but two men shot him down. They also shot Magodi through the head to make sure that he was dead. When Magodi's son came to his father's assistance the assailants wounded him in the leg. Then, they ran through the dusty streets of Rooiboklaagte, held their rifles high and shouted that they would kill anyone who came near them. The men then disappeared into the bushes. Afterwards the police were alerted and even used a helicopter to search for the assailants, but to no avail.

One of Magodi's neighbours expressed the opinion that he deserved to die. She recalled that after his funeral police came to his home and collected a revolver that was registered in his name. The police also wanted to remove a trunk that stood underneath his bed. But Magodi's wife told the police that the trunk belonged to his sister. 'People say the trunk contained human body parts, and that Magodi's sister threw the parts in the Sand river... What do the police say about this case? They should first raise Magodi from the dead to tell us from where he got the human flesh. Only then can they try those who killed Magodi.'

CONCLUSIONS

Viewed as ritual dramas, the witch-hunts of the 1990s are dynamic registers and stimulants of social change. Witch-hunts expressed the relations of opposition and alliance between different political actors, and altered the relations between the political actors and their basis of support.

The witch-hunts bear witness to an ever-widening schism between Comrades and ANC leaders. In nearly all of these anti-witchcraft movements Comrades were the most prominent participants. I see this as a response to their marginality in the new political context. While youths stood at the forefront of the liberation movement in the 1980s, they have been sidelined from ANC and Civic structures. But it is precisely such marginality that has enabled the Comrades to intervene in witchcraft. Being only loosely affiliated to the ANC, individual Comrades are not accountable to the new authorities. They have therefore been free to act in support of the victims of witchcraft. Over time, the social distance between the Comrades and other ANC structures increased and during the anti-witchcraft movement of Rooiboklaagte Comrades were obliged to act under the special banner of an independent witch-hunt committee. By staging witch-finding rituals, having witches expelled from the villages and by exposing various forms of immorality, the Comrades have compensated for their lack of influence in formal political processes. But the legitimacy of the Comrades in this role depended upon the extent to which they could articulate general rather than sectional interests. They attained greater legitimacy during the witch-hunts of Green Valley and Rooiboklaagte than in the witch-hunt of New Lines, when they were too closely identified with particular families in the village.

Witchcraft has posed a major dilemma to ANC structures, who have become representatives of the state. The attempts of ANC leaders to resolve the conflicting demands of their political superiors (who have required that they oppose witch-hunting) and of villagers (who demand their assistance in the eradication of witchcraft) have been unsuccessful. In 1990 the officials redefined the nature of the Green Valley witch-hunts. While not halting the witch-hunt, the officials prevented the expulsion and the killing of witches. In 1992 and 1993 they transferred responsibility for protecting those accused of witchcraft to the Setlhare chief. In 1994 they refrained from involving themselves in the Rooiboklaagte witch-hunt. However, villagers perceived the ANC as being responsible, at least in part, for the arrests of witch-hunters by the police. The inability of the officials to act decisively against witchcraft has placed them in opposition to the Comrades, and has meant a loss of credibility and legitimacy among villagers.

The Setlhare chief has played an increasingly prominent role in managing witchcraft accusations. The chief did not participate in the Green Valley witch-hunts of 1990. He assisted in having Elias Maluleke evicted from Green Valley in 1992 and protected the accused during the witch-hunt of New Lines in 1993. However, the chief assisted the Comrades of Rooiboklaagte in staging a witch-finding ritual in 1994. The changing nature of the chief's role is indicative of his growing political capacity. It is also a result of his appeal to 'tradition' as a source of political legitimacy (Spiegel, 1989), for there are many historical precedents for chiefly interventions in witchcraft. By insisting on letters of authorisation from the chiefs, rather than other political actors, witch-diviners have bolstered the authority of chiefship. Since they too invoke tradition, witch-diviners have an ideological affinity with the chiefs. Through managing accusations of witchcraft, the Setlhare chief has been able to act in alliance with ANC leaders and more particularly, and increasingly, with the Comrades. It seems likely that relations between the chief and Comrades that were marked by intense conflict may well become more co-operative in future. Like the Comrades, chiefs are likely to be more concerned with establishing legitimacy among villagers than with complying with the demands of outside political authorities.

# 9 CONCLUSION: WITCHCRAFT AND THE POSTCOLONIAL STATE

No person with a background in Western science can admit the reality of witchcraft or the 'breath of men' as defined by the Nyakyusa... The only solution is to kill the belief in witchcraft. As we have shown, it is somewhat weakened by elementary education and Christian teaching; and we believe that its disappearance turns on increased technical control, particularly in the field of disease, on scientific education, and on the development of interpersonal relations. (Wilson, 1967:135)

We [the black consciousness movement] do not reject it [witchcraft]. We regard it as part of the mystery of our cultural heritage.... Whites are not superstitious; whites do not have witches and witch doctors. We are the people who have this. (Biko cited in Woods, 1978:166, 167)

Belief in witchcraft and related practices form part of a basic cultural, traditional and customary principle of Africans in South Africa, and Africa as a whole. (Ralushai et al, 1996:45)

In conclusion to this monograph, I provide a brief overview of the major findings of my research and comment on a crucial question, which I have not addressed thus far, namely, 'What is to be done about witchcraft?' Or, more specifically, 'What legislative changes can be implemented to end violence against alleged witches?'

As anthropologists we might imagine that we are legislators, and formulate proposals we believe present satisfactory solutions, but we seldom have real power to enforce our prescriptions. In any case, I do not believe that there are generally acceptable solutions to this particular set of problems. Any action against witchcraft beliefs, witchcraft accusations and the killing of witches is based on prior assumptions about the meaning and morality of these phenomena. It is unlikely that a consensus would emerge between those who perceive witchcraft as a real danger, those who regard witchcraft as superstition and others for whom witchcraft beliefs, but not witch-killings, have positive value. In a fundamental sense, witchcraft involves political contestation. Under these circumstances the anthropologist might well make a more appropriate intervention by elucidating the cultural meanings and politics that are encoded in actions on witchcraft, and by predicting their likely consequences.[1]

With these ideas in mind, the conclusion of my monograph also provides a critical overview of the report by the Ralushai commission of inquiry into witchcraft.[2] The Commission was appointed in March 1995 by the Executive

Council of the Northern Province to investigate the causes of witchcraft related to violence; to review criminal cases pertaining to witchcraft over the previous ten years; and to recommend measures to be undertaken by government to combat such violence. As such the commission's report is likely to be a centre-piece in debates about witchcraft in the new South Africa. I do not merely point to scholarly errors in the report, but I endeavour to show its political significance. In short, I argue that the report presents a very important shift in official discourses about witchcraft. From the colonial notion of a civilising mission that promoted the elimination of witchcraft beliefs, the report accepts witchcraft as real and also appropriates witchcraft as a marker of a unique African identity. By counter-posing these official discourses with ethnographic material from Green Valley, I argue that the recasting of witchcraft is by no means unambiguous. New lines of contestation are likely to emerge as witchcraft becomes embroiled in politics of African nationalism.

## COLONIALISM'S CIVILISATION, APARTHEID AND WITCHCRAFT

In South Africa, the implementation of the British anti-witchcraft laws at the turn of the century and the Suppression of Witchcraft Act No. 3 of 1957 gave symbolic expression to the civilising mission of colonialism. These laws demanded no compromise with any belief or practice pertaining to witchcraft. These were perceived as baseless and even as diabolic primitive superstitions that had to be repressed and eliminated through education, Christian proselytisation and the spread of Western civilisation.

In practice, however, evidence from Green Valley clearly contradicts the assumption that witchcraft is antithetical to the so-called processes of 'civilisation' or 'modernisation'. During the earlier period of subsistence agriculture the vital importance of solidarity between the members of *metse* and their neighbours inhibited witchcraft accusations. By attributing misfortune to ancestral displeasure or states of pollution, people shifted the burden of blame onto forces that were less disruptive of interpersonal relations. These inhibitions disappeared with villagisation, the fragmentation of *metse* into smaller households and increased labour migration. Conflict between kin and neighbours and new forms of inequality favoured more personalised theories of misfortune causation. At the same time the emergence of a this-worldly and dualistic Christian worldview led to the formulation of witchcraft as the most concrete manifestation of evil.

Witchcraft may not be a discourse about modernity (Englund, 1996). None the less, it can only be understood within the frame of contemporary social and political concerns. We have seen how the symbolic meanings of the *tokolotši*, *mamlambo* and zombies are intimately related to people's dependence on money, migration and wage-labour. Stories of white familiars, the dangerous technologies of *makgoweng* and of witches with the attributes of whites, contain elements of a critique of white domination. We have also seen how witchcraft accusations arise from contemporary predicaments such as the frailty of marriage, the diffusion of wages, inheritance, competition for residential stands and rivalries among businessmen and church leaders. Witch-hunting has enabled political movements to intervene in public morality and to contest elections.

Moreover, Fields (1982) convincingly shows that, with regard to the management of witchcraft accusations, the colonial policies of indirect rule blatantly contradicted the demands of the civilising mission. Her argument is particularly pertinent to South Africa where the policies of segregation and apartheid reserved land for exclusive African occupation, ostensibly ensured African self-government and the maintenance of African institutions and culture.

In the lowveld the South African state guaranteed chiefs control over land beneath the Moholoholo mountains and juridical autonomy to deal with 'native laws and custom'. This enabled chiefs to accede to the demand by villagers for the control of witches. Out of sight and earshot of the Native Commissioners, chiefs tried cases that touched on witchcraft, and mediated in witchcraft accusations among commoners. Chiefs authorised witch-diviners to determine the guilt of the accused, condoned the ritual humiliation of those identified as witches and ensured that the bewitched were compensated in cattle for the crimes committed against them. Chiefs and their councillors also sought out and punished witches who stopped rain. By managing misfortune and protecting their subjects from harm, chiefs tapped a potent source of political legitimacy. Native Commissioners seemed to have ignored these infringements, perhaps because they involved minimal violence. Only with the establishment of Bantu Authorities in 1958 did chiefs become more directly accountable to Bantu Affairs Commissioners. This, and also the unfortunate killing of a man who had allegedly bewitched Chief Seganyane II in 1959, placed chiefs under greater pressure to comply with the stipulations of the Suppression of Witchcraft Act. But chiefs and headmen still occasionally intervened in cases of suspected witchcraft, in defiance of the Commissioners.

Fields (1982) also shows that line officers of the colonial administrations could not consistently ignore witchcraft beliefs and often revised formulations of the witchcraft laws when implementing them.[3] This too was apparent in South Africa. For example, in the 1950s, a prominent chief of the Eastern Cape complained to the Chief Native Commissioner that a man had been seen riding around his kraal at midnight, mounted on a baboon. The Commissioner saved the alleged witch from serious injury by having him removed to another district.[4] In Green Valley the South African Police diffused tensions by confining alleged witches to a locality behind the police station. Elsewhere police officers have actually investigated allegations of witchcraft. On 27 January 1995 a soot-like substance was sprinkled on a schoolgirl's food. Police sent the food to the Forensic Chemistry Laboratories in Johannesburg for analysis, but no toxic substances could be detected. Police also took statements after a child who had been missing for three days returned to his parents with a cut on his foot. Inside the wound was a small stone, a piece of wood and herbal substances. The boy's nails and hair had been cut, and he claimed that a man had pushed a piece of wire into his penis. Neither case resulted in an arrest (Ralushai et al, 1996:188, 299).

In areas now comprising the Northern Province, the Suppression of Witchcraft Act was implemented very inconsistently. A compilation of 211 cases from police dockets and court records by the Ralushai Commission show that relatively few people were prosecuted in terms of the Act, and that where they were tried and convicted, their sentences have been uneven. Only 47 (25 per cent) of the 190 people accused of having named others as witches, and of having threatened them with violence, were found guilty.[5] Nine were given suspended sentences, one received strokes with a light cane, five were sentenced to imprisonment (for periods varying from three to ten months) and 32 were given the option of a fine or imprisonment (ranging from R60 or two months, to R1,000 or twelve months). Seventy-one (31 per cent) of the 230 people accused of having perpetrated violence against alleged witches were prosecuted for contravening the Act, or for common assault, attempted murder, malicious damage to property, or arson.[6] Twenty-one were given suspended sentences; eight, strokes with a light cane; four were ordered to pay R175 in damages; five were sentenced to imprisonment (for periods of between three months and two years); and 33 were given the option of a fine or imprisonment (ranging from R30 or ten days, to R1,000 or eight months.)

Between 1985 and 1995 the courts prosecuted only 109 (52 per cent) of the 209 people accused of participating in witch-killings.[7] Twelve were given wholly suspended sentences; four, strokes with a light cane and 84 were imprisoned (for periods varying from 18 months to life). Judges often treated the belief in witchcraft as an extenuating circumstance. In the case of State v Mathabi, Justice van der Walt considered sentencing to death four accused whom had pleaded guilty, to murder. But he accepted their claim that they had thought the deceased was a witch and reduced the penalty to five years' imprisonment, of which two years were suspended.[8]

Moreover, judges have recognised witchcraft beliefs as suitable grounds for appeal. In 1985, for example, Neledzani Netshiavha woke after he heard a scratching sound on his door. Neledzani picked up an axe, walked outside and chopped down an 'animal' hanging on the rafters of his roof. After it fell to the ground, he chopped it twice more. Villagers came to see the 'animal' and described it as a donkey or a large bat, but said that it later assumed the shape of an elderly man who was a reputed witch. Neledzani had killed this man. A judge of the Venda Supreme Court sentenced him to ten years imprisonment for culpable homicide. The Bloemfontein Appeal Court, however, reduced Neledzani's sentence to four years.[9] In 1991, six men who had stoned and burnt to death four alleged witches were convicted of the murder, but sentenced to only five years imprisonment, wholly suspended on condition that they underwent 100 hours' community service.[10]

REGULATING WITCHCRAFT IN POSTCOLONIAL SOUTH AFRICA

Independence saw increased agitation in many parts of Africa for the state to remain indifferent to witchcraft no longer. Africanist intellectuals, who perceive witchcraft as real, have even reproached the courts for refusing to sentence witches.

The report of the Ralushai Commission has its roots in counter-colonial discourses which 'subvert the self-confident rationality of imperial science' (Ranger, 1996:271). It draws on the works by scholars such as Mbiti (1970), Chavunduka (1982) and Motshekga (1984) – who argue that Africans should be judged by 'African norms' rather than by 'European standards of reasonableness' and advocate that witchcraft should come under the purview of the law. These influences are apparent in lengthy citations and in some passages that follow the sources very closely.

The membership of the Ralushai Commission ensured a wide representation of African voices, previously unheard in the formulation of witchcraft laws. The commissioners – who were headed by Professor Ralushai, a social anthropologist and retired deputy principal of the University of Venda – also included a magistrate, attorney, chief, theologian, police Brigadier, organiser of traditional healers and a former ANC representative in Washington. Professor Van Heerden, a legal scholar from the University of the North, was the only white member of the Commission.

Their lengthy report (288 pages) consists of data generated from fieldwork, some recommendations and 150 pages of court material, pictures and maps. The commissioners undertook what Dederen (1996:1) calls a 'magical mystery tour', to interview representatives of 173 communities (including Acornhoek) and 43 organisations such as political parties and associations for *dingaka*, churches, health workers, the police, civic organisations, chiefs and students. They also attended eight peace rallies and three rallies of chiefs. On the basis of these investigations the authors claim that witchcraft beliefs are omnipresent among Africans in the Province. Educated people reportedly cited Shakespeare to justify their beliefs and Zionists quoted Exodus 22, Deuteronomy 18 and Acts 8. Only the leaders of European-controlled churches 'condemned witchcraft beliefs in the language of the missionaries' (Ralushai et al, 1996:18).

In presenting this data the Commissioners dissolve the spectrum of opinion into faceless references to 'many respondents' (Dederen, 1996:1). This mode of presentation supports the report's contention that witchcraft is an expression of a uniform and unique African culture. Though Indians marginally participate in these practices – for example by selling *dihlare* to Africans – whites are neither perceived to be the perpetrators or victims of witchcraft (Ralushai et al, 1996:25).[11]

By consistently using atemporal concepts, such as 'traditional', the authors represent witchcraft beliefs as primordial and invoke the past to explain the present. The report states that 'our forefathers regarded witchcraft as an integral part of our lives'; 'traditionally' mainly women were accused; and that 'traditional courts' punished witches by shaving their heads, or by roasting them in fires (ibid.: 13, 21, 28). The authors also claim that 'traditional beliefs' moulded Christianity rather than vice versa. Religious teaching reportedly had little impact, and church people 'still adhere to traditional beliefs relating to witchcraft and the ancestors' (ibid.:50).

The report only contains a short description of contemporary witchcraft beliefs. Though numerous witchcraft techniques, familiars and items of witchcraft are listed, their symbolic meanings are not explored (ibid.:22).[12] By referring to two perplexing accounts of zombies, the authors insinuate that these beliefs are factual. One account is of four naked women who called a man from his sleep, forced him to drink 'medicine' that tasted like oil and showed him people who had died long ago (ibid.:18). In the other account Jack Mafikeng, an alleged zombie, returned to his family 25 years after he was buried (ibid.:19). The authors contemplate no alternative explanations for these events.

The report none the less condemns the killing of an estimated 389 alleged witches between 1985 and 1995, the destruction of their homes, their banishment and the refusal to allow their children to attend school as 'senseless', 'brutal', 'uncivilised' and 'barbaric' (ibid.:62, 121, 270). The report offers no clear explanation for the violence, but lays blame at the door of the entire community. It acknowledges that male youths known as Comrades were at the forefront of the violence, and that political motives were sometimes involved. The execution of witches was apparently aimed to discredit bantustan governments and chiefs who had become upholders of apartheid (ibid.:32). However, the authors argue that adults manipulated the youth and delegated the responsibility for punishing witches to them because the courts treat juvenile offenders leniently (ibid.). In fact, the authors suggest that local communities saw the youth as 'heroes and protectors'.

'Traditional healers', who sniff out witches on the receipt of money, are identified as key actors in the commission of these crimes (ibid.:29). The authors none the less empathise with the healers, and explain how youths forced many healers to point out witches. Current disarray in the practice is seen to result from improper control by rival associations of healers, with conflicting rules of conduct.

The authors criticise law enforcement agencies and the Suppression of Witchcraft Act as an ineffective solution to the problems of witchcraft and witch-killings. Respondents perceived the Act as unjust because it did not aim to punish witches, but those who name others as witches. Some condoned the killings. Others felt that witches should be kept in special places, perhaps with the wild animals in the Kruger National Park (ibid.:17).

Against the backdrop of these findings, the commission recommends that 'historically black universities' should embark upon an intensive research programme dealing with witchcraft, and that government should embark upon a programme of education that would 'liberate people mentally', so that they would refrain from perpetrating violence against witches. In areas where witch-killings are common, 'experts on African customs' should design courses in school syllabi (ibid.:60). The report also emphasises that churches can play a valuable role, and commends the ZCC who formed their own commission of inquiry into witchcraft.

The report proposes two sets of legal changes. First, that the Suppression of Witchcraft Act be repealed and replaced by a Witchcraft Control Act (see Appendix I). In terms of the new Act, those who practice witchcraft would receive the harshest punishments. Any person who creates 'reasonable suspicion' that he/she practices witchcraft, puts into operation any process, which, in accordance with his/her own belief, is calculated to damage another person or thing, professes knowledge of witchcraft, advises another person how to bewitch, or supplies him/her with the 'means of witchcraft' would be liable to imprisonment for up to four years and/or a fine of up to R4,000. Persons who 'without any reasonable or justifiable cause' name, or employ 'witch-doctors' to indicate, another person as a witch, would be liable upon conviction to a fine not exceeding R3,000 and/or a prison sentence not exceeding three years. Persons who collect money to employ 'witch-doctors' to indicate others as witches, or force 'witch-doctors' to indicate other persons as witches, would be liable to a fine of up to R,2000 and/or imprisoned for up to two years (see Appendix H).

Second, that a Traditional Medical Practitioner's Council should be estab-lished to regulate the practice of 'traditional healers' in the Northern Province. The council is to be a corporate body comprising twelve members – a chairman, vice chairman, five members elected by traditional healers and five members appointed by the Minister.[13] The minister shall also appoint a registrar to serve as secretary of the council, with the right to dismiss councillors who fail to comply with their duties. The proposed council is to maintain a register of tra-ditional healers and to hold inquiries for purposes of the Act (Ralushai et al, 1996:66). Only registered healers would be allowed to practice for gain and to use the title 'Traditional Medical Practitioner' or 'Spirit Medium'. If found guilty of improper conduct, the healer could be ordered to pay a fine, suspended, or expelled. Unregistered healers who practice for gain, falsify certificates, or use unauthorised titles could be fined up to R2,000 and/or be imprisoned for two years. The Commission also proposes that a National Traditional Healers' Association, headed by a 25-member executive, be established to unite all South African 'traditional healers', 'spirit mediums' and 'faith healers' into one body.

Dederen (1996:6) describes these proposals as too vague and general to qualify as meaningful solutions. He laments the lack of specific information about the educational programmes and questions whether the condemnation of witchcraft-related violence by churches would have much of an effect, partic-ularly in the light of the earlier assertion that religious teachings have had little influence on witchcraft beliefs. Dederen states that it remains an unresolved riddle how the Witchcraft Control Act would counter witchcraft-related violence while nurturing the very ideologies in which they are rooted (Ralushai et al, 1996:7).

To these criticisms one can add that the proposals make no reference to the status of the *kgoro* of chiefs. Neither do they address the question of evidence. How would 'reasonable suspicion' of practising witchcraft or 'justifiable cause' for naming another person as a witch be determined? The proposals about traditional healers do not specifically refer to the pointing out of witches. The inclusion of the distinctively Zimbabwean category 'spirit medium', and the lack of any distinction between *dingaka* and witch-diviner (*mungoma*), raises further concern. So does the neglect of witchcraft attributions by Christian prophets and the assumption that Christian healers would sedately accept membership of a national body for 'traditional medical practitioners'.

Though not a blueprint for action, the report does indicate a general direction in the formulation of policy that might guard against the worst pitfalls that have arisen from modernisation strategies elsewhere in Africa, such as those embarked upon in Tanzania. After independence, the Tanzanian government vigorously implemented *ujamaa* villagisation schemes and replaced chiefs with appointed officials. They retained the British witchcraft laws to demonstrate their opposition to the whole complex of beliefs and practices, and made hardly any official provision for witchcraft accusations. This strategy has had disastrous effects and has led to fierce contestation between village communities and the state. In the absence of any institutional support, Tanzanian villagers have resorted to self-help to eradicate witchcraft. Between 1970 and 1988, 3,072 witch-killings occurred in Sakumuland. Yet state courts only prosecuted seven people for these killings (Mesaki, 1994:52). In the 1970s, twelve people died when the security personnel of Sakumuland rounded up 897 suspected witches and criminals. In response, the Tanzanian state imprisoned four police officers, forced two Regional Commissioners and two Ministers to resign and threatened to take severe actions against the diviners who continued to identify witches (ibid.:57). Yet these repressive actions did not have the desired outcome. In the 1980s the killings resumed, as Sungusungu vigilante groups arrogated the authority for administering justice (Bukurura, 1994).

Evidence from Green Valley shows a definite correlation between the non-recognition of witchcraft and the advent of witch-killings. Hardly any killings occurred when chiefs acted in consonance with the expectations of villagers by mediating in witchcraft accusations. The accuser's desire for vengeance was dissipated through alternative forms of punishment, and they were afforded an opportunity of being compensated for their misfortunes. At the same time those accused of witchcraft were given a chance to prove their innocence, and were provided with protection. This situation changed in the 1960s. Amidst heightened suspicions of witchcraft, the Bantu Authorities Act required chiefs to refrain from involving themselves, and a perception arose that the chiefs sided with witches. This, paradoxically, brought about greater violence. Revenge killings began when residents took justice into their own hands. The prosecution of witch-killers further enhanced conflict between villagers and government. In Chapter 7 we saw how Comrades exploited popular discontent: they attacked witches in an attempt to eliminate evil in order to attain legitimacy as a political movement. Indeed, these attacks became linked to a broader challenge to the state's control of local government, the courts and schools. Witchcraft accusations and witch-killings have certainly not abated with the unbanning of the ANC.[14] However, it is significant that no loss of life occurred in the four witch-hunts we examined that took place in the 1990s. This is because alternative forms of punishment – such as the burning of herbs and banishment – came into play. Only Magodi Thabane, who was not publicly accused by a witch-diviner, was tragically executed in Rooiboklaagte.

African governments such as those of Cameroon and Malawi, have responded very differently and have allowed state or chiefly courts to convict witches (Motsekga, 1984; Fisiy and Geschiere, 1990; Fisiy, 1998). While the official recognition and punishment of witchcraft may well suppress the killing of witches in the short-term, this strategy too can have dire consequences. This is shown in the East Province of Cameroon where state courts have imprisoned suspected witches for periods of up to ten years on the basis of testimony provided by certified *nkong* ('diviners'). This practice has not allayed the fears that ordinary villagers have of witchcraft. Villagers are alienated from the process of accusations and perceive an alliance between the *nkong* and new elites. Villagers argue that the *nkong* provide the elite with the occult means (*djambe*) to strengthen their positions and that the *nkong* can only help against witchcraft because they possess the same destructive capacity as witches. The persons convicted of witchcraft by the courts have inevitably been the less fortunate, who supposedly attack successful persons out of envy, and present an anti-modern barrier to progress.[15] By recognising *nkong* the state has thus strengthened the very same forces it tries to combat (Fisiy and Geschiere, 1990).

In the lowveld the bureaucratisation of *dingaka* – who have until now derived their powers from ancestors and alien spirits rather than from political authorities – could fundamentally alter their basis of legitimacy.[16] It could also accord the Minister, who would effectively become the chief of all diviners, new powers in the realm of the occult. More significantly, it is likely that the condoning of witchcraft accusations would entrench social inequality. As we have seen witchcraft is conceived of as the destructive power of the subordinate, activated by emotions of envy and resentment. This cultural fantasy has been manipulated by the dominant to defend their more fortunate positions, and to delegitimate the desires of the needy and deprived. Single adults, who are undesired as lovers and spouses, are imagined to keep the *tokolotši*. Persons eager to attain money are imagined to own the *mamlambo*. In political struggles, prospective members of the new ruling class attributed blame for poisoning to white farmers who feared losing their land. In the domestic sphere those accused of witchcraft have primarily been neglected elders, siblings deprived of inheritance, wives who suffer excessive domination, affines with no rights to the children of their daughters, jilted lovers and unsuccessful neighbours. Subordinate persons rarely have the capacity to use witchcraft accusations to challenge injustice and inequality.


CONCLUSIONS

The concluding chapter of this monograph has pointed to the essential ambiguities of witchcraft in apartheid (or colonial) and post-apartheid (or postcolonial) South Africa. Under apartheid official discourses about civilisation called for the suppression and elimination of superstitions such as witchcraft. In practice, however, people's experiences of proletarianisation, villagisation, Christianity and democratisation led to the proliferation of witchcraft accusations. Political authorities and apartheid courts were also far more tolerant of witchcraft beliefs and accusations than official discourses would lead one to believe.

Discourses and practices pertaining to witchcraft in the new South Africa might well be equally ambiguous. This is partly because postcolonial discourses fail to transcend a central assumption of the colonial civilising mission: that witchcraft is a residual survival of a pre-literate African culture. In the postcolonial vision of the Ralushai Commission, beliefs in witchcraft are no longer stigmatised, but are still a marker of a unique and primordial African identity.[17] This claim is not only inaccurate, but it is as improper as the argument that racism is an expression of Afrikaner culture.

Witchcraft beliefs are not unique to Africans. They are also encountered in pre-revolutionary Russian villages (Worobec, 1995), in India (Bailey, 1997), in contemporary rural France (Favret-Saada, 1980) and in England (La Fontaine, 1998). In South Africa the *tokkelosie* has on occasions been described as an Afrikaner *volkgeloof* ('folklore') (Coetzee, 1938:59), while fears of satanism and consultations of 'witch-doctors' are common present-day concerns among whites (Chidester, 1992:60–6; MacCullum, 1993). Indeed, after I participated in a discussion about witchcraft on the television programme *Two Ways* I received several telephone calls from distressed white residents of Johannesburg's affluent suburbs who earnestly believed that they had been the victims of witchcraft. As evidence the callers referred to consistent illness and misfortune, herbal substances they uncovered in their sitting rooms and inexplicable cracks in their swimming pools. In December 1999, Laviena Human, an Afrikaner woman from Louis Trichardt in the Northern Province, pleaded guilty in court to attempted murder after she paid a fellow African employee R7,000 to get a concoction from a herbalist to kill her husband. Her husband, Jasper Human, became violently ill after she sprinkled the smelly mixture in his food, but he survived (*Sunday Times*, 12 December 1999).

Moreover, witchcraft beliefs do not constitute a primordial and bounded total system, torn loose from any social context.[18] This vision fails to capture the fluid manner in which villagers situationally invoke witchcraft beliefs as they encounter perplexing events, experience prolonged conflict in marriage, or suffer unspeakable misfortune (such as the untimely deaths of their kin). For villagers witchcraft has less to do with civilisation and African identity than with their experiences of misery, marginalisation, illness, poverty and insecurity in South Africa's overcrowded former Bantustan areas. In these contexts, the law may well be more of an irrelevance than a decisive influence. There can be no lasting solution to witchcraft-related violence if the predicaments, fears and anxieties of the believers are not addressed.

# APPENDIX A: FIELDWORK REVISITED

My experiences of fieldwork bear out Sharp's (1985) suggestion that there are no natural units of study. In retrospect, my choice of a time, place and topic of research seem arbitrary. During February 1990, approximately one year after I had been employed as a junior lecturer in Social Anthropology at the University of the Witwatersrand (Wits University) in Johannesburg, two staff members of the Wits Rural Facility near Acornhoek paid an unexpected visit to the Department. The Wits Rural Facility is a unique initiative in tertiary education, which aims to facilitate the application of student skills to a rural context. Among the projects of the Facility have been law clinics, education programmes, building projects, the provision of water and electricity and small business development. Our visitors expressed a need for social scientific knowledge about the area of the Facility's operations, and invited prospective researchers, promising rondavel-type accommodation. I took up their offer, primarily because I had read Hammond-Tooke's (1981) work on the *kgaga* of the lowveld and was intrigued by his analysis of their cosmology and symbolism.

My first visit to the Rural Facility was over a weekend in March. I spent the Saturday in the company of two migrant workers whom I met outside an Acornhoek bottle store. We initially discussed South African politics. But the migrants soon invited me to a *muchongolo* dance contest in Green Valley. 'Come and see our culture', they said. I was fascinated by the dancers' costumes, their umbrellas, impala hides and kudu horns. What struck me most, however, were the lyrics of one song that called on the spirit of Shaka, the nineteenth-century Zulu king, to assist the poverty-stricken community. These impressions led me to write a proposal to study local-level politics, symbolism and ritual.

My next visits to Green Valley were during the university vacations of April and June–July. My April visit was most distressing. I gained very little insight into local culture from my conversations with *muchongolo* dancers, a cafe owner and migrant workers. I also became disheartened by episodes of political violence. One afternoon, 40 petrified women and children fled from Green Valley to seek refuge at the Rural Facility, after hearing totally unfounded rumours that Inkatha warriors would attack the village. I learnt that there had been an ongoing 'civil war' between the ANC and the Sofasonke Civic Union, which had resulted in three brutal murders.

My attention was first drawn to witchcraft in discussion with a middle-aged man. He described himself as an ANC supporter. This, he said, was because Sofasonke murdered innocent children, whereas the Comrades opposed apartheid and killed only witches. He mentioned that the Comrades had executed three witches in the village; Casteel, a man who had allegedly sent lightning to kill his own daughter; a pensioner who kept a *tokolotši*, and a headman who owned a mortuary. In each case, he said, there was irrefutable evidence of witchcraft. Baboons ran out of their homesteads when these were set alight, and human body parts were discovered underneath their beds. From his account, I deduced that witch-killings were a means whereby ANC youths terrified their political opponents.

During my June visit the need to hire interpreters became apparent. I could converse only in English and Afrikaans, and had a limited knowledge of Southern Sotho. Not much progress could be made on my own, because many villagers spoke only Northern Sotho and/or Tsonga. I therefore approached a teacher, MacDonald Mokgope, but he was unable to help because he coaches soccer each afternoon. However, he introduced me to Eliazaar Mohlala and Kally Shokane, two colleagues whom he thought would be able assistants. MacDonald was an excellent judge of character. As a 41-year-old deputy headmaster of the Green Valley Primary School, and a prominent member of the Zion Christian Church, Eliazaar was nicknamed 'Professor'. Kally, a 27-year-old university graduate and history teacher, was called 'Mr Dictionary' because of his fluency in English. Eliazaar said my appearance and accent first made him think that I was a kinsman of Eugene Terreblanche – leader of the right-wing *Afrikaner Weerstands Beweging* (Afrikaner Resistance Movement, AWB). Once I had explained my project, however, both men were eager to help. Thus began our long association as researchers and friends.

A potential problem I envisaged was that Eliazaar could act as a gatekeeper, controlling my access to information, and thereby impeding the research process. He was certainly as competent as the famous amateur anthropologists Spoon-Elias, Muchona, Doc and Tally Jackson – the men who had assisted Junod, Turner, Whyte and Liebow (see Junod, 1966:3–5; Turner, 1967:131–50; Liebow, 1967; Whyte, 1955). While I have always regarded Kally as a colleague, Eliazaar has been more of a mentor. However, another problem arose when Eliazaar invited me to his home and proceeded to explain local culture to me. For the entire day he covered topics one would expect to find in ethnology textbooks – chiefship, the ancestors, rituals and so forth. I realised that I could only progress by involving him and Kally more actively in fieldwork, as co-researchers rather than as mere interpreters or research subjects. The next day, I introduced them to ethnographic research methods. I emphasised that anthropologists were interested in different viewpoints, and highlighted the importance of case material. Subsequently, they assisted me in identifying research problems, selecting informants, doing participant observation, and fiercely debated the interpretation of information with me. We never worked in isolation, but in my absence Eliazaar and Kally noted the dates of important events.

The first task we set ourselves was to conduct a social survey of 100 of Green Valley's approximately 2,000 households. We selected an equal number of households in each village section. Standard questions were asked about life histories, household composition, the details of all household members, health, income-earning and affiliation to churches and other organisations. Though the small sample was not random, it did provide a basic indication of demographic trends. I was also, incidentally, interested to note that several informants claimed spontaneously that they had been the victims of witchcraft. Once we had completed the survey, we directed our attention to politics and cosmology. We interviewed the chief, headmen, members of the royal family and various ANC activists about local politics in past and present times. However, the Sofasonke Civic Union, which was disbanded in 1991, remained an elusive organisation. We also interviewed the leaders of all churches, ten Christian healers and ten *dingaka*. Yet it soon became apparent that the research focus was too broad.

A major breakthrough occurred on 2 January 1991. As I prepared to leave Johannesburg for the lowveld, I saw a television news report that suspected witches, who had been evicted from their homes, were being sheltered at the Acornhoek police station. To my surprise I saw that the footage had been filmed in Green Valley. Upon my arrival there, two days later, I asked Kally how he had spent Christmas. He replied, 'At night we attended parties and by day we hunted witches.' We then set to work collecting different accounts of what had transpired. Because the information we gathered was extremely rich, I decided that my study would, henceforth, focus only on witchcraft.

Throughout the period of fieldwork I held a full-time teaching position and could not secure prolonged leave. Since the assassination of my colleague, David Webster, by agents of the apartheid government in 1989, and the retirement of David Hammond-Tooke in 1991, the Wits Social Anthropology Department has been short-staffed. Instead of the conventional year in the field I became a migrant, oscillating between Johannesburg, where I taught during term-time, and the lowveld, where I conducted research over vacations. In total I spent 80 weeks carrying out research. Though I sometimes stayed with Eliazaar's nephews, I mainly slept at the Rural Facility. Since homesteads were overcrowded, I found it difficult to secure a sleeping-space in the village at short notice. My informants also feared that I would be unsafe at night: violence had not abated and whites were widely suspected of being ritual murderers. Through time I gained a basic understanding of Northern Sotho, but still had to rely on Eliazaar and Kally to translate difficult phrases. I made no attempt to learn Tsonga.

Despite the intermittent nature of fieldwork, I was widely accepted, active in various circles and able to work through participant observation. I worked as a typist at the Green Valley Primary School, assisted the ZCC with arranging funerals and attended church services and many different rituals. I invited villagers for supper, and tried to be helpful by taking people to hospital, sorting out problems with the bureaucracy and by transporting migrants to Johannesburg.

As we saw in Chapter 4, whites were widely viewed with suspicion, and were commonly referred to by the Afrikaans word *baas* ('boss'), or the derogative Sesotho and Setswana term *lekgowa*. The meaning of this word is obscure. It does not refer to the colour white (*tšhweu*) and belongs to a class of nouns (singular prefix *le*, plural prefix *ma*) reserved for animate objects and for human pests. It includes terms like *lehodu* (thief) and *lekgema* (cannibal). J.L. Comaroff (1992:53) argues that in Setswana *makgowa* originally denoted 'white bush lice'. Eliazaar suggested that *makgowa* might derive from the verb *go goa* ('to shout'). My close association with black people made me somewhat of an anomaly and I was, at times, symbolically reclassified. Villagers soon started calling me 'Sakkie' (my nickname) or '*lekgowa la Mohlala* [The white of Mohlala]'. My reception was generally very positive. This is perhaps because blacks socialising with whites subverted norms of behaviour under apartheid.

Throughout my research I presented myself as an academic and avoided political partisanship. I personally envisage an important role for exposé ethnography as exemplified by Gordon's (1992) excellent account of the victimisation of Bushmen in Namibia. Yet I believe, along with Evans-Pritchard (1966:29), that during fieldwork we should aim to play the role of a 'humble learner' rather than that of a 'militant activist'. (See Scheper-Hughes, 1995 and D'Andrade, 1995 for an extensive debate of this important issue.) My association with teachers facilitated the presentation of my research persona. The local political situation turned out to be extremely complex – marked by rivalry between different factions within the ANC, and by changing relations of conflict and co-operation between different political groupings. I maintained cordial relations not only with the ANC and the chief, but also with the Tsonga ethnic movement, *Ximiko Xa Rixaka*, and the PAC.

Only three times did I experience political intimidation. Once a man called me an AWB member and said I would be killed unless I returned to Hoedspruit. (I later learnt that he was mentally retarded.) During a consumer boycott Comrades, wielding stones in their hands, stopped my car and demanded to search the vehicle. Fortunately two young men recognised me and asked their fellow Comrades to leave me alone. On another occasion an ANC Youth League activist demanded to know what I did. The next day he apologised, saying that he had thought I was an enemy of the youth. 'I'm glad to hear you're only doing an education project. Now I don't have to kill you.'

Eliazaar, Kally and myself overcame the methodological difficulties that beset researches into witchcraft by being present where discussions of witchcraft took place (such as the *kgoro* of chief and headmen, funerals, church services and therapeutic consultations) and by interviewing persons with whom we were well acquainted. (See Chapter 1.)

Unlike Favret-Saada (1980) and Stoller and Olkes (1987), my personal experiences of fieldwork did not lead me to be 'caught up' in witchcraft to such an extent that I accept the existence of witchcraft as a reality. Their accounts are extremely valuable and closely approximate an insider's perspective. Yet I do not think that believing in witchcraft is a necessary prerequisite to understanding it. Throughout my research I was solely motivated by curiosity and by an attempt to comprehend witchcraft beliefs anthropologically. I personally consider witchcraft beliefs to be mistaken and I am appalled by violence against suspected witches. I did not hide my opinions during fieldwork. Though my personal beliefs diverged from those of my villagers, I am aware that many shared my repugnance on the question of violence. There are different kinds of understanding. For example, Kuper (1987) shows how the debate between Livingstone and a Tswana rain-doctor provides deeper insight into the unquestioned underlying assumptions, as well as the similarities and differences of their worldviews. In my approach I have tried to reflect Russel's (1946) suggestion that the right attitude is neither reverence nor contempt, but one of critical sympathy.

Much more has been written about the difficulties of commencing fieldwork than about the potentially traumatic experience of ending it. Evans-Pritchard and Turner are the all too familiar exceptions. Evans-Pritchard (1952:79) writes that during fieldwork the anthropologist is 'dependent on the natives around him for company, friendship and human understanding'. He continues, 'An anthropologist has failed unless, when he says goodbye to the natives, there is on both sides the sorrow of parting.' Turner (1967:150) describes how Muchona grieved about the loss of a friend and someone with whom to communicate upon his final departure from Ndembuland. Because the instrumental ties of friendship that I forged while producing this ethnographic monograph have become genuine, I am unable to end my fieldwork. I have therefore decided to research and write a second ethnographic study – this time on the intersections of masculinity, sexuality and power. This task should hopefully take us a very long time.

# APPENDIX B: PUBLIC PERCEPTION MAP OF SOUTH AFRICA

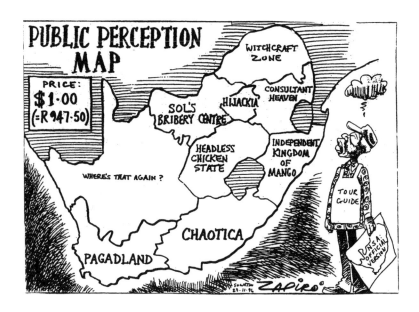

Source: *The Sowetan*, 9 July 1997.

# APPENDIX C: THE WITCHCRAFT SUPPRESSION ACT NO. 3 OF 1957

Statutes of the Republic of South Africa — Criminal Law and Procedure

## WITCHCRAFT SUPPRESSION ACT
### NO. 3 OF 1957

[Assented to 19 February, 1957]     [Date of Commencement: 22 February, 1957]

*(English text signed by the Governor-General)*

**as amended by**

Witchcraft Suppression Amendment Act, No. 50 of 1970

———————

### ACT
**To provide for the suppression of the practice of witchcraft and similar practices.**

**1. Offences relating to the practice of witchcraft and similar practices.**—Any person who—

(a) imputes to any other person the causing, by supernatural means, of any disease in or injury or damage to any person or thing, or who names or indicates any other person as a wizard;

(b) in circumstances indicating that he professes or pretends to use any supernatural power, witchcraft, sorcery, enchantment or conjuration, imputes the cause of death of, injury or grief to, disease in, damage to or disappearance of any person or thing to any other person;

(c) employs or solicits any witchdoctor, witch-finder or any other person to name or indicate any person as a wizard;

(d) professes a knowledge of witchcraft, or the use of charms, and advises any person how to bewitch, injure or damage any person or thing, or supplies any person with any pretended means of witchcraft;

(e) on the advice of any witchdoctor, witch-finder or other person or on the ground of any pretended knowledge of witchcraft, uses or causes to be put into operation any means or process which, in accordance with such advice or his own belief, is calculated to injure or damage any person or thing;

(f) for gain pretends to exercise or use any supernatural power, witchcraft, sorcery, enchantment or conjuration, or undertakes to tell fortunes, or pretends from his skill in or knowledge of any occult science to discover where and in what manner anything supposed to have been stolen or lost may be found,

shall be guilty of an offence and liable on conviction—

(i) in the case of an offence referred to in paragraph (a) or (b) in consequence of which the person in respect of whom such offence was committed, has been killed, or where the accused has been proved to be by habit or repute a witchdoctor or witch-finder, to imprisonment for a period not exceeding twenty years or to a whipping not exceeding ten strokes or to both such imprisonment and such whipping;

(ii) in the case of any other offence referred to in the said paragraphs, to one or more of the following penalties, namely, a fine not exceeding one thousand rand, imprisonment for a period not exceeding ten years and a whipping not exceeding ten strokes;

(iii) in the case of an offence referred to in paragraph (*c*), (*d*) or (*e*), to a fine not exceeding five hundred rand or to imprisonment for a period not exceeding five years, or to both such fine and such imprisonment;

(iv) in the case of an offence referred to in paragraph (*f*), to a fine not exceeding two hundred rand or to imprisonment for a period not exceeding two years.

[S. 1 substituted by s. 1 of Act No. 50 of 1970.]

**2. Presumption.**—Where any person in respect of whom an offence referred to in paragraph (*a*) or (*b*) of section 1 was committed, is killed, it shall be presumed, until the contrary is proved, that such person was killed in consequence of the commission of such offence.

[S. 2 substituted by s. 2 of Act No. 50 of 1970.]

**3. Repeal of laws.**—The laws mentioned in the Schedule to this Act are hereby repealed to the extent set out in the fourth column of that Schedule.

**4. Short title.**—This Act shall be called the Witchcraft Suppression Act, 1957.

### Schedule

LAWS REPEALED

| PROVINCE OR TERRITORY | NO. AND YEAR OF LAW | TITLE OR SUBJECT OF LAW | EXTENT OF REPEAL |
|---|---|---|---|
| Cape of Good Hope | Act No. 24 of 1886 | The Black Territories' Penal Code | Chapter XI |
| ,, | Act No. 2 of 1895 | The Witchcraft Suppression Act, 1895 | The whole |
| Natal .. .. | Law No. 19 of 1891 | Natal Code of Black Law | Section *one hundred and twenty-nine* of the Schedule as substituted by Union Proclamation No. 168 of 1932 |
| Transvaal .. | Ordinance No. 26 of 1904 | The Crimes Ordinance, 1904 | Sections *twenty-nine* to *thirty-four* inclusive |
| Zululand .. | Proclamation No. 11 of 1887 | Laws and Regulations for the Government of Zululand | Regulations *nine* and *ten* |

## WITCHCRAFT SUPPRESSION AMENDMENT ACT
## NO. 50 OF 1970

[ASSENTED TO 11 SEPTEMBER, 1970]      [DATE OF COMMENCEMENT: 18 SEPTEMBER, 1970]

(*English text signed by the State President*)

#### ACT

To amend the Witchcraft Suppression Act, 1957, so as to make it an offence for a person who pretends to exercise supernatural powers, to impute the cause of certain occurrences to another person; and to provide for incidental matters.

**1 and 2.** Substitute respectively sections 1 and 2 of the Witchcraft Suppression Act, No. 3 of 1957.

**3. Short title.**—This Act shall be called the Witchcraft Suppression Amendment Act, 1970.

# APPENDIX D: DETAILS OF THE ALLEGED WITCHES VIOLENTLY ATTACKED, GREEN VALLEY, 1971–1985

| Name | Sex | Age | Occupation | Type of Witchcraft | Alleged Victims |
|---|---|---|---|---|---|
| **1971–75** | | | | | |
| Mahwibila Tau | F | 50s | *ngaka* | *mamlambo* | affines |
| Doresela Phako | F | 50s | housewife | *mamlambo* | neighbours |
| Skukuza Makola | M | 78 | pensioner | familiars, zombies | neighbours grandchildren |
| Nduna Mobakatse | M | 60s | reverend | baboons, zombies | neighbours |
| Maureen Shokane | F | 70s | pensioner | baboons | neighbours |
| Dolf Mpuhuthi | M | 80s | pensioner | familiars zombies | neighbours |
| **1976–80** | | | | | |
| Skariot Mosoma | M | 60s | *ngaka* | familiars, *dihlare* | neighbours, cousin |
| Tulip Mbetzini | F | 40s | housewife | poison | affines |
| Lisbeth Dilebo | F | 30s | housewife | poison | husband |
| Harry Nyathi | M | 60s | pensioner | familiars, zombies | sister's co-wife cognates |
| Sarah Nkwalini | F | 70s | pensioner, *ngaka* | snake, zombies | son, affines neighbours |
| Zoka Mabaso | M | 65 | reverend | * | neighbours |
| Betty Mashego | F | 70s | widow | * | neighbours |
| Zoka Komane | M | 60s | * | *dihlare* | neighbours |
| Girly Nonyane | F | 50s | housewife | * | neighbours |
| Aaron Mashile | M | 60s | headman | *mamlambo* | affines, half-brothers, neighbours |
| **1981–85** | | | | | |
| Mabetha Maoko | M | 60s | pensioner | *tokolotši* | affines, |
| Joseph Searane | M | 50s | shop owner, soccer club manager | *dihlare*, *mamlambo* | players of rival soccer team |
| Mathews Ntimane | M | 50s | shop owner | poisoning, | wife |
| Gerry Shupe | M | 50s | security guard | dihlare, familiars | neighbours, lover's husband |
| Solly Mohlala | M | 50s | unemployed | zombies | neighbours |

# APPENDIX E: DETAILS PERTAINING TO THE VICTIMS OF WITCH-HUNTS ORGANISED BY THE COMRADES, GREEN VALLEY, 1986–1989

| Name | Sex | Age | Occupation | Type of Witchcraft | Alleged Victims |
|------|-----|-----|-----------|---------------------|------------------|
| **1986** | | | | | |
| Adam Ngobeni | M | 50s | *ngaka* | *dihlare*, zombies | brother's daughter neighbours |
| Rufus Mosoma | M | 60s | pensioner | familiars | grandson, neighbour |
| Nana Selepe | F | 60s | housewife | *dihlare*, monkey | neighbours |
| **1988** | | | | | |
| Kganeti Mamba | F | 40s | housewife | baboon | affines |
| Motombeni Tau | M | 55 | ESCOM employee | familiars | neighbours |
| Ben Nkwalini | M | 60s | builder, *ngaka* | *togolotši* | neighbours |
| Rexon Komane | M | 50s | ESCOM employee | familiars | neighbours |
| Mabatho Nonyane | F | 48 | housewife | *dihlare* | affines |
| Doris Shongwe | F | 60s | pensioner | * | neighbours |
| Phontso Banda | M | 70s | pensioner | *mamlambo* | cognates |

# APPENDIX F: DETAILS OF THOSE ACCUSED OF WITCHCRAFT, GREEN VALLEY, THE CHRISTMAS WITCH-HUNTS, 1990

| Name | Sex | Occupation | Type of Witchcraft | Alleged Victims |
|------|-----|------------|--------------------|-----------------|
| **KGAPA MADI** | | | | |
| Zacharias Ripanga | M | *ngaka* | *sefolo* | sister's son |
| Ella Lubisi | F | pensioner | *sefolo* | son-in-law |
| Nelson Selinda | M | road worker | lightning | * |
| Florence Kgwedi | F | *ngaka* | lightning | * |
| Sarafina Maatsie | F | fruitseller | *sefolo* | husband |
| Thembe Mashabane | F | pensioner | * | stepson |
| Godfrey Mnisi | M | * | *dihlare* | son |
| Tinyiko Mnisi | F | * | zombies | neighbours |
| Doris Mabuza | F | domestic | zombies | neighbours |
| Jeremy Rabothata | M | *ngaka* | baboons | neighbours |
| George Shai | M | carpenter | baboons | neighbours |
| Precious Siwele | F | housewife | poison | husband, affines |
| Mafaneseni Malebe | F | fruitseller | zombies | neighbours |
| **KHIYELANE** | | | | |
| Njojo Makone | M | shebeener | poison | customers |
| Kabi Makone | F | shebeener | poison | customers, husband |
| Afisi Ralifela | F | * | snake | affines |
| Madira Mogakane | F | *ngaka* | *dihlare* | * |
| **TSAKANE** | | | | |
| Stefina Morale | F | shebeener | murder | neighbours |
| Sindondana Nobela | M | pensioner | lightning | wife, children |
| Ben Nkwalini | M | builder | *tokolotši* | neighbours |
| Kgalipa Lubisi | M | pensioner | lightning | lover's husband |
| Benedict Sibuyi | M | pensioner | zombies | * |
| Sipho Mashego | M | pensioner | *dihlare* | chief |
| Portia Sebatana | F | housewife | zombies | co-wife |
| Sonia Manzini | F | pensioner | baboons | * |

| Name | Sex | Occupation | Type of Witchcraft | Alleged Victims |
|------|-----|-----------|--------------------|-----------------|
| MAPALENE | | | | |
| Isiah Baloyi | M | reverend | * | neighbours |
| Irvin Mashego | M | reverend | snake | daughter, affines |
| Aaron Mashile | M | headman | zombies | customers |
| Beauty Molobela | F | shebeener | *tokolotši* | * |
| Zandile Ngwenya | F | *ngaka* | poison | daughter-in-law |
| Sharon Maunye | F | * | *dihlare* | neighbours |
| Elias Maluleke | M | chief's guard | *sefolo* | neighbours |
| Linki Mogathle | F | housewife | baboons | neighbours |
| Edeline Moleme | F | * | zombies | neighbours |

# APPENDIX G: DETAILS OF THOSE ACCUSED OF WITCHCRAFT, NEW LINES, ARTHUR'S SEAT, OCTOBER 1993

| Name | Sex | Occupation | Type of Witchcraft | Alleged Victims |
|------|-----|------------|--------------------|-----------------|
| Itumeleng Magogodi | M | pensioner | familiars | son-in-law |
| Jan Maoko | M | pensioner | *letswa* | daughter-in-law |
| Joseph Moeketsi | M | reverend | *mamlambo* | neighbours |
| Kgomotso Chiloane | M | farm worker | familiars | neighbours |
| Piet Nkadimeng | M | pensioner | cat | no victims |
| Boy Dube | M | initiation master | lightning | mother |
| Thato Mohlala | M | pensioner | * | *malome* |
| Prudence Maluleke | F | housewife | poison | daughter-in-law |

# APPENDIX H: DETAILS OF THOSE PERSONS ACCUSED OF WITCHCRAFT, ROOIBOK-LAAGTE, NOVEMBER 1994

| Name | Sex | Occupation | Type of Witchcraft | Alleged Victims |
|---|---|---|---|---|
| Lucky Mohulane | M | unemployed | lightning, *tokolotši* | former lover, nephew |
| Lot Mandlazi | M | Christian healer, pensioner | lightning | neighbours |
| Izaac Ngwenyama | M | casual work, *ngaka* | zombies | mother |
| Saul Mathonsi | M | *ngaka* | zombies | * |
| Betty Mashiloane | F | reverend, tuck shop | *tokolotši* | brothers |
| Maphela Phako | M | Christian healer | * | neighbours |
| Tsakane Chiloane | F | pensioner | monkey | neighbours |
| Cinderella Shupe | F | *ngaka* | * | husband, children |
| Lucas Masilela | M | pensioner | * | daughter-in-law, lover's child |

# APPENDIX I: THE WITCHCRAFT CONTROL ACT AS PROPOSED BY THE COMMISSION OF INQUIRY INTO WITCHCRAFT VIOLENCE AND RITUAL MURDERS IN THE NORTHERN PROVINCE OF THE REPUBLIC OF SOUTH AFRICA

To provide for the control of the practice of witchcraft and similar practices.
1. Offenses relating to the practice of witchcraft and similar practices.
Any person who-
(a) without any reasonable or justifiable cause imputes any other person the causing, by supernatural means, of any death, disease or injury or damage to any person or thing, or who names or indicates any person as a wizard or witch;
(b) in circumstances indicating that he (sic) professes or pretends to use any supernatural power, witchcraft, sorcery, enchantment of conjuration, imputes the cause of death of injury or grief to disease in damage to or disappearance of any person or thing to any other person;
(c) employs or solicits any witch-doctor, witch-finder or any other person to name or indicate any person as a wizard or witch;
(d) does any act which creates a reasonable suspicion that he (sic) is engaged in the practice of witchcraft;
(e) professes a knowledge of witchcraft, or the use of charms, and advises any person how to bewitch, injure or damage any person or thing, or supplies any person with any means of witchcraft;
(f) on the advice of any witch-doctor, witch-finder or other person or on the ground of any knowledge of witchcraft, uses or causes to put into operation any means or process which, in accordance with such advice or his own belief, is calculated to injure or damage any person or thing;
(g) causes people to collect money, whether willingly or unwillingly, with the intention to employ or solicit any witch-doctor, witch-finder or any other person to name or indicate any person as a wizard or witch;
(h) causes any witch-doctor, witch-finder or any other person, against that person's wish, to name or indicate any person as a wizard or witch;
shall be guilty of an offence and liable on conviction:
(i) in the case of an offence referred to in paragraphs (a), (b) and (c) to imprisonment for a period not exceeding three years or to a fine not exceeding R3000 (Three Thousand Rand) or to both such a fine or imprisonment;

(ii) in the case of an offence referred to in paragraphs (d), (e), and (f) to imprisonment for a period not exceeding four years or to a fine not exceeding R4000 (Four Thousand Rand) or to both such a fine or imprisonment;

(iii) in the case of an offence referred to in paragraphs (g) and (h) to imprisonment for a period not exceeding two years or to a fine not exceeding R2000 (Two Thousand Rand) or to both such a fine or imprisonment.

# NOTES

## CHAPTER 1. INTRODUCTION: EXPLORING WITCHCRAFT, POWER AND POLITICS

1. This figure pertains only to the former bantustans and is obviously a vast underestimate. Ralushai et al (1996:191–239) record that 312 witchcraft-related killings were reported by the former Lebowa police, 57 by respondents in Gazankulu and that court records from Venda reveal 20 killings. These are obviously vast underestimates. According to police sources more than 73 people were killed as witches in Lebowa during 1994 alone (*New York Times*, 18 September 1994).

2. During the South African liberation struggle the 'necklace', a tyre doused in petrol, was used to execute political enemies – such as police informers – in public by burning them alive.

3. Also pertinent to the lowveld are the monographs by Kuper (1969) on the Swazi and by Mönnig (1988) on the Pedi.

4. These include the Kriges' (1965) analysis of witchcraft among the Lobedu, Wilson's (1951) comparison of Pondo and Nyakyusa witch-beliefs, Mayer's (1954) general remarks on witchcraft, Hammond-Tooke's (1970, 1974) studies on the interpretation of misfortune and of witch-familiars in the Eastern Cape and Sansom's (1972) account of witchcraft attributions in Sekhukhuneland. Studies of religion by Pauw (1960), Berglund (1989), Ngubane (1977), Hammond-Tooke (1981) and Kiernan (1990) are a valuable complement to these articles. Anderson (1990), Chidester (1992), Minnaar et al (1992), Van Kessel (1993), Ritchken (1995), Stadler (1996) and Delius (1996) investigate the recent witch-killings in the Northern Province. Of the latter authors, Stadler is the only anthropologist.

5. Harris (1994:41) argues that in the heritage of the enlightenment violence is a sign of savagery. For this reason, she suggests, anthropologists have either ignored violence or rationalised it in sociological terms.

6. The political status of the wider Bushbuckridge region continues to be extremely controversial. In 1994 the region was incorporated into the Northern Province. Yet, in response to popular demands, the provincial parliaments of the Northern Province and Mpumalanga agreed to transfer Bushbuckridge to Mpumalanga. In March 1997 the ANC decided that Bushbuckridge would remain in the Northern Province. Widespread violence erupted as Bushbuckridge residents burnt government buildings, destroyed lorries and clashed with police (Ramutsindela and Simon, 1999).

7. This population estimate was made by the Electricity Supply Commission (ESCOM), which had been supplying electricity to homes in Green Valley since 1992.

8. Instead, witchcraft beliefs have been investigated as an 'ideational system' that logically explains unfortunate events (Evans-Pritchard, 1937), or as a channel for projecting psychological emotions of guilt, desire and aggression (Kluckhohn, 1962). (See Jones, 1949; Jung, 1968; Riebe, 1987; Favret-Saada, 1980; and Bercovitch, 1989 for further elaborations of psychological perspectives on witchcraft.) Sociologically witchcraft accusations have been viewed as indices of social tensions, and as a means of terminating or adjusting social relations and affirming social boundaries (Marwick, 1952, 1965, 1970;

Turner, 1957; Middleton and Winter, 1963; Middleton, 1964; Mitchell, 1965; Douglas, 1970a; Macfarlane, 1970; Gluckman, 1972; Patterson, 1974, 1975; and Boyer and Nissenbaum, 1974). In the 1970s and 1980s neo-Marxists demonstrated the instrumentality of witchcraft in political economic struggles (Harris, 1974; Van Binsbergen, 1981; Steadman, 1985; Rowlands and Warnier, 1988) and interpretative studies delineated the place of witchcraft beliefs within wider conceptual schemes and unravelled the meanings they encoded (Lienhart, 1954; Winter, 1963; Crick, 1976; Kelly, 1976; Strathern, 1982). More recent post-structuralist studies focus on discourses of witchcraft as a cultural critique of colonialism (Lattas, 1993) or as embodying 'contested realities' arising from the interplay between global forces of modernisation and local contingencies (Comaroff, 1993; Geschiere, 1997; Ciekawy and Geschiere, 1998).

9. Weber (1978:52) defines power as 'the probability that an actor within a social relationship will be in a position to carry out his or her will despite resistance, regardless of the basis on which this probability rests'. See Wolf (1990, 1999) for a further elaboration of a materialist perspective of power.

10. Arens and Karp (1989) suggest that in African societies power is often seen to reside in the interaction between social, natural and supernatural realms; and is conceived of as the capacities of agents to transform the world.

11. For the reasons I outline in Chapter 2, I see the distinction between the 'witch' and 'sorcerer' as obscuring local concepts of occult power. I use the terms 'witch' and 'witchcraft' to denote both types of persons and modes of action. I only retain the terms 'sorcerer' and 'sorcery' when these are used by authors in the original texts.

12. See Patterson, (1974, 1975); Zelenietz and Lindenbaum (1981); Lindenbaum (1979) and Bercovitch (1989).

13. The segmentary Tiv denounced British imposed chiefs for using their power, *tsav*, destructively, and adopted anti-witchcraft cults as a means to reduce the new chiefs' authority.

14. See Marwick (1952, 1965, 1970); Turner (1957); Middleton and Winter (1963); Middleton (1964); Mitchell (1965); Douglas (1970a); Macfarlane (1970); Gluckman (1972); Patterson (1974, 1975); Boyer and Nissenbaum (1974); Harris (1974); Steadman (1985); Van Binsbergen (1981); and Rowlands and Warnier (1988).

15. Evans-Pritchard (1966) suggests that the aggressive agnosticism of many anthropologists undermined the sensitive study of religion. Scholars seldom investigated cosmological beliefs as systems of theology and have been disinclined to attribute central causality to them. Peek (1991:9) suggests that British anthropologists portrayed beliefs as derivative of social system, and understood religion with reference to kinship and government.

16. Sahlins (1976) possibly presents the most cogent argument that symbolic systems predominate over the material aspects of life and utilitarian behaviour.

17. Fox (1968), Midlefort (1972), Monter (1976) and Thomas (1971) exemplify such an approach.

18. Lett (1991) argues that absurd conclusions are generated when the principles of interpretative anthropology are applied to paranormal phenomena, and pursued to their logical ends. These include the notion that Barawa men of Sierra Leone can really turn themselves into elephants.

19. However, Geertz's actual work falls neatly into the interpretative camp (Kuper, 1999).

## CHAPTER 2. SOCIETY, COSMOLOGY AND THE MAKING OF WITCHCRAFT: CONTINUITY AND CHANGE IN THE HISTORY OF GREEN VALLEY, 1864–1995

1. The *senamane* tree (*fiscus Pretoriae*) is deemed to be very dangerous. It allegedly has power like an electric current that kills birds, animals and humans approaching it. Its stem exudes red latex resembling blood.

2.  Ritchken (1995:223) writes that the Pulana delegation to the Uys Commission, investigating border disputes in 1977, referred to the history of Maripe. 'The claim to land was based on an ideology which asserted that ownership of land came through conquest and the shedding of blood... the ideology linked land to the divine authority of the ancestors.'
3.  See Hartman (1978:38–92) and Bonner and Shapiro (1993).
4.  In 1922 Ngungunyane's son, Boyisonto, found his way into the lowveld and was officially recognised as chief (Hartman, 1978:52; Ritchken, 1995:37).
5.  Harries (1989) writes that few white farmers could farm the land themselves. 'In 1896 it was estimated that twenty-nine of the thirty white families in the lowveld were starving and had been reduced to living off locusts and honey' (p. 92).
6.  Despite this measure, rent tenancy arrangements survived on some company farms until the 1930s (Harries, 1989:94).
7.  Valuation Lands Department, 25 October 1937, LDE 115/30, V2328.
8.  In 1933 Mr McBride urged the Native Commissioner to arrest Mr Sam Sifulaentebene and his wife, who had moved from Green Valley to the farm, Dumfries, without authorisation. (Mr F. McBride, Land Agent, to Native Commissioner, Graskop, 27 November 1933, NTC 828/308 V3586).
9.  Assistant Native Commissioner, Graskop, to Native Commissioner, Pilgrim's Rest, 13 March 1934, NTS 828/308 V3586. Assistant Native Commissioner to Native Affairs Department, 18 February 1938, NTS 17/423 V10226.
10. Memorandum, Transvaal Landowners Association to Native Affairs Department, 13 August 1935, NTS 828/308 V 3586. Assistant Native Commissioner to Native Affairs Department, 18 February 1938, NTS 17/432 V10226.
11. Native Affairs Department Circular, Restricting Movement of Natives, October 1932. Assistant Native Commissioner, Graskop, to Native Commissioner, Pilgrim's Rest, 13 March 1934, NTS 828/308 V3586.
12. Valuation Lands Department, 25 October 1937, LDE 115/30 V2328.
13. Whereas the Chamber of Mines recruited mainly Mozambican workers in the 1920s, they began to focus greater attention on the Transvaal as a labour supplying area in the 1930s. In 1936 22,260 Africans from the Transvaal were employed to work on the mines (Wilson, 1972:6).
14. Reclamation and Resettlement Report, Native Affairs Department, Bushbuckridge, 9 July 1957, NTS 17/423/1, V10226.
15. Reclamation and Resettlement Report, Native Affairs Department, Bushbuckridge, 9 July 1957, NTS 17/423/1, V10226.
16. In 1938 – after an argument over beer drinking by church members – Reverend Izaac Lehman seceded from the Nazarene Church to establish the African Evangelist Mission at Casteel.
17. *Madi*, the Northern Sotho word for blood, also denotes semen.
18. Legends of the Banwalungu ancestor, Sikhonkhwane Maluleke, resemble those of Malalatuleng Mokoena. Sikhonkhwane reportedly fought the Venda with guns which he himself manufactured, abducted their women, bewitched them and disguised himself by assuming the shape of ant-heaps and trees.
19. The term *dipheko* (*mhamba* in Tsonga) denotes anything prescribed by the ancestors. These could be objects acquired for the ancestors and also the invocations and sacrifices made to appease them (Junod, 1966:420).
20. Though on a much smaller scale than the *unsindleko* ritual performed by Gcaleka migrants (McAllister, 1980), this rite dramatised a similar concern.
21. Harries (1994:156–63) argues that Spirit possession originated in Mozambique in the 1860s. He sees spirit possession as a means of coping with an oppressive situation and argues that its symptoms are similar to those of hysteria.
22. See Boersema (1984:28), Harries (1994:163) and Honwana (1997).

23. I share Turner's (1967:112–30) view that the distinction between the 'witch' and 'sorcerer', as made by the Azande, cannot readily be generalised to other cultural contexts.

24. Studies of the Northern Sotho have pointed to a difference between 'witchcraft by day' – poisoning – and 'witchcraft by night' – the use of familiars (Krige and Krige, 1965:250; Mönnig, 1988:71; Hammond-Tooke, 1981:101). My informants did not make such a distinction and insisted that poisoners mainly attacked at night.

25. Some elders mentioned that in the past chiefs immunised themselves against this kind of poison by swallowing a 'crocodile stone' upon their installation. Chiefs were expected to vomit up the stone before they died. A similar custom is purported to have existed among the Shangaan and the Kgaga (Junod, 1966:293; Hammond-Tooke, 1981:18).

26. Local beliefs resemble those of the Korekore of Zimbabwe about the illegitimate and legitimate shedding of blood. Whereas witchcraft and murder polluted the earth and caused drought, the violence of chiefs, conquerors and guerillas purified the earth and made its fertility available to descendants (Lan, 1987: 152–60).

27. Human procreation is metaphorically linked with the arable cycle. This association is apparent in the case of the Setswana word *tlhaka*, which denotes both 'seed' and 'foetus' (Comaroff, 1985:65). In Northern Sotho the word for seed is *thaka* and that of a three-month-old foetus *tlhaka*.

28. *Difeka*, *makgoma* and *mafulara* were counteracted by ritual means. To prevent *difeka* adults burnt seeds from the previous year's harvest and rubbed the ash on children's bodies, according to the correct age sequence. In the case of *makgoma* cooling substances (goat's chyme, urine and herbs) were applied. If a couple had sex during the mourning period, their pubic hair was burnt and the ashes rubbed on the bodies of all bereaved persons.

29. Given the lack of accurate information on actual claims about the transgression of taboos before 1960, it is hard to assess the comparative merits of Hammond-Tooke's (1981:125–7) theory that in the pre-Christian cosmology of the Kgaga misfortune was most commonly attributed to pollution.

30. Besonderhede vir beplanning van Zone 2, Bosbokrand Distrik, 31 May 1959.

31. Letter, Secretary Bantu Affairs Department to Bantu Affairs Commissioner, Bushbuckridge, 25 January 1959, NTS 17/423 (1) V10226.

32. Reclamation and Resettlement Report, Native Affairs Department, Bushbuckridge, 9 July 1957, NTS 17/423/1, V10226.

33. Reclamation and Resettlement Report, Native Affairs Department, Bushbuckridge, NTS 17/423/1, V10226.

34. See Hiemstra (1985), Harries (1989) and Ritchken (1995:136–231).

35. See Peel (1968) for the distinction between 'this worldly' and 'other worldly' religious orientations.

36. See Comaroff (1985:221–8) and Kiernan (1991) for more extensive discussions of Zionist colour symbolism.

37. See Kleinman and Sung (1979) and Kleinman and Kleinman (1985) for an analysis of somatisation in folk healing and biomedical practice.

38. Zulu Zionists share this conception. Kiernan (1984:225) writes, of Zulu Zionists in KwaMashu, 'the general African axiom that an illness suggests a mystical cause is accepted without question but very seldom is an offending ancestor cited as the responsible agent'.

39. A ZCC preacher argued that sacrifices were only appropriate in the days of the Old Testament. In the ultimate sacrifice, he said, Jesus died on the cross for our sins. To justify his claim that contemporary sacrifices are evil, he cited Corinthians 10:20; 'Rather than the things which gentiles sacrifice, they sacrifice to demons and not to God, and I do not want you to have fellowship with demons.'

40. Landau claims that after more than a year of his research on Christianity in Botswana he had never heard any mention of Satan. 'Tswana Christians rarely dwelled on fire and brimstone' (Landau, 1995:xvi).

41. The work of most Christian healers was similar to that of Protestant exorcists in Madagascar (Sharp, 1993:245–79). Only the St John's and Old Apostolic churches did not cast out demons, but reconciled them with God.

42. Members of the Apostolic Faith Mission and Jehovah's Witnesses could consult *dingaka*, but had to insist that the *dingaka* did not *phasa* to the ancestors when they dispensed remedies.

43. Prior to the 1960s the *twa sisa* ritual was completed in a single afternoon. A goat was slaughtered for the Malopo, and the new *ngaka* was presented with a goat's horn filled with *dihlare*.

44. Only a prophet of the Apostolic Church of Zion saw witches as emissaries of Satan. 'Witches are Satan's people', he said. 'He manages them, instructs them to mix *dihlare*, and shows them where people sleep.' The general dissociation between Satan and witchcraft in the lowveld differs from the perception among Ewe Christians in Ghana (Meyer, 1992) and from the notions that prevailed during the European and North American witch-crazes (Macfarlane, 1970; Thomas, 1971; Boyer and Nissenbaum, 1974).

45. Kiernan (1984) observes a similar tendency among Zulu Zionists in KwaMashu. He argues that sorcerers were not identified as individuals. Instead, the origin of sorcery was socially expended to coincide with the major categories of association outside the church, i.e., neighbours and co-workers. By rendering sorcery endemic to the outside, to the city as a whole, internal cohesion is ensured as a prerequisite for responding to it.

46. A survey on church membership, conducted in Lesotho during 1970, revealed that 47 per cent of all Christians were Roman Catholic, 30 per cent belonged to the Lesotho Evangelical Church, and 13 per cent to the Anglican church (Murray, 1980:132). Of all registered church members in the Tswana-speaking Tshidi Rolong chiefdom 55 per cent were members of mission-affiliated churches, and 34 per cent of Zionist-type churches (Comaroff, 1985:189). Studies of these areas do not highlight witchcraft beliefs.

## CHAPTER 3. WITCHES OF THE LOWVELD AND THEIR FAMILIARS: CONCEPTIONS OF DUALITY, POWER AND DESIRE

1. The association of witches and animals is a prominent theme in both European and African witch beliefs. Seventeenth-century pictures show European witches with black cats, dogs, pigs, goats, fish, lizards, ducks, birds and dragons. Witches obtained these animals from the devil and sent them to injure and kill people. Like werewolves, witches changed into animals as they went about at night (Parrinder, 1963:46–8). In Africa this association is apparent in the cases of the Azande, Ndembu and Nyakyusa. Among the Azande women witches kept nocturnal birds as servants and had sexual intercourse with a feared species of wild cat called *adandara* (Evans-Pritchard, 1937:56). Ndembu sorcerers conducted evil deeds through a poisonous water snake with the face of its owner (*ilomba*), and possessed the dangerous *tuyebela* which took on the diverse forms of a hyena, jackal, owl, rodent and of a man with reversed feet (Turner, 1957:95–8,148–50). The Nyakyusa imagined witchcraft to exist as pythons in the bellies of individuals (Wilson, 1951).

2. Ethnographic literature supports the perception that these familiars are not indigenous to the lowveld. Whilst studies on Nguni speakers describe the *tokološi* and the *mamlambo* (Soga, 1931; Hunter, 1979; Hammond-Tooke, 1974; McAllister, 1985), ethnographies on Northern Sotho and Tsonga-speakers do not mention them.

3. My approach draws on Douglas's (1970b, 1973) structuralist method of symbolic interpretation. Douglas insists that pattern give meaning and that items do not carry meaning by themselves in isolation from other items.

4. The distinction between *motse* and *tlhaga* in the lowveld resonates with the popular opposition in anthropological literature between 'nature' and 'culture'. See Levi-Strauss (1970) Ortner (1974) and MacCormack (1980).

5. See Comaroff (1981:370) for a similar contrast between the 'village' and 'bush' amongst the Tswana.

6. Animals of the forest (*diphoofolo tsa tlhaga*) are clearly distinguished from domestic animals (*seruiwa*). The verb *go ruiwa* ('to possess') indicates that the latter are perceived as human possessions.

7. Douglas suggests that among the Lele of Zaire sorcerers constitute a 'dangerous mediating bridge' between the contrasting domains of humans and the wild:

> The dangerous bridge is made by a wicked transfer of allegiance by humans who become sorcerers. They turn their backs on their own kind and run with the hunted, fight against the hunters, work against the diviners to achieve death instead of healing. They have moved across to the animal sphere and they have caused some animals to move in from the animal to the human sphere.
>
> (Douglas, 1970b:190)

8. These narratives resemble those of shape-shifting among the Karanko of Sierra Leone (Jackson, 1989:102–18).

9. In this respect the cultural construction of witches resembles the captivating American fictional representation of superheroes. Spiderman and Batman derive uncanny powers by appropriating the attributes of spiders and bats.

10. Patterns of witchcraft accusation in the Eastern Cape differ considerably from those prevailing in the lowveld. Wilson's (1951) impression was that during the 1930s mainly women were accused of witchcraft in Pondoland. In the late 1960s, Hammond-Tooke (1970) recorded 121 cases of witchcraft in Grahamstown and in Ciskei. 105 (87 per cent) of the accused were women. In the Northern Province men are more frequently accused of witchcraft. In the 1930s E. and J. Krige (1943:264–7) found that 18 (45 per cent) of 40 persons accused of witchcraft among the Lobedu were men. Recent fieldwork in the lowveld confirms this trend. In Green Valley men comprised 90 of the 197 (46 per cent) persons accused of witchcraft since 1960. Of the 43 people accused of witchcraft in the nearby village of Timbabati, 27 (63 per cent) were men (Stadler, 1996).

11. Zoological studies do not support the local perception that baboons are exceptionally sexually active. Eimerl and De Vore (1969) and Girolami (1989) show that for the Chamca baboon (*Papio ursinus*), which is commonly encountered in the lowveld, sexual activity is dictated by the female's hormonal cycles.

12. I discussed, with some informants, a newspaper report of Mrs Mogale from Orlando, Soweto, who claimed she was assaulted by a supernatural force (*The Sowetan*, 25 March 1992). They thought the supernatural force was indeed her husband's *mamlambo*.

13. Stories of the *mamlambo* resemble those of Satanic riches in the pentecostal churches of Ghana. In the popular Ghanian narratives human beings and human fertility are offered to Satan and snakes in exchange for money. Meyer (1995) argues that these entail both a critique of the capitalist economy in the name of the pre-capitalist ideal of mutual family assistance and an opportunity to fantasise about things which people cannot afford but nevertheless desire.

14. Hoernlé (1923) captures the ambivalent views of water amongst the Naman. 'They believe it to have great protective powers against any anti-social forces, but at the same time to be extremely dangerous to members of the society whenever they are withdrawn in any way from the powerful protection which society gives them' (p. 79).

15. See Comaroff (1985:174, 235–7) and Kiernan (1988) for more extensive discussions of the Zionist morality of money.

16.  See Werbner (1986:153) for a helpful distinction between 'protest' and 'cultural resistance'.


## CHAPTER 4. WITCHCRAFT AND WHITES: FURTHER NOTES ON THE SYMBOLIC CONSTITUTION OF OCCULT POWER

1.   This belief is not general to the African continent. In West Africa, where witchcraft is associated with dominant persons and perceived as a means of accumulation, whites are more prone to being accused of witchcraft. In northern Nigeria non-colonising whites were sometimes said to have come from an underwater world, to possess x-ray eyes and to practice witchcraft (Murray Last, personal communication). In the 1870s American missionaries in Gabon were believed to eat the souls and the life forces of Africans (John Cinnamon, personal communication).

2.   The image of the witch as a deprived and envious person is borne out in all the southern African cases that I cited. Chewa sorcerers were driven by meat hunger (Marwick, 1965:25) and Bashu witches by their desire for social and political rights (Packard, 1986:257). Witches, according to Xhosa-speaking migrants, work from envy. 'Among the special objects of their envy are a thriving herd and a thriving family' (Mayer and Mayer 1974:162). In the Dande area of Zimbabwe, Lan (1985:36) writes: 'Envy is the motive most commonly ascribed, either envy of the rich by the poor or of the fertile by the barren.' The cases that I cited also bear out Marwick's (1970:263) contention that 'both believed attacks and accusations of witchcraft and sorcery occur only between persons already linked by close social bonds'. (Also see Marwick, 1965:50; Packard, 1986:242; Mayer and Mayer, 1974:161; Lan, 1987:36.)

3.   The situation of colonists is similar to that of some African elites. In the 1920s the Avongara aristocrats in Anglo-Egyptian Sudan, who relied on tribute from commoners, enjoyed overwhelming prestige among the Azande. Commoners did not accuse the Avongara of witchcraft (Evans-Pritchard, 1937:32).

4.   Studies on witchcraft in Africa and Melanesia have been influenced by different theoretical paradigms. Scholars of Melanesia, who have been inspired by interpretive anthropology, highlight culture and cosmology. Ethnographers of Africa have been influenced by the more sociological approaches of Durkheim, Marx and Gluckman.

5.   Ashforth (1996:1220) writes: 'Until recently, state power existed, for the majority of the population subjected to it, in a world shrouded with secrecy. Government was an alien imposition experienced as a violent system whose power seemed to emanate from distant and mysterious realms.'

6.   My observation that whites are more likely to be suspected of ritual murder is not novel. Some Basotho held South African whites responsible for the Lesotho medicine murders of the 1940s (Jones, 1951). Musambachime (1988) and White (1992) document rumours of *banyama* men that spread through Zambia, Tanzania, Zimbabwe and Zaire between 1920 and 1950. According to these rumours diverse colonial actors, such as government officials, firemen, Catholic priests and European doctors, drained the blood of Africans and removed their brains. These were allegedly sold for profit to pharmacies, butcheries and museums.

7.   Other anthropologists have recorded similar experiences. When Evans-Pritchard consumed bananas and became ill his Zande friends told him he had been bewitched (Evans-Pritchard, 1937:66). Monica and Godfrey Wilson contracted malaria while conducting research among the Nyakyusa. Informants told them that a man who had previously asked them for a present, but whom they refused, bewitched them (Wilson, 1967:207).

8.   My view differs from that of Comaroff and Comaroff (1992a) who discuss the contrast between *setswana* ('ways of the Tswana') and *sekgowa* ('ways of the Europeans') in Bophuthatswana. They see the distinction as rooted in the colonial encounter, as 'carrying

a fan of associations in the collective consciousness of the dominated' and as providing an implicit critique of the colonial order (p. 156). My view more closely approximates Fischer's (1981) and Stadler's (1994) account of the uses of *xintu* ('traditions') and *xilungu* ('ways of the whites') in the Tsonga-speaking villages. In the lowveld, local African identities, such as *Sesotho* and *Xitsonga*, were contrasted to each other. *Setšo* or *xintu* (broader concepts denoting common African traditions) was contrasted to *sekgowa* or *xilungu*.

9. A middle-aged man said, 'Not all our traditions were good.' His parents told him that in the past infirm elders were placed at the kraal gates so cattle could trample them to death. They also said that women would secretly strangle the second-born of twins (Hammond-Tooke, 1981:116).

10. See Spiegel (1989) and Spiegel and McAllister (1991) for a discussion of the various uses of 'tradition' in contemporary southern Africa.

11. Lan (1985,1989) shows how Korekore spirit-mediums completely avoided contact with any European commodities during the Zimbabwean war of liberation. He sees this as due to their identification with the ancestors and their symbolic rejection of white domination. The situation in the lowveld is different. See Rodgers (1993) for an excellent discussion on the uses of material culture by *dingaka* in Timbabati.

12. See Junod (1927:514–16), Krige and Krige (1943:252), Mönnig (1967:74) and Hammond-Tooke (1981:99).

13. Here I am indebted to Boddy's (1989:337–60) attempt to view Zār possession as an allegorical construction of weddings in Northern Sudan.

14. One informant contradicted this general perception. He said that witches also cater for the sexual needs of their zombies. 'If you are a teacher, the witch will kill a teacher for you to be your wife.'

15. Foucault's (1972) description of the treatment of the insane in modern France comes to mind, especially his contention that the insane are observed but not listened to. Bastian (1993:164) also refers to the Nigerian idea that mad people are like walking dead. 'They have bodies, but there is no life force inside them.'

16. This was also the belief among the rural Ngoni-speakers in eastern Zambia (Auslander, 1993:173). However, other informants said *Moloi o nya mollo* is a proverb that means that witches cause trouble wherever they go.

17. The word *mshoshaphanzi* derives from the Zulu word *mshesha phanzi* ('quick-down'). It denotes underhand actions such as bribery and fraud.

18. See Ellsworth's (1983) analysis of the chronic deficiencies of railway transport in South Africa.

19. See Auslander (1993) and Weiss (1993) for informative discussions of the cultural meanings of mobility, highways, automobiles and sexuality in modern African contexts.

20. Peter Mokaba, former national president of the ANC Youth League, repeatedly chanted 'Kill the Farmer! Kill the Boer' during election rallies. He described the chant as 'merely part of our struggle'. Other ANC leaders said the chant was not ANC policy and that it was thus inappropriate to use it (*Argus*, 24 April 1993).

21. Right-wing Afrikaner nationalist movements – such as the AWB, Freedom Front and Conservative Party – called for the establishment of an Afrikaner *volkstaat* (lit. 'people's state'). They proclaimed several towns in the former Transvaal, including Hoedspruit, to be part of the *volkstaat*.

22. Bantu Holomisa, former South African deputy-minister of Tourism and the Environment, called on people not to eat porridge offered by the National Party because it contained ink that would disqualify them from voting. The Independent Election Commission found that Holomisa had contravened the Electoral Act (*Cape Times*, 21 April 1994). My research suggests that such claims were common, and that the assumed tactic was associated with witchcraft.

23. In his book *Biko* (1978) the liberal journalist Donald Woods describes how South African security forces sent T-shirts that had been treated with acid to his children. It is interest-

ing that Comrades recalled this incident. A possible explanation for this is that it resonates with the common belief that witches smear *dihlare* on the clothes of their victims.

24.  In the 1994 elections 1,759,597 (92 per cent) of all votes cast for the parliament of the Northern Province were for the ANC; 62,745 (3 per cent) for the National Party; 41,193 (2 per cent) for the Freedom Front; 24,360 (1 per cent) for the PAC; 6,000 for the Ximoko Progressive Party; and only 4,021 for the Democratic Party (*Weekend Star*, 7–8 May 1994).

## CHAPTER 5. WITCHES, COGNATES, AFFINES AND NEIGHBOURS: THE CHANGING DISTRIBUTION OF WITCHCRAFT ACCUSATIONS

1.  Marwick (1965) himself concedes that circumstantial evidence can lead to accusations of sorcery. In 30 per cent of sorcery accusations among the Chewa 'the blame was laid on someone not in a tense relationship with the victim and the accuser' (p. 274). Knauft (1985) found little evidence of ongoing competition in the relationships that were sorcery-prone among the Gebusi of Papua New Guinea.

2.  Affines regularly met outside the *kgoro* to settle their disputes. After one husband had been unfaithful to his wife, his siblings met with her agnates and decided that he should be reprimanded. Neighbours were more likely to resolve their differences in the *kgoro* of the chief and headmen.

3.  De Wet (1983) and McAllister (1989) both show that while relocations arising from betterment drastically eroded the support networks among neighbours, they actually strengthened the ties that bound patrilineal descendants. Manona (1991) points to the importance of cognatic relatives, such as parents, children and siblings, in facilitating the adaptation of immigrants from the farms to the townships of Grahamstown. Stadler (1994) also describes the continued importance of cognatic kin in the lowveld village of Timbabati.

4.  The situation in Green Valley differs from that which prevailed among the Gisu in one important respect. Elders above the age of 65 received civil pensions, amounting to R400 per month, and this was a valuable contribution to household income. Hence, elders were not as financially dependent on their kin.

5.  See Radcliffe-Brown (1965) for a social and structural analysis of joking-relationships between the members of alternate generations.

6.  In Tsonga the father's sister is addressed as *hahani*, elder brother as *bava lonkulu* and younger brother as *bava lontsongo*.

7.  In Northern Sotho the prefix *ra* denotes the masculine gender. This signifies the ambiguous status of the *rakgadi*. One informant commented: 'We treat the *rakgadi* as a man, but she is actually a woman.'

8.  In Tsonga the mother's brother is called *malumi*, her older sister *mhaki nkulu* and younger sister *mhaki ntsongo*.

9.  See Junod (1927), Radcliffe-Brown (1965:15–31) and Kuper (1987:105–9) for discussions of the role and status of the *malumi* among Tsonga-speakers.

10.  In Tsonga parallel-cousins are called *makweru* and cross-cousins *mzala*.

11.  Stadler (1994) investigated bridewealth payments in Timbabati more extensively. In 26 marriages, which took place between 1980 and 1990, the amounts of bridewealth demanded ranged from as little as R120, for a bride with no educational qualifications, to as much as R12,000, for a bride with a nursing diploma. The average amount of bridewealth demanded was R1,592. Only 5 of 26 men who married in the 1980s paid their bridewealth instantly.

12.  The weddings I attended smacked of elitism. A local millionaire invited more that a thousand guests to his daughter's wedding, employed caterers from Nelspruit, hired a helicopter and a Cadillac to transport the bride and groom, and gave his daughter a BMW as a wedding present.

13. One case concerned Phološo Mokone's husband, a businessman, who was murdered in 1995. After his funeral, his mother and siblings claimed that he was not legally married to Phološo, and took possession of his three vehicles.

14. See Schapera and Roberts (1975), Manona (1980), Murray (1981), Kotzé (1986), Niehaus (1988) and Bank (1994).

15. The terms 'divorce' and 'separation' denote differences in legal rather than social status. Several individuals had separated, with no intention of reuniting, but had not had their marriages annulled by the courts. The divorce rate in Green Valley may well have been higher. Some divorcees were embarrassed about their status, and concealed their previous marriages from me.

16. My definition of *bonyatši* draws on Spiegel's (1991) work on Lesotho. Yet there appears to be a slightly different conception. In Lesotho, *bonyatši* was understood to denote 'a relationship between already married persons' (Spiegel, 1991:150). The use of the term by my informants also included relationships in which only one partner was already married.

17. Parker (1990) highlights the association between subversion and sexual passion in Brazil. My male informants regarded subversive sexual relationships, rather than subversive sexual practices, as passionate. Many men found masturbation, anal and oral sex, homosexuality and unfamiliar positions in heterosexual intercourse repugnant.

18. Ten of the 31 clients whom Ketebotse Mogale, an experienced male *ngaka*, treated during February 1992 were men who complained of 'impure blood'. Ketebotse warned them about the dangers of extramarital sex, but assisted them by giving them enemas, herbs or bottles containing a mysterious red liquid.

19. Kotzé (1986) found that in the lowveld village of Dixie, women were much less committed to marriage and seldom remarried once they had separated from their husbands. However, many women in Dixie were wage-earners, employed on privately owned game farms.

20. Men told me that such *ku balo* was made by cutting a small piece from a dog's penis with a pen-knife, grinding the piece into a fine powder and by mixing it with herbs. The husband then rubbed this concoction into the wife's thighs and asked her to close the pen-knife. Should the unfaithful wife and her lover get stuck, they could be released only if she opened the pen knife.

21. The actual rates of polygyny may well be higher. It is likely that some men, who had married second wives while they worked in urban areas, concealed this fromr me during my interviews with them.

22. Dr. Alan Pugh of the Tintswalo hospital recorded 188 discharge diagnosis for the period between 1 July and 31 October 1993. Of these 108 (9 per cent) were for complications following abortion. He reports that the busiest wards were 'female medical' and 'paediatrics'.

23. Similar sentiments were expressed in the numerous anti-beerhall movements when urban youths attacked government liquor outlets and shebeens (*la Hausse*, 1988).

24. As many as 44 of those accused of witchcraft were ritual specialists: 31 were *dingaka* or initiation masters and 13 were Christian healers. Only a fraction of the accusations between them were made by rival ritual specialists and by their clients.

## CHAPTER 6. 'A WITCH HAS NO HORN': SOCIAL TENSIONS IN THE SUBJECTIVE REALITY OF WITCHCRAFT

1. This assumption is also evident in the work of Boyer and Nissenbaum (1974) on the Salem witch-craze and of Steadman (1985) on witch-killings among the Hewa of Papua New Guinea. Boyer and Nissenbaum (1974:10–20) attach greater importance to factional rivalries than to other types of the evidence used by the courts to convict witches – con-

fessions, spectral testimony and physical abnormalities. Steadman asserts that the Hewa witch-killers deemed the reality of the crime irrelevant and were 'always uncertain of the evidence to justify their accusation'. He questions explanations of witch-killing which 'assume that the killers believe in witches even though the accuracy of such accusations cannot be justified' (1985:112). Yet Steadman insists that the idiom of witchcraft is powerful enough to mobilise wide support for the killing of persons who may be distant relatives of some of the killers.

2.  This criticism is most pertinent to studies of witchcraft conducted within the Durkheimian sociological paradigm. Authors such as Heald (1986), Silverblatt (1987) and Geschiere (1988) emphasise how the instrumentality of witchcraft accusations is negotiated within local frameworks of meaning.

3.  Geertz (1973) draws our attention to a number of processes whereby religious beliefs are justified. These include placing beliefs and acts within the total framework of the religious conception, and explaining these with reference to the authority of priests and scriptures. He also emphasises the role of rituals. By enacting beliefs, rituals define images of the cosmic order, bring religious convictions to a human plane and compel the acceptance of the religious perspective. Unfortunately, Geertz does not consider any other types of evidence.

4.  In his critique of post-modernism, Gellner (1992) suggests that relativism implies an acceptance of the position that all systems of knowledge, including science, are culture-bound and should hence be accorded equal status. Gellner misrepresents the position of anti-anti relativists such as Geertz. Merely to acknowledge that science is culturally con-structed does not necessarily negate its superior explanatory capacity.

5.  Barnes (1968) and Bauner and Hinnant (1980) show how Kuhn's (1962) concept of 'paradigm' can illuminate ideas of witchcraft and spirit possession.

6.  Turner (1967:114) writes: 'a few sudden deaths in a happy village may provoke severer and sharper witchcraft accusations among its members than death in an already quarrel-some group where, so to speak, mystical harmful action is anticipated'.

7.  Shaw's (1991) comments on the status of Temne diviners in Sierra Leone inform the situation in the lowveld. Shaw suggests that by virtue of their 'four-eyed vision' Temne diviners can penetrate, and participate in, spiritual worlds that are places of vision and understanding, but are hidden from ordinary people. The revelations of diviners thus have an extra-social origin (ibid.:143).

8.  Employees of the Acornhoek bakery saw the 'small people' at the tap during a time of severe drought. In Green Valley women queued for water at all times of the night. This differed from other places such as Acornhoek, where the water shortage was less acute. The sight of small people at the tap during the night may indeed have appeared strange to outsiders.

9.  Rosenhan (1973) has shown the role of labels in psychiatric assessment. In a well known study eight sane subjects gained admission to psychiatric hospitals. Being labeled 'schizophrenic' they remained as patients an average of 19 days until they were discharged as 'in remission'. Hospital staff interpreted normal behaviours of the subjects as a manifestation of their 'condition'. Note taking was seen as evidence of a loss of memory. Pacing down corridors was not seen as due to boredom, but due to anxiety. Rosenhan argues that labels such as 'schizophrenic' carry a surplus of meanings and expectations, which colour and distort perceptions. When the reason for a patient's behaviour is unknown it is assumed to be a direct outcome of the psychodiagnostic label. 'Once the label of schizophrenia has been applied the label becomes a self fulfilling prophecy' (ibid.: 254). In Green Valley the label 'witch' had a similar distorting effect.

10. My field assistants were appalled by Albert's talk of masturbation and homosexual acts. They said that although male–male sexuality is common on the mines (*makgoweng*), these forms of sexuality are strictly taboo in the lowveld. Adolescents who are found to manipulate their own genitals are harshly punished.

11. Schoeman (1985:653–69) shows that some Pedi psychiatric patients believe that they, themselves, are witches. He argues that such patients usually experienced aggression and deep interpersonal conflicts. Through these admissions they affirmed that their behaviour was meaningful within social thought patterns.

12. Musambachime (1988:201) suggests that this effect is due to the tendency of rumours to transmit interpretations of impressions rather than impressions themselves. In times of uncertainty rumours 'are fired by a desire for meaning, a quest for clarity, and by a desire for logical explanations'. Also see White (1994) for an excellent analysis of rumour.

13. Peek (1991) suggests that the drama of divination and the diviner's liminal persona shift participants out of normal modes of thinking.

14. Heald (1991) contends that scepticism of diviners is endemic among the Gisu of Uganda. She accounts for this in terms of the social marginality of Gisu diviners and the fact that their clients have greater knowledge of their own immediate social environment than the diviners whom they consulted. Green Valley residents were not as sceptical. Diviners and prophets appear to limit their revelations and diagnosis to transcendent realms, and seldom spoke of the immediate life-worlds of their clients.

15. Criticisms of Tylor's (1871) theory of animism – which located the ultimate origins of the doctrine of the souls, spiritual beings and of religion in dreams – should not blind us to the significance of dreams in religious experiences. Studies on religion in Africa point to a prominent belief that dreams can reveal information about the transcendent realm, which is inaccessible by other means. See Lee (1958), Fabian (1966), Curley (1983) and Jedrej and Shaw (1992).

16. Emotional disturbances, exhaustion and deprivation of REM sleep are predisposing factors in sleep paralysis. Yet the syndrome can occur in individuals who are emotionally and physically healthy (see Bloom and Gelardin, 1985; Ness, 1985 and Mavromatis, 1987).

17. Sleep paralysis is a potentially pan-human neurological experience. Yet interpretations thereof, and the ideational content of hypnogogic hallucinations, are culturally variable. The Eskimo population of Alaska interpreted sleep paralysis in terms of influences from the spirit world: they perceived souls as leaving or entering the body (Bloom and Gelardin, 1985:118–19). In Newfoundland it was constructed as Old Hag syndrome: subjects saw humans or animals astride their chests (Ness, 1985:124–7).

## CHAPTER 7. WITCH-HUNTING AND POLITICAL LEGITIMACY: CHIEFS, COMRADES AND THE ELIMINATION OF EVIL, 1930–1989

1. Steadman's (1985) model may be of limited applicability to Africa. The model relies upon evidence from Oceania, where witches are believed to direct their destructive energies outside their own group. In Africa witchcraft accusations characteristically 'occur only between persons already linked by close social bonds' (Marwick, 1970:280).

2. The earliest witchcraft laws in South Africa were Act 24 of 1886 and Act 2 of 1895 (Cape of Good Hope), Law 19 (Natal), Proclamation 11 of 1887 (Zululand) and Ordinance 26 of 1904 (Transvaal). No witchcraft laws existed in the Orange Free State. See Ode Brown (1935), Malinowski (1961:94–9), Fields (1982:577) and Mombeshora (1994:75) for overviews of the British colonial witchcraft laws elsewhere in Africa. There laws were, however, implemented with different degrees of severity. In Northern Rhodesia (now Zambia) people pretending to be witches, witch-finders, and even those who commented that illness was caused by 'non-natural means' could be fined £50 and/or imprisoned for three years. In terms of the 1922 Witchcraft Ordinance of Tanganyika, the high court could impose fines of up to £200 and/or prison sentences of up to five years. Ugandans could even be punished for wearing charms.

3. Missions could not immediately provide the solution required by the African strategists. Missions produced African advocates for the empire, but also an acculturated elite who

opposed colonialism. Moreover, converts were set aside from the moral communities of the masses (Fields, 1982:574).

4.  Assistant Native Commissioner to Native Affairs Department, 2 September 1941, NTS/55, V349.

5.  The Black Administration Act of 1927 provided for the recognition of the judicial and administrative powers of chiefs over their subjects. (Native Affairs Department to Assistant Native Commissioner, 16 January 1942, NTS 187/55, V394.)

6.  An informant told me Setlhare's name is derived from for the word *setlare* (tree). He claimed that the name insinuates that Setlhare was an illegitimate child born outside the home. His claim may well be mythical. As in Zimbabwe, incest is a common theme in myths of origin and alludes to procreative power of royal lineages which can supply their own offspring (Lan, 1985:81–91). Unnatural births are also a symbol of extra-human power (Beidelman, 1971). The founder of the Moletele chiefdom was also said to have been the progeny of an incestuous union between siblings.

7.  Report into Conferment of Civil and Criminal Jurisdiction to Native Chiefs, 31 July 1946, NTS 44/55, V327.

8.  Geertz (1983:122) defines a political centre as 'a point where leading ideas come together with leading institutions to create an arena in which the events that most vitally affect its members' lives take place'.

9.  Other secondary elaborations also account for the occurrence of drought. It was widely believed that a human corpse which lay in the open veld, an aborted foetus not properly buried in cool river sand and the shedding of the blood of a pangolin could nullify the effects of rainmaking.

10. Hall (1987:68) writes of Phalaborwa, 'it seems unlikely that agriculture was ever a prosperous process in its harsh landscape, a thoroughly unpleasant place to live'.

11. Assistant Native Commissioner to Native Affairs Department, 2 September 1941, NTS 187/55 V 349. Assistant Native Commissioner to Native Affairs Department, 5 August 1941, NTS 187/55, V349.

12. Assistant Native Commissioner to Native Affairs Department, 5 August 1941, NTS 187/55 V349. Assistant Native Commissioner to Native Affairs Department, 19 September 1941, NTS 187/55, V349.

13. Report into Conferment of Civil and Criminal Jurisdiction to Native Chiefs, 31 July 1946, NTS 44/55, V327.

14. In Venda '*Phundu Malia*' means 'early winter'. In contrast to all neighbouring settlements, the village of Phundu Malia boasts lush and green vegetation. For many people this anomaly attests to the occult powers of its inhabitants. Currently Phundu Malia is situated within the boundaries of the Kruger National Park. (Personal communication, Godfried Dederen.)

15. Cattle were recognised as a form of compensation for the loss of human life. This logic was apparent in bridewealth and in murder. A grandson of Maripe's headman claimed that in the past the *kgoro* would demand that a murderer compensate the family of his victim with ten head of cattle. Likewise, in the resolution of blood feuds among the Nuer leopard-skin priests negotiated for the payment of cattle by the family of the slayer to those of the slain (Evans-Pritchard, 1970:287–310).

16. See Comaroff's (1974) insightful analysis of the implications of this process for chiefship among the Tshidi of the former Bophuthatswana bantustan.

17. Bantu Affairs Commissioner, Bushbuckridge, to Chief Bantu Affairs Commissioner, Pietersburg, 17 July 1961, 302/362/6, V9089.

18. Bantu Affairs Commissioner, Bushbuckridge, to Chief Bantu Affairs Commissioner, Pietersburg, 17 July 1961, 302/362/6, V9089.

19. Rosaldo (1980:110–20) uses the concept of a cohort to denote individuals who share a collective identity and a sense of life's possibilities by virtue of having come of age together and sharing formative historical moments when crucial life choices are made.

20. The Suppression of Witchcraft Act retained the essential clauses of the earlier laws, but provided for the imposition of harsher penalties. (The previous penalties ranged from £2 or 14 days to £10 or three months.) For the parliamentary discussions of the Suppression of Witchcraft Act see *Debates of the House of Assembly (Hansard)* 18 January to 22 June 1957, pp. 243–68, 328–30. In parliament speakers of the United Party opposition argued that by reverting to the 'tribal system' government impeded progress towards civilisation that would lead to the demise of witchcraft.

21. A next-door neighbour of Abel and Lisbeth supplied the information on which this account is based. At the time that I interviewed her the tragic events had occurred more than 15 years before. Yet she recalled them in great detail. This is because she had spoken to Abel after he became ill, her husband took him to hospital, because she assisted the bereaved family throughout the mourning period and also attended Abel's funeral.

22. This account is based on interviews with members of all the families who claimed that Skariot Mosoma bewitched them.

23. During the 1940s the Mashile brothers were migrants in Germiston and participated in the well-known strike at the AMATO textile factory (Bonner and Lambert, 1987). See Ritchken (1995:282–313) for an in-depth account of their involvement in tenant struggles and in the Lebowa Legislative Assembly.

24. In 1980 four students of the Tladishe High School in Buffelshoek went into exile and were trained as soldiers of *Umkhonto We Sizwe* (MK) – the military wing of the ANC. In 1984 they returned to the lowveld with the mission of blowing up the goods train transporting fuel to the Air Force Base at Hoedspruit. However, the timebomb they set at the Cottondale station in March 1985 detonated after the train had passed. Three days later the South African security police shot dead two of the MK soldiers and arrested two of their accomplices.

25. In May 1986 the Setlhare Crisis Committee travelled by bus to protest at the Giyani magistrate's court against the detention of Comrades who had burnt the homes of *psyanga* gangsters. Police stopped the bus and arrested all the Committee members on charges of furthering the aims of the ANC. Six committee members were imprisoned for an entire year.

26. See Ritchken et al (1990) for an account of the deficiencies of secondary schooling in the Mapulaneng area.

27. Stadler (1994) criticises the tendency to treat youth movements as homogeneous entities. He highlights divisions among the youth and points to various alliances between the youth and adults in the nearby village of Timbabati.

28. Women were under-represented in local structures of the liberation movement. Only one member of the Setlhare Crisis Committee was a woman, as were only four of the twelve of the Maripe High School student representative council members. During 1990 there were only two women on the twelve-member executive of the Green Valley Civic Association. By February 1991 both had quit. One was accused of ritual murder. The other one's husband forbade her to attend meetings. These figures are surprising, given high rates of male absenteeism and the UDF's commitment to gender equality.

29. The name *psyanga* ('rebel' in Tsonga), I was told, is derived from the Mozambican resistance movement, RENAMO.

30. There are historical parallels between the actions of Green Valley's Comrades and those of guerrillas during the Zimbabwean war of liberation. Lan (1985:167) writes that the guerrillas used witch-finding as a controversial technique to gain the support of villagers. As guerrillas entered the villages they attentively listened to complaints of witches and would interrogate them. 'The guerrillas' explicit and aggressive policy against witches was the final turn of the key in the lock. The doorway to legitimate political authority was wide open'(ibid.:170).

31. This differed from the situation in the Welsh countryside, where the institutional strength of the community remained vested with adults (Peters, 1972:120).

32. In 1986 a similar campaign in Sekhukhuneland became known as 'building soldiers'. Young men forced girls to attend their meetings and impregnated them. They also carried out attacks on the clinics that supplied contraceptives (Van Kessel, 1993:606).

33. The name possibly derives from the Sofasonke Party of James Sofasonke Mpanza – a popular leader of squatter movements in the Witwatersrand during the 1940s. After Mpanza was converted to Christianity he became an opponent of the Communist Party (French, 1982). His name has subsequently been associated with conservative political groupings on the Witwatersrand.

34. In 1989 the notorious Mankweng riot squad of the Lebowa Police was transferred to Bushbuckridge. The riot squad violently dispersed two marches organised by the Bushbuckridge Youth Congress, and arrested approximately 80 youths in Brooklyn on 24 October. The youths were charged with public violence, detained and severely assaulted. These actions coincided with Sofasonke's attacks on the Comrades (Ritchken, 1995:415).

35. See Iliffe (1979:206–7) for an important distinction between 'witch-cleansing' and 'witch-finding' movements.

## CHAPTER 8. THE ANC'S DILEMMA: THE SYMBOLIC POLITICS OF FOUR WITCH-HUNTS IN THE 1990S

1. My use of the term 'symbolic politics' does not imply that we should only interpret anti-witchcraft practices in terms of their symbolism and ignore their role in concrete political processes. See Green (1997).

2. Nelson Ramodike, the former chief minister of Lebowa, joined the ANC. His party, the United People's Front, supported the ANC at the Convention for a Democratic South Africa which preceded the South African elections of 1994. Contralesa (Council of Traditional Leaders of South Africa) is an ANC-aligned organisation of chiefs.

3. Political pluralism denotes a situation in which political power is dispersed among a variety of groups rather than concentrated in the hands of a single dominant minority. Haralambos (1980:114) and Spiegel (1992) show how co-existing political structures impinged on the lives of bantustan residents during the apartheid era.

4. The political situation in Setlhare is analogous to medical pluralism (Janzen, 1978). While there may be competition between different types of healers – physicians, prophets and *dingaka* – patients perceive them as complementary resources. An ill person may consult a physician to treat her appendix, a prophet to remove *bati* ('misfortune') and a *ngaka* to cure *sesepedi* ('boils').

5. See Richards (1935), Marwick (1950), Douglas (1963) and Willis (1968, 1970).

6. See Offiong (1983) and Auslander (1993) for accounts of the generational and gendered aspects of contemporary Nigerian and Zambian witch-cleansing.

7. Bloch (1989) and Geertz (1983) discuss the manner in which rituals legitimate and mystify the power of rulers. Kertzer (1988) analyses the use of rituals by revolutionary movements.

8. Baumann (1992) shows how in plural societies rituals are products of 'competing constituencies', involve different modes of participation and address multiple audiences.

9. Arthur's Seat and Rooiboklaagte border Green Valley and are also situated in the Setlhare chiefdom. I have included a discussion of witch-hunts in these villages because they best demonstrate ongoing political processes. The witch-hunts were very widely discussed in Green Valley and involved the participation of local political actors such as Chief Nkotobona. Central episodes of the witch-hunts took place at the police station that is located in Green Valley.

10. In 1995 Elphas Mogale was dismissed from the ANC after being charged with statutory rape. Mogale's fall from grace greatly undermined the efficacy of the local ANC leadership (*African Sun*, 6 February 1996).

11. Mogale's perception seems to be correct. My impression is that, despite their dislike of particular chiefs, adults support the institution of chiefship. See Comaroff (1974) for this important distinction. Chief German's funeral was, reportedly, the largest gathering in Green Valley's history. In his oration at the funeral, Nelson Ramodike reportedly said, 'I always heard this man was no good. But today I see the people are here in large numbers. This shows he was really very popular.'

12. An ANC leader told me chief Nkotobona had nothing to do with the attempted assassination. According to him the shooting took place after students of the Maripe High School attended a sports meeting in Phalaborwa. At the event some schoolgirls fraternised with Ovambo soldiers of the South African Defence Force. When they returned to Green Valley Comrades *sjambokked* the girls. He said that in retaliation for this the soldiers attacked the 'leader of the Comrades'.

13. My account of the events in Mbuzini is based on interviews with three of the participants – an electrician from Kgapa Madi who acted as a driver, a teacher from Mapalene who was a witness and an elderly man from Mapalene who was a suspect. None of these informants was closely associated with the Comrades.

14. Clients who consult *dingaka* could only enter the *ndumba* after they have removed their shoes, blankets and headgear. *Dingaka* said this practice identified the client with the ancestors who did not wear such items.

15. Auslander (1993:181) observes that the division of suspects into lines is a significant feature of witch-finding rituals in Zambia. He asserts that these lines create a moral map of the village, and emulate colonial practices such as census taking, tax assessment and mass inoculations. At initiation lodges in the lowveld initiates are also arranged in lines on the basis of their seniority (Hammond-Tooke, 1981:39, 64).

16. This is because money can embody dangerous qualities. Witches can place *dihlare* on money to kill its new owner.

17. *Dingaka* used switches manufactured from the hair of the blue wildebeest (*connochaetes taurinus*) to detect the problems of their clients. They attribute special power to such hair. A *ngaka* explained that wildebeest look like cattle, but have different hair. It is their hair, he said, which makes them wilder, faster and stronger than cattle.

18. Thieves were believed to use hyena tails to put night watchmen to sleep so they could steal from buildings. Such sleep was deemed to be like a temporary death. My research assistants disagreed when I suggested that the tail might offer a cure for insomnia. 'No. You'll be dead. The fumes from the tail are like chloroform.'

19. Several anthropologists equate the haircut with death and highlight its punitive potential. Leach (1958) and Mageo (1994) argue that, at a subconscious level, the haircut symbolises castration. For Hallpike (1969) the haircut symbolises social control, or living under a strict disciplinary regime. Green (1994) reports that among Pororo communities of Tanzania ritual specialists shave the body hair of alleged witches to suppress their powers. In the lowveld the haircut is also associated with transitional rituals. Babies receive haircuts when they are brought home from hospital; and initiates before they enter and leave the lodge (Hammond-Tooke, 1981:39, 59).

20. Informants suggested that, as in biblical times, torn clothing was a symbol of mourning. Nakedness also connotes images off transition, weakness, poverty, exposure and even power (Beidelman, 1968).

21. This is a widespread symbolic association in southern and central Africa (Turner, 1967:71–4).

22. My account of the New Lines witch-hunt is based on interviews with four different participants: David Morale's cousin, who was a witness and represented his family in the north; a woman suspect who was pronounced not guilty; and Boy Dube and Thabo Mohlala who were found to be witches. Only my second informant believed that the witch-diviner identified the correct witches. Yet even she expressed doubt about certain of the procedures that he adopted.

23. Boy Dube and Thabo Mohlala alleged that the Comrades appropriated a great deal of the money. They recalled that the Comrades collected R33 from nearly every household and said that the amount would have exceeded R3,000 by far. 'I am convinced the Comrades had a share of the money. They must have collected at least R9,000.'

24. I was unable to use either a cassette recorder or to take notes at the funeral. I reconstructed the orations from my own recollections and from those of my research assistants immediately after the funeral.

25. The outcome of the court case against the witch-hunters is still unknown to me. On 6 February the case was brought before the magistrate's court, but was postponed to 16 March.

## CHAPTER 9. CONCLUSION: WITCHCRAFT AND THE POSTCOLONIAL STATE

1. I have tried to emulate Ferguson's (1990) approach to development initiatives in Lesotho. Without making prescriptions about how Lesotho should be developed, Ferguson focuses on the discourses, politics and the real intended and unintended social effects of development.

2. The Ralushai Commission was also required to investigate ritual murders. Yet the report contains an overview of only eight criminal cases pertaining to ritual murders (Ralushai et al, 1996:257–67), and makes no recommendations about this phenomenon. I believe that this is because the Commission chose to emphasise witchcraft. Ritual murder is by no means trivial, but is a topic of considerable importance.

3. An interesting response is that of Frank Melland, a District Officer in Northern Rhodesia. Melland (1923) adopted a sensitive stance towards witchcraft beliefs and produced an amateur ethnographer's treatise, arguing for the coherence of witch beliefs, nearly 15 years in advance of Evans-Pritchard's *Witchcraft, Oracles and Magic Among the Azande*. Melland (1935) criticised the colonial witchcraft laws as 'politically foolish' and pointed to flaws such as the lumping together of 'witches' and 'witch-doctors'. Fields (1982:85) notes that the *bamcapi* witch-cleansing movement, which swept large parts of central Africa in the 1930s, led to manifold violations of the witchcraft laws, colonial administrators maintaining a policy of 'watchful tolerance' and allowing recognised chiefs to have their localities cleansed. Occasionally, the officers even utilised 'traditional expertise' to deal with witchcraft. In the 1940s, increased witchcraft accusations prompted the District Commissioner of Ulanga, Tanganyika, to send a *mganga* to conduct mass shavings. These were thought to suppress the powers of witches and to protect people against bewitchment (Green, 1994:29).

4. This case was brought to the attention of parliament by Dr D.L. Smit, speaker of the United Party. See *Debates of the House of Assembly (Hansard)*, 18 January to 22 June, 1957, pp. 246–7.

5. The charges against 65 people were withdrawn: 13 of the accused could not be traced, 59 were found not guilty. Two cases were transferred to chiefs and four cases were still under investigation.

6. In many cases there was insufficient evidence as the assaults were usually perpetrated by groups late at night. The charges against 29 people were withdrawn, 119 of the accused were found not guilty and police failed to trace 11 of the accused.

7. No penalties were imposed against 95 people. Charges against 13 people were withdrawn, 65 were found not guilty, one was referred to the supreme court, 14 received postponed sentences and the results of 16 cases were still outstanding.

8. See State v Mathabi and six others, Venda Supreme Court, 19–20 February 1991, Sitting at Thohoyandou before Justice Van der Walt (cited in Ralushai et al, 1996:237–9).

9. See State v Netshiavha, Venda Supreme Court, Case No. A20/1987; and Netshiavha v State 1990 (3), SACR. 331 (AD) (cited in Ralushai et al, 1996:192).

10. State v Hlanganani and others Cr No 96/12/91, Supreme Court Case No CC253/93. Sitting at Tzaneen before Justice Botha (cited in Ralushai et al, 1996:240).

11. An informant is quoted as saying that if witchcraft is effective against all races freedom fighters would have used it against colonial administrators and the supporters of apartheid (Ralushai et al, 1996:66).

12. Familiars listed by the report are the owl, bat, cat, hyena, crocodile, snake, goat, jackal, duiker, donkey, tortoise, scorpion, pig, dog, leopard, *tokolotši*, monkey and baboon. Articles used in witchcraft are purported to be razor blades, mirrors, sticks, brushes, pot lids, plates, horns, ballpoint pens, gramophone records, books, mirrors, loaves of bread and spoons (Ralushai et al, 1996:22). A curious omission is the *mamlambo*.

13. In terms of the proposed legislation 'Minister' means the Minister of Health or such other Minister to whom the Provincial Premier may from time to time assign the administration of the Act (Ralushai et al, 1996:66).

14. Comaroff and Comaroff (1999) argue precisely the opposite. They suggest that in the South African 'postcolony' 'appeals to enchantment' have intensified. The roots of such appeals can be found in a mixture of hope and hopelessness, and promise and its perversions. In the postcolonial situation glimpses of vast wealth are accompanied by a chill desperation of being left out of the promise of prosperity. They see moral panics as symptoms of an occult economy – the deployment of magical means for material ends. This view has considerable merit despite its overt economism.

15. Fisiy and Geschiere (1990:149) contend that, despite the totalitarian pretensions of Cameroon's Ahidjo regime, there was no concerted effort by government against witchcraft from above. This practice was essentially triggered by accusations from within villages. Government officials and courts intervened at the request of the local elite and *nkong*.

16. See Lan (1985:207–22) for a brief but informative discussion of the effects of the bureaucratisation of spirit-mediums in postcolonial Zimbabwe.

17. This contrasts with the manner in which witchcraft beliefs are appropriated elsewhere. The witch-museum of Salem, MA, stands as a symbol of intolerance, which reminds us, by virtue of its contrasts, of American democratic ideals.

18. See Thornton (1988) and Amselle (1988) for critiques of the bounded view of culture.

# REFERENCES

## BOOKS AND ARTICLES

Allen, T. (1991) 'Understanding Alice: Uganda's Holy Spirit Movement in Context', *Africa* 61 (3), pp. 370–99.

Amselle, J.-L. (1998) *Mestizo Logics: Anthropology of Identity in Africa and Elsewhere*. Stanford CA: Stanford University Press.

Ardener, E. (1970) 'Witchcraft, Economics and the Continuity of Belief', in M. Douglas (ed.) *Witchcraft Confessions and Accusations*. ASA Monographs 9. London: Tavistock Publications, pp. 141–60.

Arens, W. and I. Karp (1989) 'Introduction', in W. Arens and I. Karp (eds) *Creativity of Power: Cosmology and Action in African Societies*. Washington DC: Smithsonian Institution Press, pp. xi–xxix.

Ashforth, A. (1996) 'Of Secrecy and the Commonplace: Witchcraft and Power in Soweto', *Social Research* 63 (4), pp. 1183–234.

Auslander, M. (1993) '"Open the Wombs!": The Symbolic Politics of Modern Ngoni Witchfinding', in J. and J.L. Comaroff (eds) *Modernity and Its Malcontents: Ritual and Power in Postcolonial Africa*. Chicago and London: University of Chicago Press, pp. 167–92.

Austen, R.A. (1993) 'The Moral Economy of Witchcraft: An Essay in Comparative History', in J. and J.L. Comaroff (eds) *Modernity and Its Malcontents: Ritual and Power in Postcolonial Africa*. Chicago and London: University of Chicago Press, pp. 89–110.

Babcock, B.A. (1978) 'Introduction', in B.A. Babcock (ed.) *The Reversible World: Symbolic Inversion in Art and Society*. Ithaca NY: Cornell University Press, pp. 13–36.

Bailey, F.G. (1997) *Witch-Hunt in an Indian Village or the Triumph of Morality*. New Delhi: Oxford University Press.

Bank, L. (1994), 'Angry Men and Working Women: Gender, Violence, and Economic Change in Qwaqwa in the 1980s', *African Studies* 53 (1), pp. 89–114.

Barnes, S.B. (1968) 'Paradigms, Scientific and Social', *Man* (n.s.) 4 (1), pp. 94–102.

Bastian, M.L. (1993) '"Bloodhounds Who Have No Friends": Witchcraft and Locality in the Nigerian Popular Press', in J. and J.L. Comaroff (eds) *Modernity and Its Malcontents: Ritual and Power in Postcolonial Africa*. Chicago and London: University of Chicago Press, pp. 129–66.

Baumann, G. (1992) 'Ritual Implicates "Others": Rereading Durkheim in a Plural Society', in D. de Coppet (ed.) *Understanding Ritual*. European Association of Social Anthropologists. London and New York: Routledge, pp. 97–116.

Bauner, D.F. and J. Hinnant (1980) 'Normal and Revolutionary Divination: A Khunian Approach to African Traditional Thought', in I. Karp and C. S. Bird (eds) *Explorations in African Systems of Thought*. Bloomington: Indiana University Press, pp. 213–36.

Beidelman, T.O. (1968) 'Some Nuer Notions of Nakedness, Nudity and Sexuality', *Africa* 38 (2), pp. 113–31.

—— (1971) 'Nuer Priests and Prophets: Charisma, Authority and Power among the Nuer', in T.O. Beidelman (ed.) *The Translation of Culture*. London: Tavistock Publications, pp. 375–416.

Bercovitch, E. (1989) 'Moral Insights: Victim and Witch in the Nalumin Imagination', in G. Herdt and M. Stephen (eds) *The Religious Imagination in New Guinea*. New Brunswick and London: Rutgers University Press, pp. 122–59.

Berglund, A.-I. (1989) [1974] *Zulu Thought-Patterns and Symbolism*. Upsalla: Swedish Institute for Missionary Research.

Bloch, M. (1989) 'The Ritual of the Royal Bath in Madagascar: The Dissolution of Death, Birth and Fertility into Authority', in *Ritual, History and Power: Selected Papers in Anthropology*. London School of Economics. Monographs in Social Anthropology 58. London: The Athlone Press, pp. 187–211.

Bloom, J.D. and R.D. Gelardin (1985) '*Uqmairineq* and *Uqumanigianig*: Escimo Sleep Paralysis', in R.C. Simons and C.H. Hughes (eds) The *Culture-Bound Syndromes: Folk Illnesses of Psychiatric and Anthropological Interest*. Dordrecht: D. Reidel, pp. 117–22.

Boddy, J. (1989) *Wombs and Alien Spirits: Women, Men and the Zār Cult in Northern Sudan*. Madison: University of Wisconsin Press.

—— (1994) 'Spirit Possession Revisited: Beyond Instrumentality'. *Annual Review of Anthropology* (23), pp. 407–526.

Boersema, N. (1984) 'Verklaringsmoontlikhede vir die Oorspong van die Malopokultus by die Kgaga van Maake', *South African Journal of Ethnology* 7 (2), pp. 26–33.

Bohannan, P. (1958) 'Extra-Processual Events in Tiv Political Institutions', *American Anthropologist* 60 (1), pp. 1–12.

Bonner, P. and R. Lambert (1987) 'Batons and Bare Heads: the Strike at Amato Textiles, February 1958', in S. Marks and S. Trapido (eds) *The Politics of Race Class and Nationalism in Twentieth Century South Africa*. London and New York: Longman, pp. 336–56.

Bonner, P. and K. Shapiro. (1993) 'Company Town, Company Estate: Pilgrim's Rest, 1910–1932', *Journal of Southern African Studies* 19 (2), pp. 171–200.

Bourdieu, P. (1990) *The Logic of Practice* (translated by R. Nice). Stanford CA: Stanford University Press.

Boyer, P. and S. Nissenbaum (1974) *Salem Possessed: The Social Origins of Witchcraft*. Cambridge MA: Harvard University Press.

Bukurura, S. (1994) 'Sungusungu and the Banishment of Suspected Witches in Kahama', in R. Abrahams (ed.) *Witchcraft in Contemporary Tanzania*. University of Cambridge: African Studies Centre.

Bundy, C. (1987) 'Street Sociology and Pavement Politics: Aspects of Youth and Student Resistance in Cape Town, 1985', *Journal of Southern African Studies* 13 (3), pp. 303–30.

Chavunduka, G. (1982) *Witches, Witchcraft and the Law in Zimbabwe*. ZINATHA Occassional Papers 1. Harare: ZINATHA.

Chidester, D. (1992) *Shots in the Streets: Violence and Religion in South Africa*. Cape Town: Oxford University Press.

Ciekawy, D. and P. Geschiere (1998) 'Containing Witchcraft: Conflicting Scenarios in Postcolonial Africa', *African Studies Review* 41 (3), pp. 1–14.

Coetzee, A.J. (1938) *Die Afrikaanse Volksgeloof*. Amsterdam: N.V. Swets & Zeitlinger.

Cohen, A. (1979) 'Political Symbolism', *Annual Review of Anthropology* 8, pp. 87–114.

Comaroff, J. (1981) 'Healing and Cultural Transformation: The Tswana of Southern Africa', *Social Science and Medicine* 15 (2), pp. 367–78.

—— (1985) *Body of Power, Spirit of Resistance: The Culture and History of a South African People*. Chicago and London: University of Chicago Press.

Comaroff, J. and J.L. Comaroff (1992a) 'The Madman and the Migrant: Work and Labour in the Historical Consciousness of a South African People', in *Ethnography and the Historical Imagination*. Boulder CO: Westview Press, pp. 155–78.

—— (1992b) 'The Colonization of Consciousness', in *Ethnography and the Historical Imagination*. Boulder CO: Westview Press, pp. 235–64.

—— (eds) (1993) *Modernity and Its Malcontents: Ritual and Power Postcolonial Africa*. Chicago and London: University of Chicago Press.

—— (1999) 'Occult Economies and the Violence of Abstraction: Notes from the South African Postcolony', *American Ethnologist* 26 (4), pp. 279–303.

Comaroff, J.L. (1974) 'Chiefship in a South African homeland', *Journal of Southern African Studies* 1 (1), pp. 36–51.

—— (1992) 'Of Totemism and Ethnicity', in J. and J.L. Comaroff (eds) *Ethnography and the Historical Imagination*. Boulder CO: Westview Press, pp. 49–67.

Crick, M. (1976) *Explorations in Language and Meaning: Towards a Semantic Anthropology*. London: Malaby Press.

Curley, R.T. (1983) 'Dreams of Power: Social Process in a West African Religious Movement', *Africa* 53 (4), pp. 20–37.

D'Andrade, R. (1995) 'Moral Models in Anthropology'. *Current Anthropology* 36 (3), pp. 399–408.

Delius, P. (1989) 'Sebatakgomo: Migrant organization, the ANC and the Sekhukhuneland revolt' *Journal of Southern African Studies* 15 (4), pp. 581–615.

—— (1990) 'Migrants, Comrades and the Rural Revolt: Sekhukhuneland 1950–1987', *Transformations* 13 (1), pp. 2–26.

—— (1996) *A Lion Amongst the Cattle: Reconstruction and Resistance in the Northern Transvaal*. Johannesburg: Raven Press.

Development Bank Southern Africa (DBSA) (1988) *Lebowa: Introductory Economic and Social Memorandum*. Sandton: DBSA.

De Wet, C. (1995) *Moving Together, Drifting Apart: Betterment Planning Villagisation in a South African Homeland*. Johannesburg: Witwatersrand University Press.

Douglas, M. (1963) 'Techniques of Sorcery Control in Central Africa', in J. Middleton and E. H. Winter (eds) *Witchcraft and Sorcery East Africa*. London: Routledge and Kegan Paul, pp. 123–42.

—— (1970a) 'Introduction: Thirty Years after Witchcraft, Oracles Magic', in M. Douglas (ed.) *Witchcraft Confessions and Accusations*. ASA Monographs 9. London: Tavistock Publications, pp. xiii–xxxviii.

—— (1970b) *Purity and Danger*. Harmondsworth: Penguin.

—— (1973) *Natural Symbols*. Harmondsworth: Penguin.

Eimerl, S. and I. de Vore (1969) *The Primates*. The Hague, Netherlands NV, Time-Life International.

Englund, H. (1996) 'Witchcraft, Modernity and the Person: The Morality of Accumulation in Central Malawi', *Critique of Anthropology* 16 (3), pp. 257–79.

Evans-Pritchard, E.E. (1937) *Witchcraft, Oracles and Magic among the Azande*. Oxford: Clarendon Press.

—— (1948) *The Divine Kingship of the Shilluk of Nilotic Sudan*. The James Frazer Lecture of 1948. Cambridge: Cambridge University Press.

—— (1952) *Social Anthropology*. London: Routledge and Kegan Paul.

—— (1966) 'Religion and the Anthropologists', in *Social Anthropology and Other Essays*. New York: Free Press, pp. 155–71.

—— (1970) [1956] *Nuer Religion*. Oxford: Clarendon Press.

Fabian, J. (1966) 'Dream and Charisma. "Theories of Dreams" in the Jamaa-Movement (Congo)', *Anthropos* 61 (2), pp. 544–60.

Favret-Saada, J. (1980) *Deadly Words: Witchcraft in Brocage*. Cambridge: Cambridge University Press.

Ferguson, J. (1990) *The Anti-Politics Machine: 'Development', Depoliticization and Bureaucratic State Power in Lesotho*. Cape Town: David Philip.

Fields, K.E. (1982) 'Political Contingencies of Witchcraft in Colonial Central Africa: Culture and State in Marxist Theory', *Canadian Journal of African Studies* 16 (3), pp. 567–93.

Fisiy, C.F. (1998) 'Containing Occult Practices: Witchcraft Trails in Cameroon', *African Studies Review* 41 (3), pp. 143–65.

Fisiy, C.F. and P. Geschiere (1990) 'Judges and Witches, or How is the State to Deal with Witchcraft', *Cahiers d'Etudes Africaines* 118 (30), pp. 135–56.

—— (1991) 'Sorcery, Witchcraft and Accumulation: Regional variations in South and West Cameroon', *Critique of Anthropology* 11 (3), pp. 251–78.

Fortune, R.F. (1932) *Sorcerers of Dobu: The Social Anthropology of the Dobu Islanders of the Western Pacific*. London: Routledge.

Foucault, M. (1972) *Madness and Civilization: A History of Insanity in the Age of Reason*. New York: Random House.

—— (1986) *Discipline and Punish: The Birth of the Prison*. Harmondsworth: Penguin.

Fox, S. (1968) *Science and Justice*. Baltimore: Johns Hopkins University Press.

French, K. (1982) 'Squatters in the Forties', *Africa Perspective* 21, pp. 2–8.

Friedman, J. (1991) 'Consuming Desires: Strategies of Selfhood and Appropriation', *Cultural Anthropology* 6 (2), pp. 154–63.

Geertz, C. (1973) 'Religion as a Cultural System', in *The Interpretation of Cultures*. New York: Basic Books, pp. 87–125.

—— (1983) 'Centres, Kings and Charisma: Reflections on the Symbolics of Power', in *Local Knowledge: Further Essays in Interpretive Anthropology*. New York: Basic Books, pp. 121–46.

Gellner, E. (1973) *Cause and Meaning in the Social Sciences*. London: Routledge and Kegan Paul.

—— (1992) *Postmodernism, Reason and Religion*. New York: Routledge.

Geschiere, P. (1988) 'Sorcery and the State: Popular Modes of Action among the Maka of Southeast Cameroon', *Critique of Anthropology* 8 (1), pp. 35–63.

—— (1997) *The Modernity of Witchcraft: Politics and the Occult in Postcolonial Africa*. Charlottesville: University Press of Virginia.

Giddens, A. (1984) *The Construction of Society*. Berkeley: University of California Press.

Giesey, R. (1960) *The Royal Funeral in Renaissance France*. Geneva: Librairie E. Droz.

Gluckman, M. (1940) 'Analysis of a Social Situation in Modern Zululand', Bantu Studies 14: 1–30, pp. 147–74.

—— (1960) *Custom and Conflict in Africa*. Oxford: Basil Blackwell.

—— (ed.) (1972) *The Allocation of Responsibility*. Manchester: University of Manchester Press.

Gordon, R.J. (1977) *Mines, Masters and Migrants: Life in a Namibian Compound*. Johannesburg: Raven Press.

—— (1992) *The Bushman Myth: The Making of a Namibian Underclass*. Boulder CO: Westview Press.

Gordon, R.J. and A.D. Spiegel (1993) 'Southern Africa Revisited', *Annual Review of Anthropology* 22, pp. 83–105.

Gottlieb, A. (1989) 'Witches, Kings and the Sacrifice of Identity or The Power of Paradox and the Paradox of Power among the Beng of Ivory Coast', in W. Arens and I. Karp (eds) *Creativity of Power: Cosmology and Action in African Societies*. Washington DC: Smithsonian Institution Press, pp. 245–72.

Green, M. (1994) 'Shaving witchcraft in Ulanga: Kunyulewa and the Catholic Church', in R. Abrahams (ed.) *Witchcraft in Contemporary Tanzania*. Cambridge University: African Studies Centre, pp. 23–45.

—— (1997) 'Witchcraft Suppression Practices and Movements: Public Policies and the Logic of Purification', *Comparative Studies in History and Society* 40, pp. 319–45.

Hall, M. (1987) *The Changing Past: Farmers, Kings and Traders in Southern Africa*. Cape Town: David Philip.

Hallpike, C.R. (1969) 'Social Hair', *Man (n.s.)* 4 (2), pp. 256–64.

Hammond-Tooke, W.D. (1962) *Bhaca Society: A People of the Transkeian Uplands, South Africa*. Cape Town: Oxford University Press.

—— (1970) 'Urbanization and the Interpretation of Misfortune: a quantitative analysis', *Africa* 40 (1), pp. 25–39.

—— (1974) 'The Cape Nguni Witch-Familiar as a Mediatory Construct', *Man (n.s.)* 9 (1), pp. 25–39.

232Witchcraft, Power and Politics

—— (1981) *Boundaries and Belief: The Structure of a Sotho Worldview*. Johannesburg: Witwatersrand University Press.
—— (1984) 'In Search of the Lineage: the Cape Nguni Case', *Man (n.s.)* 85 (1), pp. 128–36.
—— (1989) *Rituals and Medicines: Indigenous Healing in South Africa*. Johannesburg: AD Donker.
Haralambos, M. (1980) *Themes and Perspectives in Sociology*. London: Sage.
Harries, P. (1989) 'Exclusion, Classification and Internal Colonialism: the Emergence of Ethnicity among Tsonga-speakers of South Africa', in L. Vail (ed.) *The Creation of Tribalism in Southern Africa*. London and Berkeley: James Currey, pp. 82–117.
—— (1994) *Work, Culture and Identity: Migrant labourers in Mozambique and South Africa, c. 1860–1910*. Portsmouth, London and Johannesburg: Heinemann, James Currey and Witwatersrand University Press.
Harris, M. (1974) *Cows, Pigs, Wars and Witches: The Riddles of Culture*. New York: Random House.
Harris, O. (1994) 'Condor and Bull: the Ambiguities of Masculinity in Northern Potosi', in P. Harvey and P. Gow (eds) *Sex and Violence: Issues in Representation and Experience*. London and New York: Routledge, pp. 40–65.
Hausse, P. la (1988) *Brewers, Beerhalls, and Boycotts: a History of Liquor in South Africa*. Johannesburg: Raven Press.
Heald, S. (1986) 'Witches and Thieves: Deviant Motivations in Gisu Society', *Man (n.s.)* 21 (1), pp. 65–78.
—— (1989) *Controlling Anger: The Sociology of Gisu Violence*. Manchester: University of Manchester Press.
—— (1991) 'Divinatory Failure: The Religious and Social Role of Gisu Diviners', *Africa* 61 (3), pp. 298–317.
Hirst, M.M. (1993) 'The Healer's Art: Cape Nguni Diviners in the Townships of Grahamstown, Eastern Cape, South Africa', *Curare* 16, pp. 97–114.
Hoernle, W. (1985) [1923] 'The Expression of the Social Value of Water among the Naman of South West Africa', in P. Carstens (ed.) *The Social Organization of the Nama and Other Essays*. Johannesburg: Witwatersrand University Press, pp. 77–89.
Hunter, M. (1979) [1936] *Reaction to Conquest: Effects of Contact with Europeans on the Pondo of South Africa*. Abridged Edition. Cape Town: David Philip.
Illiffe, J. (1979) *A Modern History of Tanganyika*. Cambridge: Cambridge University Press.
Jackson, M. (1989) *Paths Towards a Clearing: Radical Empiricism and Ethnographic Inquiry*. Bloomington and Indianapolis: Indiana University Press.
James, D. (1988) 'Land Shortage and Inheritance in a Lebowa Village', *Social Dynamics* 14 (2), pp. 36–51.
Janzen, J.M. (1978) *The Quest for Therapy in Lower Zaire*. (with collaboration of W. Arkinstall, MD) Berkeley, Los Angeles and London: University of California Press.
Jarvie, I.C. (1963) 'Theories of Cargo Cults: a Critical Analysis'. Part 2. *Oceania* 34 (2), pp. 109–36.
Jedrej, M.C. and R. Shaw (eds) (1992) *Dreaming, Religion and Society in Africa*. Leiden: E.J. Brill.
Jones, E. (1949) *On the Nightmare*. London: Hogarth Press.
Jung, C.G. (1968) *The Archetypes of the Collective Unconscious*. Collected Works of C. G. Jung. Volume 9. Princeton: Princeton University Press.
Junod, H. (1966) [1927] *The Life of a South African Tribe*. Two Volumes. New York: Open Books.
Junod, H. and A. Jaques (1939) *The Wisdom of the Tsonga-Shangaan People*. Cleveland Transvaal: Central Mission Press.
Kantorowicz, E.H. (1957) *The King's Two Bodies: A Study of Medieval Political Theology*. Princeton NJ: Princeton University Press.
Kapferer, B. (1988) *Myths of People, Legends of State: Violence, Intolerance, and Political Culture in Sri Lanka and Australia*. Washington and London: Smithsonian Institution Press.

Kelly, R. (1976) 'Witchcraft and Sexual Relations: An Exploration in the Social and Semantic Implications of the Structure of Belief', in P. Brown and G. Buchbinder (eds) *Man and Woman in the New Guinea Highlands*. Washington DC: AAA Special Publications No. 8, pp. 36–53.

Kertzer, D. (1988) *Ritual, Politics and Power*. New Haven CT: Yale University Press.

Kiernan, J.P. (1976) 'Prophet and Preacher: an Essential Partnership in the Work of Zion', *Man (n.s.)* 11 (3), pp. 356–66.

—— (1982) '"The Problem of Evil" in the Context of Ancestral Intervention in the Affairs of the Living in Africa', *Man (n.s.)* 17 (2), pp. 287–301.

—— (1984) 'A Cesspool of Sorcery: How Zionists Visualise and Respond to the City', *Urban Anthropology* 13 (2–3), pp. 219–36.

—— (1988) 'The Other Side of the Coin: The Conversion of Money to Religious Purposes in Zulu Zionist Churches', *Man (n.s.)* 23 (3), pp. 453–68.

—— (1990) *The Production and Management of Therapeutic Power in Zionist Churches within a Zulu City*. Lewiston NY: Mellen Press.

—— (1991) '"Wear 'n Tear and Repair": The Colour Coding of Mystical Mending in Zulu Zionist churches', *Africa* 61 (1), pp. 26–39.

—— (1994) 'Variations in a Christian Theme: The Healing Synthesis in Zulu Zionism', in C. Steward and R. Shaw (eds) *Syncretism/Anti-Syncretism: The Politics of Religious Experience*. London and New York: Routledge, pp. 69–84.

Kleinman, A. and J. Kleinman (1985) 'Somatization: the Interconnections in Chinese Society among Culture, Depressive Experiences, and the Meaning of Pain', in A. Kleinman and B. Good (eds) *Culture and Depression*. Berkeley CA: University of California Press, pp. 429–90.

Kleinman, A. and L. Sung (1979) 'Why do Indigenous Practitioners Successfully Heal?', *Social Science and Medicine* 13B, pp. 7–27.

Kluckhohn, C. (1962) [1944] *Navaho Witchcraft*. Boston: Beacon Press.

Knauft, B. (1985) *Good Company and Violence: Sorcery and Social Action in a Lowland New Guinea Society*. Berkeley CA: University of California Press.

Krige, J. (1947) 'The Social Functions of Witchcraft', *Theoria* 1, pp. 8–21.

Krige, E.J. and J.D. Krige (1965) [1943] *The Realm of a Rain-Queen: A Study of the Pattern of Lobedu Society*. London: Oxford University Press for the International Africa Institute.

Kriger, N. (1991) 'Popular Struggles in Zimbabwe's War of National Liberation', in P. Kaarsholm (ed.) *Cultural Struggles and Development in Southern Africa*. London: James Curry, pp. 125–48.

—— (1992) *Zimbabwe's Guerilla War: Peasant Voices*. Cambridge: Cambridge University Press.

Kuhn, T. (1962) *The Structure of Scientific Revolutions*. Chicago IL: Chicago University Press.

Kuper, A. (1987) *South Africa and the Anthropologist*. London: Routledge and Kegan Paul, pp. 105–9.

—— (1999) *Culture: The Anthropologist's Account*. Cambridge MA: Harvard University Press.

Kuper, H. (1969) [1947] *An African Aristocracy: Rank among the Swazi*. London: Oxford University Press for the International African Institute.

La Fontaine, J. (1998) *Speak of the Devil. Tales of Satanic Abuse in Contemporary England*. Cambridge: Cambridge University Press.

Lan, D. (1987) [1985]. *Guns & Rain: Guerillas and Spirit Mediums in Zimbabwe*. London: James Currey.

—— (1989) 'Resistance to the Present by the Past: Mediums and Money in Zimbabwe', in M. Bloch and J. Parry (eds) *Money and the Morality of Exchange*. Cambridge: Cambridge University Press, pp. 191–208.

Landau, P.S. (1995) *The Realm of the Word: Language, Gender, and Christianity in a Southern African Kingdom*. Portsmouth, NH: Heinemann; Cape Town: David Philip and London: James Currey.

Lattas, A. (1993) 'Sorcery and Colonialism: Illness, Dreams and Death as Political Languages in West New Britain', *Man (n.s.)* 28 (2), pp. 51–77.

Lawrence, P. (1987) 'De Rerum Natura: The Garia view of Sorcery', in M. Stephen (ed.) *Sorcerer and Witch in Melanesia*. Carlton, Victoria: Melbourne University Press, pp. 17–40.

Leach, E.R. (1958) 'Magical Hair', *Journal of the Royal Anthropological Institute* 88 (2), pp. 147–64.

Lee, S.G. (1958) 'Social Influences in Zulu Dreaming', *The Journal of Social Psychology* 47, pp. 265–283.

Lett, J. (1991) 'Interpretative Anthropology, Metaphysics and the Paranormal', *Journal of Anthropological Research* 47 (3), pp. 305–29.

Levi-Strauss, C. (1970) *The Raw and the Cooked*. London: Cape.

Lewis, I.M. (1971) *Ecstatic Religion: An Anthropological Study of Spirit Possession and Shamanism*. Harmondsworth: Penguin.

Liebow, E. (1967) *Tally's Corner: a Study of Negro Streetcorner Men*. Boston: Little, Brown and Company.

Lienhart, G. (1954) 'Some Notions of Witchcraft among the Dinka', *Africa* 21 (4), pp. 303–18.

Lindenbaum, S. (1979) *Kuru Sorcery: Disease and Danger in the New Guinea Highlands*. California: Mayfield Publishing Company.

Lodge, T. and B. Nasson (1991) *All, Here and Now: Black Politics in South Africa in the 1980s*. Cape Town: David Philip.

McAllister, P.A. (1980) 'Work, Homestead and the Shades: the Ritual Interpretation of Labour Migration among the Gcaleka', in P. Mayer (ed.) *Black Villagers in an Industrial Society*. Cape Town: Oxford University Press, pp. 205–54.

—— (1985) 'Beasts to beer pots: Migrant Labour and Ritual Change in Willowvale district – Transkei', *African Studies* 54 (2), pp. 121–36.

—— (1989) 'Resistance to betterment in the Transkei: a case study from Willowvale district'. *Journal of Southern African Studies* 15 (2), pp. 346–68.

MacCormack, C.P. (1980) 'Nature, Culture and Gender: A Critique', in C.P. MacCormack and M. Strathern (eds) *Nature, Culture and Gender*. Cambridge: Cambridge University Press, pp. 1–24.

MacCullum, T.G. (1993) *White Woman Witchdoctor: Tales from the African Life of Rae Graham*. Sandton, Johannesburg: Struik.

Macfarlane, A. (1970) *Witchcraft in Tudor and Stuart England*. London: Routledge and Kegan Paul.

MacGaffey, W. (1968) 'Kongo and the King of the Americans', *The Journal of Modern African Studies* 6 (2), pp. 171–81.

McLeod, M.D. (1972) 'Oracles and Accusations among the Azande', in A. Singer and B.V. Street (eds) *Zande Themes: Essays Presented to Sir Edward Evans-Pritchard*. Oxford: Basil Blackwell.

Mageo, J.M. (1994) 'Hairdo's and Don'ts: Hair Symbolism and Sexual History in Samoa', *Man (n.s.)* 29 (2), pp. 407–32.

Malinowski, B. (1961) *The Dynamics of Culture Change: An Inquiry into Race Relations in Africa*. New Haven CT: Yale University Press.

Manona, C. (1980) 'Marriage, Family Life and Migrancy in a Ciskei Village', in P. Mayer (ed.) *Black Villagers in an Industrial Society*. Cape Town: Oxford University Press, pp. 170–204.

—— (1991) 'Relying on Kin: Ex-farm Worker's Adaptation to Life in Grahamstown', in A.D. Spiegel and P.A. McAllister (eds) *Tradition and Transition in Southern Africa*. Johannesburg: Witwatersrand University Press, pp. 201–18.

Marwick, M. (1950) Another Modern Anti-Witchcraft Movement in East Central Africa', *Africa* 20 (2), pp. 100–12.

—— (1952) 'The Social Context of Cewa Witch-Beliefs', *Africa* 22 (2), pp. 120–35.

—— (1965) *Sorcery and Its Social Setting: A Study of the Northern Rhodesian Cewa.* Manchester: Manchester University Press.

—— (1970) 'Sorcery as a Social Strain-Gauge', in M. Marwick (ed.) *Witchcraft and Sorcery: Selected Readings.* Harmondsworth: Penguin.

Mavromatis, A. (1987) *Hypnagogia: the Unique State of Consciousness Between Wakefulness and Sleep.* London and New York: Routledge and Kegan Paul.

Mayer, P. (1954) *Witches.* Inaugural Lecture. Grahamstown: Rhodes University.

Mayer, P. and I. Mayer (1974) *Townsmen or Tribesmen: Conservatism and the Process of Urbanization in a South African City.* Cape Town: Oxford University Press.

Mbiti, J.S. (1970) *African Religions and Philosophy.* New York: Doubleday and Company Inc.

Melland, F. (1923) *In Witchbound Africa.* London: Secley, Service & Co.

—— (1935) 'Ethical and Political Aspects of African Witchcraft', *Africa* 8 (4), pp. 495–503.

Mesaki, S. (1994) 'Witch-killing in Sakumuland', in R. Abrahams (ed.) *Witchcraft in Contemporary Tanzania.* Cambridge University: African Studies Centre, pp. 47–60.

Meyer, B. (1992) '"If you are a Devil, you are a Witch and if you are a Witch, you are a Devil": the Interpretation of Pagan Ideas in the Conceptual Universe of Ewe Christians', *Journal of Religion in Africa* 22 (2), pp. 98–132.

—— (1995) '"Delivered from the Powers of Darkness": Confessions of Satanic Riches in Christian Ghana', *Africa* 65 (2), pp. 236–55.

Middleton, J. (1964) *Lugbara Religion: Ritual and Authority among an East African People.* London: Oxford University Press.

Middleton, J. and E.H. Winter (eds) (1963) *Witchcraft and Sorcery in East Africa.* London: Routledge and Kegan Paul.

Midlefort, H.C.E. (1972) *Witch Hunting in Southwest Germany.* Palo Alto: Stanford University Press.

Minnaar, A. de V. D. Offringa and C. Payze (1992) *To Live in Fear: Witchburning and Medicine Murder in Venda.* Pretoria: Human Sciences Research Council.

Mitchell, J.C. (1956) *The Yao Village: a Study in the Social Structure of a Nyasaland Tribe.* Manchester: Manchester University Press.

—— (1965) 'The Meaning of Misfortune for Urban Africans', in M. Fortes and G. Dieterlin (eds) *African Systems of Thought.* Oxford: Claredon Press for International African Institute, pp. 192–203.

Mombeshora, S. (1994) Witches, Witchcraft and the Question of Order: A View from a Bena Village in the Southern Highlands', in R. Abrahams (ed.) *Witchcraft in Contemporary Tanzania.* Cambridge: African Studies Centre, pp. 71–86.

Mönnig, H.O. (1988) [1967] *The Pedi.* Van Schaik: Pretoria.

Monter, W. (1976) *Witchcraft In France and Switzerland.* Ithaca NY: Cornell University Press.

Morris, B. (1987) *Anthropological Studies of Religion: An Introductory Text.* Cambridge: Cambridge University Press.

Motshekga, M.S. (1984) 'The Ideology Behind Witchcraft and the Principle of Fault in Criminal Law', *Codicillvs* XXXV (2), pp. 4–14.

Murray, C. (1980) 'Religion and Ritual', in W.F. Lye and C. Murray, *Transformations on the Highveld: The Tswana and Southern Sotho.* Cape Town: David Philip, pp. 122–33.

—— (1981) *Families Divided: the Impact of Migrant Labour in Lesotho.* Johannesburg: Raven Press.

Musambachime, M.C. (1988) 'The Impact of Rumour: the Case of the Banyama (Vampire Men) Scare in Northern Rhodesia, 1930–1964', *International Journal of African Historical Studies* 21 (2), pp. 201–17.

Ness, R. (1985) 'The Old Hag Phenomenon as Sleep Paralysis: A Biocultural Interpretation', in R.C. Simons and C.H. Hughes (eds) *The Culture-Bound Syndromes: Folk Illnesses of Psychiatric and Anthropological Interest.* Dordrecht: D. Reidel, pp. 123–46.

Ngubane, H. (1977) *Body and Mind in Zulu Medicine: An Ethnography of Health and Disease in Nyuswa-Zulu Thought and Practice.* London: Academic Press.

Niehaus, I.A. (1988) 'Domestic Dynamics and Wage Labour: a Case Study among Urban Residents in Qwaqwa', *African Studies* 47 (2), pp. 121–44.

—— (1994) 'Disharmonious Spouses and Harmonious Siblings: Conceptualising Household Formation among Urban Residents in Qwaqwa', *African Studies* 53 (1), pp. 115–36.

Ode Brown, G. (1935) 'Witchcraft and British Colonial Law', *Africa* 8 (4), pp. 481–7.

Offiong, D.A. (1983) 'Social Relations and Witch-beliefs among the Ibibio of Nigeria', *Journal of Anthropological Research* 39 (1), pp. 81–95.

Ortner, S.B. (1974) 'Is Female to Male as Nature Is to Culture?', in L. Lamphere and M.Z. Rosaldo (eds) *Women, Culture and Society* Stanford CA: Stanford University Press, pp. 67–88.

—— (1984) 'Theory in Anthropology since the Sixties', *Comparative Studies in Society and History* 26 (1), pp. 126–66.

Overing, J. (1985) 'Introduction', in J. Overing (ed.) *Reason and Morality*. ASA Monographs 29. London and New York: Tavistock Publications, pp. 1–28.

Packard, R.M. (1986) 'Social Change and the History of Misfortune among the Bashu of Eastern Zaire', in I. Karp and C. Bird (eds) *Explorations in African Systems of Thought*. Bloomington: Indiana University Press, pp. 237–67.

Parker, R. (1990) *Bodies, Pleasures and Passions: Sexual Culture in Contemporary Brazil*. Princeton NJ: Princeton University Press.

Parrinder, G. (1963) *Witchcraft: European and African*. London: Faber and Faber.

Patterson, M. (1974) 'Sorcery and Witchcraft in Melanesia', *Oceania* XLV (2), pp. 132–60.

—— (1975) 'Sorcery and Witchcraft in Melanesia: an Ethnographic Survey', *Oceania* XLV (3), pp. 212–34.

Pauw, B.A. (1960) *Religion in a Tswana Chiefdom*. Cape Town: Oxford University Press.

—— (1974) 'The Influence of Christianity', in W.D. Hammond-Tooke (ed.) *The Bantu-Speaking Peoples of Southern Africa*. London and Boston: Routledge and Kegan Paul, pp. 415–38.

Peek, P.M. (1991) 'African Divination Systems: Non-Normal Modes of Cognition', in P.M. Peek (ed.) *African Divination Systems: Ways of Knowing*. Bloomington and Indianapolis: Indiana University Press, pp. 193–212.

Peel, J.D.Y. (1968) *Aladura: A Religious Movement among the Yoruba*. London: Oxford University Press.

Perry J. and C. Perry (1991) 'Where Were the Guests? Republic Festival 1981', in A.D. Spiegel and P.A. McAllister (eds) *Tradition and Transition in Southern Africa*. Johannesburg: University of Witwatersrand Press, pp. 167–84.

Peters, E.L. (1972) 'Aspects of the Control of Moral Ambiguities: a Comparative Analysis of Two Culturally Disparate Modes of Social Control', in M. Gluckman (ed.) *The Allocation of Responsibility*. Manchester: Manchester University Press, pp. 109–62.

Radcliffe-Brown, A. (1965) *Structure and Function in Primitive Society*. London: Routledge and Kegan Paul.

Ramutsindela, M.F. and D. Simon (1999) 'The Politics of Territory and Place in Post-apartheid South Africa: The disrupted area of Bushbuckridge', *Journal of Southern African Studies* 25 (3), pp. 479–98.

Ranger, T. (1991) 'Religion and Witchcraft in Everyday life in Contemporary Zimbabwe', in P. Kaarsholm (ed.) *Cultural Struggles and Development in Southern Africa*. London: James Curry, pp. 149–66.

—— (1996) 'Postscript. Colonial and Postcolonial Identities', in R. Werbner and T. Ranger (eds) *Postcolonial Identities in Africa*. London: Zed Books, pp. 271–81.

Raphael, B. (1983) *The Anatomy of Bereavement*. New York. Basic Books.

Richards, A. (1935) 'A Modern Movement of Witch-Finders', *Africa* 8 (4), pp. 448–61.

Riebe, I. (1987) 'Kalam Witchcraft: a Historical Perspective', in M. Stephen (ed.) *Sorcerer and Witch in Melanesia*. Carlton, Victoria: Melbourne University Press, pp. 1–14.

Ritchken, E. et al. (1990) *Experiences of secondary schooling in the Mapulaneng District, Lebowa, 1989*. Learning in Limbo: Part II. Research Report No. 4. Johannesburg: Education Policy Unit, University of the Witwatersrand.

Rosaldo, R. (1980) *Ilongot Headhunting, 1883–1974: A Study in Society and History*. Stanford CA: Stanford University Press.

Rosenhahn, D.L. (1973) 'On Being Sane in Insane Places', *Science* 179, pp. 250–8.

Rowlands, M. and J.-P. Warnier (1988) 'Sorcery, Power and the Modern State in Cameroon', *Man (n.s.)* 23 (1), pp. 118–32.

Russel, B. (1946) *A History of Western Philosophy*. London: Allen and Unwin.

Sahlins, M. (1976) *Culture and Practical Reason*. Chicago: University of Chicago Press.

Sansom, B. (1972) 'When Witches are not Named', in M. Gluckman (ed.) *The Allocation of Responsibility*. Manchester: Manchester University Press, pp. 193–226.

—— (1974a) 'Traditional Economic Systems', in W.D. Hammond-Tooke (ed.) *The Bantu-Speaking Peoples of Southern Africa*. London and Boston: Routledge and Kegan Paul, pp. 135–76.

—— (1974b) 'Traditional Rulers and their Realms', in W.D. Hammond-Tooke (ed.) *The Bantu-Speaking Peoples of Southern Africa*. London and Boston: Routledge and Kegan Paul, pp. 246–83.

Schapera, I. and S. Roberts (1975) 'Rampedi Revisited: Another Look at a Kgatla Ward', *Africa* 45 (3), pp. 258–79.

Scheper-Hughes, N. (1995) 'The Primacy of the Ethical: Positions for a Militant Anthropology', *Current Anthropology* 36 (3), pp. 409–20.

Sharp, J. (1985) 'Unit of Study, Context and Culture: Towards an Historical Anthropology', *African Studies* 44 (1), pp. 65–86.

Sharp, L.A. (1993) *The Possessed and the Dispossessed: Identity and Power in a Madagascar Migrant Town*. Berkeley CA: University of Los Angeles Press.

Shaw, R. (1991) 'Splitting Truths from Darkness: Epistemological Aspects of Temne Divination', in P.M. Peek (ed.) *African Divination Systems: Ways of Knowing*. Bloomington and Indianapolis: Indiana University Press, pp. 137–52.

—— (1997) 'The Production of Witchcraft/Witchcraft as Production: Memory, Modernity and the Slave Trade in Sierra Leone', *American Ethnologist* 24 (4), pp. 856–76.

Shore, B. (1982) *Sala'ilua: A Samoan Mystery*. New York: Columbia University Press.

Silverbladt, I. (1987) *Moon, Sun and Witches: Gender Ideologies and Class in Inca and Colonial Peru*. Princeton NJ: Princeton University Press.

Soga, J.H. (1931) *The Ama-Xosa*. Lovedale: Lovedale Press.

South African Institute of Race Relations (SAIRR) (1988) *Survey of Race Relations, 1987–1988*. Johannesburg: SAIRR.

—— (1989) *Survey of Race Relations, 1988–1989*. Johannesburg: SAIRR.

Spiegel, A.D. (1989) 'Towards an Understanding of Tradition: Uses of Tradition in Apartheid South Africa'. *Critique of Anthropology* (1), pp. 49–74.

—— (1991) 'Polygyny as Myth: Towards Understanding Extramarital Relations in Lesotho', in A.D. Spiegel and P.A. McAllister (eds) *Tradition and Transition in Southern Africa*. Johannesburg: University of Witwatersrand Press, pp. 145–66.

—— (1992) 'A Trilogy of Tyranny and Tribulation: Village Politics and Administrative Intervention in Matatiele during the early 1980s'. *Journal of Contemporary African Studies* 11 (2), pp. 31–54.

Spiegel, A.D. and P.A. McAllister (eds) (1991) *Tradition and Transition in Southern Africa*. Johannesburg: University of Witwatersrand Press.

Stadler, J.J. (1996) 'Witches and Witch-Hunters: Witchcraft, Generational Relations and the Life-Cycle in a Lowveld Village', *African Studies* 55 (1), pp. 87–110.

Steadman, L. (1985) 'The Killing of Witches', *Oceania* 56 (2), pp. 106–23.

Stephen, M. (1987) 'Introduction', in M. Stephen (ed.) *Sorcerer and Witch in Melanesia*. Carlton, Victoria: Melbourne University Press, pp. 1–14.

Stoller, P. and C. Olkes (1987) in *Sorcery's Shadow: A Memoir of Apprenticeship among the Songhay of Niger*. Chicago IL: University of Chicago Press.

Strathern, A.J. (1982) 'Witchcraft, Greed, Cannibalism and Death: Some Related Themes from the New Guinea Highlands', in M. Bloch and J. Parry (eds) *Death and the Regeneration of Life*. Cambridge: Cambridge University Press, pp. 111–33.

Sundkler, B.G.M. (1961) *Bantu Prophets in South Africa*. London: Oxford University Press.

Taylor, C.C. (1992) *Milk, Honey and Money: Changing concepts in Rwandan Healing*. Washington DC: Smithsonian Institution Press.

Thomas, K. (1971) *Religion and the Decline of Magic: Studies in Popular Beliefs in Sixteenth and Seventeenth Century England*. London: Weidenfeld and Nicholson.

Thornton, R. (1988) 'Culture: A contemporary definition', in E. Boonzaier and J. Sharp (eds) *South African Keywords*. Cape Town: David Philip, pp. 17–28.

Turner, V.W. (1957) *Schism and Continuity in an African Society: a Study of Ndembu Village Life*. Manchester: Manchester University Press.

—— (1967) *The Forest of Symbols*. Ithaca, NY and London: Cornell University Press.

—— (1974) *Dramas, Fields and Metaphors: Symbolic Action in Human Society*. Ithaca NY: Cornell University Press.

Tylor, Sir E.B. (1958) [1871] *The Origion of Culture Vol. 1: Religion in Primitive Culture*. New York: Harper and Brothers.

Van Binsbergen, W.M.J. (1981) 'Religious Change and the Problem of Evil in Western Zambia', in *Religious Change in Zambia: Exploratory Studies*. London and Boston: Kegan Paul International, pp. 135–79.

Van Kessel, I. (1993) '"From Confusion to Lusaka": the Youth Revolt in Sekhukhuneland', *Journal of Southern African Studies* 19 (4), pp. 593–614.

Weber, M. (1930) [1904–5] *The Protestant Ethic and the Spirit of Capitalism* (trans. T. Parsons). London: Allen and Unwin.

—— (1949) *The Methodology of the Social Sciences* (E.A. Shils and H.A. Finch trans. and eds). Glencoe IL: The Free Press, pp. 49–112.

—— (1978) *Economy and Society: An Outline of Interpretive Sociology*. Volume 1. G. Roth and K. Wittich (eds) Berkeley CA: University of California Press.

Weiss, B. (1993) 'Money, Movement and AIDS in North-West Tanzania', *Africa* 63 (1), pp. 19–35.

Werbner, R.P. (1986) 'Review article: The Political Economy of Bricolage', *Journal of Southern African Studies* 13 (1), pp. 151–6.

West, M.E. (1975) *Bishops and Prophets in a Black City*. Cape Town and London: Philip and Collings.

—— (1988) 'Confusing Categories: Population Groups, National States and Citizenship', in E. Boonzaier and J. Sharp (eds) *South African Keywords: The Uses and Abuses of Political Concepts*. Cape Town: David Philip.

White, L. (1992) 'Bodily Fluids and Usufruct: Controlling Property in Nairobi, 1917–1939', *Canadian Journal of African Studies* 24 (3), pp. 418–38.

—— (1994) 'Between Gluckman and Foucault: Historicizing Rumour and Gossip', *Social Dynamics* 20 (2), pp. 75–92.

Whyte, W.F. (1955) *Street Corner Society: The Social Structure of an Italian Slum*. Chicago: Chicago University Press.

Willis, R.G. (1968) 'Kamcape: an Anti-Sorcery Movement in S.W. Tanzania', *Africa* 38 (1), pp. 1–15.

—— (1970) 'Instant Millenium: the Sociology of African Witch-Cleansing Cults', in M. Douglas (ed.) *Witchcraft Confessions and Accusations*. ASA Monographs 9. London: Tavistock, pp. 129–40.

Wilson, F. (1972) *Migrant Labour in South Africa*. Johannesburg: South African Council of Churches and Spro-Cas.

Wilson, M. (1951) 'Witch-Beliefs and Social Structure', *American Journal of Sociology* 56 (4), pp. 307–13.

—— (1967) [1951]. *Good Company: a Study of Nyakyusa Age-Villages*. Boston MA: Beacon Press.

Winter, E. (1963) 'The Enemy Within: Amba Witchcraft and Sociological Theory', in J. Middleton and E. Winter (eds) *Witchcraft and Sorcery in East Africa*. London: Routledge and Kegan Paul, pp. 277–99.

Wolf, E. (1990) 'Facing Power-Old Insights, New Questions', *American Anthropologist* 92 (3), pp. 586–96.

—— (1999) *Envisioning Power*. New Haven CT: Yale University Press.

Woods, D. (1978) *Biko*. Harmondsworth: Penguin Books.

Worobec, C.D. (1995) 'Witchcraft Beliefs and Practices in Pre revolutionary Russian and Ukranian Villages', *The Russian Review* (54) April, pp. 165–87.

Worsley, P. (1957) *The Trumpet Shall Sound: A Study of Cargo Cults in Melanesia*. MacGibbon and Kee.

Zelenietz, M. and S. Lindenbaum (eds) (1981) *Sorcery and Social Change in Melanesia*. Special Issue Social Analysis No. 8. Adelaide.

Ziervogel, D. (1954) *The Eastern Sotho*. Pretoria: Van Schaik.

## UNPUBLISHED PAPERS AND THESES

Anderson, R.L. (1990) '"Keeping the Myth Alive": Justice, Witches, and the Law in the 1986 Sekhukhuneland killings'. BA (Honours) dissertation. Johannesburg: Department of History, University of the Witwatersrand.

Dederen. J.M. (1996) 'Killing is easier than paperwork...A Critique of the Report of the Commission of Inquiry into Witchcraft Violence and Ritual Murders in the Northern Province of the Republic of South Africa'. Paper presented to the PAA/AASA Conference. Pretoria: University of South Africa.

De Wet, C. (1983) 'Kinship and Cooperation in two Ciskei villages'. Unpublished paper presented to the Association for Anthropology in Southern Africa, University of Port Elizabeth.

Ellsworth, R. (1983) '"The Simplicity of the Native Mind": Black Passengers on the South African Railways in the Early Twentieth Century'. Unpublished seminar paper. African Studies Institute: University of the Witwatersrand.

Fischer, A. (1981) 'Vernuwing en die rituele lewe van die Tsonga'. Unpublished paper presented to the Conference for South African Anthropologists, University of Stellenbosch.

Girolami, L. (1989) 'The Female's Role in Primate Socio-sexual Communication: a Study of the Vervet Monkey (Ceropithecus Aethiops Pygerythrus) and the Chamca Baboon (Papio Ursinus)'. PhD thesis. Johannesburg: Department of Zoology, University of the Witwatersrand.

Hartman, J.B. (1978) 'Die Samehang in die Privaatreg van die Changana Tsonga van Mhala, Met Verwysing na die Administratiefregtelike en Prosesregtelike Funksionering'. D.Phil thesis. Pretoria: Departement Volkekunde: Universiteit van Pretoria.

Hirst, M.M. (1990) 'The Healer's Art: Cape Nguni Diviners in the Townships of Grahamstown'. PhD thesis. Grahamstown: Department of Social Anthropology, Rhodes University.

Honwana, A. (1997) 'Spirit Possession and the Politics of Religious Experience in Mozambique'. Unpublished paper presented to the conference on God's Biographies in Africa. Council for the Development of Social Research in Africa, Dakar, Senegal.

James, D. (1993) '"Mino wa Setso": Songs of Town and Countryside and the Experience of Migrancy by Men and Women of the Northern Transvaal'. PhD thesis. Johannesburg: Department of Social Anthropology, University of the Witwatersrand.

Kotzé, J.C. (1986) 'Levels of Domination and a Point of Conversion in Gazankulu'. Unpublished paper presented to the Department of Social Anthropology, University of Cape Town.

240 *Witchcraft, Power and Politics*

Ritchken, E. (1995) 'Leadership and Conflict in Bushbuckridge: Struggles to Define Moral Economies Within the Context of Rapidly Transforming Political Economies'. PhD thesis. Johannesburg: Department of Political Studies, University of the Witwatersrand.

Rodgers, G. (1993) 'Healers and Ways of Healing'. BA (honours) dissertation. Johannesburg: Department of Social Anthropology, University of the Witwatersrand.

Schoeman, J.B. (1985) 'Die totaliteitsbewustheid onder Pedi psigiatriese pasiente'. Unpublished D.Phil thesis. Pretoria: University of Pretoria.

Stadler, J.J. (1994) 'Generational Relationships in a Lowveld Village: Questions of Age, Household and Tradition'. MA dissertation. Johannesburg, Department of Social Anthropology: University of the Witwatersrand.

## GOVERNMENT REPORTS

Bureau for Economic Research re Bantu Development (BENBO). (1976) *Lebowa: Ekonomiese-Economic Review*. Pretoria: BENBO.

Debates of the House of Assembly (1957) *Hansard*. Pretoria: Government Printers.

Hiemstra, V.G. (1985) *Report on Trans-Border Clashes between Subjects of Gazankulu and Lebowa*. Submitted to the Minister for Co-operation and Development, South African Government (mimeo).

Jones, G.I. (1951) *Basutholand Medicine Murder*. London: Her Majesty's Stationery Office.

Ralushai, N.V., M.V. Masinga, D.M.M. Madiba, J.A. van den Heever, T.J. Mathiba, M.E. Mphaphuli, M.W. Mokwena, V. Nolov and D. Matabane (1996) *Report of the Commission of Inquiry into Witchcraft Violence and Ritual Murders in the Northern Province of South Africa* (mimeo).

Van Warmelo, N.J. (1935) *A Preliminary Survey of the Bantu Tribes of South Africa*. Pretoria: Government Printer.

## NEWSPAPER ARTICLES

*African Sun*, 6 February 1996; *Argus*, 24 April 1993; *Cape Times*, 21 April 1994; *New York Times*, 18 September 1994 (B. Keller, 'Apartheid's grisly aftermath: "witch-burning"'); *Rand Daily Mail*, 24 April 1984; *Sunday Times*, 20 April 1986, 12 December 1999; *The Sowetan*, 25 March 1992; *Sunday Independent*, 16 June 1996 (T. Beaver, 'Gathered to stop witch-burning, priests and politicians reveal their own belief in dark forces'); *Weekend Argus*, 18/19 March 1995; *Weekly Mail and Guardian*, 1 April 1995, 9 May 1997; *Weekend Star*, 7–8 May 1994.

## ARCHIVAL RECORDS

Transvaal Archival Depot, Pretoria (TA). Select files were consulted in the following series: Native Affairs Department (NTS) and Department of Lands (LDE).

# INDEX